CAREER

Pathways
Document Literacy

CONSUMER | PERSONAL | BUSINESS | FINANCIAL

PAXEN
Learning Corporation

Melbourne, Florida
www.paxen.com

Acknowledgements

▶ **Photo Credits**

Cover (man on computer) iStockphoto © Steve Cole **iv (family buying a car)** Getty images © Barry Austin Photography; **(calculator and check register)** iStockphoto © Catherine Jones **v (employee paperwork)** Shutterstock © Goodluz; **(couple doing bills)** Shutterstock © OLJ Studio **1 (passport and map collage)** Getty Images © Richard Goerg; **(woman paying cashier at supermarket)** Getty Images © Ariel Skelley; **(family buying a car)** Getty Images © Barry Austin Photography **2 (passport and map collage)** Getty Images ©Richard Goerg **6 (hotel room interior)** iStockphoto © scibak **12 (woman paying cashier at supermarket)** Getty Images © Ariel Skelley **14 (cosmetics)** Shutterstock © Calinerie **15 (woman on mattress)** Getty Images © Vstock LLC **16 (chair)** iStockphoto © Don Joski; **(curtains)** iStockphoto © Joseph Gareri; **(dresser)** iStockphoto © Yenwen Lu; **(rug)** iStockphoto © Selahattin BAYRAM; **(dining table)** iStockphoto © Andrei Kostrioukov; **(mirror)** iStockphoto © catnap72 **17 (chocolate-chip cookies)** iStockphoto © Juanmonino **22 (family buying a car)** Getty Images © Barry Austin Photography **23 (gas pump icon)** Shutterstock © Iznogood **43 (calculator and check register)** iStockphoto © Catherine Jones; **(woman making dr. appt.)** iStockphoto © Jerry Koch; **(young man taking driving test)** iStockphoto © Rich Legg **44 (calculator and check register)** iStockphoto © Catherine Jones **60 (woman making dr. appt.)** iStockphoto © Jerry Koch **80 (young man taking driving test)** iStockphoto © Rich Legg **111 (training a new worker)** Shutterstock © Marcin Balcerzak; **(employee paperwork)** Shutterstock © Goodluz **112 (training a new worker)** Shutterstock © Marcin Balcerzak **120 (employee paperwork)** Shutterstock © Goodluz **141 (couple doing their bills)** Shutterstock © OLJ Studio; **(couple admiring their new home)** Shutterstock © Morgan Lane Photography; **(filling out tax paperwork)** © Paxen Learning – Special thanks to Sandra Bruner and Shannon McGregor **142 (couple doing their bills)** Shutterstock © OLJ Studio **154 (couple admiring their new home)** Shutterstock © Morgan Lane Photography **182 (filling out tax paperwork)** © Paxen Learning – Special thanks to Sandra Bruner and Shannon McGregor

Table of Contents

22
Whether your car is new or old, you'll find many documents involved with vehicle maintenance and insurance.

44
Learning how to manage your personal finances will help you stay within a budget, make sound financial decisions, and save for the future.

120
You'll encounter many different documents in the workplace. Knowing how to interpret these documents will help you succeed on the job.

142
Paying bills can be stressful, but understanding your charges will ensure you pay on time and don't get overcharged.

About Career Pathways

What do you want to be when you grow up? It's an innocent question, one often asked of schoolchildren. Increasingly, though, as our economy changes—and with it, entire industries—people of all ages are asking the same question. From children to young adults and on to older professionals and dislocated workers, more people than ever are attempting to find their way in today's workplace.

Often, the journey begins after high school. Whether they earn a diploma or a GED credential, potential employees often lack the proper support and guidance to make the transition from school to the workplace.

Adding to the challenge, workplaces themselves are changing. Traditional industries that once employed generations of workers have struggled to survive. Amid intense competition for available jobs, job seekers who lack necessary certifications or degrees and/or soft and career-specific skills struggle to find lasting success. Today's workers face a number of specific challenges. For example:

- Many workers, though highly skilled, may lack a market for their services.
- Although workers may have years of on-the-job experience, they could be unaware of current job-seeking techniques, such as using the Internet and in-person networking.
- Similarly, job seekers may lack a current, polished resume or sharp interviewing skills.

The solution to these challenges can be quite complex. To help people determine their next steps, Paxen offers its newest series, *Career Pathways*. This product line provides learners with strategies to survive—and thrive—in a 21st-century workforce.

Titles such as *Transitions, Job Search,* and *Greener Pastures: A Guide to Eco-Friendly Employment* aid learners in exploring and narrowing options. Others, such as *Effective Employee, Document Literacy,* and *Financial Literacy*, provide strategies for excelling inside and outside of the workplace.

Career Pathways was built in accordance with the work-readiness competencies listed in the table below.

COMPETENCIES

Pathways Essential Knowledge and Skill Statements	National Standards in K-12 Personal Finance Education
CASAS	Workforce Investment Act (WIA) Elements
Equipped for the Future (EFF)	21st Century Skills
National Career Development Guidelines (NCDG)	Pre-Employment and Work Maturity (PEWM)

CAREER Pathways

The Next Generation of Work-Readiness Materials

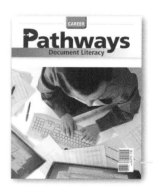

▶ Document Literacy

In *Document Literacy*, we put fine print under the microscope. A series of detailed callouts help learners decode and master complex consumer, personal, business, and financial documents. Chapter reviews allow learners to check understanding.

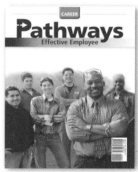

▶ Effective Employee

Effective Employee equips emerging professionals with the skills, experiences, and intangibles to excel and advance in today's workplace. An engaging narrative and high-interest features help learners unlock the secrets to lasting success.

▶ Job Search

Job Search removes the mystery—and guesswork—from the employment process. Learners receive instruction in key areas—from authoring résumés and cover letters to refining interviewing and negotiating skills—critical to employment success.

▶ Financial Literacy

For many, the world of personal finance sometimes can feel impersonal. Enter *Financial Literacy*, a color consumable title that helps learners personalize personal finance by emphasizing the essential areas of earning, spending, saving, and investing.

About Document Literacy

For the Learner

In *Document Literacy*, we put fine print under the microscope. A series of detailed callouts help learners decode and master complex consumer, personal, business, and financial documents. Chapter reviews allow learners to check understanding. *Document Literacy* contains several different components designed to enhance the learning experience.

1 Each lesson features an internal table of contents designed to help students customize their learning experience.

2 Introductory paragraphs explain the documents in context.

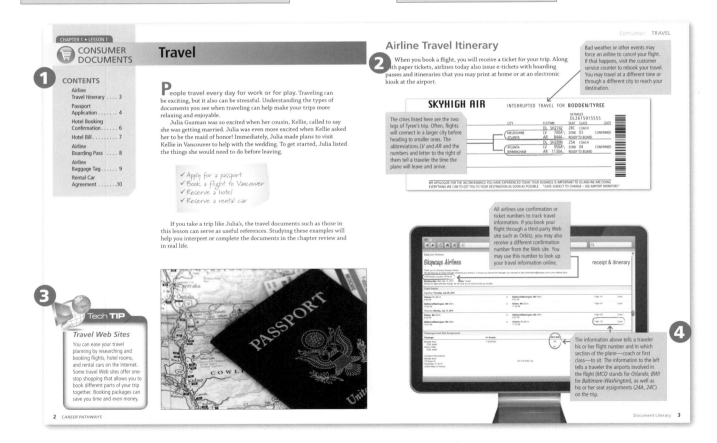

3 Tech Tips offer additional advice on utilizing the Web to manage and access documents.

4 Each document features callouts that help learners analyze and understand specific details and concepts.

Chapter Recaps and Reviews

Each chapter concludes with a recap checklist designed to ensure learner mastery. The chapter review that follows allows students to interpret or complete sample documents. These pages can be removed and submitted for assessment purposes.

1 The recap checklist highlights student goals for each lesson.

2 The chapter review contains three types of questions: short answer, true or false, and multiple choice.

3 In the chapter review, students can also practice completing sample documents.

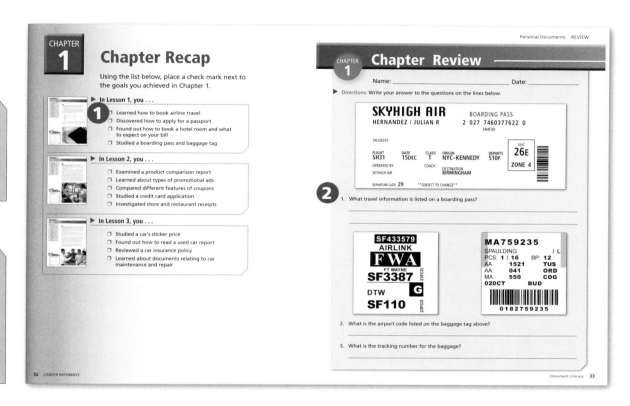

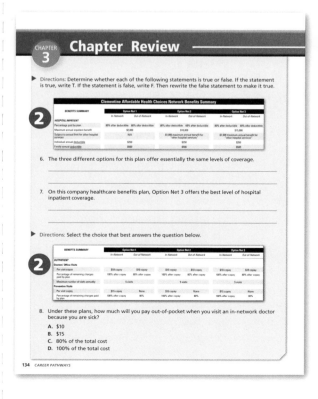

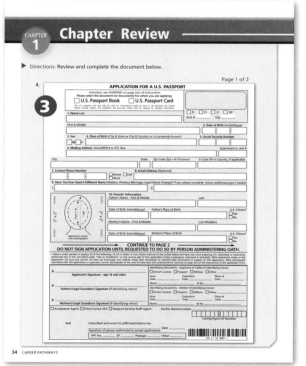

Key Words

You'll come across the words defined here throughout the documents in this book. Reviewing them ahead of time will ensure that you fully understand the documents.

CHAPTER 1: Consumer Documents

contract: a legally binding agreement between two or more parties of authority

delinquent: being overdue in payment

finance: to provide money for a purchase

insurance: a contract by which someone guarantees, for a fee, to pay someone else for the value of property if it is lost or damaged, or to pay for injury or death

interest: a charge for borrowed money that is generally a percentage of the amount borrowed

itinerary: the route of a trip or journey

model: a kind or a type of something, such as a car

premium: the amount paid for a contract of insurance

rate: a price or charge set according to a scale or standard

receipt: a written statement saying that money or goods have been received

redeem: to buy; or to remove the obligation of, by payment

void: of no legal force or effect

CHAPTER 2: Personal Documents

ATM [Automatic Teller Machine]: a computerized machine that performs basic banking functions

account: an account in a bank from which the depositor can withdraw or deposit money

arbitration: the settling of a dispute in which both sides present their arguments to a third person or group for settlement

bank statement: a brief, summarized record of activity in a financial account over a particular period of time

bankrupt: a person or company that has been declared legally unable to pay debts

beneficiary: a person who benefits or is expected to benefit from something

credit: a balance in an account in a person's favor

creditor: a person to whom a debt is owed

debit: an entry in an account representing an amount paid out or owed

dependent: a person who relies on another for financial support

direct deposit: to electronically transfer money into a bank account without first receiving a cashable check

earned income: money paid in return for labor, business, or property

landlord: the owner of land or a home that is rented to another

lease: an agreement to use real estate for a period of time in exchange for a specified rent

Medicaid: a program of medical aid designed for those unable to afford regular medical service and paid for by state and federal governments

Medicare: a government program of medical care especially for the elderly

practitioner: a person who practices a profession, such as law or medicine

tenant: one who occupies property of another, especially for rent

transaction: something transacted; in banking, an exchange of money (a deposit or withdrawal)

unearned income: money paid for which no work has been done (child support, Social Security benefits)

CHAPTER 3: Business Documents

co-pay[ment]: a small, fixed amount required by a health insurer to be paid by the insured for each outpatient visit or drug prescription

eligibility: qualified to participate

salary: money paid at regular times for work or services

taxes: charges set by federal, state, or local governments that people must pay on their earnings or property

terminate: to bring to an end

wage: a payment for work or services; usually calculated on an hourly, daily, or piecework basis

withholding: to deduct (withholding tax) from income

CHAPTER 4: Financial Documents

401(k): a savings plan that allows employees to contribute a fixed amount of income to a retirement account and to defer taxes until withdrawal

adjusted gross income: the total of an individual's wages, salaries, interest, dividends, etc., minus allowable deductions

asset: personal or corporate holdings, such as financial funds, that have monetary value and may be used in payment of debts

assessment: the assessed value of a property, usually for insurance or tax purposes

capital gains: profit from the sale of assets, such as bonds or real estate

condominium: an individually owned unit in a structure (similar to an apartment building) of many units

contribution: a sum of money contributed

dividend: a sum of money to be divided and given out

equity: the value of an owner's interest in a property in excess of claims against it (as in the amount of a mortgage)

IRA [Individual Retirement Account]: a savings plan that offers tax advantages to an individual depositor, who can use it to set aside money for retirement

lender: a bank or person who lends money, usually at a set interest rate and for a set period of time

mortgage: a transfer of rights to a piece of property (such as as to a house), usually in return for a loan

mutual funds: a collection of shares of various stocks managed by a financial company

premises: a building or part of a building usually with its grounds

principal: a sum of money on which interest is computed, such as a loan

risk: possibility of the loss of money, especially in financial investments

Roth IRA: an individual retirement account in which investments are made with taxable dollars, but earnings are tax-free and withdrawals are tax-free after age 59 ½

stock: the ownership element of a corporation divided to give the owners an interest and usually voting power, or a portion of such stock

taxable income: money paid in return for labor, business, or property that can be taxed by the government

transfer: to move to a different place or situation (as in to move money from one account to another)

withdrawal: the removal of money from a bank account

Consumer Documents

CONSUMER DOCUMENTS

Travel

CONTENTS

People travel every day for work or for play. Traveling can be exciting, but it also can be stressful. Understanding the types of documents you see when traveling can help make your trips more relaxing and enjoyable.

Julia Guzman was so excited when her cousin, Kellie, called to say she was getting married. Julia was even more excited when Kellie asked her to be the maid of honor! Immediately, Julia made plans to visit Kellie in Vancouver to help with the wedding. To get started, Julia listed the things she would need to do before leaving.

✔ Apply for a passport
✔ Book a flight to Vancouver
✔ Reserve a hotel
✔ Reserve a rental car

If you take a trip like Julia's, the travel documents such as those in this lesson can serve as useful references. Studying these examples will help you interpret or complete the documents in the chapter review and in real life.

Travel Web Sites

You can ease your travel planning by researching and booking flights, hotel rooms, and rental cars on the Internet. Some travel Web sites offer one-stop shopping that allows you to book different parts of your trip together. Booking packages can save you time and even money.

Airline Travel Itinerary

When you book a flight, you will receive a ticket for your trip. Along with paper tickets, airlines today also issue e-tickets with boarding passes and itineraries that you may print at home or at an electronic kiosk at the airport.

Bad weather or other events may force an airline to cancel your flight. If that happens, visit the customer service counter to rebook your travel. You may travel at a different time or through a different city to reach your destination.

SKYHIGH AIR

INTERRUPTED TRAVEL FOR **BODDEN/TYREE**

SKYMILES
DL2615915555

CITY	FLT/TIME	SEAT	CLASS	GATE
	DL SH2742	28C	COACH	
MELBOURNE	LV 700A	ZONE 03	CONFIRMED	
ATLANTA	AR 844A		READY TO BOARD	
	DL SH2890	25A	COACH	
ATLANTA	LV 950A	ZONE 04	CONFIRMED	
BIRMINGHAM	AR 1130A		READY TO BOARD	

The cities listed here are the two legs of Tyree's trip. Often, flights will connect in a larger city before heading to smaller ones. The abbreviations *LV* and *AR* and the numbers and letter to the right of them tell a traveler the time the plane will leave and arrive.

WE APOLOGIZE FOR THE INCONVENIENCE YOU HAVE EXPERIENCED TODAY. YOUR BUSINESS IS IMPORTANT TO US AND WE ARE DOING EVERYTHING WE CAN TO GET YOU TO YOUR DESTINATION AS SOON AS POSSIBLE.   *GATE SUBJECT TO CHANGE – SEE AIRPORT MONITORS*

All airlines use confirmation or ticket numbers to track travel information. If you book your flight through a third-party Web site such as Orbitz, you may also receive a different confirmation number from the Web site. You may use this number to look up your travel information online.

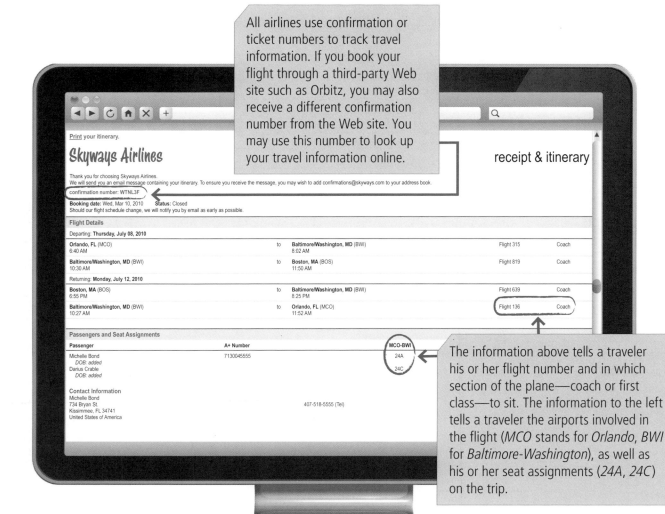

Print your itinerary.

Skyways Airlines

Thank you for choosing Skyways Airlines.
We will send you an email message containing your itinerary. To ensure you receive the message, you may wish to add confirmations@skyways.com to your address book.

confirmation number: WTNL3F

Booking date: Wed, Mar 10, 2010   **Status:** Closed
Should our flight schedule change, we will notify you by email as early as possible.

receipt & itinerary

Flight Details

Departing: **Thursday, July 08, 2010**

Orlando, FL (MCO) 6:40 AM	to	**Baltimore/Washington, MD** (BWI) 8:02 AM	Flight 315	Coach
Baltimore/Washington, MD (BWI) 10:30 AM	to	**Boston, MA** (BOS) 11:50 AM	Flight 819	Coach

Returning: **Monday, July 12, 2010**

Boston, MA (BOS) 6:55 PM	to	**Baltimore/Washington, MD** (BWI) 8:25 PM	Flight 639	Coach
Baltimore/Washington, MD (BWI) 10:27 AM	to	**Orlando, FL** (MCO) 11:52 AM	Flight 136	Coach

Passengers and Seat Assignments

Passenger	A+ Number	MCO-BWI
Michelle Bond *DOB: added*	7130045555	24A
Darius Crable *DOB: added*		24C

Contact Information
Michelle Bond
734 Bryan St.
Kissimmee, FL 34741
United States of America

407-518-5555 (Tel)

The information above tells a traveler his or her flight number and in which section of the plane—coach or first class—to sit. The information to the left tells a traveler the airports involved in the flight (*MCO* stands for *Orlando, BWI* for *Baltimore-Washington*), as well as his or her seat assignments (*24A, 24C*) on the trip.

Passport Application

Are you planning to travel outside the United States? If so, you'll need to apply for a passport several weeks in advance so that you may receive it in time for your trip. Be sure to collect the necessary documents and submit two photos with your application.

Page 1 of 2

APPLICATION FOR A U.S. PASSPORT

Attention: see WARNING on page two of instructions
Please select the document (or documents) for which you are applying:

[X] **U.S. Passport Book**   [ ] **U.S. Passport Card** ◄

The U.S. passport card may only be used for international travel by land or sea between the United States, Canada, Mexico, the Caribbean and Bermuda. Please visit our website for detailed information.

> You may apply for either a traditional passport book or a newer passport card. Passport cards are less expensive than passport books, but only allow for travel to Canada, Mexico, Bermuda, and the Caribbean in a car or on a ship. If you wish to travel to other countries or travel by air, apply for a passport book.

1. Name *Last*

Ramirez

First & Middle

Mercedes Renee

3. Sex   **4. Place of Birth** *(City & State or City & Country as it is presently known)*

[ ] M [X] F   Tucson, Arizona

6. Mailing Address: *Street/RFD # or P.O. Box*

10342 Mirage Dr.

City	State	Zip Code *(Zip + 4 if known)*	In Care Of or Country, if applicable
Phoenix	AZ	85010	

7. Contact Phone Number

602 - 555 - 6872   [ ] Home [X] Cell [ ] Work

8. Email Address *(Optional)*

9. Have You Ever Used A Different Name *(Maiden, Previous Marriage, Legal Name Change)? If yes, please complete. (Attach additional pages if needed)*

1. Mercedes Renee Brown   2.

STAPLE STAPLE

2" x 2"   From 1" to 1 3/8"   2" x 2"

STAPLE STAPLE

Submit two recent, color photographs

10. Parents' Information

Father's Name – First & Middle   **Last**

Roberto James   Brown

Date of Birth (mm/dd/yyyy)   **Father's Place of Birth**   **U.S. Citizen?**

07/02/1956   Atlanta, Georgia   [X] Yes [ ] No

Mother's Name – First & Middle   **Last (Maiden)**

Patricia Rose   Stephens

Date of Birth (mm/dd/yyyy)   **Mother's Place of Birth**   **U.S. Citizen?**

11/11/55   Macon, Georgia   [X] Yes [ ] No

→ **CONTINUE TO PAGE 2** ←
DO NOT SIGN APPLICATION UNTIL REQUESTED TO DO SO BY PERSON ADMINISTERING OATH.

I declare under penalty of perjury all of the following: 1)I am a citizen or non-citizen national of the United States and have not, since acquiring U.S. citizenship or nationality, performed any of the acts listed under "Acts or Conditions" on the reverse side of this application (unless explanatory statement is attached); 2)the statements made on the application are true and correct; 3)I have not knowingly and willfully made false statements or included false documents in support of this application; 4)the photograph submitted with this application is a genuine, current, photograph of me; and 5)I have read and understood the warning on page two of the instructions to the application form.

X _____
Applicant's Signature – age 16 and older

> Because a passport serves as proof of citizenship, you must provide official documents as proof of citizenship when you apply. You may show a certified copy of your birth certificate, an old U.S. passport, a naturalization certificate, or a certificate of citizenship.

Identifying Documents – Applicant or Father (if identifying minor)
[ ] Driver's License [ ] Passport [ ] Military [ ] Other ____

Issue Date ____ Expiration Date ____ Place of Date ____
Name ____ ID No ____

Identifying Documents – Mother (if identifying minor)
[ ] Driver's License [ ] Passport [ ] Military [ ] Other ____

Issue Date ____ Expiration Date ____ Place of Date ____
Name ____ ID No ____

Facility Name/Location ____

Facility/Agent ID Number

Seal   Subscribed and sworn to (affirmed) before me:

____ Date ____

Signature of person authorized to accept applications

PPT Fee ____ EF ____ Postage ____ Other ____

DS 11 10 2007 1

Passport Application

Name of Applicant (Last, First & Middle)	2. Date of Birth (mm/dd/yyyy)
Ramirez, Mercedes Renee	03/22/1982

11. Height	12. Hair Color	13. Eye Color	14. Occupation	15. Employer
5'4	Black	Brown	customer service representative	First Regional Bank

16. Additional Contact Phone Numbers

602-555-8280 ☐ Home ☐ Cell ☒ Work ☐ _____ ☐ Home ☐ Cell ☐ Work ☐ _____

17. Permanent Address: *Street/RFD # (No P.O. Box)*

	Apartment or unit #
10342 Mirage Dr.	3

City	State	Zip Code (Zip + 4 if known)
Phoenix	AZ	85010

18. Emergency Contact – *Provide the information of a person not traveling with you to be contacted in the event of an emergency.*

Name	Address: Street/RFD # or P.O. Box	Apartment or unit #
Patricia Brown	8255 Peach St.	

City	State	Zip Code	Phone Number	Relationship
Atlanta	GA	30311	404-555-2462	mother

19. Travel Plans

Date of Trip (mm/dd/yyyy)	Length of Trip	Countries to be visited
03/20/2011	10 days	Costa Rica

> If you have travel planned when applying for your passport, you can add information about it in question 19. However, this is not required.

20. Have you ever been married? ☒ Yes ☐ No

Current spouse's or most recent former spouse's name	Place of birth	Date of marriage (mm/dd/yyyy)		Date (mm/dd/yyyy)
Michael Ramirez	Dallas, Texas	06/24/2006	☐ Widowed? ☐ Divorced?	

21. Have you ever been issued a U.S. Passport Book? ☐ Yes ☒ No   If yes, complete the remaining items in #21.

Your name as listed on your most recent passport book _____   Most recent passport book number _____

Status of your most recent passport book
☐ In My Possession ☐ Stolen ☐ Lost ☐ Other _____   Approximate date your most recent passport book was issued or date you applied (mm/dd/yyyy) _____

22. Have you ever been issued a U.S. Passport Card? ☐ Yes ☒ No   If yes, complete the remaining items in #22.

Your name as listed on your most recent passport card _____   Most recent passport card number _____

Status of your most recent passport card
☐ In My Possession ☐ Stolen ☐ Lost ☐ Other _____   Approximate date your most recent passport card was issued or date you applied (mm/dd/yyyy) _____

STOP! PLEASE DO NOT WRITE BELOW THIS LINE

FOR ISSUING OFFICE ONLY ☐ Sole Parent ☐ Both

Name as it appears on citizenship evidence _____

☐ Birth Certificate	SR	CR	City	Filed/Issued:
☐ Report of Birth	240	545	1350	Filed/City:

> When applying for a passport, include information about any of your previous U.S. passport books or cards, even if they are expired or you lost them.

DS 11 10 2007 1

Hotel Booking Confirmation

While you may book a room on-site at a hotel, it can be easier to reserve a room ahead of time. You may use the hotel's Web site or call the hotel directly to book a room. If you're traveling during a busy time or to a popular destination, reserving a room in advance will ensure that you have a place to stay.

You may be eligible for discounts if you belong to certain groups. For example, members of AAA often receive discounts on hotel stays, and many chains give discounts to members of the military.

Most hotel rooms feature two full-size beds—enough room to comfortably sleep four people. You can request a room with a king-size bed, but you might have to pay more for the room. Also, many hotels allow children to stay free in a room with their parent or guardian.

Your confirmation number provides proof of your reservation in the event you need to make changes to or even cancel your plans.

Hotel Bill

Whether you stay at a hotel for a night or for a week, you will receive a bill at the end of your stay. At many hotels, you may choose to present a credit card at check-in on which your hotel purchases will be charged. On the morning of your check-out, you will receive a bill from the hotel. You will want to double-check the bill for accuracy.

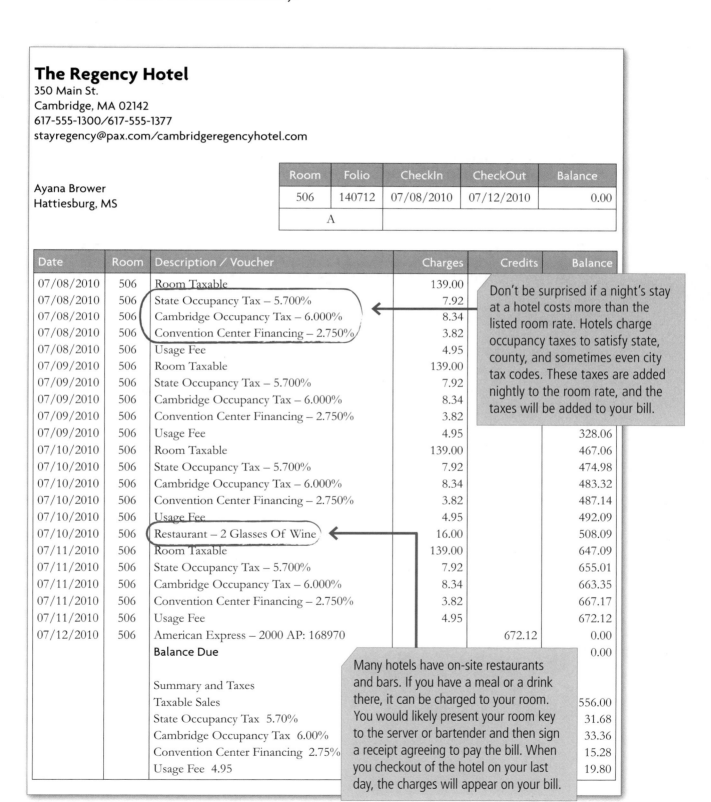

The Regency Hotel
350 Main St.
Cambridge, MA 02142
617-555-1300/617-555-1377
stayregency@pax.com/cambridgeregencyhotel.com

Ayana Brower
Hattiesburg, MS

Room	Folio	CheckIn	CheckOut	Balance
506	140712	07/08/2010	07/12/2010	0.00
A				

Date	Room	Description / Voucher	Charges	Credits	Balance
07/08/2010	506	Room Taxable	139.00		
07/08/2010	506	State Occupancy Tax – 5.700%	7.92		
07/08/2010	506	Cambridge Occupancy Tax – 6.000%	8.34		
07/08/2010	506	Convention Center Financing – 2.750%	3.82		
07/08/2010	506	Usage Fee	4.95		
07/09/2010	506	Room Taxable	139.00		
07/09/2010	506	State Occupancy Tax – 5.700%	7.92		
07/09/2010	506	Cambridge Occupancy Tax – 6.000%	8.34		
07/09/2010	506	Convention Center Financing – 2.750%	3.82		
07/09/2010	506	Usage Fee	4.95		328.06
07/10/2010	506	Room Taxable	139.00		467.06
07/10/2010	506	State Occupancy Tax – 5.700%	7.92		474.98
07/10/2010	506	Cambridge Occupancy Tax – 6.000%	8.34		483.32
07/10/2010	506	Convention Center Financing – 2.750%	3.82		487.14
07/10/2010	506	Usage Fee	4.95		492.09
07/10/2010	506	Restaurant – 2 Glasses Of Wine	16.00		508.09
07/11/2010	506	Room Taxable	139.00		647.09
07/11/2010	506	State Occupancy Tax – 5.700%	7.92		655.01
07/11/2010	506	Cambridge Occupancy Tax – 6.000%	8.34		663.35
07/11/2010	506	Convention Center Financing – 2.750%	3.82		667.17
07/11/2010	506	Usage Fee	4.95		672.12
07/12/2010	506	American Express – 2000 AP: 168970		672.12	0.00
		Balance Due			0.00
		Summary and Taxes			
		Taxable Sales			556.00
		State Occupancy Tax 5.70%			31.68
		Cambridge Occupancy Tax 6.00%			33.36
		Convention Center Financing 2.75%			15.28
		Usage Fee 4.95			19.80

Don't be surprised if a night's stay at a hotel costs more than the listed room rate. Hotels charge occupancy taxes to satisfy state, county, and sometimes even city tax codes. These taxes are added nightly to the room rate, and the taxes will be added to your bill.

Many hotels have on-site restaurants and bars. If you have a meal or a drink there, it can be charged to your room. You would likely present your room key to the server or bartender and then sign a receipt agreeing to pay the bill. When you checkout of the hotel on your last day, the charges will appear on your bill.

Airline Boarding Pass

If you have access to a printer, you can save time by printing your boarding pass before leaving for the airport. Twenty-four hours before your flight leaves, the airline will send you an e-mail with a Web link to check in for your flight. After checking in online, you may print your boarding pass. Then, you should be able to bypass the airport check in—unless you want to check luggage.

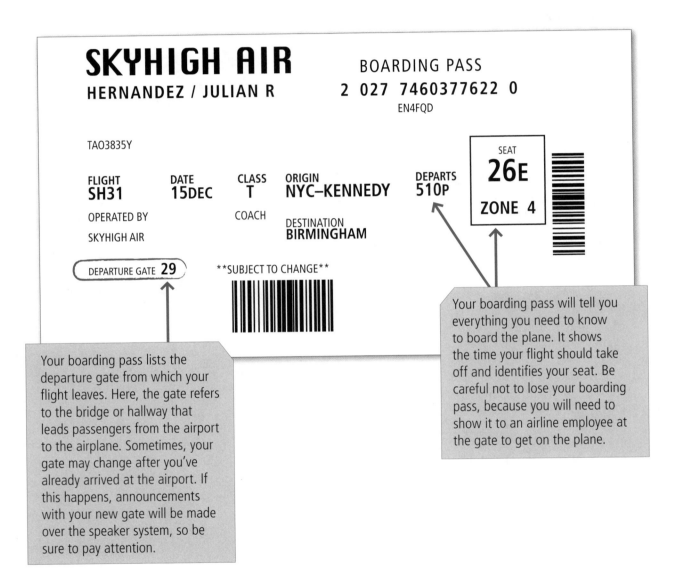

SKYHIGH AIR

HERNANDEZ / JULIAN R

BOARDING PASS

2 027 7460377622 0

EN4FQD

TAO3835Y

| FLIGHT | DATE | CLASS | ORIGIN | DEPARTS | SEAT |
| SH31 | 15DEC | T | NYC–KENNEDY | 510P | 26E |

OPERATED BY

SKYHIGH AIR

COACH

DESTINATION
BIRMINGHAM

ZONE 4

DEPARTURE GATE 29

SUBJECT TO CHANGE

Your boarding pass lists the departure gate from which your flight leaves. Here, the gate refers to the bridge or hallway that leads passengers from the airport to the airplane. Sometimes, your gate may change after you've already arrived at the airport. If this happens, announcements with your new gate will be made over the speaker system, so be sure to pay attention.

Your boarding pass will tell you everything you need to know to board the plane. It shows the time your flight should take off and identifies your seat. Be careful not to lose your boarding pass, because you will need to show it to an airline employee at the gate to get on the plane.

Airline Baggage Tag

If you're traveling for a short period of time, you may be able to fit all of your personal items into a small carry-on bag. If you are bringing a larger suitcase or more than one bag, you'll need to check the bag(s) with the airline, which in turn will store your bags in the aircraft's cargo section.

When you check a bag at the airport, an airline employee will attach a tag to your bag to tell handlers where to send your luggage. You will also receive a baggage slip that will help you identify your bag in the event it gets misdirected. After you arrive at your final destination, you'll pick up your checked bags at baggage claim.

Notice an unusual code on your baggage tag? Airlines use standard three-digit codes to identify different airports. The "FWA" here indicates the Fort Wayne airport.

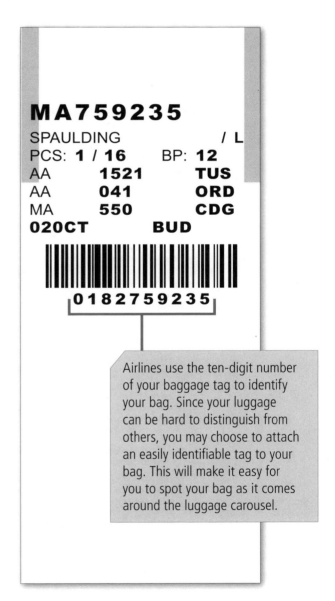

Airlines use the ten-digit number of your baggage tag to identify your bag. Since your luggage can be hard to distinguish from others, you may choose to attach an easily identifiable tag to your bag. This will make it easy for you to spot your bag as it comes around the luggage carousel.

Rental Car Agreement

You may decide to rent a car as part of your travel plans. Any time you rent a car, you will need to sign a contract with the rental company. This contract explains your rights and responsibilities, so be sure to keep a copy.

General Policies

1. **GENERAL RENTAL REQUIREMENTS***

THESE ARE THE GENERAL RENTAL REQUIREMENTS OF RENT A CAR. THE RENTAL COMPANY OPERATING THE LOCATION MAY HAVE OTHER REQUIREMENTS. THE REQUIREMENTS OF THE RENTAL LOCATION WILL CONTROL. **CHECK THE LOCAL POLICIES OF THE RENTING LOCATION FOR MORE INFORMATION ON THEIR TERMS AND CONDITIONS.** FOR RENTALS OUTSIDE OF THE UNITED STATES AND CANADA, PLEASE REFER TO THE LOCAL POLICIES WHERE YOU INTEND TO RENT THE VEHICLE.

A. Rental Rates: Daily Rental rates are based on a 24-hour rental day starting at the time of rental. The minimum charge is one day, plus mileage, if applicable. The renter will be charged for each hour and/or any part of an hour in excess of a rental day the renter keeps the vehicle until the vehicle is returned, up to the applicable daily rate.

A. Rental Rates: Daily Rental rates are based on a 24-hour rental day starting at the time of rental. The minimum charge is one day, plus mileage, if applicable. The renter will be charged for each hour and/or any part of an hour in excess of a rental day the renter keeps the vehicle until the vehicle is returned, up to the applicable daily rate.

Typically, you may rent a car by the day or by the week. Weekly rates are a better value if you need the car for a longer period of time. Keeping the car for a longer or a shorter period of time may cause your rates to change.

C. Authorized Drivers: The vehicle may be driven only by an authorized driver. An authorized driver is the renter and any additional person who appears at the time of rental and signs the rental agreement. All authorized drivers must satisfy our age requirements, have a valid drivers license, and fulfill our other qualifications, which vary by location. Employers and co-employees of renters renting on corporate rate plans, if properly licensed and meet our age requirements, are authorized to drive the vehicle while acting within the scope of their employment duties.

E. Underage Driver's Fee: An authorized driver 21 to 24 years of age may be charged an Underage Drivers fee because of such driver's age in addition to the additional driver fee, if applicable. Because the requirements vary by location, please refer to the Local Policies for specific information on additional authorized or underage drivers at the location where you intend to rent a vehicle.

How old are you? Most rental companies require drivers to be at least 21 years of age to rent a car. They typically charge drivers under 25 an additional fee. If you are under 25 years old, you may want to shop around to find a company that does not charge this fee.

E. Underage Driver's Fee: An authorized driver 21 to 24 years of age may be charged an Underage Drivers fee because of such driver's age in addition to the additional driver fee, if applicable. Because the requirements vary by location, please refer to the Local Policies for specific information on additional authorized or underage drivers at the location where you intend to rent a vehicle.

F. Credit Qualifications/requirement: To qualify to rent the vehicle, the renter must present at the time of rental a major credit card or debit card (See Debit Card Usage below) in the renters own name with available credit.

F. Credit Qualifications/requirement: To qualify to rent the vehicle, the renter must present at the time of rental a major credit card or debit card (See Debit Card Usage below) in the renters own name with available credit.

Even if you want to pay your rental fees in cash, you will need to provide a credit or debit card number when you pick up the car. Rental companies will charge this card if you damage the vehicle or receive any traffic tickets.

Our debit card policy complies with all applicable U.S. federal and state laws. Debit cards are accepted for payment at the end of rental without a credit inquiry. Debit cards may not be accepted in Canada except for payment at the end of rental. Since credit requirements vary by location, please refer to the Local Policies for specific information on the acceptance and usage of debit cards where you intend to rent a vehicle.

Rental Car Agreement

L. Driver's Licenses: The renter or any additional authorized driver's wanting to drive the rental vehicle must present (at the beginning of the rental) a motor vehicle driver's license that is valid for the entire rental period. A valid motor vehicle drivers license means a drivers license that has not been suspended, expired, surrendered or revoked and includes an expiration date occurring after the end of the rental period. The following motor vehicle drivers licenses are generally acceptable in the U.S.

1. A valid motor vehicle driver's license issued by any state, territory or possession of the U.S.
2. A valid temporary driver's license issued by any state, territory or possession of the U.S.
3. A traffic citation issued by any state, territory or possession of the U.S., as a temporary license, valid for the entire rental period (the court date being the expiration date) accompanied with a second form of photo identification with signature (excluding the credit card used for rental).
4. A valid U.S. military identification card plus an expired driver's license for active duty U.S. military personnel in those states where active duty U.S. military can drive on an expired driver's license.

M. Driver Record Checks: In the U.S., before we will rent a vehicle and when the customer arrives at our location, the customer and any additional authorized drivers may be subject to a driving record and license check with the DMV. In the rare instance the driving record and license check fails to meet our criteria, we reserve the right to deny the rental based on the DMV report.

Expect a rental car company to check your driving record before providing you with a car. If you have been involved in too many accidents or have been cited for driving under the influence, the rental company may refuse to rent you a car.

M. Driver Record Checks: In the U.S., before we will rent a vehicle and when the customer arrives at our location, the customer and any additional authorized drivers may be subject to a driving record and license check with the DMV. In the rare instance the driving record and license check fails to meet our criteria, we reserve the right to deny the rental based on the DMV report.

- The drivers have a valid license that is not currently suspended, revoked, expired, or surrendered; and,
- The drivers have not, during the last 24 months, pled guilty or paid a fine for, or otherwise been convicted, of:
  - accrued 8 or more points; or
  - one or more reckless driving; or
  - three or more moving violations; and
- The drivers have not, during the last 36 months, pled guilty or paid a fine for, or otherwise been convicted, of:
  - two or more accidents; or
- The drivers have not, during the last 48 months, pled guilty or paid a fine for, or otherwise been convicted, of:
  - one or more accidents with a fatality or bodily injury, operating a vehicle, or permitting the operation of a vehicle without a license or without insurance; or
  - possession of a stolen vehicle or using a vehicle in a crime; or
  - failure to report an accident or leaving the scene of an accident, and
- The drivers have not, during the last 72 months, been convicted of a DWI, DWAI or DUI.

N. One-way Rentals: One-way rentals within the U.S. and within Canada vary by location and vehicle availability. A one-way drop fee will apply.

O. Optional Equipment:

1. **Child Safety Seats:** For an additional charge, which varies by location, infant, toddler and child/youth safety seats are available at many locations.

O. Optional Equipment:

1. **Child Safety Seats:** For an additional charge, which varies by location, infant, toddler and child/youth safety seats are available at many locations.

You may choose to add certain optional services to your rental, such as roadside assistance or prepaid tolls. These features may be convenient but will cost you some extra money.

2. **Electronic toll by-pass option:** In a few cities, we offer an option to purchase an electronic toll bypass service for a per/day charge that allows the driver to bypass all toll booths and avoid electronic toll charges on all the toll roads in the city or state, as applicable; and, as many times a day as necessary. If you decline to purchase the toll bypass option, you will pay us for all unpaid toll road violations (including violations captured by camera) charged by the toll authority plus a $25.00 administrative fee per violation. If you have a personal transponder or account, it may not transfer to the rental vehicle and you will be charged a toll violation. Please be advised that some toll roads are managed electronically and have no manned booths. GPS units rented from us can be programmed to avoid toll roads.

CONSUMER DOCUMENTS

Purchasing

CONTENTS

Being an informed consumer involves understanding documents related to purchases. Whether you're buying a bottle of soda or a new living room furniture set, you need to know how to read consumer documents, such as advertisements and receipts, to make sound purchasing decisions.

Advertisements can be misleading, so it's important to read all the details and fine print before making a purchase. Product comparison reports help you compare aspects of the same item made by different companies. These types of reports can be especially helpful when making a large purchase, such as an appliance or a piece of furniture.

Purchase-related documents provide important information for planning and making purchases. Understanding the terms and conditions of payment plans and credit card offers can also help you save money while keeping your monthly bills manageable. You may also get great deals using a payment plan or a credit card to purchase items, but as with other documents, you should read them thoroughly before taking action. Studying these examples will help you interpret or complete the documents in the chapter review and in real life.

Online Bargain Shopping

If you're planning to make a purchase, you may want to research prices and sales on the Internet. Some stores offer special coupons or sale prices exclusively on their Web sites. Many stores also have versions of their weekly advertisements that you can access online.

Product Comparison Report

Magazines such as *Consumer Reports* regularly publish reviews of different types of products. You may see reviews for everyday products such as dishwashing soap or for major purchases such as cars. Using these reviews can help you make smart buys and get the most for your money.

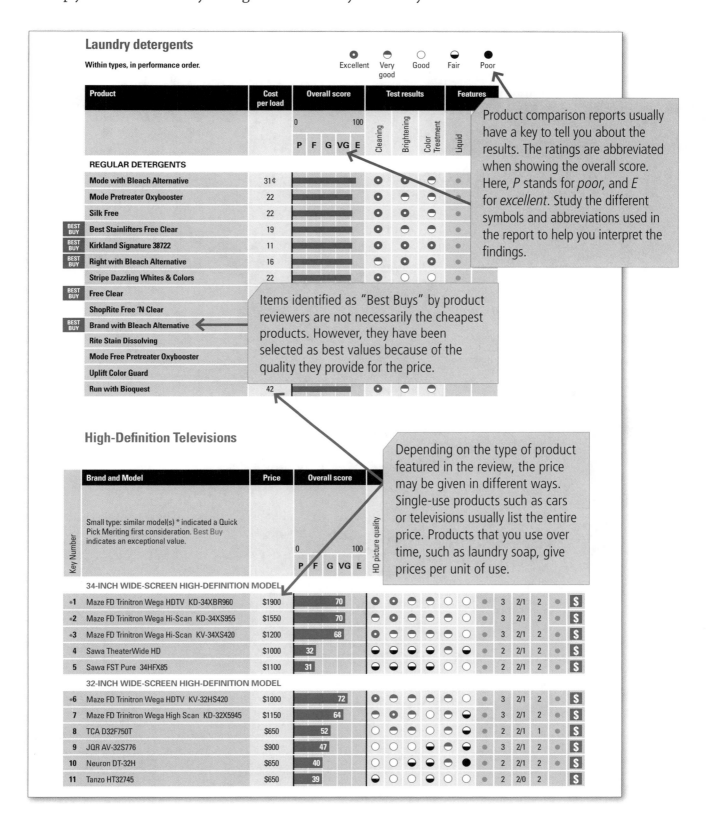

Laundry detergents

Within types, in performance order.

Key: ⊙ Excellent ◖ Very good ○ Good ◑ Fair ● Poor

Product	Cost per load	Overall score P F G VG E	Cleaning	Brightening	Color Treatment	Liquid
REGULAR DETERGENTS						
Mode with Bleach Alternative	31¢		⊙	◖	○	●
Mode Pretreater Oxybooster	22		⊙	◑	○	
Silk Free	22		⊙	◖	○	●
BEST BUY Best Stainlifters Free Clear	19		⊙	◖	○	●
BEST BUY Kirkland Signature 38722	11		⊙	◖	⊙	●
BEST BUY Right with Bleach Alternative	16		◑	◖	⊙	●
Stripe Dazzling Whites & Colors	22		⊙	○	○	●
BEST BUY Free Clear						
ShopRite Free 'N Clear						
BEST BUY Brand with Bleach Alternative						
Rite Stain Dissolving						
Mode Free Pretreater Oxybooster						
Uplift Color Guard						
Run with Bioquest	42		⊙	○	○	●

Product comparison reports usually have a key to tell you about the results. The ratings are abbreviated when showing the overall score. Here, *P* stands for *poor*, and *E* for *excellent*. Study the different symbols and abbreviations used in the report to help you interpret the findings.

Items identified as "Best Buys" by product reviewers are not necessarily the cheapest products. However, they have been selected as best values because of the quality they provide for the price.

High-Definition Televisions

Key Number	Brand and Model	Price	Overall score P F G VG E	HD picture quality											
	Small type: similar model(s) * indicated a Quick Pick Meriting first consideration. Best Buy indicates an exceptional value.														
	34-INCH WIDE-SCREEN HIGH-DEFINITION MODEL														
*1	Maze FD Trinitron Wega HDTV KD-34XBR960	$1900	70	⊙	⊙	◖	◖	◖	○	○	●	3	2/1	2	$
*2	Maze FD Trinitron Wega Hi-Scan KD-34XS955	$1550	70	⊙	◖	◖	◖	◖	○	○	●	3	2/1	2	$
*3	Maze FD Trinitron Wega Hi-Scan KV-34XS420	$1200	68	⊙	◖	◖	◖	◖	○	○	●	3	2/1	2	$
4	Sawa TheaterWide HD	$1000	32	◖	◖	◖	◖	◖	◖	○	●	2	2/1	2	$
5	Sawa FST Pure 34HFX85	$1100	31	◖	◖	◖	◖	◖	○	○	●	2	2/1	2	$
	32-INCH WIDE-SCREEN HIGH-DEFINITION MODEL														
*6	Maze FD Trinitron Wega HDTV KV-32HS420	$1000	72	⊙	◖	◖	◖	◖	○	○	●	3	2/1	2	$
7	Maze FD Trinitron Wega High Scan KD-32X5945	$1150	64	◖	⊙	◖	◖	◖	○	◑	●	3	2/1	2	$
8	TCA D32F750T	$650	52	○	○	◖	◖	○	○	○	●	2	2/1	1	$
9	JQR AV-32S776	$900	47	○	○	○	◖	◖	◖	◑	●	3	2/1	2	$
10	Neuron DT-32H	$650	40	○	○	◑	◖	◑	●	○	●	2	2/1	2	$
11	Tanzo HT32745	$650	39	◖	○	○	◑	◖	○	○	●	2	2/0	2	$

Depending on the type of product featured in the review, the price may be given in different ways. Single-use products such as cars or televisions usually list the entire price. Products that you use over time, such as laundry soap, give prices per unit of use.

Fine-Print Ad

Have you ever gone to a store that was having a big sale only to discover that the product you wanted to buy wasn't part of it? Checking the fine print on sale advertisements may help you avoid disappointment or surprise when it comes time to pay.

40% off

ALL COSMETICS FROM:
- Restore
- Cici
- NYT
- Heal

NOW $2.09–8.99

Includes mascara, eye shadow, liner, foundation, powder, nail color, blush, eye makeup remover, lip color, and brow color.

Offer excludes implements, beauty tools, and clearance. MAX.com: Use brand name as keyword in search box

MAX BEAUTY

Sales Sunday, Sept. 26th through Saturday, Oct. 2nd

This ad states those products that are part of this sale and those that are not. Even though the sale covers many products and brands, it does not cover items such as brushes or makeup cases.

MAX Gift Certificate
VALID 9/26/12 – 10/2/12

Use this certificate in-store or online

$3.50 off

ANY PURCHASE OF $10 OR MORE*

For online purchases, enter the coupon code 41863 in the space provided in your shopping basket and click "apply."

*Coupon offer valid on all regular price, sale, and clearance merchandise. Excluding salon services, fragrance, hair artistry brands, prestige cosmetics, prestige skincare. **Cannot be redeemed for cash or gift cards. This offer cannot be combined with any other MAX coupon offer. Not valid on prior purchases. Limit one per customer. **See in-store for exclusions. Void if copied or transferred and where prohibited by law. ©2012 MAX salon.

This ad also includes a coupon for $3.50 off a purchase of $10 or more. However, by reading the fine print you can learn that the coupon fails to cover some expensive items, such as designer-brand perfume or salon haircuts.

Buy Now, Pay Later Ad

For many buy now, pay later purchases, you must open a credit account with the store selling the item. Terms vary, but most deals offer zero percent interest for a specific amount of time. If you pay the balance before the period ends, you won't have to pay any interest. In that case, the purchase will be same as cash.

CALLEN
HOME FURNISHINGS
THE BETTER SLEEP SHOP

Sleep Tite Cushion Firm

$299
QUEEN
2PC. SET
Compare†
$889

TWIN set . . . Compare† $629 . . . . . SALE $249
FULL set . . . . Compare† $849 . . . . . SALE $279
KING set . . . . Compare† $1559 . . . . SALE $349

Sleep Tite Plush Pillowtop

$399
QUEEN
2PC. SET
Compare†
$1119

TWIN set . . . Compare† $849 . . . . . SALE $349
FULL set . . . . Compare† $1069 . . . . SALE $379
KING set . . . . Compare† $1779 . . . . SALE $699

Sleep Tite Posturepedic Luxury Plush Euro Pillowtop

$799
QUEEN
2PC. SET
Compare†
$2669

TWIN set . . . Compare† $2239 . . . . SALE $599
FULL set . . . . Compare† $2639 . . . . SALE $799
KING set . . . . Compare† $3559 . . . SALE $1199

Sleep Tite Premium Posturepedic Firm OR Plush Euro Pillowtop

$999
QUEEN
2PC. SET
Compare†
$2889

TWIN set . . . Compare† $2449 . . . . SALE $799
FULL set . . . . Compare† $2849 . . . . SALE $999
KING set . . . . Compare† $3779 . . . SALE $1399

To take advantage of buy now, pay later sales, you usually need to pay for your purchase with the store's credit card. Interest fees on the purchase are waived if you pay off your debt within a certain period of time, usually over several weeks or months. If you fail to pay off the purchase, however, you will owe the entire amount of interest that has built up over the grace period. Paying off such purchases on time can save you hundreds of dollars in interest charges.

50% OFF AND MORE
†Compare Price
ALL Sleep Tite Mattresses Including Posturepedics

50% OFF† plus, take an extra 10% OFF
ALL Stem & Franks and Soul by Sleep Tite Mattresses

SLEEP INTEREST FREE
FOR UP TO 36 MONTHS*
On Purchases pf $799–$1,999 with your More For You Card. Equal Fixed Minimum Monthly Payments Required. Penalty APR may apply if you make a late payment. See store for complete details.

As with any major purchase, read the fine print on the advertisement and on the credit card agreement, should you decide to use one. In the fine print, you'll find information about the interest rate, length of the interest-free portion of the loan, and other important details.

Finance Offer: Valid on furniture and mattress purchase with your More for You credit card on or before November 16, 2010. No minimum purchase required. On promo purchase balance, 12 minimum monthly payments are required until expiration or termination of promotion, but no Finance Charges will be assessed if (1) promo purchase balance paid in full in 12 months or less, and (2) all minimum monthly payments on account paid when due. Otherwise, promo may be terminated and treated as a non-promo balance. Regular rates apply to non-promo balances, including optional charges. Promo purchases on existing accounts may not receive full benefit of promo terms, including reduced APR if applicable, or account is subject to Penalty APR. Payments over the minimum will be applied as required by applicable law. As of 6/28/10. APR 29.99% & on all accounts in default. Penalty APR: 29.99%. Minimum Finance Charge $2.00. Subject to approval by GE Money Bank. †Compare prices: Sale prices and percentage savings offered in this advertisement on furniture and mattresses are discount from the compare price. The compare price is the regular price or original price for the item or comparable item at another retailer. Actual sales may or may not have been made at the compare prices and intermediate markdowns may have been taken.

New and improved • callenathome.com

Callen Home Furnishings – Centerville
5695 Wilmington Pike
Centerville, OH 45459
937-555-0500

Callen Home Furnishings – Dayton
2121 Harshman Road
Dayton, OH 45424
937-555-7000

Coupons

Coupons are good for more than just groceries. Stores or manufacturers may offer coupons for certain items. Using coupons can help you save money on a variety of goods and services. You may even find coupons for discounts on big-ticket items such as televisions or game systems.

Coupons like this one offer a set percent-off discount on a variety of products at a certain store. Because you can use the coupon on only one item, be sure to apply it to your most expensive purchase.

Valid 9/5/2011 – 9/28/2011 only at Home Max stores

GET 10% OFF any single item from the following catagories:

HOME THEATER TVs $399 & up; Blu-ray Disc™ and HD DVD players; home audio; audio and video accessories; furniture $99 & up; Home Theater installation; **COMPUTER ACCESSORIES** DVD-RW drives; flash and external hard drives; printers $149 & up; scanners $99 & up; networking; speakers, mice, and keyboards; PC cameras and gaming controllers; digital recorders $99 & up; surge protectors; flash memory; cables; graphic and sound cards; software; blank media; ink cartridges; printer docks; paper; **DIGITAL CAMERAS** $249 & up; **CAMCORDERS** $279 & up; digital camera accessories; camcorder accessories; blank media; camcorder batteries; premium photo services; digital photo frames; photo gifts; Photo Center Gift Cards; batteries; **MP3 Players & Car Electronics** MP3 accessories; GPS hardware; car audio; satellite radio hardware; musical instruments; CD/DVD storage; toys; **Phones & Accessories** pay-as-you-go phones; cordless phones; answering machines; landline and cellular phone accessories; phone cards; two-way radios; **Major and Small Appliances & More**

HOME MAX

This coupon offers $15 off any purchase of $75 or more. Regardless of the amount of money you spend after that amount, you will still receive $15 off. This coupon differs from the coupon above, which gives you a bigger dollar discount as you spend more money.

GLOBAL MARKET

Over 1000 locations. Find one near you at globalmarket.com

Visit globalmarket.com to see the six most popular ways to decorate after the move. Then bring in this offer to save $15 on your purchase of $75 or more.

Bring this offer to a U.S. Global Market store and save $15 off on your next purchase of $75 or more. Offer does not apply to delivery or other service charges. Offer does not apply to prior purchases and cannot be used on Gift Card, UNICEF or other non-discountable merchandise purchases. Offer is not valid in combination with any other offer or discount and is not valid at stores closing sales. Offer must be surrendered at the time of purchase. Limit one per customer, void if copied and no cash value. Expires 09/20/11

2800

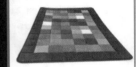

Coupons

QuikService

We Care About Your Car!

5601 N. ASHLAND

(at Bryn Mawr)

773-555-1188

Monday – Friday: 8 am – 7 pm
Saturday: 8 am – 6 pm
Sunday: 9 am – 4 pm

We Accept Competitor's Coupons!

No Appointment Needed!

QuikService
OIL CHANGE
$7 OFF

Includes:
- Change Oil Up to 5 qts.
- Install New Oil Filter
- Check Air Filter
- Check Brake Fluid
- Check Wiper Blades
- Vacuum Interior Floors
- Wash Exterior Window

As Needed:
- Lubricate Chassis
- Check and Fill Transmission/Transaxle Fluid
- Check and Fill Differential Fluid, Power Steering Fluid, Battery, Washer Fluid
- Check and Inflate Tires

Valid only at
5601 N. Ashland Ave.

Some stores will take not only their own coupons but also those of competing local stores. If you prefer one business over another, don't hesitate to take the competitor's coupon to the place where you'd rather buy the product or service. Some stores will also match their competitors' prices.

Be sure to check to see what the coupon covers. You may need additional services that the coupon does not cover.

Nearly all coupons carry an expiration date. Check this date to ensure that it remains valid. If you plan to use a coupon beyond its expiration date, it never hurts to ask the store if it will still honor the coupon. Some stores will apply the discount after the expiration date.

MANUFACTURER'S COUPON

Expires 10/20/2011

SAVE $.50

when you buy TWO (2) packages of Decadence Morsels any variety

0009 2098 1842 7801

Consumer: One coupon per purchase. Good only on product indicated. Consumer pays any sales tax. Coupon void if altered, copied, sold, purchased, exchanged, transferred, or where prohibited or restricted by law.

RETAILER: Redeem on terms stated for consumer upon purchase of product indicated.

0 00000 00026 0

0028000–014431

Be sure to read the coupon carefully for specific details. For example, this coupon offers 50 cents off *two packages* of chocolate chips; the coupon wouldn't apply to just one package.

Credit Card Application

Millions of Americans have at least one credit card. Credit cards are a convenient way to pay for purchases, but these cards can quickly become overwhelming. Understanding the responsibilities that come with credit card use will help you become a better consumer.

NOBU

Apply   Confirm   Results

NOBU Credit is issued by TM Money Bank ("TMMB"). The TMMB Privacy Policy governs the use of NOBU Credit. This privacy policy may be different from the Privacy Policy of NOBU.

You should be able to answer "YES" to these statements in order to increase your chances of approval:

- Your credit history is clear of bankruptcies and seriously delinquent accounts.

- You are at least 18 years old and have a valid social security number.

- You have not submitted an application for a NOBU Credit Card in the past 90 days.

About You – **Federal law requires GEMB to obtain, verify, and record information that identifies you when you open an account. We will use your name, address, date of birth, and other information for this purpose.**

First Name `Kealoha`   Initial `  `   Last Name `Enos`

Address `15689 Kaniau Road, #4` (street name and number required)

`                    `

City `Lahaina`   State `HI`   Zip `96761`

Home Phone* `808` – `555` – `6491`

Business Phone* `808` – `555` – `3200`

Cell / Other Phone* `808` – `555` – `4878`

*You authorize us to contact you at any number you provide.

Email Address `enosk@opax.com`

☐ Yes! I want to receive emails from you and NOBU.

Annual Income
(from all sources) `34,250` .00

Alimony, child support, or separate maintenance income need not be included unless relied upon for credit. You may include the annual amount that you have available to spend from any assets.
WI Residents only: If you are applying for an individual account, combine your and your spouse's financial information.

> Credit card companies will check your credit history before deciding whether to issue you a card. Your credit history shows a record of your borrowing and repayment. A good credit history will help you qualify for credit cards and get better interest rates.

> This application does not require you to list all your income, such as alimony from an ex-spouse, child support payments, or maintenance income (government assistance). You don't need to include that income unless you would use it to help pay your credit card bill.

Credit Card Application

Most credit cards offer an optional protection plan that will cancel your balance if you lose your job or suffer a serious illness. To participate in this program, you must pay a monthly fee based on your credit card balance.

As part of a credit card application, companies usually ask for your social security number and driver's license number so that they can find information about your credit history. Companies ask for personal information, such as your mother's maiden name, so that they can verify your identity if you call to make changes to your account. It'd be hard for a stranger to guess your mother's maiden name.

Complete if at current residence for less than 2 years:

Previous Address

Previous City   Previous State

Verification – Your personal information is safe. To help us protect you, please enter your date of birth, social security number, driver's license information, and mother's maiden name.

Date of Birth   5 / 15 / 1975

Social Security Number   XXX – XXX – XXXX

Driver's License Number   E00685555   State HI   Expiration   5 / 15 / 2016

Mother's Maiden Name   Taketa

Optional Card Security – Up to **$10,000** in **Protection on your NOBU Credit Card.**

With the opening of your new NOBU Credit Card Account, feel secure knowing you are financially protected. Enroll in the Card Security program and we will cancel your Account balance up to $10,000 if you experience a qualifying unemployment, approved leave of absence, disability, hospitalization, nursing home care, terminal illness or loss of life.

Click Here for Summary of Terms

I acknowledge that I do not need to purchase Card Security to obtain credit. Per the Card Security agreement. I agree that you may bill my NOBU Account a monthly fee of $1.68 per $100 to the monthly ending balance on my Account. I may cancel at any time. I have read and agree to the Summary of Terms above. By clicking the enrollment button below, I intend to purchase optional Card Security and this constitutes my signature. Residents of MS are not eligible.

☐ Yes! I would like to enroll in Card Security.

Important Information – Please see below for **Key Terms** and **Consent to Electronic Communications**. You may **Print or Download** these disclosures here. **Print or Download in Spanish**.

Pay attention to the stated interest rate on the credit card application. A high interest rate like this one may cost you lots of money over time. By paying off your balance each month, you can avoid paying interest on your purchases.

TM MONEY BANK NOBU CREDIT CARD ACCOUNT	
Interest Rates and Interest Charges	
Annual Percentage Rate (APR) for Purchases	**25.99%** This APR will vary with the market based on the Prime Rate.
How to Avoid Paying Interest on Purchases	Your due date is at least 23 days after the close of each billing cycle. We will not charge you interest on purchases if you pay your entire balance by the due date of each month.

Applicant Signature By applying for this account, I am asking TM Money Bank ("TMMB") to issue me a NOBU Credit Card (the "Card"), and I agree that:

- I am providing the information in this application to TMMB and to NOBU North American Services LLC (and its affiliates) so that they can create and update their records, and provide me with service and special offers.

Receipts

Whenever you purchase a product or a service, you should get a receipt for it. Receipts give information about your purchase, including the product or service you bought, its cost, the form of payment you used to purchase it, and any change, if appropriate, you received.

FRESH FARE

```
FRESH FARE XXXXXXXXXXXXXXXXXXXXXXXXXX
XXXXXXXXXXXXXXXXXXXXXXXXXXXXXXXXXX

            GROCERY
KIDNEY BEAN                      .79  F
RegPrice    .89      Card Save   .10
2 @ 2.19   VEG SOUP MIX         4.38  F

         REFRIG / FROZEN
1 @ 3.99 EA / 2 FOR 7.00
RD FAT MILK                     3.99  F
SFY SEL 3 CHSE RAV              3.00  F
RegPrice   3.59      Card Save   .59

          BAKED GOODS
6 @ .79   JUMBO CKY            4.74  F

            PRODUCE
0.65 lb @ $1.99 / lb
WT        PEPPER GREEN BELL     1.29  F
1.56 lb @ $4.99 / lb
WT        TOMATOES HOTHOUSE     7.78  F
**** TAX          .00 BAL      25.97
XXX XXX XXXXXXXXXXXXXXXXX       25.97

          CHANGE                .00
       NUMBER OF ITEMS  =  13
2/01/11  18:19  1539 04 0055 9501

Club Card Savings            $  .69
     Look for the # sign on your receipt
     for possible Health Care Flex Spending
        Account items for reimbursement.

Healthy Eating just got easier. Visit freshfare.com/
foodflex for a free Nutrition Snapshot of your Fresh
Fare Club Card purchase and to identify healthier
alternatives.

         LET US HEAR FROM YOU!
  1-888-555-3929 or visit FRESHFARE.COM
```

Some items may be on sale at a special price, like 2 items for $2.19 instead of 89 cents apiece. Other items, like produce, are sold by the pound. You'll see the price listed per pound rather than by items, such as $1.99/lb.

Many grocery stores now have club card programs. Registering for a free card allows you to pay lower prices for many items. Some stores allow you to access information on their Web sites about your purchases, such as menu suggestions and coupons.

TERMINAL 742

```
              4374711285 1024

          THANK YOU FOR SHOPPING AT
          STANTON*S, HERALD SQUARE

     TERMINAL 742  CUSTOMER COPY   PURCHASE
     S003 ASSC 266234 TR3278 10/12/10 649P

     COOKWARE            QTY 1    16.99
     636189000013
     NY 8.25% TAX                  1.40

     TOTAL AMOUNT DUE STORE       18.39

     ACCOUNT NUMBER   XXXXXXXXXXXX
        DEBIT TENDER              18.39
```

```
              0037423278

268234      0037423278       10/12/11
KEEP THIS RECEIPT         SEE REVERSE SIDE
```

KEEP THIS RECEIPT
FOR RETURN/EXCHANGE

Want an Employee Discount?
And How About A New Career?
Visit StantonJobs.com And Apply Today

States and cities levy different sales taxes on purchases. This receipt is from New York, which has a state sales tax of 8.25%. The item the buyer purchased cost $16.99. To calculate the sales tax, multiply 16.99 by .0825, which equals 1.4. The total for the purchase is $16.99 plus $1.40, or $18.39.

Don't throw away your receipts! Most stores require your original purchase receipt if you wish to return or exchange an item. You may find the store's return policy printed on the back of your receipt.

Restaurant Receipts

Many restaurants allow you to pay with a debit or credit card instead of cash. If you choose to pay with a card, your server will bring you two copies of the bill. You should leave one copy for the restaurant and take the other as your receipt.

BALANCE BISTRO — TAMPA
4134 E. Shore Dr.
(813) 555-3838

Date : 11/5/2012   Time: 9:447:53 PM

Status: Approved

Card Type: Visa
Card Number: XXXXXXXXXXXX5561
Swipe/Manual: Swipe
Server ID: 327
Server Name   Rebecca
Check Number: 412278
Tab Number: 96
Profil Center: Table Sales
Number Of Covers: 2
Persons: 1, 2
Card Owner   landry/melissa.

AMOUNT   19.80

TIP   4.00

TOTAL   23.80

****
*****CREDIT CARD VOUCHER*****
Manny's Tuscan Grille
787 42nd St. W
Tampa, FL
Ph: (813) 555-3939
Date: Nov06' 11   10:31PM
Card Type: Visa
Acct #:   XXXXXXXXXXXXX2437
Card Entry: SWIPED
Trans Type: PURCHASE
Trans Key: EIE003381061245
Auth Code: 15313
Check: 253
Table: 93/1
Server: 824 Tabitha

Subtotal: 35.45
Gratuity: 6.—
Total: 41.45
Signature:

X   Will Darcy

Guest Copy
Visit www.guest-feedback.com and tell us about your experience. Enter survey ID 737898.

When paying with a debit or credit card, you have the option of adding a tip to your total bill. Simply write the amount you'd like to tip on the tip line of your receipt. Then add that amount to the total. You also may choose to leave a cash tip. Most people tip between 15 and 20 percent of the bill. It's easy to figure the percentage: moving the decimal one place to the left of the total will tell you what 10 percent of the bill is. For this bill, a $4 tip is 20 percent, and a 15 percent tip would be $3.

If you pay with a credit card, you'll get a receipt like this from your server after he or she runs your credit card. The server also will present you with an itemized bill listing your food and drinks. Check the itemized receipt to ensure the accuracy of your bill.

Sometimes your receipt will provide the address for a Web site on which you can complete a survey about your dining experience. By completing this survey, you may earn you a coupon toward your next meal.

CONSUMER DOCUMENTS

Automobiles

CONTENTS

Some people use the bus or subway to get around each day, but a great many people drive cars. If you already own a car, you know that proper maintenance will ensure that it runs reliably and lasts as long as possible. If you are looking to purchase a vehicle, you'll need to understand the many documents related to buying, registering, and insuring your car.

After Eduardo Washington landed his first job as an HVAC technician, he realized that borrowing his father's car wasn't going to suit his needs anymore. He needed to drive to and from work every day and wanted to run errands and hang out with his friends. It was time for him to buy a car.

Since a new car was out of his price range, Eduardo researched used cars to determine those that were most reliable. He looked up reports about specific used cars so that he could make the best choice. Eduardo looked both online and at local dealerships for the perfect used car. He also knew that once he purchased the car, he'd need to take good care of it. He would need to change the oil regularly. He also would need to register his car with the state motor vehicle agency and obtain car insurance.

Whether you're looking to buy a car or already own one, the documents in this chapter may serve as helpful references. Studying these examples will help you interpret or complete the documents in the chapter review and in real life.

Online Classifieds

If you want to buy a used car, check classified Web sites such as Craigslist. Every day owners and dealers alike post cars for sale on these types of Web sites. You can browse hundreds of cars online to help you find just the right one.

Car Sticker

When you visit a car dealership, you will notice that each car has a sticker in its window. This sticker gives you the price and other helpful information about the vehicle. Take all this information into consideration before you decide to purchase the car.

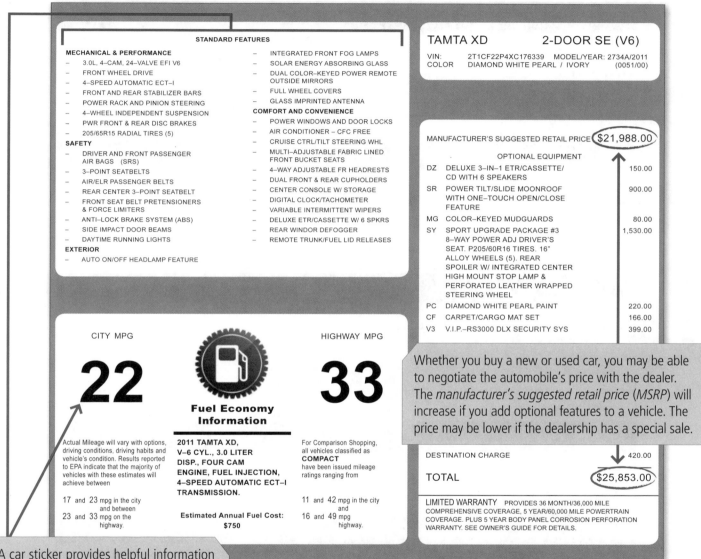

STANDARD FEATURES

MECHANICAL & PERFORMANCE
- 3.0L, 4–CAM, 24–VALVE EFI V6
- FRONT WHEEL DRIVE
- 4–SPEED AUTOMATIC ECT–I
- FRONT AND REAR STABILIZER BARS
- POWER RACK AND PINION STEERING
- 4–WHEEL INDEPENDENT SUSPENSION
- PWR FRONT & REAR DISC BRAKES
- 205/65R15 RADIAL TIRES (5)

SAFETY
- DRIVER AND FRONT PASSENGER AIR BAGS (SRS)
- 3–POINT SEATBELTS
- AIR/ELR PASSENGER BELTS
- REAR CENTER 3–POINT SEATBELT
- FRONT SEAT BELT PRETENSIONERS & FORCE LIMITERS
- ANTI–LOCK BRAKE SYSTEM (ABS)
- SIDE IMPACT DOOR BEAMS
- DAYTIME RUNNING LIGHTS

EXTERIOR
- AUTO ON/OFF HEADLAMP FEATURE
- INTEGRATED FRONT FOG LAMPS
- SOLAR ENERGY ABSORBING GLASS
- DUAL COLOR–KEYED POWER REMOTE OUTSIDE MIRRORS
- FULL WHEEL COVERS
- GLASS IMPRINTED ANTENNA

COMFORT AND CONVENIENCE
- POWER WINDOWS AND DOOR LOCKS
- AIR CONDITIONER – CFC FREE
- CRUISE CTRL/TILT STEERING WHL
- MULTI–ADJUSTABLE FABRIC LINED FRONT BUCKET SEATS
- 4–WAY ADJUSTABLE FR HEADRESTS
- DUAL FRONT & REAR CUPHOLDERS
- CENTER CONSOLE W/ STORAGE
- DIGITAL CLOCK/TACHOMETER
- VARIABLE INTERMITTENT WIPERS
- DELUXE ETR/CASSETTE W/ 6 SPKRS
- REAR WINDOR DEFOGGER
- REMOTE TRUNK/FUEL LID RELEASES

TAMTA XD   2-DOOR SE (V6)

VIN: 2T1CF22P4XC176339   MODEL/YEAR: 2734A/2011
COLOR   DIAMOND WHITE PEARL / IVORY   (0051/00)

MANUFACTURER'S SUGGESTED RETAIL PRICE **$21,988.00**

OPTIONAL EQUIPMENT

DZ	DELUXE 3–IN–1 ETR/CASSETTE/ CD WITH 6 SPEAKERS	150.00
SR	POWER TILT/SLIDE MOONROOF WITH ONE–TOUCH OPEN/CLOSE FEATURE	900.00
MG	COLOR–KEYED MUDGUARDS	80.00
SY	SPORT UPGRADE PACKAGE #3 8–WAY POWER ADJ DRIVER'S SEAT. P205/60R16 TIRES. 16" ALLOY WHEELS (5). REAR SPOILER W/ INTEGRATED CENTER HIGH MOUNT STOP LAMP & PERFORATED LEATHER WRAPPED STEERING WHEEL	1,530.00
PC	DIAMOND WHITE PEARL PAINT	220.00
CF	CARPET/CARGO MAT SET	166.00
V3	V.I.P.–RS3000 DLX SECURITY SYS	399.00

DESTINATION CHARGE   420.00

TOTAL   **$25,853.00**

LIMITED WARRANTY   PROVIDES 36 MONTH/36,000 MILE COMPREHENSIVE COVERAGE, 5 YEAR/60,000 MILE POWERTRAIN COVERAGE. PLUS 5 YEAR BODY PANEL CORROSION PERFORATION WARRANTY. SEE OWNER'S GUIDE FOR DETAILS.

CITY MPG

22

Actual Mileage will vary with options, driving conditions, driving habits and vehicle's condition. Results reported to EPA indicate that the majority of vehicles with these estimates will achieve between

17 and 23 mpg in the city and between
23 and 33 mpg on the highway.

Fuel Economy Information

2011 TAMTA XD, V–6 CYL., 3.0 LITER DISP., FOUR CAM ENGINE, FUEL INJECTION, 4–SPEED AUTOMATIC ECT–I TRANSMISSION.

Estimated Annual Fuel Cost: **$750**

HIGHWAY MPG

33

For Comparison Shopping, all vehicles classified as **COMPACT** have been issued mileage ratings ranging from

11 and 42 mpg in the city and
16 and 49 mpg highway.

> Whether you buy a new or used car, you may be able to negotiate the automobile's price with the dealer. The *manufacturer's suggested retail price* (*MSRP*) will increase if you add optional features to a vehicle. The price may be lower if the dealership has a special sale.

> A car sticker provides helpful information about the vehicle. It lists the car's mechanical specifications and any special optional features. The sticker also gives the car's average gas mileage to help you estimate your possible fuel costs.

Used Car Report

If you're considering buying a used car, you may want to obtain a copy of the car's history to make an informed decision. Car histories tell about a car's maintenance, including its accident history. It will even let you know whether the car has been in a flood or other damaging event.

Page 1 of 2

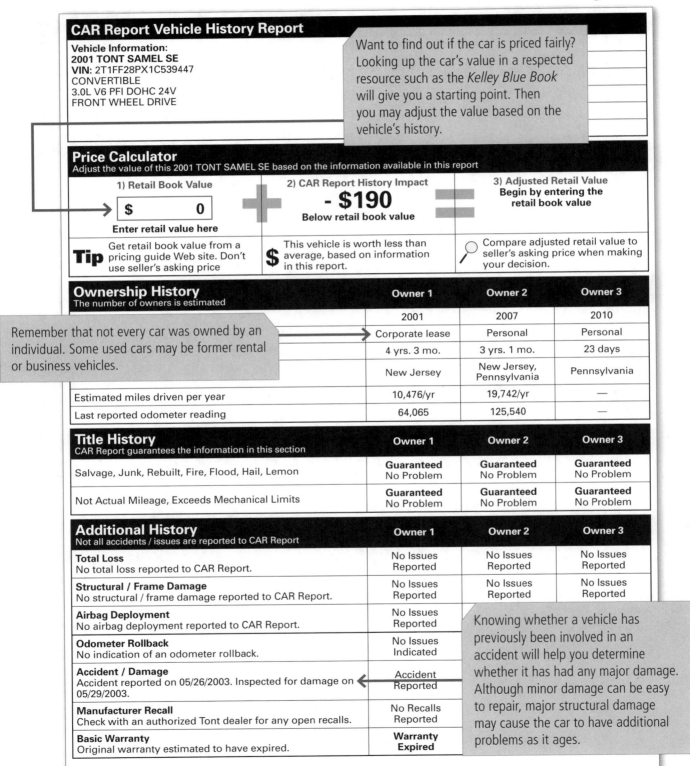

CAR Report Vehicle History Report

Vehicle Information:
2001 TONT SAMEL SE
VIN: 2T1FF28PX1C539447
CONVERTIBLE
3.0L V6 PFI DOHC 24V
FRONT WHEEL DRIVE

Want to find out if the car is priced fairly? Looking up the car's value in a respected resource such as the *Kelley Blue Book* will give you a starting point. Then you may adjust the value based on the vehicle's history.

Price Calculator
Adjust the value of this 2001 TONT SAMEL SE based on the information available in this report

1) Retail Book Value	2) CAR Report History Impact	3) Adjusted Retail Value
$ 0	**- $190**	**Begin by entering the retail book value**
Enter retail value here	Below retail book value	

Tip Get retail book value from a pricing guide Web site. Don't use seller's asking price

$ This vehicle is worth less than average, based on information in this report.

🔍 Compare adjusted retail value to seller's asking price when making your decision.

Ownership History
The number of owners is estimated

	Owner 1	Owner 2	Owner 3
	2001	2007	2010
	Corporate lease	Personal	Personal
	4 yrs. 3 mo.	3 yrs. 1 mo.	23 days
	New Jersey	New Jersey, Pennsylvania	Pennsylvania
Estimated miles driven per year	10,476/yr	19,742/yr	—
Last reported odometer reading	64,065	125,540	—

Remember that not every car was owned by an individual. Some used cars may be former rental or business vehicles.

Title History
CAR Report guarantees the information in this section

	Owner 1	Owner 2	Owner 3
Salvage, Junk, Rebuilt, Fire, Flood, Hail, Lemon	**Guaranteed** No Problem	**Guaranteed** No Problem	**Guaranteed** No Problem
Not Actual Mileage, Exceeds Mechanical Limits	**Guaranteed** No Problem	**Guaranteed** No Problem	**Guaranteed** No Problem

Additional History
Not all accidents / issues are reported to CAR Report

	Owner 1	Owner 2	Owner 3
Total Loss No total loss reported to CAR Report.	No Issues Reported	No Issues Reported	No Issues Reported
Structural / Frame Damage No structural / frame damage reported to CAR Report.	No Issues Reported	No Issues Reported	No Issues Reported
Airbag Deployment No airbag deployment reported to CAR Report.	No Issues Reported		
Odometer Rollback No indication of an odometer rollback.	No Issues Indicated		
Accident / Damage Accident reported on 05/26/2003. Inspected for damage on 05/29/2003.	Accident Reported		
Manufacturer Recall Check with an authorized Tont dealer for any open recalls.	No Recalls Reported		
Basic Warranty Original warranty estimated to have expired.	**Warranty Expired**		

Knowing whether a vehicle has previously been involved in an accident will help you determine whether it has had any major damage. Although minor damage can be easy to repair, major structural damage may cause the car to have additional problems as it ages.

Used Car Report

Owner 1
Purchased: 2001
Type: Corporate lease
Where: New Jersey
Est. miles/year: 10,476/yr
Est. length owned:
7/23/01 – 11/3/05
(4 yrs. 3 mo.)

Date:	Mileage:	Source:	Comments:
06/25/2001		NICB	Vehicle manufactured and shipped to original dealer.
07/23/2001	25	New Jersey Motor Vehicle Dept. Phoenix, AZ Title #WT20012040366	Title issued or updated. First owner reported. Registered as corporate lease vehicle. Registered as lease vehicle.
05/26/2003		New Jersey Damage Report	Accident reported involving rear impact. It hit another motor vehicle.
05/29/2003		New Jersey Damage Report	Vehicle inspected after an accident or other incident. Damage to rear. A vehicle inspection completed by your dealer or professional inspector is recommended.
11/03/2004	44,890	Dealer Inventory Blackwood, NJ	Vehicle offered for sale.
12/01/2005		New Jersey Motor Vehicle Dept. Blackwood, NJ Title #WT20053350469	Title issued or updated. Owner purchased from leasing company.
12/15/2005	44,895	New Jersey Motor Vehicle Dept. Deptford, NJ Title #RV20053490226	Title issued or updated. Registration issued or renewed. Loan or lien reported. Vehicle color noted as Silver.
05/24/2007	64,045	Dealer Inventory	Vehicle offered for sale.
05/25/2007	64,065	Richardson Imports Turnersville, NJ 856-842-0500	Oil and filter changed, chassis lubricated. Washed/detailed.
06/13/2007		Dealer Inventory	Vehicle sold.
06/15/2007		New Jersey Motor Vehicle Dept. Maple Shade, NJ Title #DB20071660798	Title issued or updated. Dealer took title of this vehicle while it was in inventory.
06/29/2007		New Jersey Motor Vehicle Dept. Swedesboro, NJ	Registration issued or renewed. Vehicle color noted as Silver.

> A car history report will tell you when a vehicle changes owners. If you decide to buy a car from its original owner, you may receive better information about the car's history directly from that person.

Owner 2
Purchased: 2007
Type: Personal
Where: New Jersey, Pennsylvania
Est. miles/year: 19,742/yr
Est. length owned:
6/29/07 – 8/7/10
(3 yrs. 1 mo.)

Date:	Mileage:	Source:	Comments:
06/29/2007	64,100	New Jersey Motor Vehicle Dept. Mullica Hill, NJ Title #GD20071800535	Title issued or updated. New owner reported. Loan or lien reported.
02/01/2008	77,034	TONT of Runnemede Runnemede, NJ 856-939-3400	Automatic transmission fluid and filter changed. Air filter replaced. Lights checked
06/15/2008		New Jersey Motor Vehicle Dept. Swedesboro, NJ	Registration updated when owner moved the vehicle to a new location.
10/01/2009	106,901	Mabel of Cherry Hill Maple Shade, NJ 856-727-1111	Washed/detailed. Maintenance inspection completed.
08/07/2010	125,490	Online Listing	Vehicle offered for sale.
08/11/2010		Scott Sonta of West Chester West Chester, PA 610-692-6000	Vehicle sold.
08/13/2010	125,540	Scott Sonta of West Chester West Chester, PA 610-692-6000	State inspection completed. Emissions inspection completed.
09/09/2010		Pennsylvania Motor Vehicle Dept. West Chester, PA Title #68715341SC01	Vehicle purchase reported. Title issued or updated. Dealer took title of this vehicle while it was in inventory.

Owner 3
Purchased: 2010
Type: Personal
Where: Pennsylvania
Est. miles/year: 10,476/yr
Est. length owned:
10/22/10 – present
(25 days)

Date:	Mileage:	Source:	Comments:
10/22/2010		Pennsylvania Motor Vehicle Dept. Coatesville, PA Title #68715341AL02	Title issued or updated. New owner reported.
10/27/2010		Scott Sonta of West Chester West Chester, PA 610-692-6000	Vehicle serviced.

> Check maintenance records to learn about the level of the car's care. However, be mindful that car owners who change their own oil or take the car to a private mechanic rather than to a dealer will not see such maintenance efforts appear on the car history report.

Car Insurance Quote

States require you to have car insurance in order to be a legal driver. Driving without insurance may cause you to have your license suspended. It can also cost you thousands of dollars if you were to get into an accident while uninsured.

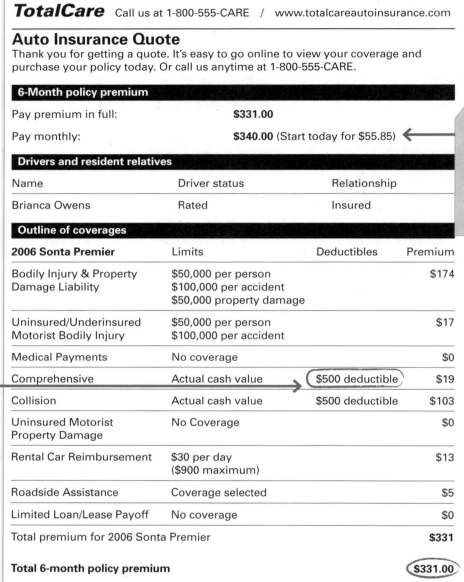

TotalCare   Call us at 1-800-555-CARE / www.totalcareautoinsurance.com

Auto Insurance Quote
Thank you for getting a quote. It's easy to go online to view your coverage and purchase your policy today. Or call us anytime at 1-800-555-CARE.

Quote # 645663977

Brianca Owens
6937 Augusta, Ave. SE
Atlanta, GA 30315

6-Month policy premium

Pay premium in full:	**$331.00**
Pay monthly:	**$340.00** (Start today for $55.85)

Most insurance companies will let you make monthly payments if you cannot afford to pay for several months at one time. However, they may charge you a few extra dollars for this convenience of paying your bill over time.

Drivers and resident relatives

Name	Driver status	Relationship
Brianca Owens	Rated	Insured

Outline of coverages

2006 Sonta Premier	Limits	Deductibles	Premium
Bodily Injury & Property Damage Liability	$50,000 per person $100,000 per accident $50,000 property damage		$174
Uninsured/Underinsured Motorist Bodily Injury	$50,000 per person $100,000 per accident		$17
Medical Payments	No coverage		$0
Comprehensive	Actual cash value	$500 deductible	$19
Collision	Actual cash value	$500 deductible	$103
Uninsured Motorist Property Damage	No Coverage		$0
Rental Car Reimbursement	$30 per day ($900 maximum)		$13
Roadside Assistance	Coverage selected		$5
Limited Loan/Lease Payoff	No coverage		$0
Total premium for 2006 Sonta Premier			**$331**
Total 6-month policy premium			**$331.00**

Different insurance policies have different deductibles, or the amount of money you are responsible for paying if your car requires a repair. Although a higher deductible may mean a lower policy payment, it also may cover fewer repair costs than a more expensive, lower deductible.

Most car insurance policies span a quarter year (three months) or a half year (six months). At the end of your term, you may choose to renew your policy or shop for a new one. You may also cancel your policy at any time during the term if you find a better policy elsewhere.

Car Insurance Statement

Whenever you take out a new car insurance policy or renew an existing one, your insurance company will send you a statement explaining your coverage. Review this statement carefully so that you understand your plan's coverage.

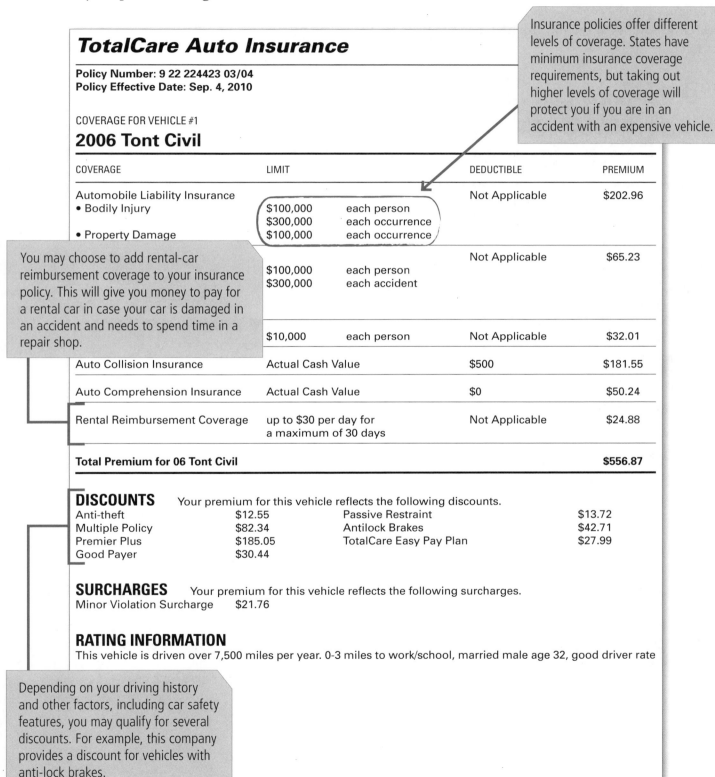

Insurance policies offer different levels of coverage. States have minimum insurance coverage requirements, but taking out higher levels of coverage will protect you if you are in an accident with an expensive vehicle.

TotalCare Auto Insurance

Policy Number: 9 22 224423 03/04
Policy Effective Date: Sep. 4, 2010

COVERAGE FOR VEHICLE #1
2006 Tont Civil

COVERAGE	LIMIT		DEDUCTIBLE	PREMIUM
Automobile Liability Insurance			Not Applicable	$202.96
• Bodily Injury	$100,000	each person		
	$300,000	each occurrence		
• Property Damage	$100,000	each occurrence		
	$100,000	each person	Not Applicable	$65.23
	$300,000	each accident		
	$10,000	each person	Not Applicable	$32.01
Auto Collision Insurance	Actual Cash Value		$500	$181.55
Auto Comprehension Insurance	Actual Cash Value		$0	$50.24
Rental Reimbursement Coverage	up to $30 per day for a maximum of 30 days		Not Applicable	$24.88
Total Premium for 06 Tont Civil				**$556.87**

You may choose to add rental-car reimbursement coverage to your insurance policy. This will give you money to pay for a rental car in case your car is damaged in an accident and needs to spend time in a repair shop.

DISCOUNTS   Your premium for this vehicle reflects the following discounts.

Anti-theft	$12.55	Passive Restraint	$13.72
Multiple Policy	$82.34	Antilock Brakes	$42.71
Premier Plus	$185.05	TotalCare Easy Pay Plan	$27.99
Good Payer	$30.44		

SURCHARGES   Your premium for this vehicle reflects the following surcharges.
Minor Violation Surcharge $21.76

RATING INFORMATION
This vehicle is driven over 7,500 miles per year. 0-3 miles to work/school, married male age 32, good driver rate

Depending on your driving history and other factors, including car safety features, you may qualify for several discounts. For example, this company provides a discount for vehicles with anti-lock brakes.

Automobile Repair Estimate

If you get into an accident or your car is not working properly, you should take it to a repair shop. Once you do, ask for an estimate before the shop begins work on your car to prevent unpleasant surprises on the bill. A mechanic will examine your car for any issues and provide an estimate of the cost to repair it. After you agree to the estimate, the mechanic will begin repairs. You will pay the final bill when you pick up your car.

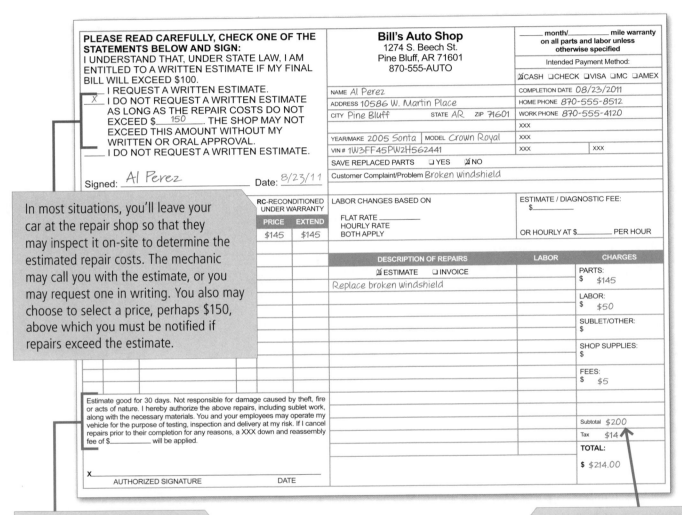

In most situations, you'll leave your car at the repair shop so that they may inspect it on-site to determine the estimated repair costs. The mechanic may call you with the estimate, or you may request one in writing. You also may choose to select a price, perhaps $150, above which you must be notified if repairs exceed the estimate.

An estimate is only good for a certain period of time. If you wait too long to complete repairs after receiving an estimate, you may pay a different price.

Keep in mind that an estimate is just that—an estimate. Your actual bill may vary somewhat from the estimated price. However, the repair shop should discuss any significant differences with you before beginning those repairs.

Automobile Repair Invoice

After you've received and agreed to an estimate for a car repair, the mechanic will begin work. You will pay for any parts needed to repair your car and also for the labor of the people working on your vehicle. The majority of repair costs will be due when you pick up your car.

UPTOWN AUTO CARE
2217 S. Maple Dr.
Minneapolis, MN 55405
Phone: 612–555–7545   Fax: 612–555–8708
You will never pay for a repair you didn't need

INVOICE
789
Org. Est #001574

INVOICE   Print Date: 08/27/2012

Ref #:		2004 Road – Lee SE	
		4.0L, In-Line, VIN (S)	
		Lic # KBZ535	Odometer In: 82612
		Vin#:	Odometer Out: 82612
		Hat #	

Part Description / Number	Qty	Sale	Extended	Labor Description	Hours	Extended
SPARK PLUG				OVER HEATING CHECK COOLING SYSTEM		
7561	6.00	4.46	26.76	SCOPE CHECK	0.70	59.50
REBUILD HEAD				SCOPE CHECK		
3345	1.00	450.00	450.00	NEEDS RADIATOR, LEAKING AT TOP,		
ANTI-FREEZE COOLANT				NEED SERP BELT VERY CRACKED,		
HS57134	1.00	168.40	168.40	ENGINE, MISSING BADLY,		
CYLINDER HEAD GASKET SET				REC SCOPE CHECK		
AF	2.00	18.50	37.00	CYLINDER HEAD GASKET –	14.00	1,200.00
CYLINDER HEAD BOLTS				Remove & Replace – [Includes: Remove carbon,		
ES71102	1.00	91.59	91.59	check surfaces for warpage, adjust valves and		
Shop Supplies		58.03	58.03	ignition timing.] – In-Line 6		
				(Additional time) – Where Air Cond	N/A	N/C
				interferes add		
				CUSTOMER MUST RETURN IN		
				1200 MILES FOR CHECK		

Your invoice will show the price of each part used to repair your car. It will also tell you how long technicians spent working on your car. Together, parts and labor will make up your total bill.

Many repair shops guarantee their work for a period of time or for a certain number of miles. If a repaired part breaks during this warranty period, you may be able to return it to the shop and have it fixed again for free.

Technicians: ANDERSON, SCOTT   PUFFER, MARK

Org Estimate $2.150.75	Revision $0.00	Current Estimate $2,150.75	Additional Cost	Revised Estimate		

Labor:	$1,259.5
Parts:	$831.78
Sublet:	$0.00
Sub:	$2,091.28
Tax:	$59.47
Total:	$2,150.75
Bal Due:	$0.00

Payments – Check (#7655) – $2,150.75

I hereby authorize the above repair work to be done along with the necessary material and hereby grant you and/ or your employees permission to operate the car or truck herein described on street, highways, or elsewhere for the purpose to testing and/or inspection. As express mechanic's lien is hereby acknowledged on above car or truck to secure the amount of repairs thereto. Warranty on parts and labor is one year or 12,000 miles, whichever comes first. Warranty work has to be performed in our shop & cannot exceed the original cost of repair.

SIGNATURE *Stacy Walker*   Date 8/27/12   Time

Automobile Oil Change Invoice

Your car will run better and last longer with regular maintenance, such as oil changes. You may decide to get your oil changed at a dealership or at a business that specializes in oil changes.

You may use several different types of oil in your vehicle. Synthetic oil is more expensive than traditional oil, but it lasts longer. Synthetic oil is a good choice if you often forget to have your oil changed or you drive a lot.

Burnet Fast Lube

Burnet Fast Lube
7120 Burnet Road
Austin, TX

DATE 7-21-10

NAME: Shawn Chastain

STREET ADDRESS:

CITY, STATE, & ZIP: Austin, TX 73301

PHONE:

MILEAGE 6590

YEAR 02 | MAKE Lansing | MODEL Storm

Wherever you get your oil changed, the mechanics will do a routine inspection on other parts of your car, such as your tires, battery, and turn signals. You'll be notified if any of these other parts need repair. Many oil-change shops will also replace or repair these items for you.

I HEREBY AUTHORIZE THE ABOVE NAMED TO DO THE ABOVE WORK.

X _Shawn Chastain_

HOOD	PT	TECH
LT	TT	

OIL CHANGE ( ) ROTELLA T (X) 10W/30 ( ) 10W/40 ( ) HD30 ( ) 5W/20 ( ) 5W/30 ( ) 20W/50	AMOUNT	
COUPON'S TYPE: _____	21	95
OIL OVER 5 QUARTS		
AIR FILTER # Good	/	
BREATHER ELEMENT #	n/a	
PCV VALUE #	n/a	
BRAKE FLUID	/	
POWER STEERING FLUID	/	
TRANSMISSION FLUID	/	
DIFFERENTIAL	n/a	
WASH CAR	No FS 3	00
VACUUM	No	
TIRES _32_ PSI	/	
WIPER BLADES	/	
WASHER FLUID	/	
BATTERY	/	
FUEL FILTER #		
RADIATOR (FILL/FLUSH)		

Expect to pay a small, separate fee to cover disposal of your old oil. Remember that if you change your oil yourself, you cannot simply throw away the used oil. It must be disposed of properly.

DISPOSAL FEE, OIL, FILTER, FLUIDS	1	50
CASH CHECK SUBTOTAL		
CC _____ TAX	1	85
TOTAL	28	30

NO. 66871

Insurance Card

You will receive an insurance card in the mail after you purchase a car insurance policy. Keep this card in your car or your wallet so that you have it with you whenever you're driving. In most states, driving without proof of insurance is illegal.

Insurance cards provide a variety of auto-related information, such as proper steps to take if involved in an auto accident.

Insurer: Enterprising Select Insurance Co - 02960
Policy Number: 15810255-0   Effective Date: 07/17/2011 to 01/17/2012
[X] Personal Injury Protection   [X] Bodily Injury Liability
    Benefits/Property Damage Liability   See policy and outline of coverage;
                                                damage to a rental vehicle is covered
                                                to the extent shown therein.

Named Insured:
    CASSIE HOPKINS
    TREMEL HOPKINS
Vehicles: Year   Make   Model   VIN
           2000   Ram   R210   1FTNN00P5PMT15628
           2007   Lansing   FT Mobil   QHMKO02183S0055778

Customer Service: 800-555-4737
    Misrepresentation of insurance is a first degree misdemeanor.
    NOT VALID FOR MORE THAN ONE YEAR FROM EFFECTIVE DATE.
Form 4950 FL (12/07)

IF YOU'RE IN AN ACCIDENT
1. Remain at the scene. Don't admit fault.
2. Call the police to report the accident.
3. Exchange information with the other driver(s).
4. Report your claim to Enterprising immediately.

TO REPORT A CLAIM
Auto: claims.enterprising.com or 1-800-555-5298
Commercial Auto and Non-auto: 1-800-555-5298

Ask about our concierge-level claims service and network of repair shops, both backed by our Limited Lifetime Guarantee.

ENTERPRISING

KEEP THIS CARD IN YOUR VEHICLE WHILE IN OPERATION.

Your insurance card provides important information about your policy, including the names of the insured drivers on your policy and descriptions of the covered vehicles.

If you need to make a claim on your policy, you may call the number printed on your card. You can also sometimes file and manage your claims online.

Vehicle Registration

States require automobile owners to pay a fee to register their vehicles at the Department of Motor Vehicles (DMV). This is also where you and other automobile owners can obtain license plates for your vehicles.

States, counties, and cities may levy taxes on your vehicle registration. Examine this section to see the different fees that make up your yearly registration total.

FLORIDA VEHICLE REGISTRATION

CO/AGY 19 / 7   T# 625570613
                   B# 1866473

PLATE	**510AAA**	DECAL	**45555102**	Expires	**Midnight Sat 7/9/2011**	Reg. Tax	45.15	Class Code	1
YR/MK	**2007/LANS**	BODY	**5D**	COLOR	**SIL**	Init. Reg.		Tax Months	12
VIN	**JHMGD37497S055914**	TITLE	99027915			County Fee	0.50	Back Tax Mos	0
Plate Type	**RGR**	NET WT	**2450**			Mail Fee	0.70	Credit Class	
DL/FEID	**H569102741208**			2ND DL#	**H1502458406655**	Sales Tax		Credit Months	0
Date Issued	**6/4/2010**	Plate Issued	**6/29/2009**			Voluntary Fees			
						Grand Total	(46.35)		

HOPKINS

IMPORTANT INFORMATION

1. The Florida license plate must remain with the registrant upon sale of vehicle.
2. The registration must be delivered to a Tax Collector or Tag Agent for transfer to a replacement vehicle.
3. Your registration must be updated to your new address within 20 days of moving.
4. Registration renewals are the responsibility of the registrant and shall occur during the 30-day period prior to the expiration date shown on this registration. Renewal notices are provided as a courtesy and are not required for renewal purposes.

Remember to renew your vehicle registration each year. You may have to provide proof of insurance when you renew your registration. For that and other reasons, keep your vehicle registration in your car's glove box.

Chapter Recap

Using the list below, place a check mark next to the goals you achieved in Chapter 1.

▶ **In Lesson 1, you . . .**

☐ Learned how to book airline travel

☐ Discovered how to apply for a passport

☐ Found out how to book a hotel room and what to expect on your bill

☐ Studied a boarding pass and baggage tag

▶ **In Lesson 2, you . . .**

☐ Examined a product comparison report

☐ Learned about types of promotional ads

☐ Compared different features of coupons

☐ Studied a credit card application

☐ Investigated store and restaurant receipts

▶ **In Lesson 3, you . . .**

☐ Studied a car's sticker price

☐ Found out how to read a used car report

☐ Reviewed a car insurance policy

☐ Learned about documents relating to car maintenance and repair

Chapter Review

Name: _____ Date: _____

▶ Directions: Write your answer to the questions on the lines below.

1. What travel information is listed on a boarding pass?

_____

_____

2. What is the airport code listed on the baggage tag above?

_____

3. What is the tracking number for the baggage?

_____

▶ Directions: Review and complete the document below.

Page 1 of 2

4.

APPLICATION FOR A U.S. PASSPORT

Attention: see WARNING on page two of instructions
Please select the document (or documents) for which you are applying:

☐ **U.S. Passport Book**   ☐ **U.S. Passport Card**

The U.S. passport card may only be used for international travel by land or sea between the United States, Canada, Mexico, the Caribbean and Bermuda. Please visit our website for detailed information.

☐ R   ☐ D   ☐ O   ☐ DP

End. # _____   Exp _____

1. Name *Last*

First & Middle

2. Date of Birth *(mm/dd/yyyy)*

3. Sex   ☐ M ☐ F

4. Place of Birth *(City & State **or** City & Country as it is presently known)*

5. Social Security Number

6. Mailing Address: *Street/RFD # or P.O. Box*

Apartment or unit #

City

State

Zip Code *(Zip + 4 if known)*

In Care Of or Country, if applicable

7. Contact Phone Number

☐ Home ☐ Cell
☐ Work

8. Email Address *(Optional)*

9. Have You Ever Used A Different Name *(Maiden, Previous Marriage, Legal Name Change)? If yes, please complete. (Attach additional pages if needed)*

1.

2.

STAPLE   STAPLE

From 1" to 1 3/8"

2" x 2"   2" x 2"

STAPLE   STAPLE

Submit two recent, color photographs

10. Parents' Information

Father's Name – First & Middle

Last

Date of Birth (mm/dd/yyyy)

Father's Place of Birth

U.S. Citizen?
☐ Yes
☐ No

Mother's Name – First & Middle

Last (Maiden)

Date of Birth (mm/dd/yyyy)

Mother's Place of Birth

U.S. Citizen?
☐ Yes
☐ No

CONTINUE TO PAGE 2
DO NOT SIGN APPLICATION UNTIL REQUESTED TO DO SO BY PERSON ADMINISTERING OATH.

I declare under penalty of perjury all of the following: 1)I am a citizen or non-citizen national of the United States and have not, since acquiring U.S. citizenship or nationality, performed any of the acts listed under "Acts or Conditions" on the reverse side of this application (unless explanatory statement is attached); 2)the statements made on the application are true and correct; 3)I have not knowingly and willfully made false statements or included false documents in support of this application; 4)the photograph submitted with this application is a genuine, current, photograph of me; and 5)I have read and understood the warning on page two of the instructions to the application form.

X _____
   Applicant's Signature – age 16 and older

X _____
   Father's/Legal Guardian's Signature (if identifying minor)

X _____
   Mother's/Legal Guardian's Signature (if identifying minor)

Identifying Documents – Applicant or Father (if identifying minor)
☐ Driver's License ☐ Passport ☐ Military ☐ Other _____

Issue
Date _____

Expiration
Date _____

Place of
Date _____

Name _____   ID No _____

Identifying Documents – Mother (if identifying minor)
☐ Driver's License ☐ Passport ☐ Military ☐ Other _____

Issue
Date _____

Expiration
Date _____

Place of
Date _____

Name _____   ID No _____

☐ Acceptance Agent ☐ (Vice) Consul USA ☐ Passport Services Staff Agent

Facility Name/Location

Facility/Agent ID Number

Seal   Subscribed and sworn to (affirmed) before me:

_____ Date _____
Signature of person authorized to accept applications

PPT Fee _____   EF _____   Postage _____   Other _____

DS 11 10 2007 1

Name: _____ **Date:** _____

Name of Applicant *(Last, First & Middle)*

2. Date of Birth *(mm/dd/yyyy)*

11. Height | **12. Hair Color** | **13. Eye Color** | **14. Occupation** | **15. Employer**

16. Additional Contact Phone Numbers

☐ Home ☐ Cell
☐ Work ☐ _____

☐ Home ☐ Cell
☐ Work ☐ _____

17. Permanent Address: *Street/RFD # (No P.O. Box)*

Apartment or unit #

City

State

Zip Code *(Zip + 4 if known)*

18. Emergency Contact – *Provide the information of a person not traveling with you to be contacted in the event of an emergency.*

Name

Address: Street/RFD # or P.O. Box

Apartment or unit #

City

State

Zip Code

Phone Number

Relationship

19. Travel Plans

Date of Trip *(mm/dd/yyyy)*

Length of Trip

Countries to be visited

20. Have you ever been married? ☐ Yes ☐ No   If yes, complete the remaining items in #20.

Current spouse's or most recent former spouse's name

Place of birth

Date of marriage *(mm/dd/yyyy)*

☐ Widowed?
☐ Divorced?

Date *(mm/dd/yyyy)*

21. Have you ever been issued a U.S. Passport Book? ☐ Yes ☐ No   If yes, complete the remaining items in #21.

Your name as listed on your most recent passport book

Most recent passport book number

Status of your most recent passport book
☐ In My Possession ☐ Stolen ☐ Lost ☐ Other _____

Approximate date your most recent passport book was issued or date you applied (mm/dd/yyyy)

22. Have you ever been issued a U.S. Passport Card? ☐ Yes ☐ No   If yes, complete the remaining items in #22.

Your name as listed on your most recent passport card

Most recent passport card number

Status of your most recent passport card
☐ In My Possession ☐ Stolen ☐ Lost ☐ Other _____

Approximate date your most recent passport card was issued or date you applied (mm/dd/yyyy)

STOP! PLEASE DO NOT WRITE BELOW THIS LINE

FOR ISSUING OFFICE ONLY ☐ Sole Parent ☐ Both

Name as it appears on citizenship evidence _____

☐ Birth Certificate	SR	CR	City	Filed/Issued:
☐ Report of Birth	240	545	1350	Filed/City:
☐ Passport	Issue Date:			
☐ Other:				
☐ Attached:				

DS 11 10 2007 1

Chapter Review

▶ Directions: Determine whether the following statement is true or false. If the statement is true, write T. If the statement is false, write F. Then rewrite the false statement to make it true.

NOBU

Apply   Confirm   Results

NOBU Credit is issued by TM Money Bank ("TMMB"). The TMMB Privacy Policy governs the use of NOBU Credit. This privacy policy may be different from the Privacy Policy of NOBU.

You should be able to answer "YES" to these statements in order to increase your chances of approval:

- Your credit history is clear of bankruptcies and seriously delinquent accounts.

- You are at least 18 years old and have a valid social security number.

- You have not submitted an application for a NOBU Credit Card in the past 90 days.

About You – Federal law requires GEMB to obtain, verify, and record information that identifies you when you open an account. We will use your name, address, date of birth, and other information for this purpose.

First Name `Kealoha`   Initial `   `   Last Name `Enos`

Address `15689 Kaniau Road, #4`   (street name and number required)

`                    `

City `Lahaina`   State `HI`   Zip `96761`

Home Phone* `808` – `555` – `6491`

Business Phone* `808` – `555` – `3200`

Cell / Other Phone* `808` – `555` – `4878`

*You authorize us to contact you at any number you provide.

Email Address `enosk@opax.com`

☐ Yes! I want to receive emails from you and NOBU.

Annual Income (from all sources) `34,250` .00

Alimony, child support, or separate maintenance income need not be included unless relied upon for credit. You may include the annual amount that you have available to spend from any assets. **WI Residents only:** If you are applying for an individual account, combine your and your spouse's financial information.

Length of Time at Current Address `3` (in years)

Residence `Rent`

5. When revealing your income on a credit application, you must list all sources of income, including any child support payments you receive.

Name: _____ Date: _____

▶ Directions: Write your answer to the questions on the lines below.

Optional Card Security – Up to $10,000 in Protection on your NOBU Credit Card.

With the opening of your new NOBU Credit Card Account, feel secure knowing you are financially protected. Enroll in the Card Security program and we will cancel your Account balance up to $10,000 if you experience a qualifying unemployment, approved leave of absence, disability, hospitalization, nursing home care, terminal illness or loss of life.

Click Here for Summary of Terms

I acknowledge that I do not need to purchase Card Security to obtain credit. Per the Card Security agreement. I agree that you may bill my NOBU Account a monthly fee of $1.68 per $100 to the monthly ending balance on my Account. I may cancel at any time. I have read and agree to the Summary of Terms above. By clicking the enrollment button below, I intend to purchase optional Card Security and this constitutes my signature. Residents of MS are not eligible.

☐ Yes! I would like to enroll in Card Security.

Important Information – Please see below for Key Terms and Consent to Electronic Communications. You may Print or Download these disclosures here. Print or Download in Spanish.

TM MONEY BANK
NOBU CREDIT CARD ACCOUNT

Interest Rates and Interest Charges	
Annual Percentage Rate (APR) for Purchases	**25.99%** This APR will vary with the market based on the Prime Rate.
How to Avoid Paying Interest on Purchases	Your due date is at least 23 days after the close of each billing cycle. We will not charge you interest on purchases if you pay your entire balance by the due date of each month.

Applicant Signature By applying for this account, I am asking TM Money Bank ("TMMB") to issue me a NOBU Credit Card (the "Card"), and I agree that:
- I am providing the information in this application to TMMB and to NOBU North American Services LLC (and its affiliates) so that they can create and update their records, and provide me with service and special offers.

6. If Kealoha Enos has a $300 balance and has the card security plan, how much is her monthly fee?

_____

7. What is the interest rate on this card, and will it ever change? How do you know?

_____

_____

▶ Directions: Answer the questions below.

FRESH FARE

FRESH FARE XXXXXXXXXXXXXXXXXXXXXXXXX
XXXXXXXXXXXXXXXXXXXXXXXXXXXXXXXXXX

GROCERY

KIDNEY BEAN		.79 F
RegPrice .89	Card Save	.10
2 @ 2.19 VEG SOUP MIX		4.38 F

REFRIG / FROZEN

1 @ 3.99 EA / 2 FOR 7.00		
RD FAT MILK		3.99 F
SFY SEL 3 CHSE RAV		3.00 F
RegPrice 3.59	Card Save	.59

BAKED GOODS

6 @ .79 JUMBO CKY	4.74 F

PRODUCE

0.65 lb @ $1.99 / lb	
WT PEPPER GREEN BELL	1.29 F
1.56 lb @ $4.99 / lb	
WT TOMATOES HOTHOUSE	7.78 F
**** TAX .00 BAL	25.97
XXX XXX XXXXXXXXXXXXXXXXX	25.97
CHANGE	.00
NUMBER OF ITEMS = 13	
2/01/11 18:19 1539 04 0055 9501	

Club Card Savings $ .69
Look for the # sign on your receipt
for possible Health Care Flex Spending
Account items for reimbursement.

Healthy Eating just got easier. Visit freshfare.com/
foodflex for a free Nutrition Snapshot of your Fresh
Fare Club Card purchase and to identify healthier
alternatives.

LET US HEAR FROM YOU!
1-888-555-3929 or visit FRESHFARE.COM

FRESH FARE STORE #XXXXX
XXXXXXXXXXXX XXXXXX
XXXXXXXXXXXX XXXXXX

TERMINAL 742

4374711285102 4

THANK YOU FOR SHOPPING AT
STANTON*S, HERALD SQUARE

TERMINAL 742 CUSTOMER COPY   PURCHASE
S003 ASSC 266234 TR3278 10/12/10 649P

COOKWARE	QTY 1	16.99
636189000013		
NY 8.25% TAX		1.40

TOTAL AMOUNT DUE STORE   18.39

ACCOUNT NUMBER   XXXXXXXXXXXX
             DEBIT TENDER   18.39

0037423278

268234   0037423278   10/12/11
KEEP THIS RECEIPT   SEE REVERSE SIDE

KEEP THIS RECEIPT
FOR RETURN/EXCHANGE

Want an Employee Discount?
And How About A New Career?
Visit StantonJobs.com And Apply Today

8. Based on the information in the receipt above, how much would one pound of green bell peppers cost?

_____

9. You should keep your sales receipt in order to

    A. find out when an item goes on sale.

    B. know how much tax to pay on an item.

    C. return or exchange an item at a store.

    D. join a grocery store savings club.

10. If the cookware on the second receipt above cost $20, how much would the tax on that item be?

_____

Name: _____   Date: _____

▶ Directions: Determine whether each of the following statements is true or false. If the statement is true, write T. If the statement is false, write F. Then rewrite the false statement to make it true.

STANDARD FEATURES

MECHANICAL & PERFORMANCE
- 3.0L, 4–CAM, 24–VALVE EFI V6
- FRONT WHEEL DRIVE
- 4–SPEED AUTOMATIC ECT–I
- FRONT AND REAR STABILIZER BARS
- POWER RACK AND PINION STEERING
- 4–WHEEL INDEPENDENT SUSPENSION
- PWR FRONT & REAR DISC BRAKES
- 205/65R15 RADIAL TIRES (5)

SAFETY
- DRIVER AND FRONT PASSENGER AIR BAGS (SRS)
- 3–POINT SEATBELTS
- AIR/ELR PASSENGER BELTS
- REAR CENTER 3–POINT SEATBELT
- FRONT SEAT BELT PRETENSIONERS & FORCE LIMITERS
- ANTI–LOCK BRAKE SYSTEM (ABS)
- SIDE IMPACT DOOR BEAMS
- DAYTIME RUNNING LIGHTS

EXTERIOR
- AUTO ON/OFF HEADLAMP FEATURE

- INTEGRATED FRONT FOG LAMPS
- SOLAR ENERGY ABSORBING GLASS
- DUAL COLOR–KEYED POWER REMOTE OUTSIDE MIRRORS
- FULL WHEEL COVERS
- GLASS IMPRINTED ANTENNA

COMFORT AND CONVENIENCE
- POWER WINDOWS AND DOOR LOCKS
- AIR CONDITIONER – CFC FREE
- CRUISE CTRL/TILT STEERING WHL
- MULTI–ADJUSTABLE FABRIC LINED FRONT BUCKET SEATS
- 4–WAY ADJUSTABLE FR HEADRESTS
- DUAL FRONT & REAR CUPHOLDERS
- CENTER CONSOLE W/ STORAGE
- DIGITAL CLOCK/TACHOMETER
- VARIABLE INTERMITTENT WIPERS
- DELUXE ETR/CASSETTE W/ 6 SPKRS
- REAR WINDOR DEFOGGER
- REMOTE TRUNK/FUEL LID RELEASES

TAMTA XD   2-DOOR SE (V6)

VIN: 2T1CF22P4XC176339   MODEL/YEAR: 2734A/2011
COLOR   DIAMOND WHITE PEARL / IVORY   (0051/00)

MANUFACTURER'S SUGGESTED RETAIL PRICE **$21,988.00**

OPTIONAL EQUIPMENT

DZ	DELUXE 3–IN–1 ETR/CASSETTE/ CD WITH 6 SPEAKERS	150.00
SR	POWER TILT/SLIDE MOONROOF WITH ONE–TOUCH OPEN/CLOSE FEATURE	900.00
MG	COLOR–KEYED MUDGUARDS	80.00
SY	SPORT UPGRADE PACKAGE #3 8–WAY POWER ADJ DRIVER'S SEAT. P205/60R16 TIRES. 16" ALLOY WHEELS (5). REAR SPOILER W/ INTEGRATED CENTER HIGH MOUNT STOP LAMP & PERFORATED LEATHER WRAPPED STEERING WHEEL	1,530.00
PC	DIAMOND WHITE PEARL PAINT	220.00
CF	CARPET/CARGO MAT SET	166.00
V3	V.I.P.–RS3000 DLX SECURITY SYS	399.00

DESTINATION CHARGE   420.00

TOTAL   **$25,853.00**

LIMITED WARRANTY   PROVIDES 36 MONTH/36,000 MILE COMPREHENSIVE COVERAGE, 5 YEAR/60,000 MILE POWERTRAIN COVERAGE. PLUS 5 YEAR BODY PANEL CORROSION PERFORATION WARRANTY. SEE OWNER'S GUIDE FOR DETAILS.

CITY MPG

22

Fuel Economy Information

HIGHWAY MPG

33

Actual Mileage will vary with options, driving conditions, driving habits and vehicle's condition. Results reported to EPA indicate that the majority of vehicles with these estimates will achieve between

17 and 23 mpg in the city and between
23 and 33 mpg on the highway.

2011 TAMTA XD, V–6 CYL., 3.0 LITER DISP., FOUR CAM ENGINE, FUEL INJECTION, 4–SPEED AUTOMATIC ECT–I TRANSMISSION.

Estimated Annual Fuel Cost: $750

For Comparison Shopping, all vehicles classified as **COMPACT** have been issued mileage ratings ranging from

11 and 42 mpg in the city and
16 and 49 mpg highway.

---

11. The car described in the sticker above includes many safety features, including an anti-lock brake system.

_____

12. The price of this car without any additional equipment or features is $25,853.00.

_____

► Directions: Write your answer to the question on the lines below.

CAR Report Vehicle History Report

Vehicle Information:
2001 TONT SAMEL SE
VIN: 2T1FF28PX1C539447
CONVERTIBLE
3.0L V6 PFI DOHC 24V
FRONT WHEEL DRIVE

Accident / Damage reported
3 Previous owners
5 Service records available
Types of owners: Corporate lease, Personal
125,540 Last reported odometer reading
$190 Below retail book value

Price Calculator
Adjust the value of this 2001 TONT SAMEL SE based on the information available in this report

1) Retail Book Value	2) CAR Report History Impact	3) Adjusted Retail Value
$ 0	**- $190**	**Begin by entering the retail book value**
Enter retail value here	Below retail book value	

Tip Get retail book value from a pricing guide Web site. Don't use seller's asking price

$ This vehicle is worth less than average, based on information in this report.

🔍 Compare adjusted retail value to seller's asking price when making your decision.

Ownership History
The number of owners is estimated

	Owner 1	Owner 2	Owner 3
Year purchased	2001	2007	2010
Type of owner	Corporate lease	Personal	Personal
Estimated length of ownership	4 yrs. 3 mo.	3 yrs. 1 mo.	23 days
Owned in the following states/provinces	New Jersey	New Jersey, Pennsylvania	Pennsylvania
Estimated miles driven per year	10,476/yr	19,742/yr	—
Last reported odometer reading	64,065	125,540	—

Title History
CAR Report guarantees the information in this section

	Owner 1	Owner 2	Owner 3
Salvage, Junk, Rebuilt, Fire, Flood, Hail, Lemon	**Guaranteed** No Problem	**Guaranteed** No Problem	**Guaranteed** No Problem
Not Actual Mileage, Exceeds Mechanical Limits	**Guaranteed** No Problem	**Guaranteed** No Problem	**Guaranteed** No Problem

Additional History
Not all accidents / issues are reported to CAR Report

	Owner 1	Owner 2	Owner 3
Total Loss No total loss reported to CAR Report.	No Issues Reported	No Issues Reported	No Issues Reported
Structural / Frame Damage No structural / frame damage reported to CAR Report.	No Issues Reported	No Issues Reported	No Issues Reported
Airbag Deployment No airbag deployment reported to CAR Report.	No Issues Reported	No Issues Reported	No Issues Reported
Odometer Rollback No indication of an odometer rollback.	No Issues Indicated	No Issues Indicated	No Issues Indicated
Accident / Damage Accident reported on 05/26/2003. Inspected for damage on 05/29/2003.	Accident Reported	No New Issues Reported	No New Issues Reported
Manufacturer Recall Check with an authorized Tont dealer for any open recalls.	No Recalls Reported	No Recalls Reported	No Recalls Reported
Basic Warranty Original warranty estimated to have expired.	**Warranty Expired**	**Warranty Expired**	**Warranty Expired**

13. According to the report, the car is worth how much less than the retail book value?

_____

_____

Name: _____   Date: _____

▶ Directions: Determine whether each of the following statements is true or false. If the statement is true, write T. If the statement is false, write F. Then rewrite the false statement to make it true.

TotalCare   Call us at 1-800-555-CARE   /   www.totalcareautoinsurance.com

Auto Insurance Quote

Thank you for getting a quote. It's easy to go online to view your coverage and purchase your policy today. Or call us anytime at 1-800-555-CARE.

Quote # 645663977

Brianca Owens
6937 Augusta, Ave. SE
Atlanta, GA 30315

6-Month policy premium

Pay premium in full:	**$331.00**
Pay monthly:	**$340.00** (Start today for $55.85)

Drivers and resident relatives

Name	Driver status	Relationship
Brianca Owens	Rated	Insured

Outline of coverages

2006 Sonta Premier	Limits	Deductibles	Premium
Bodily Injury & Property Damage Liability	$50,000 per person $100,000 per accident $50,000 property damage		$174
Uninsured/Underinsured Motorist Bodily Injury	$50,000 per person $100,000 per accident		$17
Medical Payments	No coverage		$0
Comprehensive	Actual cash value	$500 deductible	$19
Collision	Actual cash value	$500 deductible	$103
Uninsured Motorist Property Damage	No Coverage		$0
Rental Car Reimbursement	$30 per day ($900 maximum)		$13
Roadside Assistance	Coverage selected		$5
Limited Loan/Lease Payoff	No coverage		$0
Total premium for 2006 Sonta Premier			**$331**
Total 6-month policy premium			**$331.00**

---

14. Car insurance policies all offer the same level of coverage.

_____

15. Your car insurance statement will list your deductible.

_____

▶ Directions: Write your answer to the question on the lines below.

Burnet Fast Lube

Burnet Fast Lube
7120 Burnet Road
Austin, TX

HOOD	PT	TECH
LT	TT	

DATE 7-21-10

NAME: Shawn Chastain

STREET ADDRESS:

CITY, STATE, & ZIP: Austin, TX 73301

PHONE:

MILEAGE 6590

YEAR 02	MAKE Lansing	MODEL Storm
ENGINE 2.4	TAG#	MILEAGE (NEXT SERV)

OIL FILTER: 29   CHASSIS FITTINGS

COMMENTS:

I HEREBY AUTHORIZE THE ABOVE NAMED TO DO THE ABOVE WORK.

X___Shawn Chastain___

OIL CHANGE ( ) ROTELLA T (X) 10W/30 ( ) 10W/40 ( ) HD30 ( ) 5W/20 ( ) 5W/30 ( ) 20W/50		AMOUNT	
COUPON'S TYPE: _____		21	95
OIL OVER 5 QUARTS			
AIR FILTER # Good	/		
BREATHER ELEMENT #	n/a		
PCV VALUE #	n/a		
BRAKE FLUID	/		
POWER STEERING FLUID	/		
TRANSMISSION FLUID	/		
DIFFERENTIAL	n/a		
WASH CAR	No FS	3	00
VACUUM	No		
TIRES ___32___ PSI		/	
WIPER BLADES	/		
WASHER FLUID		/	
BATTERY	/		
FUEL FILTER #			
RADIATOR (FILL/FLUSH)			
DISPOSAL FEE, OIL, FILTER, FLUIDS		1	50
CASH CHECK	SUBTOTAL		
CC _____	TAX	1	85
	TOTAL	28	30

NO. 66871

16. Why might you pay more for an oil change beyond just the price of the oil change itself?

_____

_____

Personal Documents

▶ **LESSON 1:**

Money Management
pages 44–59

▶ **LESSON 2:**

Health and Medicine
pages 60–79

▶ **LESSON 3:**

Lifestyle and Living
pages 80–99

Chapter Recap	Chapter Review
☑ _____	_____
☑ _____	_____
☑ _____	_____

▶ **CHAPTER 2:**

Recap/Review
pages 100–110

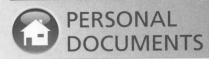

PERSONAL DOCUMENTS

Money Management

CONTENTS

For some people, just thinking about a budget can cause anxiety. They may have a wallet filled with automated teller (ATM) receipts and a drawer filled with old check stubs. For others, balancing a checkbook may come naturally. They organize their finances and track their spending. Whether you're organized or not, your mailbox may be stuffed with notices and offers from your bank and various credit card companies. These documents can be confusing. Knowing how to read them can help you manage money effectively.

Today, consumers pay for goods and services through the use of a check, debit card, or credit card. Although more people today are likely to use a debit card for purchases or payments, they can still benefit by writing deductions (and deposits) in a check register. Consumers should keep receipts any time they use a debit or ATM card and then record them in a check register as soon as possible. This will help consumers track their spending. Another option involves online banking, which provides automated account balances. Studying the examples in this lesson will help you interpret and complete the documents in the chapter review and in real life.

Online Budget Management

Have a hard time sticking to a budget? You may want to sign up for a free online financial management tracker. These services securely track spending from your bank accounts and credit cards. Some also alert you as you approach or exceed your budgeted amounts in various categories.

Online Bank Statement

Nearly all banks today offer online banking. These services often allow users to view recent purchases, transfer money between two accounts, and even pay bills. Sometimes, you may choose to replace printed, mailed bank statements with online statements.

Many banks allow users to quickly access and print traditional statements in .pdf form from the Internet. Statements may be available for the previous months or even years, depending on the bank.

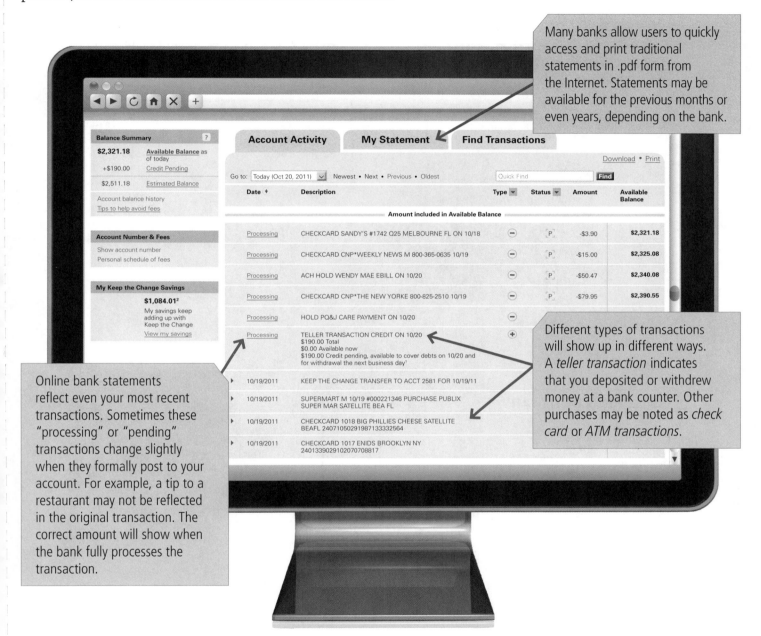

Online bank statements reflect even your most recent transactions. Sometimes these "processing" or "pending" transactions change slightly when they formally post to your account. For example, a tip to a restaurant may not be reflected in the original transaction. The correct amount will show when the bank fully processes the transaction.

Different types of transactions will show up in different ways. A *teller transaction* indicates that you deposited or withdrew money at a bank counter. Other purchases may be noted as *check card* or *ATM transactions*.

Paper Bank Statement

Reviewing your monthly paper bank statement can help you track your money. By verifying your debits and credits on a regular basis, you can closely monitor your account balances and avoid any embarrassing overdrafts.

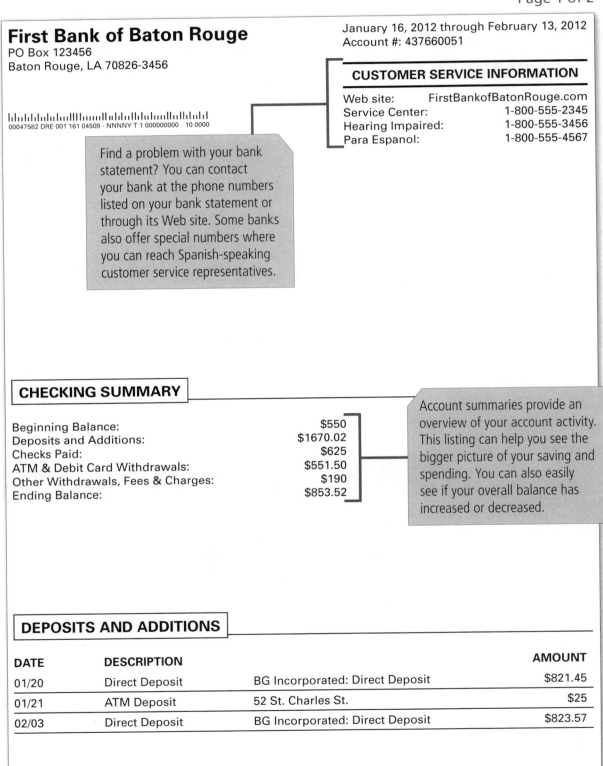

First Bank of Baton Rouge
PO Box 123456
Baton Rouge, LA 70826-3456

January 16, 2012 through February 13, 2012
Account #: 437660051

00047582 DRE 001 161 04509 - NNNNY T 1 000000000 10 0000

CUSTOMER SERVICE INFORMATION

Web site:	FirstBankofBatonRouge.com
Service Center:	1-800-555-2345
Hearing Impaired:	1-800-555-3456
Para Espanol:	1-800-555-4567

Find a problem with your bank statement? You can contact your bank at the phone numbers listed on your bank statement or through its Web site. Some banks also offer special numbers where you can reach Spanish-speaking customer service representatives.

CHECKING SUMMARY

Beginning Balance:	$550
Deposits and Additions:	$1670.02
Checks Paid:	$625
ATM & Debit Card Withdrawals:	$551.50
Other Withdrawals, Fees & Charges:	$190
Ending Balance:	$853.52

Account summaries provide an overview of your account activity. This listing can help you see the bigger picture of your saving and spending. You can also easily see if your overall balance has increased or decreased.

DEPOSITS AND ADDITIONS

DATE	DESCRIPTION		AMOUNT
01/20	Direct Deposit	BG Incorporated: Direct Deposit	$821.45
01/21	ATM Deposit	52 St. Charles St.	$25
02/03	Direct Deposit	BG Incorporated: Direct Deposit	$823.57

Paper Bank Statement

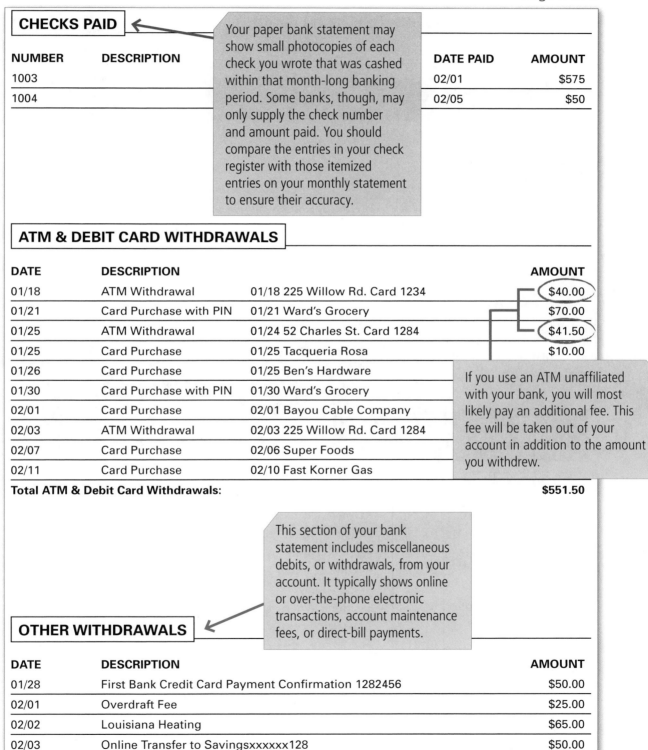

CHECKS PAID

NUMBER	DESCRIPTION	DATE PAID	AMOUNT
1003		02/01	$575
1004		02/05	$50

> Your paper bank statement may show small photocopies of each check you wrote that was cashed within that month-long banking period. Some banks, though, may only supply the check number and amount paid. You should compare the entries in your check register with those itemized entries on your monthly statement to ensure their accuracy.

ATM & DEBIT CARD WITHDRAWALS

DATE	DESCRIPTION		AMOUNT
01/18	ATM Withdrawal	01/18 225 Willow Rd. Card 1234	$40.00
01/21	Card Purchase with PIN	01/21 Ward's Grocery	$70.00
01/25	ATM Withdrawal	01/24 52 Charles St. Card 1284	$41.50
01/25	Card Purchase	01/25 Tacqueria Rosa	$10.00
01/26	Card Purchase	01/25 Ben's Hardware	
01/30	Card Purchase with PIN	01/30 Ward's Grocery	
02/01	Card Purchase	02/01 Bayou Cable Company	
02/03	ATM Withdrawal	02/03 225 Willow Rd. Card 1284	
02/07	Card Purchase	02/06 Super Foods	
02/11	Card Purchase	02/10 Fast Korner Gas	

Total ATM & Debit Card Withdrawals: **$551.50**

> If you use an ATM unaffiliated with your bank, you will most likely pay an additional fee. This fee will be taken out of your account in addition to the amount you withdrew.

> This section of your bank statement includes miscellaneous debits, or withdrawals, from your account. It typically shows online or over-the-phone electronic transactions, account maintenance fees, or direct-bill payments.

OTHER WITHDRAWALS

DATE	DESCRIPTION	AMOUNT
01/28	First Bank Credit Card Payment Confirmation 1282456	$50.00
02/01	Overdraft Fee	$25.00
02/02	Louisiana Heating	$65.00
02/03	Online Transfer to Savingsxxxxxx128	$50.00

Credit Card Statement

Unless you choose to only receive e-bills, you will get a monthly credit card statement in the mail. These statements show your purchases, account information, and the amount you owe. The statement also will tell you when to submit payment.

To avoid fees and penalties, be sure to pay at least the minimum payment. If you pay only the minimum, however, it will take a longer time to pay off your entire debt. Making even a slightly larger payment will help you erase your debt more quickly.

Statement of Personal Credit Card

☐ Check here if address or telephone number has changed. Please note changes on reverse side.

Account Number	Statement Closing Date	Current Amount Due
5129-885-650	01-31-11	$278.49

JILLIAN COOPER
5812 SKYVIEW DRIVE
ATLANTA, GA 30310
872919345   0017825500000003

MAIL PAYMENT TO:
EA BANK
132 GINGHAM STREET
ATLANTA, GA 30310

Detach here and return upper portion with check or money order. Do not staple or fold.

Statement of Personal Credit Card Account

Don't forget to make your payment! Late fees can add up quickly, and late payments may cause your interest rate to rise and your credit score to fall. If you're late with your payment, call your credit card company to ask if it will waive your fees and penalties. If you have a good payment history, many companies will forgive an occasional late payment.

Account Number	Statement Closing Date
5129-885-650	01-31-11

02-01-11	Payment Due Date:	03-01-11
01-31-11		
$1,500.00	Credit Available:	$1221.50
$278.50	Minimum Payment Due:	$20.00

Transaction Fees:	+3.00
Annual Fees:	+25.00
Current Amount Due:	+250.49
Amount Past Due:	+0
Amount Over Credit Line:	+0
NEW BALANCE:	**$278.49**

Payments:	-74.25
Finance Charge:	+00
Late Charge:	+0

Reference Number	Sold	Posted	Activity Since Last Statement		Amount
43210987	01-03	01-13	Payment, Thank You		-74.25
01234567	01-12	01-13	Wings 'N' Fries	Atlanta, GA	$25.25
78901234	01-14	01-17	Record Release	Atlanta, GA	$40.00
45678901	01-14	01-17	Hamm's Sporting Goods	Atlanta, GA	$75.25
32109879	01-22	01-23	Home Supply	Atlanta, GA	$20.75
76543210	01-29	01-30	Electronic World		
23455678		01-30	Transaction Fees		
34567890		02-01	Annual Fee		

Some credit cards, especially those that offer airline miles or other rewards, charge users an annual fee for the use of the card. Comparing plans before you sign up may help you find a card without an annual fee.

Rate Summary

Finance Charge Summary	Purchase	Advances
Periodic Rate	20.45%	20.45%
Annual Percentage Rate	19.80%	19.80%

For account information and customer services, please call 1-800-555-1085

Payments or credits received after closing date above will appear on next month's statement.

Online Credit Card Statement

Like banks, many credit card companies allow you to view your statement and make payments online. Be sure to check the credit company's Web site to find out how late in the evening you may post a payment that will be credited that day.

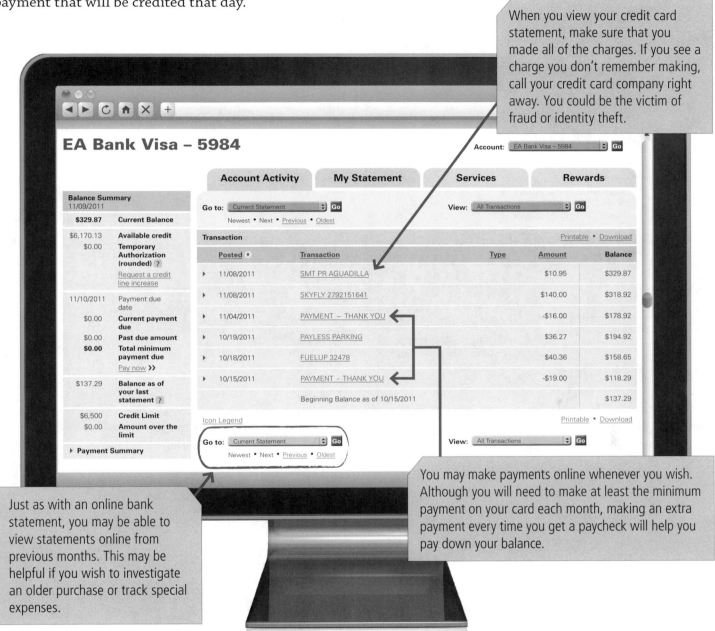

When you view your credit card statement, make sure that you made all of the charges. If you see a charge you don't remember making, call your credit card company right away. You could be the victim of fraud or identity theft.

Just as with an online bank statement, you may be able to view statements online from previous months. This may be helpful if you wish to investigate an older purchase or track special expenses.

You may make payments online whenever you wish. Although you will need to make at least the minimum payment on your card each month, making an extra payment every time you get a paycheck will help you pay down your balance.

Printed Check

You can use printed checks to make payments from your checking account, including withdrawals of cash at a bank counter. If you do, carefully log and track payments to ensure their accuracy.

Each check has a unique identifying number in the upper right corner. Use this number to track each check that you write in your financial records.

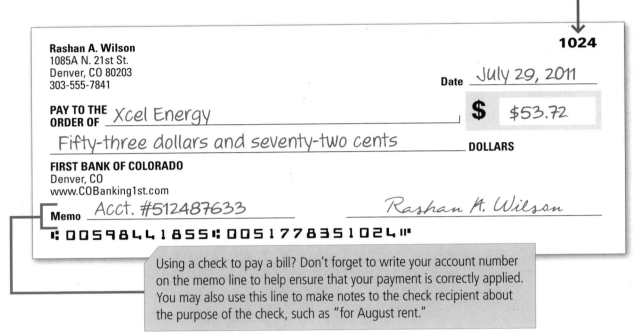

1024

Rashan A. Wilson
1085A N. 21st St.
Denver, CO 80203
303-555-7841

Date July 29, 2011

PAY TO THE
ORDER OF Xcel Energy

$ $53.72

Fifty-three dollars and seventy-two cents

DOLLARS

FIRST BANK OF COLORADO
Denver, CO
www.COBanking1st.com

Memo Acct. #512487633

Rashan A. Wilson

⑆ 005984418 55⑆ 00517783 51024 ⑈

Using a check to pay a bill? Don't forget to write your account number on the memo line to help ensure that your payment is correctly applied. You may also use this line to make notes to the check recipient about the purpose of the check, such as "for August rent."

Deposit Slip

You may use deposit slips to add money to your checking or savings account at a bank. You'll find deposit slips at the back of your checkbook, with additional ones available at your bank or ATM.

If you are depositing more than two checks, turn the deposit slip over and list each one separately on the back. Then write the subtotal from the back section on the front of the slip.

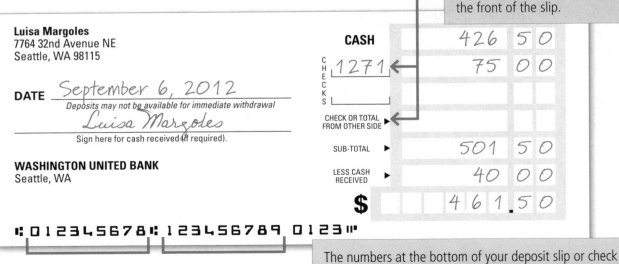

Luisa Margoles
7764 32nd Avenue NE
Seattle, WA 98115

DATE September 6, 2012
Deposits may not be available for immediate withdrawal

Luisa Margoles
Sign here for cash received (if required).

WASHINGTON UNITED BANK
Seattle, WA

CASH | 426 | 50
CHECKS | 1271 | 75 | 00
| |
CHECK OR TOTAL FROM OTHER SIDE |
SUB-TOTAL ▶ | 501 | 50
LESS CASH RECEIVED ▶ | 40 | 00
$ | 461 . 50

⑆ 012345678 ⑆ 123456789 0123 ⑈

routing number   account number

The numbers at the bottom of your deposit slip or check identify your bank and account numbers. The first group of numbers, known as your routing number, specifies the bank branch at which you opened your account. The second group of numbers gives your account number at that bank.

Check Register

Even if you choose to manage your bank account online, you can still use a check register to track your finances more effectively. Balance, or check, your records against your printed or online bank statement at least once a month.

DC	Debit Card	ATM	Teller Withdrawal	AD	Automatic Deposit	AP	Automatic Payment	BP	Online Bill Pay	XFER	Online or Phone Transfer

NUMBER OR CODE	DATE	TRANSACTION DESCRIPTION	PAYMENT AMOUNT		✓	DEPOSIT AMOUNT		$ BALANCE	
AD	04/01/2011	Paycheck	$			$ 842	16	1687	54
874	04/01/2011	Home Properties	675	00				1012	54
DC	04/01/2011	Food Savers	34	52				978	02
BP	04/02/2011	Central Electric	27	23				950	79
ATM	04/02/2011	Cash	40	00				910	79

Checkbook registers may provide different codes to track each type of transaction. Use the system described at the top of each page for quick reference. The space in the far left column can also house the number of your check.

Be careful with your math! A simple calculation error can lead to additional fees and interest if you were to overdraw your account. You may want to use a calculator to be safe.

Pay Stub

Pay stubs contain valuable information about your pay history. On a pay stub, you can find information about that pay period and for the year to date. You may want to keep your pay stubs, especially the last one you receive each year for tax purposes.

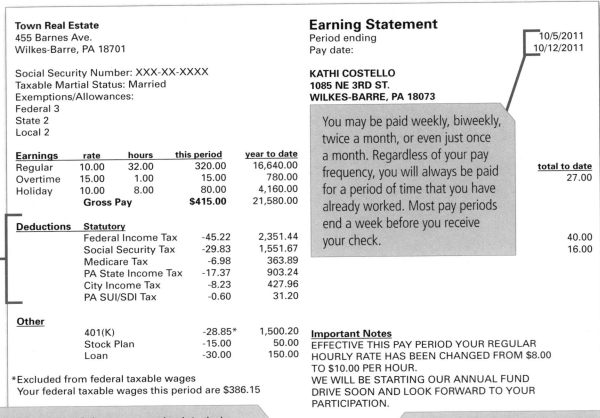

Town Real Estate
455 Barnes Ave.
Wilkes-Barre, PA 18701

Social Security Number: XXX-XX-XXXX
Taxable Martial Status: Married
Exemptions/Allowances:
Federal 3
State 2
Local 2

Earning Statement
Period ending
Pay date: 10/5/2011
                                        10/12/2011

KATHI COSTELLO
1085 NE 3RD ST.
WILKES-BARRE, PA 18073

You may be paid weekly, biweekly, twice a month, or even just once a month. Regardless of your pay frequency, you will always be paid for a period of time that you have already worked. Most pay periods end a week before you receive your check.

Earnings	rate	hours	this period	year to date
Regular	10.00	32.00	320.00	16,640.00
Overtime	15.00	1.00	15.00	780.00
Holiday	10.00	8.00	80.00	4,160.00
Gross Pay			**$415.00**	21,580.00

total to date
27.00

Deductions	Statutory		
	Federal Income Tax	-45.22	2,351.44
	Social Security Tax	-29.83	1,551.67
	Medicare Tax	-6.98	363.89
	PA State Income Tax	-17.37	903.24
	City Income Tax	-8.23	427.96
	PA SUI/SDI Tax	-0.60	31.20

40.00
16.00

Other			
	401(K)	-28.85*	1,500.20
	Stock Plan	-15.00	50.00
	Loan	-30.00	150.00

*Excluded from federal taxable wages
Your federal taxable wages this period are $386.15

Important Notes
EFFECTIVE THIS PAY PERIOD YOUR REGULAR HOURLY RATE HAS BEEN CHANGED FROM $8.00 TO $10.00 PER HOUR.
WE WILL BE STARTING OUR ANNUAL FUND DRIVE SOON AND LOOK FORWARD TO YOUR PARTICIPATION.

You've probably noticed that your paycheck includes deductions from your total pay. Most employers withhold from each check taxes that you owe the government so you do not have to pay them at once when taxes come due. Some of your earnings, however, are untaxed. These include funds you use to pay for health insurance.

If you sign up for direct deposit, the "check" that you receive will only be for your records— you cannot cash it. Otherwise, you will receive a live check that you can cash or deposit into your bank account.

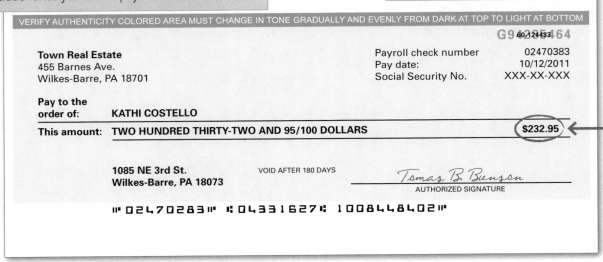

VERIFY AUTHENTICITY COLORED AREA MUST CHANGE IN TONE GRADUALLY AND EVENLY FROM DARK AT TOP TO LIGHT AT BOTTOM

G9   64   60-124433

Town Real Estate
455 Barnes Ave.
Wilkes-Barre, PA 18701

Payroll check number   02470383
Pay date: 10/12/2011
Social Security No.   XXX-XX-XXX

Pay to the
order of: **KATHI COSTELLO**

This amount: **TWO HUNDRED THIRTY-TWO AND 95/100 DOLLARS** $232.95

1085 NE 3rd St.
Wilkes-Barre, PA 18073

VOID AFTER 180 DAYS

Tomas B. Benson
AUTHORIZED SIGNATURE

⑆ 02470283 ⑆ ⑈ 04331627 ⑈ 1008448402 ⑆

Personal Budget Worksheet

To some, setting up a personal budget may seem intimidating. However, using a template like the one below can help you easily plan your monthly income and expenses. Sticking to your budget will help ensure that you live within your means.

> A good budget will reflect reality as well as your plan. Sometimes your actual expenses may be higher or lower than planned. By tracking actual expenses, you can see whether you need to adjust your budget.

PERSONAL BUDGET

INCOME	Budget	Actual	Difference
Wages	1,525.00	1,525.00	0.00
Interest/dividends	0.00	0.00	0.00
Miscellaneous	250.00	250.00	0.00
Income totals	**1,775.00**	**1,775.00**	**0.00**

EXPENSES

Home

	Budget	Actual	Difference
Mortgage/rent	550.00	550.00	0.00
Utilities	85.00	107.00	(22.00)
Home telephone	0.00	0.00	0.00
Cellular telephone	40.00	40.00	0.00
Internet service	20.00	20.00	0.00
Home improvement	20.00	0.00	20.00
Other home	0.00	0.00	0.00
Home totals			

Daily

Groceries			
Child care			
Eating out			
Other daily			
Daily totals			

> Some expenses, such as your mortgage or rent will remain largely the same from month to month. Others may change. For example, a rise in gas prices will probably lead to an increase in your overall transportation costs. Be sure to update your budget regularly to reflect real-world changes.

Transportation

	Budget	Actual	Difference
Gas	125.00	136.00	(11.00)
Car payment	165.00	165.00	0.00
Insurance	45.00	45.00	0.00
Car maintenance	25.00	20.00	5.00
Public transportation	10.00	7.50	2.50
Other transportation	10.00	5.00	5.00
Transportation totals	**380.00**	**378.50**	**1.50**

Entertainment

	Budget	Actual	Difference
Cable TV	55.00	55.00	0.00
Video/DVD rentals	15.00	10.50	4.50
Movies/plays	15.00	9.00	6.00
Concerts/clubs	15.00	0.00	15.00
Magazines/books/newspapers	15.00	10.00	5.00
Other entertainment expenses	15.00	10.00	5.00
Entertainment totals	**130.00**	**94.50**	**35.50**

Health

	Budget	Actual	Difference
Health club/gym dues	20.00	20.00	0.00
Medications	25.00	30.00	(5.00)
Co-payments/out-of-pocket	25.00	15.00	10.00
Life insurance	5.00	5.00	0.00
Other health expenses	25.00	20.00	5.00
Health totals	**100.00**	**90.00**	**10.00**

Personal

	Budget	Actual	Difference
Clothing	50.00	125.00	(75.00)
Gifts	15.00	25.00	(10.00)
Hair care			
Music (CDs, etc.)			
Toiletries and personal goods			
Charitable giving			
Other personal expenses			
Personal totals			

> Don't forget to save! You might choose to save for a vacation or holiday shopping. Many people also automatically deduct retirement savings from each paycheck they receive.

Finance

	Budget	Actual	Difference
Long-term savings	50.00	50.00	0.00
Retirement (401k, Roth IRA)	25.00	25.00	0.00
Credit card payments	50.00	50.00	0.00
Other obligations	0.00	0.00	0.00
Finance totals	**125.00**	**125.00**	**0.00**

	Budget	Actual	Difference
Total expenses	**1,760.00**	**1,741.50**	**(17.50)**

Credit Report and Score

Your credit score rates among the most important numbers in your financial life. A good score will help you secure loans and credit cards and help you receive low interest rates and favorable credit terms.

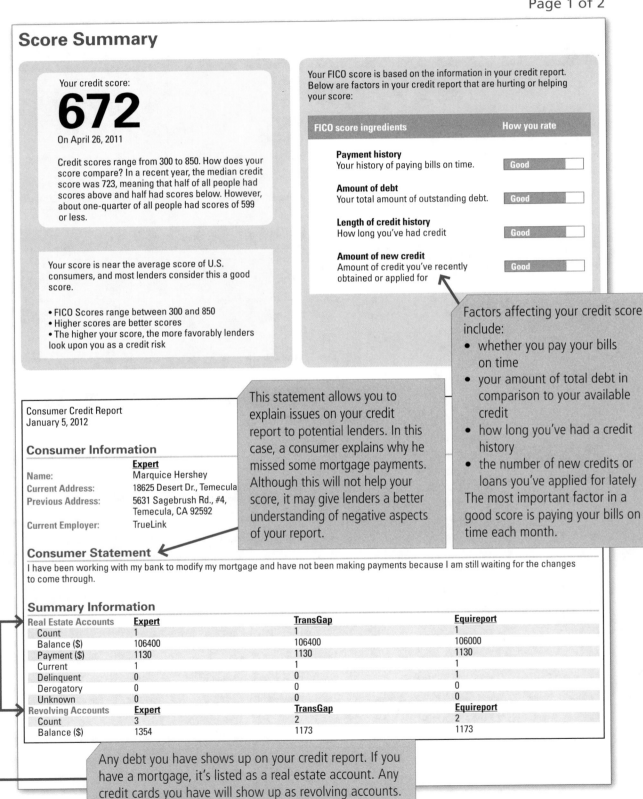

Score Summary

Your credit score:

672

On April 26, 2011

Credit scores range from 300 to 850. How does your score compare? In a recent year, the median credit score was 723, meaning that half of all people had scores above and half had scores below. However, about one-quarter of all people had scores of 599 or less.

Your score is near the average score of U.S. consumers, and most lenders consider this a good score.

- FICO Scores range between 300 and 850
- Higher scores are better scores
- The higher your score, the more favorably lenders look upon you as a credit risk

Your FICO score is based on the information in your credit report. Below are factors in your credit report that are hurting or helping your score:

FICO score ingredients	How you rate
Payment history Your history of paying bills on time.	Good
Amount of debt Your total amount of outstanding debt.	Good
Length of credit history How long you've had credit	Good
Amount of new credit Amount of credit you've recently obtained or applied for	Good

Factors affecting your credit score include:
- whether you pay your bills on time
- your amount of total debt in comparison to your available credit
- how long you've had a credit history
- the number of new credits or loans you've applied for lately

The most important factor in a good score is paying your bills on time each month.

This statement allows you to explain issues on your credit report to potential lenders. In this case, a consumer explains why he missed some mortgage payments. Although this will not help your score, it may give lenders a better understanding of negative aspects of your report.

Consumer Credit Report
January 5, 2012

Consumer Information

	Expert
Name:	Marquice Hershey
Current Address:	18625 Desert Dr., Temecula
Previous Address:	5631 Sagebrush Rd., #4, Temecula, CA 92592
Current Employer:	TrueLink

Consumer Statement

I have been working with my bank to modify my mortgage and have not been making payments because I am still waiting for the changes to come through.

Summary Information

Real Estate Accounts	Expert	TransGap	Equireport
Count	1	1	1
Balance ($)	106400	106400	106000
Payment ($)	1130	1130	1130
Current	1	1	1
Delinquent	0	0	1
Derogatory	0	0	0
Unknown	0	0	0
Revolving Accounts	**Expert**	**TransGap**	**Equireport**
Count	3	2	2
Balance ($)	1354	1173	1173

Any debt you have shows up on your credit report. If you have a mortgage, it's listed as a real estate account. Any credit cards you have will show up as revolving accounts.

Credit Report and Score

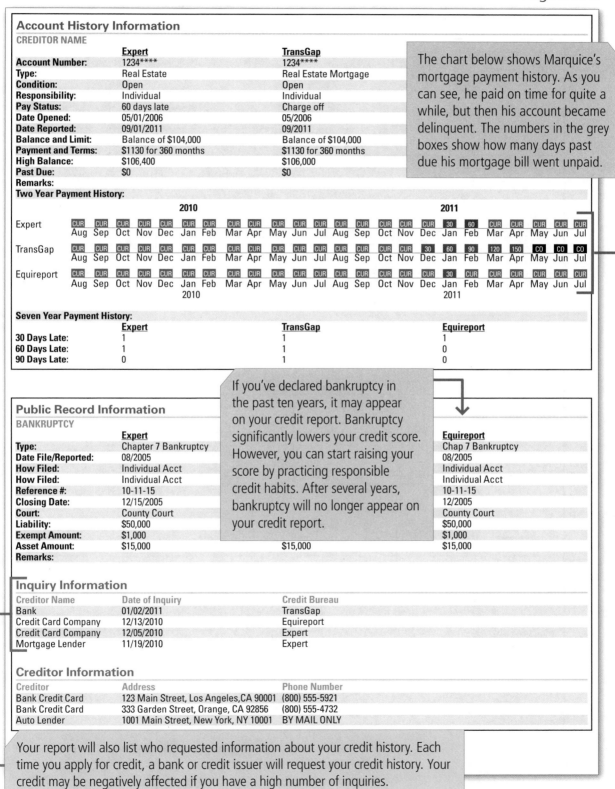

Account History Information

CREDITOR NAME

	Expert	TransGap
Account Number:	1234****	1234****
Type:	Real Estate	Real Estate Mortgage
Condition:	Open	Open
Responsibility:	Individual	Individual
Pay Status:	60 days late	Charge off
Date Opened:	05/01/2006	05/2006
Date Reported:	09/01/2011	09/2011
Balance and Limit:	Balance of $104,000	Balance of $104,000
Payment and Terms:	$1130 for 360 months	$1130 for 360 months
High Balance:	$106,400	$106,000
Past Due:	$0	$0
Remarks:		

Two Year Payment History:

> The chart below shows Marquice's mortgage payment history. As you can see, he paid on time for quite a while, but then his account became delinquent. The numbers in the grey boxes show how many days past due his mortgage bill went unpaid.

	2010																	**2011**						
Expert	CUR	CUR	CUR	CUR	CUR	CUR	CUR	CUR	CUR	CUR	CUR	CUR	CUR	CUR	CUR	CUR	CUR	30	60	CUR	CUR	CUR	CUR	CUR
	Aug	Sep	Oct	Nov	Dec	Jan	Feb	Mar	Apr	May	Jun	Jul	Aug	Sep	Oct	Nov	Dec	Jan	Feb	Mar	Apr	May	Jun	Jul
TransGap	CUR	CUR	CUR	CUR	CUR	CUR	CUR	CUR	CUR	CUR	CUR	CUR	CUR	CUR	CUR	CUR	30	60	90	120	150	CO	CO	CO
	Aug	Sep	Oct	Nov	Dec	Jan	Feb	Mar	Apr	May	Jun	Jul	Aug	Sep	Oct	Nov	Dec	Jan	Feb	Mar	Apr	May	Jun	Jul
Equireport	CUR	CUR	CUR	CUR	CUR	CUR	CUR	CUR	CUR	CUR	CUR	CUR	CUR	CUR	CUR	CUR	CUR	30	CUR	CUR	CUR	CUR	CUR	CUR
	Aug	Sep	Oct	Nov	Dec	Jan	Feb	Mar	Apr	May	Jun	Jul	Aug	Sep	Oct	Nov	Dec	Jan	Feb	Mar	Apr	May	Jun	Jul
						2010												2011						

Seven Year Payment History:

	Expert	TransGap	Equireport
30 Days Late:	1	1	1
60 Days Late:	1	1	0
90 Days Late:	0	1	0

Public Record Information

BANKRUPTCY

> If you've declared bankruptcy in the past ten years, it may appear on your credit report. Bankruptcy significantly lowers your credit score. However, you can start raising your score by practicing responsible credit habits. After several years, bankruptcy will no longer appear on your credit report.

	Expert		Equireport
Type:	Chapter 7 Bankruptcy		Chap 7 Bankruptcy
Date File/Reported:	08/2005		08/2005
How Filed:	Individual Acct		Individual Acct
How Filed:	Individual Acct		Individual Acct
Reference #:	10-11-15		10-11-15
Closing Date:	12/15/2005		12/2005
Court:	County Court		County Court
Liability:	$50,000		$50,000
Exempt Amount:	$1,000		$1,000
Asset Amount:	$15,000	$15,000	$15,000
Remarks:			

Inquiry Information

Creditor Name	Date of Inquiry	Credit Bureau
Bank	01/02/2011	TransGap
Credit Card Company	12/13/2010	Equireport
Credit Card Company	12/05/2010	Expert
Mortgage Lender	11/19/2010	Expert

Creditor Information

Creditor	Address	Phone Number
Bank Credit Card	123 Main Street, Los Angeles, CA 90001	(800) 555-5921
Bank Credit Card	333 Garden Street, Orange, CA 92856	(800) 555-4732
Auto Lender	1001 Main Street, New York, NY 10001	BY MAIL ONLY

> Your report will also list who requested information about your credit history. Each time you apply for credit, a bank or credit issuer will request your credit history. Your credit may be negatively affected if you have a high number of inquiries.

Payday Loan Application

Car break down? Credit card at its limit? You may find yourself turning to a payday loan advance company to help cover unexpected expenses. However, before you grab the quick cash, ensure that you completely understand all of the loan's terms and conditions.

A payday advance company will want information about your current employment. They can use that information to determine how much money you can afford to repay quickly. If you are unemployed, you may not be approved for a loan.

APPLICANT INFORMATION

Last Name, First Name

Customer Number in Transaction System

Name			Date of Birth	Social Security Number
Last	*First*	*Middle*	02 / 15 / 1986	XXX – XX – XXXX
Young	Terek	Charles		

Residence

Street	*City*	*State*	*Zip Code*	*If own, monthly mortgage amount*	*If rent, monthly rent amount*	*Months at residence*
565 Lincoln Ave., Apt. B,	Springfield	IL	62705		$625	14

Phone and Email

Evening Phone	*Daytime Phone*	*Email*
(217) 555-6423	(217) 555-4350	youngtc@pax.com

INCOME INFORMATION

Income Frequency		Income Source	Income Amount

Intervals (check only one)

Day Received (check day(s), then specify next pay date)

☐ Mon., ☐ Tues., ☐ Wed., ☐ Thurs., ☐ Fri.

☐ Weekly

Next pay date:

☒ Bi-weekly ☐ Mon., ☐ Tues., ☐ Wed., ☐ Thurs., ☒ Fri.

(26/year)

Next pay date: 05-11-2012

☐ Semi-monthly (26/year) ☐ 1ˢᵗ and 15th, ☐ 15th and last business day of the month, ☐ 5th and 20th, or ☐ other _____

Next pay date:

☐ Monthly ☐ 1ˢᵗ, ☐ 3ʳᵈ, the _____ Wednesday of the month, or ☐ other _____

Next pay date:

Source Type (check general source, then specific source)

☒ Wage income.
Specify (check more than one, if appropriate)
☐ Salary ☒ Overtime
☒ Hourly ☐ Bonus
☐ Commissions ☐ Private pension
Other. Specify: _____

☐ Government benefit income.
Specify (check more than one, if appropriate)
☐ Social Security
☐ Disability
☐ Other. Specify: _____

☐ Other income source.
Specify: _____

Amount of income received each pay period

Gross income $ $1346

Net income** $ $970

Income direct deposited?
☐ Yes ☐ No

Not including monthly mortgage or rent payment, total amount of all other monthly debt payments

$ $275

*You need not disclose to us any income you may receive from alimony, child support, or separate maintenance. We will treat one of those payments as income only if you ask us to do so and we can verify the regularity of the payment.
**For wage income, net income means your gross pay minus taxes, insurance premiums, retirement an 401(k) contributions, garnishment (if any).

EMPLOYMENT INFORMATION

Current Position

Employer	*Job Title*	*Department or Shift*	*Hire Date*	*Work Phone*
A1 Electronics	Assistant Manager	Varies	11/01/2010	(217) 555-4350 Ext..

Employment Verification

Supervisors Name	*Employment Verification Phone*	*Employer Address* 8665 Mall Dr.,
Angelo Patrick	(217) 555-4350	Ste. 170, Springfield IL 62703

COVERED BORROWER IDENTIFICATION STATEMENT. Federal law provides important protections to active duty members of the Armed Forces and their dependents. To ensure that these protections are provided to eligible applicants, we require you to sign one of the following statements as applicable:
I AM a regular or reserve member of the Army, Navy, Marine Corps, Air Force or Coast Guard, serving on active duty under a call or order that does not specify a period of 30 days or fewer.

I AM a dependent of a member of the Armed Forces on active duty as described above, because I am the member's spouse, the member's child under the age of eighteen years old, or I am an individual for whom the member provided more that one-half of my financial support for 180 days immediately proceeding today's date.
-OR-
I AM NOT a regular or reserve member of the Army, Navy, Marine Corps, Air Force or Coast Guard, serving on active duty under a call or order that does not specify a period of 30 days or fewer (or dependent of such a member).
Warning: It is important to fill out this form accurately. Knowingly making a false statement on a credit application is a crime.

BANKING INFORMATION

Bank Name	*Account Number*	*Account Balance*	*Date Account Opened*
Bank of Springfield	529963210	$355	05/2004

CONTACTS FOR LOCATION INFORMATION

Name (we prefer that at least one contact be a relative)	*Phone Number*	*Relationship*
Tanya Young	(217) 555-7842	mother
Harold Young	(217) 555-3321	brother
Whitney Franklin	(217) 555-1489	girlfriend

FOR OFFICE USE ONLY

Heard of Payday Advance Plus
☐ Drive-by ☐ Direct mail
☐ Internet
☐ Referred by friend/family
☐ Yellow pages ☐ Brochure/flyer
☐ Other. Specify: _____

Processing Checklist
☐ Pay stub, award letter, or court order ☐ Bank Statement ☐ Checkbook
☐ Mail ☐ Photo ID
Form of ID: _____
Issuer and Expiration Date: _____
Unique ID Number _____

Employee Signature

Manager Signature

Think you can avoid repaying your loan by ignoring calls from credit companies? Companies will try very hard to locate you. If they can't reach you, they will begin contacting friends and family members listed on your application.

Payday Loan Application

Read the arbitration agreement or other claim settlement agreement before signing a payday loan application. This section explains the process for any disagreements you might have with the company issuing the payday loan. By accepting the loan, you also agree to the company's terms to settle any disagreements.

ARBITRATION AGREEMENT

1. DEFINITIONS. We, our and us each means Payday Advance Plus and you and your each means the credit applicant identified above. Transaction means, collectively, the account with us for which you are applying and each and every credit transaction that you and we ever complete following your submission of this Credit Application. Claim means any claim, dispute, or controversy arising from or relating to this Agreement, this Transaction, any other agreement or transaction that you and we have ever entered into or completed in the past, or any other conduct or dealing between you and us. A court or arbitrator interpreting the scope of this Arbitration Agreement should broadly construe the meaning of Claim so as to give effect to your and our intention to arbitrate any and all claims, disputes, or controversies that may arise between you and us. Consistent with this broad construction, Claim includes (but is not limited to) each of the claims, disputes, or controversies listed below.

➤ A Claim includes any dispute of controversy regarding the scope, validity, or enforceability of this Arbitration Agreement. For example, a clam includes any assertion by you or us that this Arbitration Agreement is unenforceable because applicable usury, lending, or consumer protection laws render the underlying Transaction void or unenforceable. A Claim also includes any assertion by you or us that this Arbitration Agreement is unenforceable because it lacks fairness or mutuality of obligations, conflicts with bankruptcy or other federal laws, improperly limits your or our remedies for the others violation of laws or unduly restricts your or our access to the court system. Finally, a Claim includes any assertion by you or us that this Arbitration Agreement is unenforceable because you or we did not receive notice or understand its provisions, you or we need to discover the filing fees or administrative costs associated with commencing an arbitration proceeding, or you or we believe the arbitration firm or the arbitrator will be unfair or biased.

➤ A Claim includes any claim that you assert against a person or entity related to us–including our parent company, affiliated companies, directors, officers, employees, agents, and representatives–and any claim that we assert against a person or entity related to you. For the purpose of this Arbitration Agreement, reference to we, our and us and references to you and your include such related persons or entities. You and we agree that these related persons and entities may elect to arbitrate any Claim asserted against them even though they have not signed this Arbitration Agreement.

➤ A Claim includes any statutory, tort, contractual, or equitable (i.e., non-monetary) claim. For example, a Claim includes any claim arising under the following: a federal or state statute, act, or legislative enactment; a federal or state administrative regulation or rule; common law (i.e., non-statutory law based on court cases); a local ordinance or zoning code; this Agreement or another contract; a judicial or regulatory decree, order, or consent agreement; or any other type of law.

➤ A Claim includes (but is not limited to) any claim based on your or our conduct before you and we consummated this Transaction. For example, a Claim includes any dispute or controversy regarding our advertising, application processing, or underwriting practices, our communication or credit decisions, or our provision of cost-of-credit or to the consumer protection disclosures.

A Claim includes any request for monetary damages or equitable remedies, whether such request is asserted a claim, counterclaim, or cross-claim.

2. RIGHT TO REJECT ARBITRATION. If you do not want to arbitrate all Claims as provided in this Arbitration Agreement, then you have the right to reject the Arbitration Agreement. To reject arbitration, you must deliver written notice to us at the following address within 30 days following the date of this Credit Application: Payday Advance Plus, Attn: Arbitration Opt-Out, 7755 Montgomery Road, Suite 400, Cincinnati, Ohio 45236. Nobody else can reject arbitration for you; this method is the only way you can reject the Arbitration Agreement. Your rejection of the Arbitration Agreement will not affect your right to credit, how much credit you receive, or any contract term other than the Arbitration Agreement.

3. MANDATORY ARBITRATION UPON ELECTION. Subject to your right to reject arbitration (explained in Section 2 above) and subject to the small claims court exception (explained in Section 4 below), you and we agree to arbitrate the Claim, then neither you nor we may file or maintain a lawsuit in court except a small claims court and neither you nor we may join or participate in a class action, act as a class representative or private attorney general, or consolidate a Claim with claims of others. A person or entity against whom a Claim is asserted may elect to arbitrate the Claim by providing oral or written notice to the person asserting the Claim (i.e., the claimant). Such notice need not follow any particular format but must reasonably inform the claimant that arbitration has been elected. For example, if you or we file a lawsuits against the other, then the other provides sufficient notice if the other orally informs the claimant that the other elects to arbitrate the Claim or if the other files a pleading (i.e., a document filed in court) requesting the court to stay (i.e., freeze) the court case and refer the Claim to arbitration.

4. SMALL CLAIMS COURT EXCEPTION. You and we may ask a small claims court to decide a Claim so long as no party to the small claims court lawsuit seeks to certify a class, consolidate the claims of multiple person, or recover damages beyond the jurisdiction of the small claims court. If you file a small claims court lawsuit against us, then we lose the right to elect arbitration of your Claim (but not of other person's Claims). In contrast, if we file a small claims court lawsuit against you, then you retain the right to elect arbitration of our Claim.

5. ARBITRATION FIRM. The American Arbitration Association (AAA) (1-800-555-7879, www.adr.org) will administer the arbitration of Claims. The AAA will normally apply its Consumers Arbitration Rules then in effect to a Claim but may apply other types of procedural rules–such as the AAA is Commercial Arbitration Rules then in effect–if a party to the arbitration proceeding demonstrates that the application of such other procedural rules is appropriate. No matter what the arbitration firm's procedural rules provide, you and we agree that the arbitrator must issue a written decision and may award any type of remedy; including punitive damages and equitable relief; that a court or jury could award if the Claim were litigated. You and we also agree that an arbitration firm may not arbitrate a Claim as a class action or otherwise consolidate the Claims of multiple persons. You may request a copy of the AAA's Consumer Arbitration Rules and other procedural rules at the toll-free number or URL (universal resource locator) identified above. If you object to the AAA as the arbitration firm, then the parties may agree to select a local arbitrator who is a retired judge or registered arbitrator in good standing with an arbitration firm, provided that such local arbitrator must enforce all the terms of this arbitration agreement, including the class-action waiver. The parties may not select a local arbitrator who refuses to enforce this arbitration agreement, including the class action waiver, because you and we waived any rights to arbitrate a Claim on a class-action, representative action, or consolidated basis. When attempting to contact AAA or another arbitration firm, please recognize that phone numbers and URLS change frequently; you may need to update the contact information provided above with your own research.

6. PAYMENT OF ARBITRATION FEE; SELECTION OF FORUM. If you file a Claim with the AAA or another arbitration firm, the firm will usually ask you to pay a filing fee and may also ask you to pay in advance for some of the expenses the firm will incur when administering the arbitration proceeding. Upon your written request, we will pay to the arbitration firm any fees or advance administrative expenses that the arbitration firm requires you to pay as a condition to your filing a Claim with the firm. Additionally, we will pay any fees or expenses the arbitration firm charges for administering the arbitration proceeding, any fees or expenses the individual arbitrator or arbitrators charge for attending the arbitration hearing, and any fees a court charges you to file a lawsuit appealing the arbitration decision. We will pay these fees and expenses whether or not you prevail in the arbitration proceeding. Finally, we agree to hold the arbitration proceedings in the county of your residence or in any different location of your choice in the United States.

---

6. PAYMENT OF ARBITRATION FEE; SELECTION OF FORUM. If you file a Claim with the AAA or another arbitration firm, the firm will usually ask you to pay a filing fee and may also ask you to pay in advance for some of the expenses the firm will incur when administering the arbitration proceeding. Upon your written request, we will pay to the arbitration firm any fees or advance administrative expenses that the arbitration firm requires you to pay as a condition to your filing a Claim with the firm. Additionally, we will pay any fees or expenses the arbitration firm charges for administering the arbitration proceeding, any fees or expenses the individual arbitrator or arbitrators charge for attending the arbitration hearing, and any fees a court charges you to file a lawsuit appealing the arbitration decision. We will pay these fees and expenses whether or not you prevail in the arbitration proceeding. Finally, we agree to hold the arbitration proceedings in the county of your residence or in any different location of your choice in the United States.

According to this agreement, you are required to pay any arbitration fees if you have a dispute with the company. You could avoid this fee by submitting a written request for the company to pay the fees. If you did not read the agreement, you may needlessly spend money in a dispute.

If you obtain one or more Transactions from us, you further authorize us to service your Transactions by obtaining information about your location from the contact persons you have listed. By signing to the immediate right, you agree to all the terms of both the Arbitration Agreement and the Notice-of-Grievance Agreement set forth above. You also represent and warrant that all the information contained in this two-page Credit Application is true and correct, including your answers to the bankruptcy questions immediately below.

Are you currently a debtor in a pending bankruptcy proceeding (i.e., a bankruptcy in which debts have not yet been discharged)? ☐ yes ☒ no

Will you file a bankruptcy petition under any chapter of the U.S. Bankruptcy Code either during the tem of a Transaction or within the 90-day period following your repayment of a Transaction? ☐ yes ☒ no

Terek C. Young

Applicant's Signature

4/30/2012

Date

Payday Loan Interest Rates and Terms

Payday loans may help you out of a jam, but their rates are significantly higher than those for credit cards. You might be surprised to find out how much a short-term loan will end up costing you.

These rates and terms limit your maximum loan amount to one-quarter of your paycheck or $1,000, whichever is less. Only you will know how much you can afford to comfortably repay. Be careful to only take out an amount than you can afford to repay.

Illinois Payday Loan Rates and Terms

Availability of Payday Loan

Payday Advance Plus offers payday loans both online and at a store location near you.

Governing Law

The loan agreement will be governed by the applicable laws of Illinois. Questions or complaints should be directed to your state's regulatory agency.

Maximum Payday Loan Amount

The maximum loan amount for Illinois residents will be 25% of gross monthly income or $1,000.00, whichever is less.

Fax of Pay Stub

Illinois regulation states that all Illinois customers have their most recent pay stub on file with Payday Advance Plus when receiving a payday loan. For online customers, please fax or e-mail Payday Advance Plus your latest pay stub when applying to ensure timely processing of your loan. If you receive income by means other than an employer, please fax or e-mail other proof of your Social Security, disability, child support or alimony payments. All materials may be sent via fax to (800) 555-7032 or via email to customerservice@pax.com. When applying for a payday loan at a store location, please take the above documentation with you.

Payday Loan Terms

For a Payday Advance Plus online loan and a store loan, the minimum loan term is 13 days and the maximum loan term is 35 days.

Only one loan is permitted at Payday Advance Plus, whether online or at a store.

Illinois state law mandates a 7-day cooling off period after a customer has been in a payday loan product for 45 consecutive days.

Illinois state law mandates a 14-day cooling off period after a customer has paid an extended payment plan and any transaction that was outstanding during the extended payment plan period.

Extensions
Extended Payment Plan

A customer who has an outstanding payday transaction for 35 or more consecutive days may request an extended payment plan

Illinois
MINIMUM QUALIFICATIONS AND REQUIREMENTS*

QUALIFICATIONS

- A regular, verifiable source of income
- An active checking account
- A working phone

*Additional qualification or requirements may apply. See Web site for details.

REQUIRED ITEMS

- Your most recent pay stub (if you are employed)

  OR

- Your most recent bank statement (if you have another source of income)
- Your checkbook
- Proof of current address (phone or utility bill)
- Driver's license or government-issued photo ID

State regulations differ for payday loan companies. Learn about rules in your state by reviewing rates and terms online or at your closest payday loan location.

Payday Loan Interest Rates and Terms

The annual percentage rates (APR) for even small loans at a payday loan company may exceed 400 percent. This means that if you borrow $50 and repay it over the course of a year, it would end up costing you more than $2,000!

The fee that you pay is usually calculated over just a two-week term, since two weeks is a common time frame between pay checks. Your APR reflects the ratio of that fee to the amount that you borrowed over an entire year.

FINANCE CHARGE SCHEDULE*

*The APR calculation is based on a transaction with a 14-day term. Your APR may be different if your transaction term is not 14 days. The APR of your transaction will be disclosed in the federal Truth-In-Lending Statement contained in your contract.

Annual Percentage Rates The cost of your credit as yearly rated (assumes a 14-day term)	Finance Charge The dollar amount the credit will cost you	Amount financed The amount we pay to you or on your behalf	Total of Payments The amount you will have paid payments as scheduled	Number of Payments
404.11%	$7.75	$50.00	$57.75	1
403.93%	$11.62	$75.00	$86.62	1
404.11%	$15.50	$100.00	$115.50	1
404.00%	$19.37	$125.00	$144.37	1
404.11%	$23.25	$150.00	$173.25	1
404.03%	$27.12	$175.00	$202.12	1
404.11%	$31.00	$200.00	$231.00	1
404.05%	$34.87	$225.00	$259.87	1
404.11%	$38.75	$250.00	$288.75	1
404.06%	$42.62	$275.00	$317.62	1
404.11%	$46.50	$300.00	$346.50	1
404.07%	$50.37	$325.00	$375.37	1
404.11%	54.25	$350.00	$404.25	1
404.07%	$58.12	$375.00	$433.121	1
404.11%	$62.00	$400.00	$462.00	1
404.08%	$65.87	$425.00	$490.87	1
404.11%	$69.75	$450.00	$519.75	1
404.08%	$73.62	$475.00	$548.62	1
404.11%	$77.50	$500.00	$577.50	1
404.11%	$85.25	$550.00	$635.25	1
404.11%	$93.00	$600.00	$693.00	1
404.11%	$100.75	$650.00	$750.75	1
404.11%	$108.50	$700.00	$808.50	1
404.11%	$116.25	$750.00	$866.25	1
404.11%	$124.00	$800.00	$924.00	1
404.11%	$131.75	$850.00	$981.75	1
404.11%	$139.50	$900.00	$1,039.50	1
404.11%	$147.25	$950.00	$1,097.25	1
404.11%	$155.00	$1,000.00	$1,155.00	1

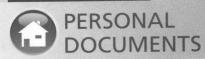

PERSONAL DOCUMENTS

Health and Medicine

CONTENTS

No one enjoys being ill, but understanding what to expect after you visit a doctor or hospital at least can put your mind at ease. Different types of medical visits or procedures incur varying fees. What seems like a simple procedure may in fact be quite expensive. For instance, you may be billed separately for lab tests or medications prescribed by the doctor. Learning how to read a medical bill may help you better understand the various fees involved.

A health insurance policy may help you pay for preventive care, illnesses, or injuries. Not all insurance policies have agreements with every health care provider. Under some insurance plans, you may have to visit doctors, hospitals, and labs covered by your insurance network. Providing a complete and accurate medical history may help you find a policy most likely to serve your medical needs. Even if you are young and in good health, having medical and life insurance can help you withstand an unexpected illness, accident, or another unforeseen event. Studying the examples in this lesson will help you interpret and complete the documents in the chapter review and in real life.

Tech TIP

Online Medical Web Sites

If you start to feel sick, you may go online to look up your symptoms on medical Web sites, such as WebMD. Although these sites can provide valuable information, keep in mind that self-diagnosis cannot replace a visit to the doctor.

Doctor's Office Bill

If you have health insurance, you won't have to pay the full bill after a doctor appointment. You might pay a standard portion of the bill, called a co-pay. If your insurance company does not cover the rest of the bill, you will be responsible for any uncovered costs.

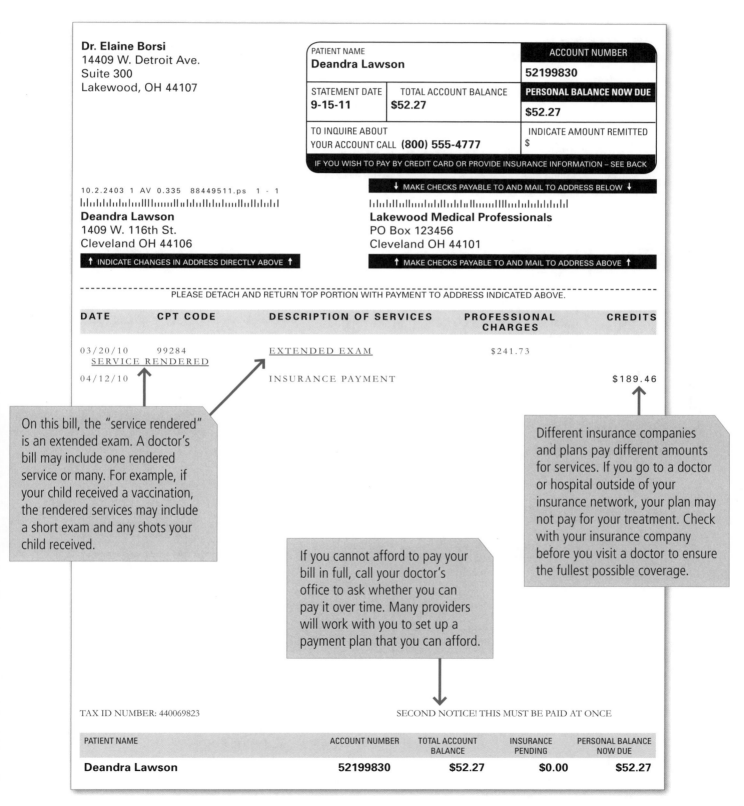

Dr. Elaine Borsi
14409 W. Detroit Ave.
Suite 300
Lakewood, OH 44107

PATIENT NAME	ACCOUNT NUMBER
Deandra Lawson	**52199830**

STATEMENT DATE	TOTAL ACCOUNT BALANCE	**PERSONAL BALANCE NOW DUE**
9-15-11	**$52.27**	**$52.27**

TO INQUIRE ABOUT YOUR ACCOUNT CALL **(800) 555-4777**	INDICATE AMOUNT REMITTED $

IF YOU WISH TO PAY BY CREDIT CARD OR PROVIDE INSURANCE INFORMATION – SEE BACK

↓ MAKE CHECKS PAYABLE TO AND MAIL TO ADDRESS BELOW ↓

10.2.2403 1 AV 0.335 88449511.ps 1 - 1

Deandra Lawson
1409 W. 116th St.
Cleveland OH 44106

Lakewood Medical Professionals
PO Box 123456
Cleveland OH 44101

↑ INDICATE CHANGES IN ADDRESS DIRECTLY ABOVE ↑

↑ MAKE CHECKS PAYABLE TO AND MAIL TO ADDRESS ABOVE ↑

------- PLEASE DETACH AND RETURN TOP PORTION WITH PAYMENT TO ADDRESS INDICATED ABOVE. -------

DATE	CPT CODE	DESCRIPTION OF SERVICES	PROFESSIONAL CHARGES	CREDITS
03/20/10	99284	EXTENDED EXAM	$241.73	
SERVICE RENDERED				
04/12/10		INSURANCE PAYMENT		$189.46

On this bill, the "service rendered" is an extended exam. A doctor's bill may include one rendered service or many. For example, if your child received a vaccination, the rendered services may include a short exam and any shots your child received.

Different insurance companies and plans pay different amounts for services. If you go to a doctor or hospital outside of your insurance network, your plan may not pay for your treatment. Check with your insurance company before you visit a doctor to ensure the fullest possible coverage.

If you cannot afford to pay your bill in full, call your doctor's office to ask whether you can pay it over time. Many providers will work with you to set up a payment plan that you can afford.

TAX ID NUMBER: 440069823

SECOND NOTICE! THIS MUST BE PAID AT ONCE

PATIENT NAME	ACCOUNT NUMBER	TOTAL ACCOUNT BALANCE	INSURANCE PENDING	PERSONAL BALANCE NOW DUE
Deandra Lawson	**52199830**	**$52.27**	**$0.00**	**$52.27**

Hospital Bill

When you visit a hospital, you will probably receive at least two bills. One bill will come from the hospital itself and another from the doctor or doctors who treated you. You may also receive additional bills from any companies that provided lab services, tests, or transportation.

Health insurance companies often have special agreements with hospitals and other providers. These providers accept lower payment rates from insurance companies than you could negotiate on your own. Just like at the doctor's office, you must pay any part of the bill not covered by your insurance.

Eugene City Hospital
and Eugene City Health Network

PO Box 9127
Eugene, OR 97024

877-555-5555
800-555-5555 Toll Free Oregon
877-555-5555 Toll Free U.S.

frankmed 121109_42255

TO: William Guzman
745 Timber Rd., #7
Eugene, OR 97024

Thank you for your payment. Please don't hesitate to call at 1-877-555-5555 whenever we can be of any assistance.

PATIENT'S NAME	ACCOUNT #	STATEMENT DATED
William Guzman	V12345678	10/17/11
DUE DATE	TOTAL DUE	PENDING INSURANCE
11/6/11	$108.13	$0.00
Payments made less than 10 days before the date on this statement may not appear on this bill.		PLEASE PAY THIS AMOUNT
		$108.13

This is a statement for HOSPITAL SERVICES only. You may receive an additional statement for any services you received from your physician.

DATE	DESCRIPTION	AMOUNT CHARGED	INS. PAYMENTS & ADJUSTMENTS	BALANCE DUE
	CARDIOLOGY	991.00		
06/26/11	MEDICARE ADJUSTMENT		-609.72	
06/26/11	MEDICARE PAYMENT		-207.72	
07/18/11	COMPRA TX ADJUSTMENT		0.00	
07/18/11	COMPRA TX PAYMENT		-65.43	
	Charges to date:	991.00		
	Receipts to date:		273.15	
	Adjustments to date:	0.00	609.72	
	Total due:			
	Estimated insurance due:			108.13
	Your insurance company has processed this claim. They have notified us that the remainder is your balance.			

PLEASE RETAIN THIS PORTION FOR YOU RECORDS

- -

CREDIT CARD INFORMATION

ACCOUNT NUMBER   CARD VERIFICATION #

☐☐☐☐☐☐☐☐☐☐☐☐☐☐☐☐☐   ☐☐☐

Expiration Date ___/___/___   Amount Paid $_____

Signature X _____

* The card verification # is the 3-digit number in the signature area on the back of your card. Please see an example on the back of this statement.

Please return this section with your payment.

PATIENTS NAME	ACCOUNT #	STATEMENT DATED
William Guzman	V12345678	10/17/11
DUE DATE	TOTAL DUE	PLEASE PAY THIS AMOUNT
11/6/07	$108.13	$108.13
		AMOUNT ENCLOSED

Pay online at
www.eugenecityhospital.com/billing

☐ **HAVE YOU MOVED? HAS YOUR INSURANCE CHANGED?**
Then check box and enter changes to your address or insurance on the reverse side of this bill.

To set up a payment plan, please call
Patient Account Services 877-555-5555

Eugene City Hospital
PO Box 9127
Eugene, OR 97024
||ı|ıı|ıı|ıı|ııı|ııı|||ıııı||ı|ı|ı|ı|ı|ıı|ı|ı||ıı|ı|ıı|ıı|

Many hospitals allow you to pay your bill online instead of mailing a check or money order. You can also often pay over the phone by calling the hospital's billing department.

Lab Procedure Bill

If you have blood drawn or a tissue sample sent out for tests, you will probably receive a bill from a laboratory company. This bill only reflects charges associated with processing tests ordered by your doctor. You may receive an additional bill for your doctor's services.

Some people may be covered by two insurance policies. For example, you may have one insurance policy from your job and another one from your spouse's job. If so, your secondary insurance may cover some of the fees that your primary insurance did not. Be sure to provide information about both policies to receive your full benefits.

Laboratory Testing Corporation

Tax ID # 47-6529907

Regina Cusack
18205 Coastal Lane
Wilmington NC 28403

Test requested by:
Insurance that has been filed is listed below:
Golden Rule
ID #: 47-6529907
Policy Group #:

Laboratory Bill

Due upon receipt

Payment made via an online banking service must include this invoice #

Your invoice #: 45003950

Amount Due: $19.95

Patient Name: Regina Cusack
Invoice Date   09/24/10

Important Notice

THIS BILL REPRESENTS THE CO-INSURANCE, DEDUCTIBLE OR CO-PAY AMOUNT DUE AFTER NOTIFICATION FROM YOUR INSURANCE COMPANY. PLEASE REMIT PROMPT PAYMENT. IF YOU HAVE SECONDARY INSURANCE PLEASE CALL 1-800-555-4567. THANK YOU.

Summary of Activity

Date of Service	Description	Charges	Adjustments	Medicare/ Medicaid Paid	Insurance Paid	Patient Paid	You Pay
09-08-10	Chol+Trig+HDL+LDL_D	169.00					169.00
09-08-10	Comp. Metabolic Panel (14)	46.00					46.00
09-08-10	Drawing Fee	24.00					24.00
	Adjustments(s)		(219.05)				
Web payment and insurance filing options are available at: www.pax.com/billing or 1-800-555-4567		239.00					$19.95

If you received an Explanation of Benefits from your insurance company and the patient responsibility is less than the amount of this bill, please pay the lesser amount. Call our Customer Service Department at 1-800-555-4567 with any questions. Only your doctor can answer questions concerning diagnosis and results.

TEST PERFORMED BY: LABORATORY TESTING CORPORATION OF WILMINGTON, 245 RIVER ST., WILMINGTON NC 28401

We accept credit cards. Insurance and credit card payment information is located on the back of this invoice. For proper credit, return the below portion with payment.

DO NOT SEND CASH
Make check or money order payable to:

Laboratory Testing Corporation
PO Box 506955
Jacksonville, NC 28540

Your insurance company will send you an Explanation of Benefits (EOB) for each claim submitted. This statement shows the charges that the company received, what it paid, and the amount you owe as the patient. The EOB is not a bill. However, if there's a balance, you can expect a bill from the provider soon.

The codes in the description column are for medical blood tests. The charges are paid to the lab that ran the tests. The drawing fee pays the phlebotomist, or the person who drew your blood. The adjustments show how much of the bill your insurance company paid. You are responsible for the balance.

Health Insurance Application

Whether you get insurance through your employer or buy it on your own, you must fill out a health insurance application. Be sure to provide a complete summary of your medical history. Insurance companies can end your coverage if you misrepresent your medical past.

EXQUISITE HEALTH

Individual & Family Enrollment Application

PART I. Tell us who you are enrolling and select the product:
Application must be typed or completed in blue or black ink.
THE APPLICATION MUST BE COMPLETED BY THE APPLICANT.

Requested Effective Date

A. Reason for Application

FAMILY TYPE
- ☐ Self
- ☑ Self & Child
- ☐ Self, Spouse/Domestic Partner and Child(ren)
- ☐ Self & Spouse/Domestic Partner
- ☐ Self & Children

☐ *Please check for Domestic Partner enrollment*
☐ Process as separate policies

ENROLLMENT TYPE
- ☑ New Enrollment
- ☐ Change Plan*
- ☐ Add Dependent*

*Member ID number (listed on your ID card): _____

> You may be able to apply for insurance that covers both you and your family. The number of people covered under the policy will affect the cost of the plan.

☐ Credit card (Please complete the credit card section on application)

☐ Credit card (Please complete credit card section; **not available with Term Life**)

C. Choice of Coverage

PPO* – Exquisite Health Life Insurance Company: Available for 1st and 15th of the month effective dates

SimpleValue ☐ 30 ☑ 40 ☐ 50
with ☑ Generic Rx *or* ☐ Combo Rx

HSA (Compatible Plans) ☐ SimpleChoice ☐ SmartChoice

SimpleChoice ☐ 15 ☐ 25 ☐ 35 ☐ 40 ☐ 50
☐ FirstChoice PPO ☐ ValueChoice 1500

*As a convenience to you, if you have applied for Individual PPO coverage and do not meet the underwriting requirements for preferred premiums for the PPO plan for which you applied, Exquisite Health may elect to offer you our Modified Issue PPO option. The Modified offer may be a plan that will have a rate that is 20% or 50% higher than the standard rate for which you applied. You will be automatically enrolled unless otherwise specified. Please check this box should you not wish to be automatically enrolled into the Modified Issue PPO option and the new rate.
☐ **NO, do not enroll me**

HMO – Exquisite Health of California: Only available for the 1st of the month effective dates ☐ HMO 15 ☐ HMO 40

Add – Term Life Insurance Coverage
(Part VI must be completed)
☑ $15,000 ☐ $30,000 ☐ $50,000

Add – Dental and Vision Plus
☐ Dental & Vision Plus
Primary Dentist Number (HMO plans only): _____

PART II. Applicant Information (Note: For the most favorable rate, make the younger spouse/domestic partner the primary applicant.)

Primary Applicant's Last Name	First Name	MI	
Lazio	Julia	R	☐ Male ☑ Female

Home Address: 1502 Redwood Rd., #2C

City	State	ZIP	County applicant resides in
Sacramento,	CA	95833	Sacramento

Home Phone Number	Work Phone Number	Email address
(916)555-2774	(916)555-3122	juliarl@domain.com

Primary Applicant's Birth Date (mo/day/year): 03/03/1968

Primary Applicant's Social Security Number: XXX XX XXXX

Height	Weight (lbs)	Primary Care Physician ID # (if applicable)	Current Patient	Physician Group ID#
5'4"	145		☐ Yes ☐ No	

Type of Business:
- ☑ Self Employed/Consultant
- ☐ Professional/Management
- ☐ Employed (Non-managerial)
- ☐ Unemployed (between jobs)
- ☐ Student
- ☐ Retired
- ☐ Other: _____

Occupation: Home healthcare provider

Salary Range (optional):
- ☑ $18,000–30,000
- ☐ $30,001–45,000
- ☐ $45,001–60,000
- ☐ $60,001–75,000
- ☐ $75,001–90,000
- ☐ $90,001+

Would you be interested in other Exquisite Health or affiliated entities, products and services May we contact you by email? ☑ Yes ☐ No
The release of your information may result in an Exquisite Health representative or Authorized Agent contacting you.

In the past 6 months, have you been a resident of the United States? ☑ Yes ☐ No
If no, where was your last residence? _____

> Health factors, such as your height-to-weight ratio, may affect your insurance rates. Living a healthy lifestyle by avoiding tobacco, excessive alcohol consumption, and unhealthy foods will improve your overall health. It will also reduce your health insurance costs.

> Most insurance companies offer a number of different policies. Review the informational materials you receive about each policy. This will help you choose the one that's right for you. Keep in mind that less expensive policies come with higher deductibles (the portion of the bill you're responsible for) and more restrictive coverage.

Health Insurance Application

List each applicant for the policy separately, even if that person is a child. You may be enrolling more people than will fit in the space provided. If so, attach an extra sheet of paper with information for those applicants.

EXQUISITE HEALTH

Primary's Social Security Number
X X X X X X X X X

PART III. Family member(s) to be enrolled

List all eligible family members to be enrolled other than yourself. If a listed family member's last name is different from yours, please explain on a separate sheet of paper. For Domestic Partner coverage all requirements for eligibility, as required by the applicable laws of the State of California, must be met and a joint Declaration of Domestic Partnership must be filed with the California Secretary of State. **To be processed under one Subscriber, all family members must reside at the same address.** *HMO only*: If you are applying for HMO coverage, you must select a Physician Group and Primary Care Physician. You may choose the same or different Physician Group and Primary Care Physician for each family member you are enrolling. If you do not select a Primary Care Physician, one will be selected for you within your regional area.

Relation	Last Name First Name MI	Social Security No.	Date of Birth	Height	Weight (lbs)	Primary Care Physical ID#	Current Patient	Physician Group ID#
☐ Husband ☐ Wife	Spouse/Domestic Partner	— —					☐ Yes ☐ No	
☑ Son ☐ Daughter	Child 1 Lazio Thomas M	XXX–XX–XXXX	08/05/1997	5'8"	140		☐ Yes ☐ No	
Full Time Student? ☑ Yes ☐ No	Units Carried	Name of School Sacramento City High School						
☐ Son ☐ Daughter	Child 2	— —					☐ Yes ☐ No	
Full Time Student? ☐ Yes ☐ No	Units Carried	Name of School						
☐ Son ☐ Daughter	Child 3	— —					☐ Yes ☐ No	
Full Time Student? ☐ Yes ☐ No	Units Carried	Name of School						
☐ Son ☐ Daughter	Child 4	— —					☐ Yes ☐ No	
Full Time Student? ☐ Yes ☐ No	Units Carried	Name of School						

For additional dependents please attach another sheet with the requested information.

PART IV. (a) Statement of health (All questions must be answered. Include information for yourself and each family member applying for coverage. Please answer all questions "Yes" or "No." (IF "YES," PLEASE CIRCLE THE SPECIFIC **CONDITIONS**.) Complete Part B on page 4.

	Yes	No
1) A. Is either the applicant or spouse/domestic partner or female dependent, whether or not listed on the application, currently pregnant?	☐	☑
B. If you are a male listed on this application, are you expecting a child with anyone, even if the mother is not listed on this application?	☐	☑
C. If you are a male listed on this application, has your spouse, even if not listed on this application, performed a home pregnancy test that has reacted positive during the previous 90 days?	☐	☑
D. During the previous 90 days, has any female applicant performed a home pregnancy test that has reacted positive?	☐	☑
2) Have you or any applying family member had an abnormal physical exam, laboratory results, EKG, X-ray(s), MRI, CT scan or other diagnostic test(s), or been advised to have diagnostic test(s), treatment(s), surgery or hospitalization(s), or are you waiting for the results of any diagnostic test(s)?	☐	☑
3) Have you or any applying family member been seen by a health care practitioner, been a patient in a hospital, clinic, surgicenter, sanatorium or other medical facility as an inpatient or outpatient?	☑	☐

Some health conditions may be grouped together on the medical history form. If only one of the conditions applies to an applicant circle or indicate the relevant one.

	Yes	No
	☐	☑
A. Chest pain, high or low blood pressure, heart disease, heart murmur, palpitations or irregular heart beat, peripheral vascular disease, blood clot, phlebitis, varicose veins, blood disorder, anemia, enlarged lymph nodes, or any other heart, cardiovascular, or circulatory disorder?	☑	☐
B. Headaches, dizziness, paralysis, stroke, loss of consciousness, seizure disorder, sleep apnea, multiple sclerosis, cerebral palsy, or any other disorder of the brain or nervous system?	☐	☑

Health Insurance Application

Keep in mind that you will not necessarily be rejected for health insurance just because of past medical problems. If you or another applicant has a specific condition, it is important to list it. This ensures that a claim will not be denied later because it was an unreported pre-existing condition.

EXQUISITE HEALTH

Primary's Social Security Number
X X X X X X X X X

PART IV. (a) Statement of health (continued)

	Yes	No
5) C. Disorder of the mouth, throat or esophagus, tonsillitis, ulcer(s), colitis, ulcerative colitis, spastic colitis, Crohn's disease, gall bladder disorder, chronic diarrhea, hernia, hemorrhoids, hepatitis, pancreatitis, intestinal or rectal problems, liver disease, cirrhosis, stomach disorder, or any other disorder of the digestive system?	✔	
D. Allergy, sinusitis, bronchitis, emphysema, chronic obstructive pulmonary disease (COPD), pneumonia, tuberculosis, coughing up blood, or any other lung or respiratory disorder?		✔
E. Asthma?	✔	
If "Yes," have you been hospitalized or been to an emergency room in the past 24 months?		✔
Have you received any adrenaline or epinephrine injections?		
F. Disorder of the kidney or bladder, infections, blood in urine, pyelonephritis, or any other disorder of the urinary tract?		✔
G. Arthritis, rheumatoid arthritis, bursitis, gout, disorder of the back, spine, bone or joint, herniated, ruptured, or bulging disc, muscle or tendon pain, carpal tunnel syndrome, muscular dystrophy, fixation device or any other disorder of the musculoskeletal system?		✔
H. Jaw problems, temporal mandibular joint syndrome (TMJ), pain or difficulty breathing, chewing or swallowing?		✔
I. Diabetes, thyroid disorder, adrenal disorder, lupus, Raynaud's disease, chronic fatigue syndrome, Epstein-Barr virus, unintentional weight loss or any other disorder of the metabolic system?		✔
J. Cancer, melanoma, tumor, cyst, growth, leukemia, Hodgkin's disease, or any other malignancy or any unbiopsied or undiagnosed tumor, cyst or growth?		✔
K. Psoriasis, keratosis, herpes, burn(s), birthmark(s), warts, or any other disorder of the skin?	✔	
L. Disorder of the eyes or sight, glaucoma, cataracts, disorder of the ears or hearing, ear infection (otitis media), disorder of the nose or breathing, deviated nasal septum?		✔
M. Nervous, mental, emotional or obsessive compulsive disorder, behavioral disorder, panic attack(s), anxiety, depression, manic depression, schizophrenia, attention deficit disorder, ADHD, or eating disorder?		✔

	Yes	No
N. Alcohol or substance abuse/dependency, counseling, member of a support group?		✔
(i) Do you consume alcoholic beverages?	✔	
If "yes", please indicate the number of alcoholic beverages you consume weekly (a beverage is 12 ounces of beer, 6 ounces of wine, 1 ounce of liquor). Applicant 3 Spouse/Domestic Partner____		
O. Premature birth, developmental delay, congenital abnormalities, clubfoot, cleft lip or palate, or Down's syndrome?		✔
P. Cosmetic or reconstructive surgery, including breast implants?		✔
Q. Male reproductive system: disorder of the prostate, infections, impotency, sexual dysfunction, infertility, sexually transmitted disease or any other disorder of the reproductive system?		✔
R. Female reproductive system: disorder of the breast, fibroid tumors, infertility, menstruation disorders, abnormal Pap test, infections, sexually transmitted disease, abnormal bleeding, endometriosis or any other disorder of the uterus or reproductive system?		✔
6) Have you or any applying family member been diagnosed as having or been treated for AIDS (Acquired Immune Deficiency Syndrome) or ARC (AIDS-Related Complex)?		✔
7) Have you or any applying family member consulted any health care practitioner for any condition or symptom(s) for which a diagnosis has not been established?		✔
8) During the past 12 months, have you or any applying family member smoked cigarettes, cigars, pipes, or used chewing tobacco?		✔
9) During the past three years, have you or any applying family member consulted any health care practitioner for any reason not listed on this form?		✔
10) During the past 12 months, have you or any applying family member experienced symptoms for which any health care practitioner has not been consulted?		✔
11) Is the applicant or any applying family member currently taking medication? If "Yes," please complete section IV (b).	✔	
12) Has the applicant or any applying family member taken a prescription medication during the past 12 months for a period of more than two weeks? If "Yes," please complete Part IV (b).		✔

Questions such as these only refer to symptoms that may be unusual. You do not need to report a common cold or an occasional headache.

3

SAP 6013215 (3/07)

Health Insurance Application

EXQUISITE HEALTH

Primary's Social Security Number

☒☒☒ ☒☒ ☒☒☒☒

PART IV. (a) Statement of health (continued)
Female applicants only (applicable to all females listed on the application). Attach another page if more than two females are listed on the application.

Applicant Name: Julia Lazio			Applicant Name:		
13) A. Have you had a menstrual period in each of the last six months, including within the last 30 days? If "No," please explain:	Yes ☑	No ☐	13) A. Have you had a menstrual period in each of the last six months, including within the last 30 days? If "No," please explain:	Yes ☐	No ☐
B. (i) Have you had a pelvic exam? If yes, date of last pelvic exam (Mo/Dy/Yr): 08/24/2011	Yes ☑	No ☐		Yes ☐	No ☐
(ii) Have you had a pap smear? If yes, date of last pap smear (Mo/Dy/Yr): 08/24/2011	Yes ☑	No ☐		Yes ☐	No ☐
(iii) Were the results of the exam(s) normal? If "No," please explain:	Yes ☑	No ☐		Yes ☐	No ☐

> Health insurance applications may ask for information that you consider personal. Keep in mind that providing your medical information to a health insurance company is much like providing it to your doctor; it's confidential.

PART IV. (b) Statement of health – If you answered "Yes" to any questions in Section IV (a), please identify the question number and explain in FULL DETAIL below. If additional space is necessary, please attach extra pages.

Question Number	Family member name and name used on doctor's records	Diagnosis, signs or symptoms, condition, treatment or recommendation	Still under treatment?	Dates of treatment or Hospitalization (Mo/Yr) Began	Ended	Full name, address & telephone number of every health care practitioner, clinic, hospital or any other medical facility (include ZIP code)
Q#: 3	Julia R Lazio	Gave birth	☐ Yes ☑ No	08/97	08/97	Dr. Aziz Singh, Sacramento General Hospital, 123 Main St., Sacramento CA 95801
Q#: 5E	Thomas M Lazio	Asthma	☐ Yes ☑ No	03/2000		Dr. Rochelle Jackson, 5225 Center St., Ste. 300, Sacramento CA 95833
Q#: 5K	Julia R Lazio	Migraines	☐ Yes ☑ No	04/2002	09/2006	Dr. Marc Brune, 5236 Center St., Ste. 215, Sacramento CA 95833
			☐ Yes ☐ No			
			☐ Yes ☐ No			
			☐ Yes ☐ No			

DOCTOR'S VISITS – Please provide information regarding the last health care practitioner visit or physical examination for ALL family members you wish to cover.

Name of Individual	Date of Visit	Reason for visit	Result of Visit	Full name, address & telephone number of every health care practitioner, clinic, hospital or any other medical facility (include ZIP code)
Julia R Lazio	10/04/2011	Annual checkup	Normal	Dr. Marc Brune, 5236 Center St., Ste. 215, Sacramento CA 95833
Thomas M Lazio	05/22/2011	Asthma checkup	Normal	Dr. Rochelle Jackson, 5225 Center St., Ste. 300, Sacramento CA 95833

> Include as much information as you can about your last doctor's visit. If you have trouble remembering dates or other details, call your doctor's office for that information.

4

SAP 6013215 (3/07)

Health Insurance Application

Many health insurance companies offer special policies for people who have difficulty obtaining other coverage. Discuss your options with a health insurance broker or representative to learn more.

EXQUISITE HEALTH

Primary's Social Security Number
X X X X X X X X X

PART IV. (b) Statement of health (continued)

MEDICATIONS – Please list all medications taken currently or within the last year by anyone listed on this application.

Name of Individual	Condition	Name of Medication	Prescribing Physician	Most Recent Refill Date	Strength (No. of milligrams)	Dosage & Frequency (How many pills and how often take)	Number of refills per year
Thomas	Strep throat	Amoxicillin	Brune	02/18/2011	500	1 pill 2x day	0

You do not need to include common over-the-counter medications such as Tylenol in this listing. However be sure to include any prescription medication.

PART V. Prior health coverage.

A. During the previous 62 days, have you been covered by health insurance? ☑ Yes ☐ No

If "Yes," Current Carrier: HealthOne   Effective date: 06/2007 Expected termination date: 11/30/2011
☐ Individual & Family HMO   ☐ Group HMO
☑ Individual & Family PPO   ☐ Group PPO
☐ Disability, Short Term or Interim   ☐ Other: _____

B. Has anyone on this application been a Health Net or Foundation Health Member in the last five years? ☐ Yes ☑ No

If "Yes," former Health Net or Foundation Health Member name: _____

Group Number (listed on your ID card): _____

Member ID Number (listed on your ID card): _____

C. **HIPAA Guaranteed Issue Coverage**
You may be considered for coverage under the HIPAA Guaranteed Issue plans. The plan does not require medical underwriting and the rates are higher compared to the other Individual Plans. If you qualify please request the complete benefit details and rates. If you meet every condition below you are eligible for guaranteed issue in accordance with HIPAA.

1. Have you had a total of at least 18 months of health care coverage (including COBRA or Cal-COBRA, if applicable) without more than a 63-day break (excluding any employer imposed waiting periods) in coverage? ☐ Yes ☑ No

2. Was your most recent coverage through a group health plan (COBRA and Cal-COBRA are considered group coverage)? ☐ Yes ☑ No

3. Currently are you eligible for coverage under a group health plan, Medicare or Medicaid? *(If yes, you are not eligible for HIPAA coverage.)* ☐ Yes ☑ No

4. Was your most recent coverage terminated because of nonpayment or fraud? ☐ Yes ☑ No

5. Were you eligible under COBRA or Cal-COBRA? ☐ Yes ☑ No

Yes, start date: _____   End Date: _____

If Yes, did you accept and exhaust all benefits that were available? ☐ Yes ☑ No
If No, please explain: Self-employed, COBRA not available
_____

PART VI. Individual Term Life Insurance – Underwritten by Health Net Life Insurance Company – Applicant Only.

Applicant Only
This insurance is not intended to replace any Life Insurance Policy currently in force. **Life Insurance requires an additional premium. (Must be at least 19 years old to enroll). The percentage indicated must equal 100%.**

Beneficiary (Full Name)	Relationship		
Thomas Michael Lazio	son	100%	%
Beneficiary (Full Name)	Relationship		
			%
Beneficiary (Full Name)	Relationship		
			%
SIGNATURE of APPLICANT Julia R. Lazio		DATE 11/2/2011	

SAP 6013215 (3/07)

You may choose to sign up for additional insurance coverage. Health insurance companies may offer life, dental, or vision coverage for an additional fee.

Health Insurance Application

If you do not read, write, or speak English well, you can have a translator fill out the form on your behalf. You will need to tell this person the information to include on the form.

EXQUISITE HEALTH

Primary's Social Security Number

X X X | X X | X X X X

PART VII. Individual & Family Plans Exception to Standard Enrollment – Statement of Accountability.

This is to be used when the Applicant cannot complete the application because of the reason(s) indicated below. The applicant must complete the appropriate section that applies to their enrollment. This form must be submitted with the Individual & Family Enrollment Application when applicable.

I, _____, personally read and completed the Individual & Family Enrollment Application for the Applicant named above because:

☐ Applicant does not read English   ☐ Applicant does not speak English   ☐ Applicant does not write English

Other (explain) _____

Under the penalty of perjury I attest that, I translated/read to the applicant the contents of the Individual & Family Enrollment Application, including Part IX "Conditions of Enrollment" and Part X "Important Provisions" of the Individual & Family Enrollment Application. I accurately listed all the requested personal and medical history disclosed by:

_____ (Name of applicant)

Signatures and date (required in ink).

SIGNATURE of APPLICANT	Today's Date
SIGNATURE of TRANSLATOR	Today's Date
TRANSLATOR'S/READER'S NAME (PRINT)	TRANSLATOR'S/READER'S PHONE NUMBER
TRANSLATOR'S/READER'S ADDRESS	
TRANSLATOR'S/READER'S CITY	STATE	ZIP

PART VIII. Writing agent information – Without complete agent name and address, correspondence will not be sent.

Health Net Broker ID: J431

Kathy Hope
Name (Print)
5922 Midiron Circle
Address
Huntington Beach, CA 92649

Sub – Agent ID: _____
(Must be completed only if Sub-Agent Agreement is approved)
800-555-9114
Phone number
800-555-0057
Fax Number
kathy@exquisitehealth.com
Email address

Writing Agent's Signature/Number (Required)

Date Signed (Required)

Writing Agent Certification

Are you aware of any information not disclosed in this application that might have a bearing on the risk?   ☐ Yes ☐ No

If "Yes," please explain: _____

Just because you apply for health insurance with a company does not mean that it will necessarily accept you. Sometimes, companies will accept one applicant but not others. Wait until you receive an acceptance letter before attempting to use your new policy.

PART IX. Conditions of enrollment

GENERAL CONDITIONS: Exquisite Health reserves the right to reject any application for enrollment. Exquisite Health may selectively accept the Applicant or only a dependent(s). There is no coverage unless this Application is accepted by Exquisite Health's Underwriting Department and a Notice of Acceptance is issued to the Applicant even though you paid money to Exquisite Health for the first month's premium. Cashing your check does not mean your application is approved. If rejected, your money will be returned to you. No other department, officer, agent or employee of Exquisite Health is authorized to grant enrollment. An insurance agent cannot grant approval, change terms or waive requirements. Exquisite Health may require that you take a medical examination and you will be responsible for payment of any related fees in such event. This application and all medical information or examination reports shall become a part of the Plan Contract or Insurance Policy.

Family Members who are covered under another Exquisite Health Individual plan are not eligible for coverage hereunder. Should a Family Member enrolling for coverage, become covered under another Exquisite Health Individual plan at a later date, his or her coverage under this plan will terminate on the effective date of coverage under the other Exquisite Health Individual plan.

IFPAPP022007   6   SAP 6013215 (3/07)

Health Insurance Application

Be truthful when filling out your application. If you aren't, the company can cancel your coverage. They can also charge you fees, including additional policy premiums for the period during which you were covered under the plan.

EXQUISITE HEALTH

Primary's Social Security Number
⊠⊠⊠ ⊠⊠ ⊠⊠⊠⊠

PART IX. Conditions of enrollment (continued)

Any intentional or unintentional nondisclosure or misstatement of fact in application materials is cause for disenrollment and rescission of the Plan Contract or Insurance Policy, and Exquisite Health may recoup from the Subscriber (or from You or from the Applicant) any amounts paid for Covered Services obtained as a result of such nondisclosure or misstatement of fact. In addition, if a Subscriber makes a false statement or omission as to the Subscriber's or Family Member's health status or history on application materials, Exquisite Health shall have no liability for the provision of coverage under the Plan Contract or Insurance Policy.

USE AND DISCLOSURE OF PROTECTED HEALTH INFORMATION: I acknowledge and understand that health care providers may disclose health information about me or my dependents to Exquisite Health. Exquisite Health uses and may disclose this information for purposes of treatment, payment and health plan operations, including but not limited to utilization management, quality improvement, disease or case management programs. Exquisite Health's Notice of Privacy Practices is included in the Plan Contract and Insurance Policy, and I may also obtain a copy of this Notice on the Web site at www.healthnet.com or through Exquisite Health Customer Contact Center. Authorization for use and disclosure of protected health information shall be valid for a period of 30 months from the date of my signature below.

IF SOLE APPLICANT IS A MINOR: If the sole Applicant under this application is under 18 years of age, the Applicant's parent or legal guardian must sign as such. By signing, he or she does hereby agree to be legally responsible for the accuracy of information in this Application and for payments of premiums. If such responsible party is not the natural parent of the Applicant, copies of the court papers authorizing guardianship must be submitted with this Application.

IF APPLICANT CANNOT READ ENGLISH: If an Applicant does not read English, the translator and Applicant must sign and submit the **Statement of Accountability** for translating this entire Application (on page 6, PART VII of this Application).

PART X. Important Provisions

NOTICE: For your protection, California law requires the following to appear on this form. Any person who knowingly presents a false or fraudulent claim for the payment of a loss is guilty of a crime and may be subject to fines and confinement in state prison. California law prohibits an HIV test from being required or used by health care services plans or insurance companies as a condition of obtaining coverage.

ACKNOWLEDGEMENT AND AGREEMENT: I, the applicant, understand and agree that by enrolling with or accepting services from Health Net, I and any enrolled dependents are obligated to understand and abide by the terms, conditions and provisions of the Plan Contract or Insurance Policy. I, the applicant, have read and understand the terms of this Application and my signature below indicates that the information entered in this Application is complete, true and correct, and I accept these terms.

BINDING ARBITRATION: I, the applicant, understand and agree that any and all disputes or disagreements between me (including any of my enrolled family members or heirs or personal representatives) and Exquisite Health regarding the construction, interpretation, performance or breach of the Exquisite Health Plan Contract or Insurance Policy, or regarding other matters relating to or arising out of my Exquisite Health membership, whether stated in tort, contract or otherwise, and whether or not other parties such as health care providers, or their agents or employees, are also involved, must be submitted to final and binding arbitration in lieu of a jury or court trial. I understand that, by agreeing to submit all disputes to final and binding arbitration, all parties, including Exquisite Health, are giving up their constitutional right to the extent permitted by law to have their dispute decided in a court of law before a jury. I also understand that disputes that I may have with Exquisite Health involving claims or medical malpractice (that is, whether any medical services rendered were unnecessary or unauthorized or were improperly, negligently or incompetently rendered) are also subject to final and binding arbitration. A more detailed arbitration provision is included in the Plan Contract or Insurance Policy. My signature below indicates that I understand the terms of this Binding Arbitration Clause and agree to submit disputes to binding arbitration.

APPLICANT OR PARENT OR LEGAL GUARDIAN'S SIGNATURE IF APPLICANT IS UNDER 18 YEARS OLD	Date Signed
SPOUSE/DOMESTIC PARTNER'S SIGNATURE	Date Signed
SIGNATURE OF APPLICANT'S DEPENDENT	Date Signed
SIGNATURE OF APPLICANT'S DEPENDENT	Date Signed

It's a good idea to photocopy your health insurance application for your records. If later disputes arise, you can refer to your original application.

Applicant's Signatures (the applicant must personally sign his/her name and agree to the Arbitration Clause in order for the application to be processed), *required in ink.*

Exquisite Health reserves the right to cancel, rescind, or terminate any policy where this Application and Agreement was signed by anyone other than the applicant. Neither Broker nor any other person may sign this Application and Agreement.

Make personal check payable to "Exquisite Health." Return Completed Application to:
Exquisite Health Individual and Family Enrollment, Post Office Box 1000 Calabasis, California 90011

You may submit a photocopy or facsimile of the Application and Authorizations. Exquisite Health recommends that you retain a copy of this Application and Authorizations for your records.

All references to "Exquisite Health" herein include the affiliates and subsidiaries of Exquisite Health which underwrite or administer the coverage to which this Enrollment Application applies. "Plan Contract" refers to the Exquisite Health of California, Inc. Combined Contract and Evidence of Coverage; "Insurance Policy" refers to Exquisite Health Life Insurance Company Explanation of Your Insurance Plan, Exquisite Health PPO Policy.

IFPAPP022007

7

SAP 6013215 (3/07)

Health Insurance Application

Many insurance companies allow you to set up automatic payment arrangements. This ensures that you won't forget to submit a premium payment. For this policy, you can set up automatic bank drafts or regular charges to your credit card. Many people have health insurance covered by their employer. If so, the charges are normally deducted from their paychecks.

Page 8 of 8

EXQUISITE HEALTH

Primary's Social Security Number

X X X X X X X X X

Exquisite Health's Pay Option – Monthly Automatic Payment for Individual & Family Plans

SIMPLE PAYMENT OPTION (Automatic Bank Draft) ☐ First month's payment   ☑ Monthly premium payment

Monthly premium charge can be withdrawn directly from your personal checking account. The premium will be withdrawn from your bank account about ten days in advance of the due date.

Account Holder's Social Security Number	Transit Routing Number	Account Number
XXX-XX-XXXX	55620048	456789001

Bank Name	State
Bank of Sacramento	California

As a convenience, I request and authorize Exquisite Health to pay and charge to the above account checks drawn on that account by and payable to the order of "**Exquisite Health**" provided there are sufficient collected funds in said account to pay the same upon presentation. I understand that the Premium withdrawn from my account will be for the future bill period plus any past due balances and my first month's withdraw maybe for multiple periods if I did not submit a binder check or due to the timing of the set-up. I agree that Exquisite Health's rights in respect to each such check shall be the same as if it were a check written to Exquisite Health and signed personally by me. This authority is to remain in effect until revoked by me in writing and until Exquisite Health actually receives such notice, I agree that Exquisite Health shall be fully protected in honoring any such check. *(Note: A 30-day notice is required to discontinue this service due to the time required to initiate this change with your bank.)*

Automatic Bank Draft (ABD) transmissions are submitted to the bank on approximately the 20th of every month, for the following month's premium. It can take upwards of 6 weeks to process an ABD request. Therefore, your premium should be submitted with your request for ABD, and/or manual payment should continued to be remitted to Exquisite Health, until such time that you receive confirmation of ABD commencement in writing from Exquisite Health.

I further agree that if any such check be dishonored, whether with or without cause and whether intentionally or inadvertently, I will be charged a $25 service charge for each occurrence. I understand Exquisite Health shall be under no liability whatsoever even though such dishonor may result in the forfeiture of health coverage.

SIGNATURE of ACCOUNT HOLDER (Required to Process).	Date
Julia R. Lazio	11/2/2011

CREDIT CARD   ☐ First month's payment   ☐ Monthly premium payment

Monthly premium charge can be charged directly to your credit card account. The premium will be charged to your credit card account approximately ten days in advance of the due date.

First Name (as on card)	Middle (as on card)	Last Name (as on card)	Card Type ☐ Visa ☐ MasterCard
Account Number 16-digits (complete)	Expiration Date (MM/YYYY)	*Signature Panel Code	Cardholder's email address
Billing Address	City	State	ZIP[1]

Signature Panel Code can be found on the back of your credit card. This 3-4 digit code is usually the last three digits located in the signature panel. This information is required in order for the credit card to be processed.

As a convenience, I request and authorize Exquisite Health or Exquisite Health Life Insurance Company ("Exquisite Health") to charge my credit cardaccount identified above for the payment of my initial premium and/or my monthly premium. I understand that the Premium charged to my account will be for the future bill period plus any past due balances and that my first month's withdraw / charge may be for multiple periods depending upon date of approval and the bill period. This authority is to remain in effect until revoked by me in writing and until Exquisite Health actually receives such notice, I agree that Exquisite Health shall be fully protected in honoring any such charge. *(Note: A 30-day notice is required to discontinue this service due to the time required to initiate this change with your credit card company.)* I further agree that if my credit card is declined for payment, whether with or without cause and whether intentionally or inadvertently, I will be charged a $25 service charge for each occurrence. Credit card transmissions are submitted to the bank on approximately the 20th of every month for the following month's premium.

[1]The zip code must match the cardholder's address, otherwise the credit card cannot be processed.

SIGNATURE of CREDIT CARD ACCOUNT HOLDER (Required to Process).	Date

SAP 6013215 (3/07)

If you decide to change your payment plan, be sure to give the insurance company plenty of notice. This policy requires 30-day notice to make changes to the payment arrangements.

Medicaid Application

If you're pregnant or have children, you may be eligible to apply for your state's Medicaid program. This will provide coverage if you cannot afford health insurance or do not have access to a plan through your job. Call your state's Medicaid office or visit its Web site to learn about eligibility requirements.

> You do not need to be a U.S. citizen to qualify for Medicaid. However, be sure to provide your immigration documents to prove your eligibility to the Medicaid provider.

Application
FOR MISSISSIPPI HEALTH BENEFITS

Mississippi Division of **MEDICAID**

> Having a hard time understanding the application form? Call your closest Medicaid office or visit its site online to determine whether it offers special translating or other services to help you complete the form.

For Office Use Only

Regional Office: _____
Worker: _____
☐ Application   ☐ Review
Case Name: _____
Case Number: _____
Date Received: _____
Interviewed By: _____
Interview Date: _____

1. HEAD OF HOUSEHOLD (This is the primary contact for the case)

You must be interviewed before we can make a decision about you or your child(ren)'s eligibility.

Rebecca	R	Stout
First Name	Middle Initial	Last Name

What is the language most spoken in your home? _English_ If not English and you need assistance, contact your Regional Office or call 1-800-421-2408. An interpreter service will be provided free of charge.
If you are hearing or visually impaired and need special assistance, contact your Medicaid Regional Office or call 1-800-421-2408.

Marital Status: ☐ Single ☐ Married ☐ Separated (Date_____) ☑ Divorced (Date _9/2010_) ☐ Widowed
Home Address: _5455 S. School St._ Apt or Lot # _3_
City: _Jackson_ County: _Hinds_ State: _MS_ Zip: _39203_
Mailing address (if different from Home address) _____
City_____ County _____ State _____ Zip _____
Home Phone or Cell # _(601) 555-8531_ Message # if no phone _____ Whose # is this? _____
Work Phone # _(601) 555-2210_ May we contact you at work? ☐ Yes ☑ No

2. HOUSEHOLD MEMBERS (List everyone applying, starting with yourself even if you are not applying)

Are you applying for this person? Yes No	Full Name NOTE:Legal parents & spouses living in the home must be listed, even if not applying	Social Security Number *	How is this person related to you?	Date of Birth (MM/DD/YY) (for all applying, attach proof of birth) **	Sex (M/F)	Race *** (Indicate all that apply)	US Citizen? **** (for all applying) Yes No	Pregnant? (For all applying) Yes No
☑ ☐	Rebecca Renee Stout	XXX-XX-XXXX	self	12/06/1983	F	White	☑ ☐	☐ ☑
☑ ☐	Madison Emma Stout	XXX-XX-XXXX	child	06/15/2007	F	White	☑ ☐	☐ ☑
☑ ☐	Alexander Patrick Stout	XXX-XX-XXXX	child	01/03/2010	M	White	☑ ☐	☐ ☑
☐ ☐							☐ ☐	☐ ☐
☐ ☐							☐ ☐	☐ ☐
☐ ☐							☐ ☐	☐ ☐
☐ ☐							☐ ☐	☐ ☐
☐ ☐							☐ ☐	☐ ☐

*You must give us the Social Security Number (SSN) for any person who wants to be eligible for Health Benefits. See the back of this form for more information on the use of Social Security Numbers.
**Proof of Birth is required for any person applying for Health Benefits.
*** Tell us all that apply: American Indian, Alaska Native, Asian, Black or African American, Native Hawaiian or other Pacific Islander, White, Hispanic or Latino, Other. If 'Other', be specific.
****If you mark "No" to US Citizen, alien status for all applying must be verified to determine qualified alien status. This does not apply to aliens seeking emergency Medicaid services.

Revised 09/01/2008

Medicaid Application

Are you paying for the care of a child or sick parent who lives with you? Be sure to list the costs of that care on your application to help determine your income verification.

You may be divorced or not living with the other parent of your child or children. If so, you do not need to count that person's income as part of your eligibility.

3. EARNED INCOME INFORMATION

List all earnings from employment and self-employment that you, your spouse and children in your household receive. You must provide proof of your household's most recent income. Your worker will explain to you what is acceptable verification for your family. Only the income of legal parent(s) living in the home is used to determine children's eligibility.

Name of Person Working	Gross Amount Paid (include tips, recurring overtime)	Name of Employer, Address & Phone Number	How often paid?	Employment Start Date?	Is Insurance Available?*
Rebecca Stout	$320.00	ABC Office, 150 Main St. Jackson MS 39203 601-555-2210	weekly	10/01/2007	no

*If you could get insurance for your children through this employer if you had the money to pay the premiums, answer "Yes"

4. CHILD/ADULT CARE EXPENSES

Do you pay someone to care for a child or incapacitated adult living in your home while you work? ☑ Yes ☐ No. If yes, complete:

Name of Person Paying Child/Adult Care Expenses	Name of Child/Adult	Age	Amount Paid	How often paid	Name & Telephone # of Daycare Provider
Rebecca Stout	Madison	4	$50.00	weekly	Ollia Carter
Rebecca Stout	Alexander	1	$50.00	weekly	601-555-4265

5. UNEARNED INCOME INFORMATION

List all unearned income received by you, your spouse and children in your household. Examples include Social Security benefits, SSI, TANF, Veteran's benefits, unemployment benefits, worker's compensation, child support, alimony, cash contributions, interest, royalties, dividends, rental income and educational income.

Name of Person Receiving Payments	Type of Payment	Gross Amount of Payment	How Often Received
Rebecca Stout	child support	$500.00	monthly

If you are eligible for certain benefits, such as unemployment compensation, you must apply if you want to be eligible.

6. INSURANCE INFORMATION

Does any person you are applying for already have health insurance coverage, other than Medicaid or CHIP?
☐ Yes ☑ No
If yes, attach a copy of the front and back of the insurance card(s) and provide the following information:

Name of person Insured	Policy Holder's Name	Insurance Company or Employer Plan	Group or Policy #	Effective Date of Coverage	If coverage expected to end, give end date

If you have some other form of insurance coverage, list it on your application. If that coverage ends at some point in the future due to a job change or other event, be sure to list that date on your application as well.

Medicaid Application

Did you pay out-of-pocket for health care while uninsured? If so, Medicare may reimburse you for the cost of those visits.

Has any person you are applying for had health insurance coverage, other than Medicaid or CHIP, that ended within the last 6 months?
☐ Yes ☑ No. If yes, provide the person's name and coverage information.

_____
_____

7. RETROACTIVE COVERAGE FOR MEDICAID ONLY (RETROACTIVE COVERAGE IS NOT AVAILABLE FOR THE CHIP PROGRAM)

Did anyone included in your application receive medical services within the last 3 months? ☑ Yes ☐ No. If yes, list the people and the months the medical expenses were incurred if you want Medicaid eligibility considered for these months.

Name: Madison _____ Alexander _____ _____
Months: June _____ July _____ _____

_____ _____ _____

8. CHILD SUPPORT COOPERATION

If you are an adult (not pregnant) applying for Medicaid, you are required to cooperate with child support services in order for you to get Medicaid for yourself (your children's eligibility will not be affected if you choose not to cooperate). You must cooperate unless the Department of Human Services tells us you have good reason not to cooperate.

Do you agree to cooperate? ☑ Yes ☐ No. If yes, provide the following information about the absent parent(s) of the children included in your application.

Name of Absent Parent	Child(ren) of this Parent	Absent Parent's Date of Birth	Absent Parent's Address	Absent Parent's Employer
Christopher Stout	Madison, Alexander	03/02/1982	6841 W. 15th St., #2 Jackson, MS 39204	A1 Plumbers

NOTE: Assistance in establishing paternity and obtaining support is available for Medicaid-eligible children through the Department of Human Services. If you are not required to cooperate as a condition of eligibility, you can request to be referred for child support services. You must tell us if you want this service.

9. PREGNANCY VERIFICATION

If you are applying because you are pregnant, you must provide a written statement from your doctor or health care provider stating you are pregnant and your expected due date. Use this space or provide a separate statement.

Patient's Name _____ Pregnant? ☐ Yes ☐ No

Expected Date of Delivery _____ # of Births Expected _____

First Maternity Visit _____

_____ _____
Signature of Medical Practitioner (MD/RN)   Date

If you are applying for Medicaid because you are expecting a child, you will need to have your doctor verify that you are pregnant. This is to help ensure your eligibility for Medicaid insurance.

Medicaid Application

Each applicant on your Medicaid application must have his or her own Social Security number. If you have a child who doesn't have a Social Security number, you may wish to apply for one on their behalf before applying for Medicaid. Your Medicaid office may be able to help you complete the Social Security application.

10. USE OF SOCIAL SECURITY NUMBERS

Pursuant to the authority found in federal law at 42 U.S.C. 1320b-7(a) and federal regulations at 42 CFR 435.910, you are required to disclose the Social Security Number (SSN) for each person applying for Health Benefits. This is a mandatory requirement in order to be eligible for Medicaid benefits, unless an applicant is a non-qualified alien seeking emergency Medicaid services. If you cannot recall the SSN for each applicant or if the applicant does not have a SSN, the agency can assist you in applying for an SSN for each applicant. If the applicant has a well established religious objection for not providing his or her SSN, he or she should state the basis for such objection and the agency will review this request. The SSN will be used to verify information such as income and insurance coverage and to help maintain files regarding eligibility pursuant to the authority described in federal regulations 42 CFR 435.940 through 42 CFR 435.960. The SSN may also be used to match with records within the State Medicaid agency and in other state, federal, and/or local agencies, such as the Social Security Administration, Internal Revenue Services, and Employment Security.

11. RIGHTS AND RESPONSIBILITIES (Please read carefully)

- Children under 21 who are eligible for health benefits under Medicaid are eligible for a free health care prevention program called Cool Kids. It provides a way for children to get medical exams, check-ups, follow up treatment and special care to make sure they maintain good health. You will be asked to select an approved screening provider at your interview.
- Adults eligible for Medicaid should get a yearly health screening (physical exam) from your doctor or clinic. This exam will not count against your annual doctor visit limit under Medicaid.
- Information about Family Planning Services and WIC food services are available from your local Health Department.
- Information you share is confidential. Your medical information can only be released if needed to administer the Medicaid or CHIP programs. If you receive care or treatment under Medicaid or CHIP, you authorize the health care provider to release to Medicaid and the CHIP insurer your medical records and information relating to your diagnosis, examination and treatment.
- Information that you give may be reviewed and verified by state and federal staff. You must fully cooperate with state and federal workers if your case is reviewed. No additional permission is needed to get verification or other information.
- Your application will be considered without regard to race, color, sex, age, handicap, religion, national origin, political belief, or Limited English Proficiency.
- An annual review is required for all recipients of Medicaid and CHIP. Failure to complete the review process may result in the termination of benefits for the individual(s) due for review.
- Face to face interviews are required for new applications and annual reviews.
- You may ask for a hearing if you are not satisfied with any action taken by the State of Mississippi in connection with your application for health benefits.
- Medicaid does not pay medical expenses that a third party, such as private health insurance, should pay. By accepting Medicaid, you agree to give your rights to any third party payment to the Division of Medicaid. These payments include payments from hospital and health insurance policies.

12. SIGNATURE

Please sign this statement:

I certify that the information I have provided above is true to the best of my knowledge, and I give permission for the State of Mississippi to make any necessary contact to check my statements. I have read the list of my rights and responsibilities that is printed above. If I knowingly give false statements or leave out information asked for on this application, such as income or household members, I commit a crime that is punishable under federal and/or state law.

Rebecca Stout	*9-4-2011*
Signature of Applicant	Date

If you want to register to vote or update your voter registration information, you may do so at your interview.

After you are approved for Medicare, you will have to meet with someone at the Medicaid office once a year. This meeting will determine your continued eligibility. Be sure not to miss this interview! If you do, you may have your coverage cancelled even if you remain eligible.

Life Insurance Policy

Life insurance provides a payment to beneficiaries, or people chosen by the insured party to receive benefits in the event of the insured person's death. This money may help pay for funeral costs or any outstanding bills the deceased person may have.

OAK INSURANCE COMPANY

LIFE INSURANCE POLICY

POLICY NUMBER 1262435-9

Type of policy: Risk 5 years – non-smoking
Receivers of Scholarships

The Policyholder	:	James Humphreys
The insured	:	James Humphreys
I.D. number	:	1541549 Gender: male
Date of birth	:	1/10/1983 Age: 28
Occupation	:	restaurant manager

Inception date : 1/10/2011   Term of insurance : 35 years
Expiration date : 1/10/2046   The premium shall be paid until : 1/10/2046

> The cost of your life insurance differs depending on your sex and your age at the time of application. Younger people and women typically receive lower rates than older people and men.

> **BASIC SUM INSURED**
> $75,000   seventy-five thousand dollars

The Base Sum Insured shall be paid upon the occurrence of the following event:
Upon the death of the Insured – immediately subsequent to his/her death.

<u>The Beneficiary:</u>
Upon the death of the Insured – as specified in the Insurance Proposal.

For the purposes of the "Linkage Terms" clause in the General Conditions section of the Policy, the base index was set at 9.967.00 points (hereinafter: "the Base Index"), adjusted to the basic index of 100 points of January 1959 and divided by 1000.

> Life insurance policies normally pay immediately after the death of the covered person. This way the beneficiaries—the people who receive the insurance payout—have money right away to pay funeral costs.

Life Insurance Policy

You may be able to add coverage to your life insurance policy. This policy has special additions to cover the insured in the event he becomes disabled and can no longer work.

The use of tobacco is an important factor in the cost of a life insurance policy. If you smoke, do not lie on your life insurance application simply to get better rates. Insurance companies may require you to take a blood test to verify that you are a non-smoker.

Page 2 of 4

OAK INSURANCE COMPANY

LIFE INSURANCE POLICY

POLICY NUMBER 1262435-9

Type of policy: Risk 5 years – non-smoking

INSURANCE SCHEDULE – continued

COVERS AND EXTENSIONS

It is hereby agreed and declared that this policy includes the additional covers and extensions specified in the following appendices, which constitute an integral part thereof.

No. Insured	Appendix Code	Description of the Addl. Insurance/Extension	Inception date of Insurance	Term of Insurance	Sum Insured	Monthly Premium
		The Premium for Basic Insurance	10/11	35	100,165	11.39
1	107	Life insurance – 5 years – non-smoking	10/11	35		
1	121	Accidental disability	10/11	35	1,000,000	6.93
1	162	Working incapacity insurance, without NII offsetting, extended professional, six months (6-month waiting period)	10/11	35	4,000	41.68

The inclusive monthly premium $60.00

The inclusive monthly premium shall be paid on the first of each month.

The monthly premium for a first Insured for 5-year risk insurance – non-smoking – shall be increased, as follows:

As of the following date:	Premium:
1/10/2011	13.47
1/10/2016	18.07
1/10/2021	26.66
1/10/2026	41.85
1/10/2031	68.33
1/10/2036	111.82

In some life insurance policies, the monthly premium stays the same for the length of the insurance. Some policies, like this one, have a premium that increases over time. Payments may be lower in the beginning and increase as your assumed ability to pay rises.

This rider replaces all previous riders.

Should the policyholder change the method by which he/she pays the premium, the premium shall change according to the Company's customary procedures at the time.

Life Insurance Policy

A number of amendments (changes) may be made to the standard insurance policy. Be sure that you read and understand all of these amendments before you accept the coverage. This ensures that you know what will and will not be covered.

The legal terms an insurance company uses may be difficult to understand. If you do not know what different clauses mean, ask your insurance agent to explain them to you. This clause, for example, explains the conditions under which the insured person is considered partially unable to work.

OAK INSURANCE COMPANY

LIFE INSURANCE POLICY

POLICY NUMBER 1262435-9

Type of policy: Risk 5 years – non-smoking

INSURANCE SCHEDULE – continue

Notwithstanding that stated in the Insurance Schedule, the waiting period, in the instance of work incapacity, shall be three months.

It is hereby agreed and declared that the following amendments shall apply to appendix 161 or 162 or 163:

1. Clause 10 (a) shall be replaced by the following:
    The Insured shall be deemed as having partial work incapacity if he/she fulfills the eligibility requirements for a monthly compensation and/or release from payment of the premiums specified in clause 4 at the rate of 25% or more, and provided that the Insured has been recognized as temporarily or permanently disabled by the National Insurance Institute and/or by an occupational physician.

2. Clause 10 (e) is cancelled.

3. Clause 6 (a) is cancelled.

4. Clause 4 (a) (b) is cancelled and replaced by:
    If, due to an illness or accident (hereinafter: "the Insured Event"), the Insured is deprived – at the rate of at least 75% – of the ability to continue to engage in research and/or in the occupation detailed in the Insurance Proposal, it is hereby agreed and declared that, for each percent of work incapacity exceeding 25% and up to 75%, a monthly compensation shall be paid at the rate of the disability percentages from the stipend.

5. Contrary to that stated in clause 6 (b), the total of all monthly compensation payments that shall become due to the Insured from the Company or from any other insurance company or from a pension fund, shall be at the rate of 100% of the stipend.

6. In the instance of work incapacity due to a terrorist attack, the amount of the compensation shall be paid after offsetting all payments from government sources.

It is hereby agreed and declared that the following amendments shall apply to appendix 161 or 162:

1. Clause 6 (a) is cancelled.

2. Clause 4 (a) (b) is cancelled and replaced by:
    If, due to an illness or accident (hereinafter: "the Insured Event"), the Insured is deprived – at the rate of at least 75% – of the ability to continue in the profession he had been engaged in, as specified in the Insurance Proposal, until the Insured Event occurred, and due to

Life Insurance Policy

which, he was prevented from engaging in any profession or occupation at which he had been engaged during the five years preceding the date of that same illness or accident.

It is hereby agreed and declared that the following amendments shall apply to appendix 161 or 162. Or 163:

1. Clause 10 (a) shall be replaced by:
The Insured shall be deemed as having partial work incapacity if he fulfills the eligibility requirements for a monthly compensation and/or release from payment of the premiums specified in clause 4 at the rate of 25% or more, and provided that the Insured has been recognized as temporarily or permanently disabled by the National Insurance Institute.

2. Clause 10 (e) is cancelled.

Look familiar? This amendment repeats much of the same information from the first Clause 1 on the previous page. Both describe when the insured person is considered partially unable to work. Notice that this clause makes that person eligible if he or she is so acknowledged by the National Insurance Institute. The previous clause also establishes eligibility through the diagnosis of a doctor. Expect insurance policies to use a great deal of similar—but not exactly the same—information.

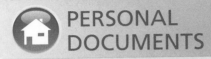

PERSONAL DOCUMENTS

Lifestyle and Living

CONTENTS

Keisha Fullerton couldn't wait to begin her new job as a medical technician at City Hospital. Keisha lived with her mom while attending school. Now that she had a full-time job, Keisha couldn't wait to get her own apartment.

As soon as Keisha found an apartment she liked, she filled out a lease application. The next morning the landlord called to tell her that she had been approved. She stopped at the post office to get a money order for her security deposit and first month's rent on her way to sign the lease at the property management office. Then, after signing the lease, Keisha went back to the post office to fill out a change of address form so that her mail would be forwarded to her new apartment.

If you apply for a driver's license, change your address, or perform a number of other common life tasks, you will need to fill out certain forms. Many of these forms contain complicated legal language that may be difficult to understand. In such cases, ask the person to whom you are giving the forms to explain any unfamiliar concepts or terms. Studying the examples in this lesson will help you interpret or complete the documents in the chapter review and in real life.

Managing Your Life Online

Many of the documents in this lesson, such as the change of address form, may be filled out on the Internet. Check the appropriate agency's Web site to learn whether it offers an online option. This will save you time and paper.

Postal Money Order

All post offices sell money orders. You can use postal money orders, just like personal checks, to pay bills. Usually you must pay for money orders with cash or with a debit card.

If you use a postal money order to pay a bill, you should note your account number on this line.

Postal money orders are only valid in the United States and its possessions, such as Puerto Rico. You can use money orders to send money to a different country. If you do, you must buy a special international money order.

Mailing Receipt Confirmation

Sometimes it is important to know whether a package or document that you have mailed has been received. For a small fee, the post office offers delivery confirmation. However, if you want someone to sign for your package, you will need to add the signature confirmation service.

Fill out the name of the person or company and the complete address to which you are sending your mail. This will help you remember the recipient of your delivery.

You can use your delivery confirmation number to look up the status of your mail on the United States Postal Service Web site.

Mailing Insurance

If you are mailing something valuable or breakable, you may wish to purchase special postal insurance coverage. Although very few packages are damaged in transit, this can provide you with extra peace of mind.

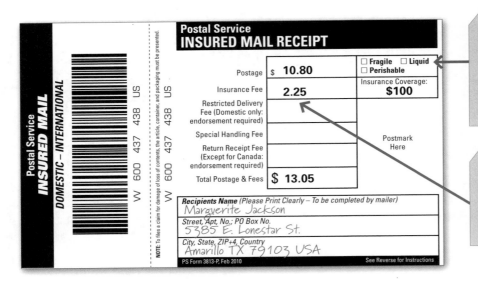

Sending a bottle of perfume to your mother as a gift? Mailing your best friend her favorite hometown potato chips? Be sure to check these special boxes if you are mailing more delicate items.

Costs for mailing insurance vary depending on the amount of coverage you purchase. Greater levels of coverage come with higher fees.

Address Label

Sometimes you may wish to send papers or packages through a private shipping company such as UPS or FedEx. These shippers have their own special labels that you will need to fill out for each package you send.

You can use a tracking number to locate your package in real time. Visit the shipper's Web site and follow the directions on-screen to track your package to its final destination.

Be sure to completely fill out the shipping information section. Private shippers offer different services to help you get your package to its destination on time. Remember that overnight shipping may be much more expensive than ground shipping.

Change of Address Form

If you move, you'll want to file a change of address form with the post office. This will allow your mail to be automatically forwarded to your new address. You may fill out a paper form for free or pay a small fee to file online or over the phone.

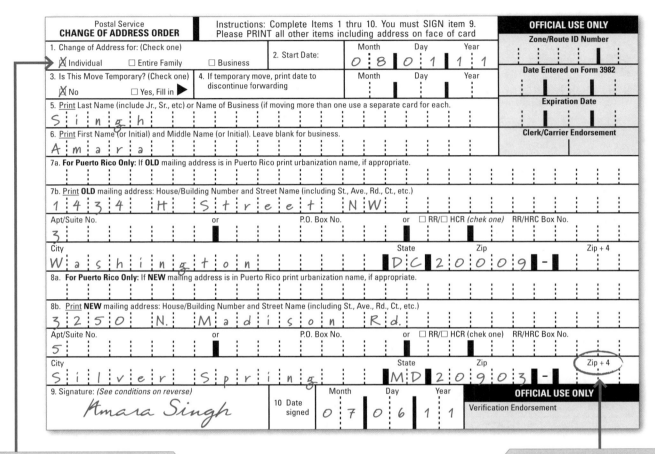

If you live alone or are moving out of a place where others will remain, you should choose the "individual" option. If you are moving with your family, select "entire family." Everyone who lives in your household with the same last name will be covered under the change of address form.

If you don't know the Zip + 4 for your old or new address, you can look it up online. But don't worry—the postal service can forward your mail without this information.

Driver's Permit Application

Regardless of your age, if you are learning to drive, you must first apply for a driver's permit rather than a license. This permit allows you to drive under certain conditions that vary from state to state. Check with your state's department of motor vehicles for the exact conditions of your permit.

> What kind of vehicle are you learning to drive? If it's a motorcycle, you must apply for a different class of license. Some states simply add a motorcycle endorsement to an existing driver's license.

> This application is for a non-commercial, or personal, driving permit. If you are learning to drive a bus, truck, or other commercial vehicle for your job, you would apply for a different type of permit or license.

DL-180 (7-10)

pennsylvania
DEPARTMENT OF TRANSPORTATION
BUREAU OF DRIVER LICENSING

NON-COMMERCIAL LEARNER'S PERMIT APPLICATION
PLEASE TYPE OR PRINT ALL INFORMATION IN BLUE OR BLACK INK

YOU MUST APPLY IN PERSON

DRIVER'S LICENSE NUMBER/I.D. NUMBER: _____

JR., ETC.

MIDDLE NAME
Louise

SOCIAL SECURITY NUMBER	SEX	TELEPHONE (8 a.m. to 4:30 p.m.)
XXX-XX-XXXX	F	412-555-3982

[X] BROWN ☐ GREEN ☐ HAZEL ☐ PINK ☐ BLACK ☐ GRAY ☐ DICHROMATIC ☐ OTHER

STREET ADDRESS - A Post Office Box number may be used in addition to the actual residence address but cannot be used as the only address.
625 W. Clark St.

CITY	STATE	ZIP CODE
Pittsburgh	PA	15205

CHECK DESIRED PERMIT(S)	PERMIT(S) DESIRED	FEE	ENTER FEE FOR EACH ITEM CHECKED
	☐ CLASS A (Combination Vehicle over 26,000), ☐ CLASS B (Truck or Bus over 26,000), [X] CLASS C (Automobile)	$5.00	$5.00
	☐ CLASS M (Motorcycle) MSEA Fee is included	$15.00	

MUST CHECK ONE	LICENSE REQUIRED	FEE	ENTER FEE FOR LICENSE CHECKED
	[X] 4-Year Photo	$28.00	$28.00
	☐ 2-Year Photo (Age 65 & Over)	$17.50	
[X] Organ Donation Awareness Trust Fund (I wish to contribute $1.00)		$1.00	$1.00

PAID BY: ☐ Check ☐ Money Order Payable to PennDOT (Cash **CANNOT** be accepted) | **TOTAL** | $ 34.00

ALL QUESTIONS MUST BE ANSWERED | (Check [✔] Applicable Block) YES NO

1. Have you ever held or possessed a PA Driver's License/Learner's Permit/Photo Identification Card?........... ☐ [X]

2. Is your right to apply for a license or your privilege to operate a vehicle in this or any other state currently suspended, revoked, or subject to installation of an ignition interlock device?........... ☐ [X]
   If yes, give state _____ date _____, and reason _____

3. Have you been arrested or cited in this state or any other state for any violation, which carries a possible penalty of suspension or revocation of your driver's license or driving privilege?........... ☐ [X]
   If yes, give state _____ date _____, and reason _____

4. Do you hold a valid license or ID card from any other state?........... ☐ [X]

AUTHORIZATION AND CERTIFICATION

I certify under penalty of law that this information contained herein is true and correct. I hereby authorize the Social Security Administration to release to the Department of Transportation information concerning my Social Security Identification Number for the purpose of identification. I hereby acknowledge this day that I have received notice of the provisions of Section 3709 of the Vehicle Code. (See back for provisions)
WARNING: Misstatement of fact is a misdemeanor of the third degree punishable by a fine of up to $2,500 and/or imprisonment up to 1 year (18 Pa. C.S. Section 4904[b]).

☐ I am under the age of 18 years and I hereby request Organ Donor designation on my PA Driver's License. Parent must check consent block on the ParenGuardian Consent Form (DL-180TD). (Applicants 18 years of age or older will have the opportunity to request Organ Donor designation at the Photo Center at the time they have their photo taken.)
I hereby certify that I am a resident of the Commonwealth of Pennsylvania.

SIGN HERE
May Ling
(APPLICANT'S SIGNATURE IN INK)

10/02/2011
(DATE)

FOR OFFICIAL USE ONLY

VISION SCREENING	CHECK (✓) YES NO
20/40 vision or less in better eye with correction ...	☐ ☐
Report of Eye Examination (attached)..................	☐ ☐
☐ Qualified with Restrictions	
☐ Corrective Lenses	
☐ Other: _____	
☐ Qualified Without Restrictions	

COMPLETE ALL ITEMS		
Uncorrected		Corrected
20/	Right Eye	20/
20/	Left Eye	20/
20/	Both Eyes	20/
R L	Fields	R L

Classes which should be endorsed on the Driver's PA License.
☐ A ☐ B ☐ C ☐ M

EXAMINER'S DRIVER CERTIFICATION
This is to certify that the above applicant has applied for and passed the examination for the above class(es) for a Pennsylvania Driver's License.

_____
(SIGNATURE OF EXAMINER)   (DLE NO.)

DATE OF ISSUE:
MONTH	DAY	YEAR

EXAM CENTER:

Driver's Permit Application

This state requires a medical exam to verify that you are healthy enough to drive safely. Not all states have this requirement. Check with your state office to find out your state's requirements.

You need to prove your identity and age in order to receive a permit. If you are a U.S. citizen, you may show documents such as a certified copy of your birth certificate or a passport. If you are not a citizen, you must bring several documents.

Page 2 of 2

DL-180 (7-10)

ALL INFORMATION IN THIS SECTION MUST BE COMPLETED IN FULL BY A HEALTH CARE PROVIDER

Please check any of the following that **would** prevent control of a motor vehicle.

- ❏ Neurological disorders
- ❏ Neuropsychiatric disorders
- ❏ Circulatory disorder
- ❏ Cardiac disorder
- ❏ Hypertension
- ❏ Uncontrolled Epilepsy
- ❏ Uncontrolled Diabetes
- ❏ Cognitive Impairment
- ❏ Alcohol abuse
- ❏ Drug abuse
- ❏ Conditions causing repeated lapses of consciousness (e.g. epilepsy, narcolepsy, hysteria, etc.)

Specify: _____   If seizure disorder, date of last seizure: _____

- ❏ Impairment or Amputation of an appendage. If so, list: _____
- ❏ Other: _____

NOTE: Any recommendations/additional comments must accompany this certificate on a health care provider's letterhead.

Documents such as gas or electric bills, leases, or tax records can prove your residency status. This state also allows a roommate to provide an official document. You can then provide something more informal, such as a bank statement or a magazine label.

	STATE LICENSE #
	STATE	ZIP CODE
FAX	

I hereby state that the facts above set forth are true and correct to the best of my knowledge, information and belief. I understand that the statements made herein are made subject to the penalties of 18 Pa. C.S. § 4904 (relating to unsworn falsification to authorities) punishable by a fine up to $2,500 and/or imprisonment up to 1 year.

Examinee's Signature (SIGN ONLY IN PRESENCE OF PROVIDER)   Provider's Signature   Physical Date

TO MEET IDENTIFICATION REQUIREMENTS YOU MUST PRESENT THE FOLLOWING:

U.S. Citizens -

Social Security Card (card cannot be laminated) AND **ONE** of the following:
- Birth Certificate with raised seal (**U.S. issued by an authorized government agency, including U.S. territories or Puerto Rico. Non-U.S. Birth Certificates will not be accepted**)
- Certificate of U.S. Citizenship (**BCIS/INS Form N-560**)
- Certificate of Naturalization (**BCIS/INS Form N-550 or N-570**)
- Valid U.S. Passport

NOTE: *Only valid U.S. Passports and original documents will be accepted.*

✦ If you have an Out-of-State Driver's License, you should present it along with your Social Security Card and one of the above forms.

Non-U.S. Citizens – You must bring **ALL** of the following:
- Social Security Card
- Valid Passport
- All original **USCIS/immigration** documents
- Written verification of attendance from school (**Student Status Only**)
- Written verification from employer (**Employment Status Only**)

To obtain detailed information regarding "identity/residency requirements," you can:
- Visit the Identity/Security Info Center at www.dmv.state.pa.us
- Call us at 1-800-932-4600 or 1-800-228-0676 (TDD) Monday through Friday from 8 a.m. to 5 p.m., or
- Visit one of our Driver License Centers.

All documents must show the same name and date of birth or an association between the information on the documents. Additional documentation may be required if a connection between documents cannot be established (e.g. Marriage Certificate, Court Order of name change, Divorce Decree, etc.)

TO MEET RESIDENCY REQUIREMENTS YOU MUST PRESENT TWO OF THE FOLLOWING (for customers 18 years of age or older):

- Current Utility Bills *(water, gas, electric, cable, etc.)*
  * Cellular/mobile or pager bills are not acceptable
- W-2 Form
- Tax Records
- Current Weapons Permit (U.S. citizen only)
- Lease Agreements
- Mortgage Documents

Note: If you reside with someone and have no bills in your name, you will still need to provide two proofs of residency. One proof is to bring the person with whom you reside along with their Driver's License or Photo ID to the Driver License Center. You will also need to provide a second proof of residency such as official mail (bank statement, tax notice, magazine etc.) that has your name and address on it. The address must match that of the person with whom you reside.

ORGAN DONATION AWARENESS TRUST FUND (ODTF): You have the opportunity to contribute $1.00 to the Fund. The additional $1.00 contribution must be **added** to the fee above and included in your payment by check/money order.

Permit Fee: Additional permit fee of $5.00 for each permit requested.

MSEA Fee: These additional fees are required under the Pennsylvania Vehicle Code Section 7904 and will be used to support a Motorcycle Safety Education Program in the Commonwealth of Pennsylvania.

PROVISIONS OF SECTION 3709 OF THE VEHICLE CODE

Section 3709 provides for a fine of up to $300 for dropping, throwing or depositing, upon any highway, or upon any other public or private property without the consent of the owner thereof or into or on the waters of this Commonwealth, from a vehicle, any waste paper, sweepings, ashes, household waste, glass, metal, refuse or rubbish or any dangerous or detrimental substance, or permitting any of the preceding without immediately removing such items or causing their removal.

Driver's License Application

Whether applying for your first-ever driver's license or one in a new state, you will need to complete an application. Usually, you don't need to reapply each time you renew your license in the same state.

Under federal law, you can register to vote or update your voter registration information when you apply for or renew your driver's license.

Completion of this section is requested but not required to apply for a driver's license or ID Card. (Virginia Code §2.2-3806)

INFORMATION FOR THE STATE BOARD OF ELECTIONS

Are you a citizen of the United States of America?

YES (INITIAL BOX) `LAS`   **NO** (INITIAL BOX)

Do you want to apply to register to vote or change your voter registration address?

YES (INITIAL BOX) `LAS`   **NO** (INITIAL BOX)

INFORMATION FOR THE VIRGINIA TRANSPLANT COUNCIL

☐ Yes, I would like to remain or become an organ, eye and tissue donor.

dmv Now.com
www.dmvNow.com
Virginia Department of Motor Vehicles
Post Office Box 27412
Richmond, Virginia 23269-0001

DRIVER'S LICENSE AND IDENTIFICATION CARD APPLICATION

LOG #

Purpose: Use this form to apply for a Virginia Driver's License or Identification Card.

Instructions: Applicants complete the front and back of this application.

Note: Va. Code §§46.2-323 and 46.2-342 require that you provide DMV with the information on this form (including your social security number). It is not necessary to provide a social security number for an identification card. This social security number is for record-keeping purposes and may be disseminated only in accordance with Va. Code §§46.2-208 and 46.2-209. Persons convicted of certain sexual offenses (as listed in Va. Code §9.1-902) must register or re-register with the Virginia Department of State Police as provided in Va. Code §§9.1-901, 9.1-903, and 9.1-904. If you provide a non-Virginia residence/home address or non-Virginia mailing address, your application for a driver's license or identification (ID) card may be denied.

APPLICATION TYPE (Check one)

1. ☒ Driver's License   2. ☐ Learner's Permit and Driver's License   3. ☐ CDL Learner's Permit or License   4. ☐ Motorcycle Learner's Permit
5. ☐ Driver's License with Motorcycle (Class M)   6. ☐ CDL with Motorcycle (Class M)   7. ☐ Driver's License with School Bus Endorsement (to carry less than 16 passengers)
8. ☐ Identification Card   9. ☐ Hearing Impaired ID Card   10. ☐ Emancipated Minor ID Card   11. ☐ Driver's License Testing for Foreign Diplomats

If you are applying for a replacement license or identification card check one of the following:
☐ I am surrendering my current license or identification card.
☒ I hereby certify any current license or ID card is unavailable for surrender because it is   ☐ Lost   ☒ Stolen   ☐ Destroyed or Mutilated

Do you currently have or have you ever held a driver's license or learner's permit from Virginia, another state, U.S. territory or foreign country?   ☐ Yes   ☐ No
If yes, provide the following:

LICENSE NUMBER	ISSUE DATE (mm/dd/yyyy)	EXPIRATION DATE (mm/dd/yyyy)	STATE/COUNTRY
A12345678	04/12/2009	04/12/2013	Virginia, USA

APPLICANT INFORMATION

NOTE: YOUR ADDRESS BELOW MUST BE CURRENT. THE U.S. POSTAL SERVICE WILL NOT FORWARD.

FULL LEGAL NAME (last, first, middle, suffix)	SOCIAL SECURITY NUMBER	BIRTHDATE (mm/dd/yyyy)
Smith, Lathan Anthony	XXX-XX-XXXX	04/12/1972

DAYTIME TELEPHONE NUMBER	GENDER (check one)	HEIGHT	WEIGHT	EYE COLOR	HAIR COLOR
(815) 555-4879	☒ MALE ☐ FEMALE	6 FT. 1 IN.	205 LBS.	brown	black

STREET ADDRESS	APT NO.	CITY	STATE	ZIP CODE
341 W. Jefferson St.		Richmond	VA	23218

IF YOUR NAME HAS CHANGED, PRINT YOUR FORMER NAME HERE

NAME OF CITY OR COUNTY OF RESIDENCE   ☒ CITY ☐ COUNTY OF ____   Richmond

MAILING ADDRESS (if different from above)   APT NO.   CITY

DRIVER'S LICENSE APPLICANTS

	YES	NO
1. Do you wear glasses or contact lenses?	☒	☐
2. Do you have a physical or mental condition which requires that you take medication?	☐	☒
3. Have you ever had a seizure, blackout, or loss of consciousness?	☐	☒
4. Do you have a physical condition which requires you to use special equipment in order to drive?	☐	☒
5. Have you been convicted within the past ten years in this state or elsewhere of any offense resulting from your operation of, or involving, a motor vehicle? (Do not include parking tickets.)	☒	☐
6. Has your license or privilege to drive ever been suspended, revoked, or disqualified in this state or elsewhere, or is it currently suspended, revoked or disqualified?	☐	☒

Applying for a driver's license because you have moved to a new state? You will have to turn in your old license to your new state's licensing authority. You may also need to take a brief written or driving test.

FOR DMV USE ONLY — DO NOT WRITE BELOW THIS LINE

FAILED   REMARKS/PAID STAMP

ENTER CUSTOMER NUMBER

TRANSACTION TYPE   ☐ ORIGINAL   ☐ REISSUE   FEE
☐ RENEWAL   ☐ DUPLICATE

PROOF OF ID (secondary)   PROOF OF SOCIAL SECURITY NUMBER (specify)

PROOF OF LEGAL PRESENCE (specify)

DOCUMENT VERIFIER SIGNATURE AND NUMBER

You can use this application to apply for either a driver's license or a state identification card. You can use a state ID card just like a driver's license to officially prove your identity and age. However, it does not grant you driving privileges. You may wish to apply for a state ID if you do not drive.

Driver's License Application

You may drive a truck, bus, taxi, or other commercial vehicle for your job. If so, you'll need to apply for a commercial driver's license. Depending on your state, you may need to take an additional written or driving test to receive this type of license.

Page 2 of 2

PARENT OR GUARDIAN CONSENT FOR APPLICANTS UNDER 18 (Unless applicant is married - marriage certificate required)

I authorize issuance of a learner's permit/driver's license/identification card. I certify that the applicant is a resident of Virginia. I certify that the applicant is attending school regularly and is in good academic standing, but if not, I authorize issuance of a learner's permit/driver's license. I certify that this applicant will operate a motor vehicle for at least 45 hours (15 of which will occur after sunset) while holding a learner's permit.

If my child attends public school, I authorize the principal or designee of the public school attended by the applicant to notify the juvenile and domestic relations district court (within whose jurisdiction the applicant resides) when the applicant has had 10 or more unexcused absences from school on consecutive school days.

I certify that the statements made and the information submitted by me regarding this certification are true and correct.

PARENT/GUARDIAN NAME (print)	PARENT/GUARDIAN SIGNATURE	DATE (mm/dd/yyyy)

APPLICANT UNDER AGE 18 Have you ever been found not innocent of any offense in a Juvenile and Domestic Relations Court in this or any other state? ☐ YES ☐ NO
If you answered YES, a court within your jurisdiction must provide court consent below.

COURT CONSENT In my opinion the applicant's request for a learner's permit/driver's license ☐ should be granted. ☐ should not be granted.
Remarks:

JUDGE NAME (print)	JUDGE SIGNATURE	DATE (mm/dd/yyyy)

COMMERCIAL DRIVER'S LICENSE APPLICANTS

Complete this CERTIFICATION OF QUALIFICATION by checking the box for the category that applies. (For requirements refer to the Code of Federal Regulations or VA Motor Carrier Safety Regulations).

INTERSTATE DRIVER
☐ I meet the qualification requirements of Part 391 of the Federal Motor Carrier Safety Regulations.
☐ I am exempt from the qualification requirements of Part 391 of the Federal Motor Carrier Safety Regulations.

INTRASTATE DRIVER
☐ I meet the qualification requirements of the Virginia Motor Carrier Safety Regulations.
☐ I am exempt from the qualification requirements of the Virginia Motor Carrier Safety Regulations.

VEHICLE TYPE
I want to be licensed to operate the type of vehicle(s) checked below:

☐ A - Combination vehicle with GVWR or GCWR of 26,001 lbs. or more
☐ B - Single vehicle with GVWR of 26,001 lbs. or more, or towing a vehicle less than 10,000 lbs. GVWR.
☐ C - Any vehicle that does not fit the definition of a Class A or Class B vehicle and is either used to transport hazardous materials or designed to carry 16 or more passengers, including the driver.

AIR BRAKES ☐ With ☐ Without

ENDORSEMENT
I want to apply for the following vehicle endorsement(s):
☐ H - Hazardous Materials
☐ N - Tank
☐ P - Passenger Carrying Vehicle (16 or more passengers)
☐ S - School Bus (16 or more passengers)
☐ T - Double/Triple Trailer

Identify any state(s) in which you have been previously licensed within the past 10 years. Provide additional information using the Supplemental Driver's Licensing History Sheet, form DL1PA.

STATE(S)

LICENSE NUMBER

LICENSE ISSUE DATE (mm/dd/yyyy)

LICENSE EXPIRATION DATE (mm/dd/yyyy)

GOVERNMENT EMPLOYEES - (Fee waiver certification)

I certify that I am employed by the:
☐ Commonwealth of Virginia or ☐ City of ☐ County of ☐ Town of _____

to operate a motorcycle or commercial motor vehicle and, because of such employment, I am entitled to the waiver of the motorcycle class and/or commercial motor vehicle endorsement fee, provided I have paid for and hold a valid Virginia driver's license or have made application for such.

SELECTIVE SERVICE

All males under the age of 26 are required to check one of the following. Failure to provide a response will result in denial of your application.
☐ I am already registered with Selective Service.
☐ I am a non-immigrant alien in the U.S. and not required to register.
☐ I authorize DMV to forward to the Selective Service System personal information necessary to register me with Selective Service.

By signing this application, I consent to be registered with Selective Service, if required by federal law. If under age 18, an appropriate adult must complete and sign below: I authorize DMV to send information to Selective Service which will be used to register applicant when he is 18 years old.

SIGNATURE (check one and sign) ☐ PARENT/GUARDIAN ☐ JUDGE, JUVENILE DOMESTIC RELATIONS COURT ☐ EMANCIPATED MINOR

CERTIFICATION AND SIGNATURES

I certify and affirm that I am a resident of Virginia, that all information presented in this application is true and correct, that any documents I have presented to DMV are genuine, and that my appearance, for purpose of my DMV photograph, is a true and accurate representation of how I generally appear in public. I make this certification and affirmation under penalty of perjury and understand that knowingly making a false statement on this application is a criminal violation

APPLICANT NAME (print)	APPLICANT SIGNATURE	DATE (mm/dd/yyyy)
Lathan A. Smith	Lathan A. Smith	09/06/2011

Just as you can register to vote when you apply for a driver's license, you can also sign up for the Selective Service if required. You must sign up for the Selective Service if you are a male between the ages of 18 and 25. You only need to sign up once.

Social Security Application

Social Security numbers officially track your tax information with the federal government. You will find that many companies now use them for other financial and identification purposes.

> You may have changed your name due to marriage, divorce, or some other reason. If so, don't forget to apply for a new Social Security card with your new personal information. You will keep the same Social Security number but receive a new card showing your new name.

SOCIAL SECURITY ADMINISTRATION
Application for a Social Security Card

Form Approved
OMB No. 0960-0066

1

NAME TO BE SHOWN ON CARD	First Ana	Full Middle Name Maria	Last Martinez
FULL NAME AT BIRTH IF OTHER THAN ABOVE	First	Full Middle Name	Last
OTHER NAMES USED ON YOUR SOCIAL SECURITY CARD			

2 Social Security number previously assigned to the person listed in item 1 ➡ ☐☐☐ - ☐☐ - ☐☐☐☐

3 PLACE OF BIRTH (Do Not Abbreviate) — Albuquerque, New Mexico
City / State or Foreign Country

Office Use Only — FCI

4 DATE OF BIRTH — 02/02/2011 MM/DD/YYYY

5 CITIZENSHIP (Check One)
- ☒ U.S. Citizen
- ☐ Legal Alien Allowed To Work
- ☐ Legal Alien **Not** Allowed To Work (See Instructions On Page 3)
- ☐ Other (See Instructions On Page 3)

6 ETHNICITY
Are You Hispanic or Latino? (Your Response is Voluntary)
☒ Yes ☐ No

7 RACE Select One or More (Your Response is Voluntary)
- ☐ Native Hawaiian
- ☐ Alaska Native
- ☐ Asian
- ☐ American Indian
- ☐ Black/African American
- ☐ Other Pacific Islander
- ☒ White

8 SEX ➡ ☐ Male ☒ Female

9

A. MOTHER'S NAME AT HER BIRTH	First Martha	Full Middle Name Maria	Last Name At Her Birth Diaz

B. MOTHER'S SOCIAL SECURITY NUMBER (See instructions for 9 B on Page 3) ➡ ☒☒☒ - ☒☒ - ☒☒☒☒ ☐ Unknown

10

A. FATHER'S NAME ➡	First Armando	Full Middle Name Pedro	Last Martinez

B. FATHER'S SOCIAL SECURITY NUMBER (See instructions for 10B on Page 3) ➡ ☒☒☒ - ☒☒ - ☒☒☒☒ ☐ Unknown

11 Has the person listed in item 1 or anyone acting on his/her behalf ever filed for or received a Social Security number card before?
☐ Yes (If "yes" answer questions 12-13) ☒ No ☐ Don't Know (If "don't know," skip to question 14.)

12 Name shown on the most recent Social Security card issued for the person listed in item 1 ➡
First | Full Middle Name | Last Name

13 Enter any different date of birth if used on an earlier application for a card ➡ ___ MM/DD/YYYY

14 TODAY'S DATE — 05/15/2012 MM/DD/YYYY

15 DAYTIME PHONE NUMBER — 505 Area Code — 555-8912 Number

16 MAILING ADDRESS (Do Not Abbreviate) ➡ Street Address, Apt. No., PO Box, Rural Route No. 24318 Canyon Way, #1 — City Albuquerque, — State/Foreign Country NM — ZIP Code 87107

I declare under penalty of perjury that I have examined all the information on this form, and on any accompanying statements or forms, and it is true and correct to the best to my knowledge.

17 YOUR SIGNATURE ➤ *Martha Diaz*

18 YOUR RELATIONSHIP TO THE PERSON IN ITEM 1 IS:
☐ Self ☒ Natural Or Adoptive Parent ☐ Legal Guardian ☐ Other Specify ___

DO NOT WRITE BELOW THIS LINE (FOR SSA USE ONLY)

NPN			DOC	NTI
PBC	EVI	EVA	EVC	PRA
EVIDENCE SUBMITTED				

> Parents or guardians can apply for Social Security numbers on behalf of their dependents. Many people apply for Social Security numbers for their children shortly after they are born.

Name Change Form

Usually, you do not need to apply for a name change with the court if you get married. Instead, your marriage license serves as your legal name change. However, name changes due to divorce or adoption are typically processed through the courts.

_____Supreme_____ Court of the State of New York

County of_____Erie_____

In the Matter of the Application of a

_____Yolanda Mechelle Berry_____,

Petitioner,

FOR LEAVE TO CHANGE __Her__ NAME TO:
(His/Her)

Yolanda Mechelle Lawson

_____Yolanda Mechelle Lawson_____.
(Proposed New Name)

> Name changes are usually handled by county courts. Check with your own county's or municipality's court system to find out how to handle a name change in your area.

**PETITION FOR
NAME CHANGE**

Index # _____

> Be sure to print or type your proposed new name very clearly on your form. A spelling mistake or misread handwriting can result in your new name being different from the one you actually want! In many cases, a lawyer may fill this form out for you.

TO THE _____Supreme_____ COURT OF THE STATE OF NEW YORK:

The Petition of Yolanda Berry respectfully shows this court:

1. The petitioner resides at No. _____2434 Niagara Way_____, in

The __city__ of _____Buffalo_____, County of _____Erie_____, and has so resided for a

period of __0__ years and __2__ months prior to the making of this application.

2. The petitioner _____Yolanda Berry_____ was born at _____Buffalo_____

on the __24th__ day of __1978__ and is now __33__ years of age. (Attached hereto

and made a part hereof is a copy of the petitioner's birth certificate.)

3. The petitioner proposed to change said His/Her name to _____Yolanda Mechelle Lawson_____.

4. The petitioner is a natural born citizen of the United States.

5. The petitioner _____ is/ __X__ is not married and has/has not been married previously.

Name Change Form

The court will wish to ensure that you are not changing your name in order to avoid paying a debt, child support or other payments, or serving a criminal sentence. If any of these situations apply to you, be sure to explain your circumstances to the court.

6. The petitioner : (Check One)

___X___ has never been convicted of a crime

_____ has been convicted of a crime, the details of which are attached in a separate statement, annexed hereto and made a part hereof.

7. The petitioner has never been adjudicated a bankrupt.

8. There are no judgments or liens of record and no actions pending against your in petitioner in any court of this state or of the United States, or of any governmental subdivision thereof, or elsewhere whether the court be of record or not. There are no bankruptcy or insolvency proceedings, voluntary or involuntary, pending against your petitioner in any court whatsoever or before any officer, person, body or board having jurisdiction thereof and your petitioner has not, at any time, made any assignments for the benefit of creditor. (If there have been, enter details instead of previous statement).

9. There are no claims, demands, liabilities or obligations of any kind whatsoever on a written instrument or otherwise against your infants under the only names by which they have been known, which are the names sought herein to be abandoned, and your infants have no creditors who may be adversely affected or prejudiced in any way by the proposed change of name. (If there have been, enter details instead of previous statement).

10. The petitioner _____ is/___X___ is not responsible for child support obligations. (If there are child support obligations, details are attached in a separate statement).

11. The petitioner _____ is/___X___ is not responsible for spousal support obligations. (If there are spousal support obligations, details are attached in a separate statement).

12. The grounds of this application to change the petitioner's name are as follows:

Wish to use maiden name again after being divorced _____

_____

_____ .

13. No previous application has been made for the relief sought herein.

WHEREFORE, petitioner respectfully prays for an order permitting the

petitioner ____Yolanda Berry____ to assume the name ____Yolanda Mechelle Lawson____

in place of that of ____Yolanda Mechelle Berry____ .
(Current Name)

DATED: __09/12__ , 20 __11__

_____
Yolanda Berry
(Signature of petitioner)

Although most people change their names for reasons relating to family changes, you may choose to take a new name simply because you like it better.

Name Change Form

STATE OF NEW YORK

INDIVIDUAL VERIFICATION

COUNTY OF _____Erie_____

    THIS IS TO CERTIFY that **I,** _____, being duly sworn deposes and says: your deponent is the Petitioner in the within action; your deponent has read the foregoing Petition and knows the contents thereof. The same is true to deponent's own knowledge, except as to the matters therein stated to be alleged on information and belief, and as to those matters deponent believes it to be true.

Sworn to before me this

    day of _____ , 20__11__

> The legal language in this statement means that you have read the application and completed it fully and truthfully.

_____
(Signature of petitioner)

_____
Notary Public

> You may need to have certain legal documents, such as this one, signed and stamped by a notary public. Notary publics are specially licensed and authorized to formally identify people. Your bank or insurance agency office probably has a notary public on staff. If you use a notary public, make sure you wait to sign the document in their presence.

Apartment Lease Application

To lease an apartment, you will have to fill out an application. This gives your potential landlord the information that he or she needs to make a decision about whether to rent to you.

RENTAL APPLICATION

Every occupant over the age of 18 MUST fill out a separate application (even if married)
Please fill out this form COMPLETELY and sign where indicated

PERSONAL INFORMATION

FIRST NAME Leslie	MIDDLE Elizabeth	LAST Muller	S.S.# XXX-XX-XXXX

DATE OF BIRTH 05/12/1985	MARITAL STATUS single		DRIVERS LICENSE # 1122334-4	STATE TN

PHONE 615-555-6568	HOME	PHONE	CELL	EMAIL lesliem@pax.com

PRESENT HOME ADDRESS 875 N. Grove St., Apt. 2B		CITY/STATE/ZIP Nashville, TN 37426

LENGTH OF TIME 2 years	PRESENT LANDLORD A1 Apartments

REASON FOR LEAVING want to be closer to work	AMOUNT OF RENT $550

PREVIOUS HOME ADDRESS 682 W. 27th St., Apt. 16		CITY/STATE/ZIP Nashville, TN 37422

LENGTH OF TIME 2 years	PREVIOUS LANDLORD Nashville Properties

REASON FOR LEAVING got place without roommates	AMOUNT OF RENT $350

NEXT PREVIOUS HOME ADDRESS	CITY/STATE/ZIP

LENGTH OF TIME	PREVIOUS LANDLORD	LANDLORD PHONE

REASON FOR LEAVING	AMOUNT OF RENT	WAS YOUR RENT UP TO DATE?

> Potential landlords want to know where you lived before. They may contact your current or previous landlords to ask whether you paid your rent regularly and maintained your apartment.

PROPOSED OCCUPANT(S)

NAME Leslie Muller	OCCUPATION child care worker	AGE 26
NAME	OCCUPATION	AGE
NAME	OCCUPATION	AGE
NAME	OCCUPATION	AGE
NAME	OCCUPATION	AGE

> Have a pet? Many apartments allow you to have a cat or a small dog. You may have to pay an extra security deposit or a small amount of additional rent each month to cover any damage caused by your pet. Be sure to talk about any pets to your landlord before you move in.

PROPOSED PET(S)

NAME Paws		☒ INDOOR ☐ OUTDOOR	AGE 4
NAME		☐ INDOOR ☐ OUTDOOR	AGE
NAME	TYPE/BREED	☐ INDOOR ☐ OUTDOOR	AGE

VEHICLE(S) INFORMATION

YEAR 2001	MAKE Solva	MODEL Strong	COLOR black	PLATE# QR4 501	STATE TN
YEAR	MAKE	MODEL	COLOR	PLATE#	STATE

EMPLOYMENT

CURRENT EMPLOYER Best Daycare	OCCUPATION child care worker	HOURS/WEEK 40
SUPERVISOR Doreen Washington	PHONE 615-555-6437	EXT:	YEARS EMPLOYED
ADDRESS 6345 N. Eastern St.	CITY/STATE/ZIP Nashville TN 37425	
CURRENT EMPLOYER	OCCUPATION	HOURS/WEEK
SUPERVISOR	PHONE	EXT:	YEARS EMPLOYED
	CITY/STATE/ZIP	

> Your potential landlord will want to know whether you earn enough money to pay your rent. If you do not currently have a job, your landlord may ask for a co-signer or proof of income.

SOURCE employment	PROOF OF INCOME pay stub
SOURCE	PROOF OF INCOME
SOURCE	PROOF OF INCOME

Apartment Lease Application

CREDIT CARD/FINANCIAL INFORMATION

CAR LOAN LIEN HOLDER	BALANCE OWED	MONTHLY PAYMENT	CREDITOR'S PHONE #
n/a			
CREDIT CARD COMPANY Bank1	BALANCE OWED $450.00	MONTHLY PAYMENT $20.00	CREDITOR'S PHONE # 800-555-1221
CREDIT CARD COMPANY StoreCard	BALANCE OWED $125.00	MONTHLY PAYMENT $10.00	CREDITOR'S PHONE # 800-555-2112
CREDIT CARD COMPANY n/a	BALANCE OWED	MONTHLY PAYMENT	CREDITOR'S PHONE #
CHILD SUPPORT/OTHER CREDIT OWED n/a	BALANCE OWED	MONTHLY PAYMENT	CREDITOR'S PHONE #
BANK ACCOUNT NAME OF BANK FirstBank	BALANCE $1500	MONTHLY PAYMENT	ACCOUNT NUMBER 123456789

EMERGENCY/PERSONAL REFERENCE INFORMATION

EMERGENCY CONTRACT Karen Dewitt	PHONE 615-555-7990
RELATION mother	ADDRESS 8550 E. Flowering Trail
EMERGENCY CONTRACT Steve Muller	PHONE 615-555-2421
RELATION father	ADDRESS 6213 S. Lincoln St.
PERSONAL REFERENCE Carmella Garcia	PHONE 615-555-2002
RELATION former supervisor	ADDRESS Kids Castle
PERSONAL REFERENCE Adrian Thompson	PHONE 615-555-5879 ext. 12
RELATION former instructor	ADDRESS Nashville Community College

> Your potential landlord will want to talk to references. References are people who know you and can speak to your character and personal habits. You might want to tell the people you chose that you listed them as references. That way, they know to expect a phone call from your potential landlord.

APPLICANT QUESTIONNAIRE/ AUTHORIZATION

HAS APPLICANT EVER BEEN SUED FOR BILLS?	○ YES ⊗ NO	HAS APPLICANT EVER BEEN LOCKED OUT OF HIS OR HER APARTMENT BY THE SHERIFF?	○ YES ⊗ NO
HAS APPLICANT EVER BEEN BANKRUPT?	○ YES ⊗ NO	HAS APPLICANT EVER BEEN BROUGHT TO COURT BY ANOTHER LANDLORD?	○ YES ⊗ NO
HAS APPLICANT EVER BEEN GUILTY OF A FELONY?	○ YES ⊗ NO	HAS APPLICANT EVER MOVED OWING RENT OR DAMAGED AN APARTMENT?	○ YES ⊗ NO
HAS APPLICANT EVER BROKEN A LEASE?	○ YES ⊗ NO	IS THE TOTAL MOVE-IN AMOUNT AVAILABLE NOW (RENT AND DEPOSIT)?	⊗ YES ○ NO

Applicant authorizes the landlord to contact past and present landlords, employers, creditors, credit bureaus, neighbors and any other sources deemed necessary to investigate applicant. All information is true, accurate and complete to the best of applicant's knowledge. Landlord reserves the right to disqualify tenants if information is not as represented.

ANY PERSON OR FIRM IS AUTHORIZED TO RELEASE INFORMATION ABOUT THE UNDERSIGNED UPON PRESENTATION OF THIS FORM OR A PHOTOCOPY OF THIS FORM AT ANY TIME.

X _____Leslie Muller_____   _____7/18/2011_____
APPLICANTS SIGNATURE   DATE

If you have any questions about the interpretation or legality of this form, please consult an attorney or other qualified person.

NOTES:

> Questions such as these help your potential landlord feel confident about your rental history. If you have had problems with an apartment or landlord in the past, it's better to explain the situation to your potential landlord up front.

Apartment Lease

Before you move into a new apartment, be sure to sign a formal lease agreement that explains your rights and responsibilities as a tenant. Most lease agreements are for one year, but some may be for shorter or longer periods of time.

Residential Lease Agreement

This agreement, dated October 01, 2011, is between Best Properties and Sandra Margoles, Benjamin Margoles

1. **Landlord:**
   The Landlord(s) and/or agent(s) is/are and will be referred to in this Lease Agreement as "Landlord".
   Best Properties (Landlord)

2. **Tenant:**
   The Tenant(s) is/are:
   Sandra Margoles
   Benjamin Margoles
   And will be referred to in this Lease as "Tenant".

3. **Rental Property:**
   The Landlord agrees to rent the Tenant the property described as a(n) house located at _____ which will be referred to in this Lease as the "Leased Premises."

4. **Term of Lease Agreement:**
   The Lease Agreement will begin on October 1, 2011 and will end on October 1, 2012.

5. **Use & Occupancy of Property:**
   A. The only person(s) living in the property is/are: Sandra Margoles, Benjamin Margoles.
   B. Any changes in the occupancy will require written consent of the Landlord.
   C. The Tenant will use the property only as a residence.

6. **Amount of Rent:**
   A. The amount of the Rent is $775.00, to be paid monthly.

> Your lease agreement will state the amount of your monthly rent. This amount should match the rental payment agreed upon between you and the landlord.

7. **Date rent is due:**
   A. The rent is due in advance on or before the 5th day of each month. The rent due date is the date the Landlord must receive the Tenant's payment.
   B. Rental payments are made payable to: Best Properties.
   C. Rental payments may be delivered to the Landlord at: Best Properties, 1250 S. 51st St., Salt Lake City, UT 84104.

8. **Late Fee:**
   A. If the rent or any other charges are not received by the Landlord on or before 5 days after the rent due date, Tenant must pay a late fee of $25 in addition to the rent.
   B. Rental payments paid late 3 times within a 12-month period creates a default of the Lease Agreement.
   C. Payments received by Landlord when there are arrearages shall be credited first to any outstanding balance and then applied to the current amount due.

> You usually have to pay a security deposit to move into a rental unit. Although this amount is often the same as your monthly rent, it may be less or more.

> Be sure to pay your rent by the date listed on your lease to avoid being charged a late fee. If you can't pay your rent on time, contact your landlord or leasing agency to explain why. You may be able to have any late fees waived if you have an emergency.

10. **Security Deposit**
    A. The Tenant(s) have paid to the Landlord a Security Deposit of $775.00, to be held in an Escrow Account.
    B. The Security Deposit is intended to pay the cost of damages, cleaning, excessive wear and tear, and unreturned keys once the Lease Agreement has ended and/or for any unpaid charges or attorney fees suffered by the Landlord by reason of Tenant's default of this Lease Agreement.
    C. Tenant may be responsible for any unpaid charges or attorney fees, suffered by the Landlord by reason of Tenant's default of this Lease in accordance to state and local laws and regulations.
    D. Under no circumstance can the Security Deposit be used as a payment for rent and/or for charges due during the term of this Lease Agreement.
    E. The Leased Premises must be left in good, clean condition, with all trash, debris, and Tenant's personal property removed. The Leased Premises shall be left with all appliances and equipment in working order.
    F. Landlord's recover of damages will not be limited to the amount of the Security Deposit.

Apartment Lease

Your lease will explain the repairs for which the landlord is responsible and those that are your responsibility. Normally, the landlord takes care of all major repairs. If you have carelessly broken or damaged something, it will probably be your responsibility to repair it.

Page 2 of 4

11. **Utilities & Services: None included**

12. **Appliances:**
    A. Landlord will supply and maintain: refrigerator, stove, heater
    B. Tenant must have written approval before installing any appliance. Landlord accepts no responsibility for the maintenance, repair or upkeep of any appliance supplied by the Tenant. Tenant agrees he/she is responsible for any damage that occurs to the Leased Premises resulting from the addition of any appliance that is supplied by the Tenant.

13. **Maintenance and Repairs:**
    Landlord shall be responsible for repairs in or about the Leased Premises unless caused by the negligence of the Tenant. Tenant will be responsible for any repairs caused by his/her negligence.
    A. It is the responsibility of the Tenant to promptly notify the Landlord of the need for any such repair of which the Tenant becomes aware.
    B. If any required repair is caused by the negligence of the Tenant and/or Tenant's guests, the Tenant will be fully responsible for the cost of the repair and/or replacement that may be needed.
    C. The Tenant must keep the Leased Premises clean and sanitary at all times and remove all rubbish, garbage, and other waste in a clean, tidy and sanitary manner.
    D. Tenant must abide by all local recycling regulations.
    E. The Tenant shall properly use and operate all electrical cooking and plumbing fixtures and keep them clean and sanitary.
    F. The Tenant is not permitted to paint, make any alterations, improvements or additions to the premises without first obtaining the written permission of the Landlord. The Landlord's permission to a particular painting, alteration, improvement, or addition shall not be deemed as consent to future painting, alterations, improvements, or additions.
    G. The Tenant is responsible for removing snow and ice from stairs and walkways.

14 **Condition of Property:**
    A. The Tenant acknowledges that the Tenant has inspected the Leased Premises and at the commencement of this Lease Agreement, the interior and exterior of the Leased Premises, as well as all equipment and any appliances are found to be in an acceptable condition and in good working order.
    B. The Tenant agrees that neither the Landlord nor his agent has made promises regarding the condition of the Leased Premises.
    C. The Tenant agrees to return the Leased Premises to Landlord at end of the Lease Agreement in the same condition it was at the beginning of the Lease Agreement.

15. **Pets:**
    Pets are not allowed.

16. **Parking**
    Parking is provided. Two assigned spaces.

Some apartments allow small pets, while others may not allow pets of any size. Parking is normally available for free or for a small additional monthly fee for those living in an apartment complex.

17. **Rules and Regulations:**
    A. Late fees are strictly enforced and any unpaid fees will not be waived.
    B. The Tenant may not interfere with the peaceful enjoyment of the neighbors.
    C. The Tenant will be responsible for any fine and/or violation that is imposed on the Landlord due to the Tenant's negligence.
    D. The Tenant shall abide by Federal, State, and Local Laws.
    E. The Tenant agrees not to use the Leased Premises for any unlawful purpose, including but not limited to the sale, use or possession of illegal drugs on or around the Lease Premises.
    F. The Tenant must report any malfunction with smoke detector(s) immediately to the Landlord. The Tenant agrees not to remove, dismantle or take any action to interfere with the operation of any smoke detector(s) installed on the Leased Premises.
    G. Absolutely no hazardous materials are permitted to be in or around the Leased Premises at any time.
    H. Under no circumstance may a store, oven or range be used as a source for heat.
    I. The Tenant shall notify Landlord of any pest control problems.
    J. The Tenant must obtain written permission to install a satellite system or antenna on or around the Leased Premises.
    K. The Tenant may not block the fire escape at any time.

18. **Addendums:**
    The following Addendums, attached to this Lease Agreement, shall become part of this Lease Agreement:
    none

19. **Insurance:**
    Tenant agrees to be solely responsible for any damage to or loss of the Tenant's personal property. Accordingly, the Tenant is strongly encouraged to obtain personal property/renter's insurance with an insurance company properly licensed to do business in the State. The policy must become effective on or before the beginning date of this Lease Agreement.

Apartment Lease

If your landlord wants to enter your apartment in a non-emergency situation, he or she must legally give you notice. Usually, this notice must occur 24 hours beforehand. You do not have to let your landlord into your apartment if he or she has not given you notice, unless there's a major problem that needs to be addressed.

20. **Security not Promised:**
The Tenant has inspected and acknowledges that all door and window locks, fire extinguishers, security alarm systems and/or carbon monoxide detectors are in sound working order. Tenant further understands and acknowledges that although the Landlord makes every effort to make the Leased Premises sage and secure, this in now way creates a promise of security.

21. **Right of Entry:**
   A. Landlord and/or his agents, with 24-hour written notice have the right during the term of this Lease Agreement to enter during reasonable hours to inspect the premises, make repairs or improvements or show prospective buyers and/or Tenant(s) the property.
   B. In the event of an emergency, Landlord reserves the right to enter Leased Premises without notice. It is required that Landlord have a working set of keys and/or security codes to gain access to the Leased Premises.
      I. Tenant will not change, or install additional locks, bolts, or security systems without the written permission of the Landlord.
      II. Unauthorized installation or changing of any locks will be replaced at the Tenant's expense.
      III. Tenant shall be responsible for any and all damages that may occur as a result of forcible entry during an emergency where there is an unauthorized placement of a lock.

22. **Ending or Renewing the Lease Agreement:**
   A. At the end of the Lease term, the Lease Agreement shall automatically continue on a month to month basis. The Landlord or Tenant may end this Lease Agreement by giving to the other 30 days prior written notice before the end of the Lease Agreement.

23. **Notices:**
   A. Any notices required by the terms of this Lease Agreement shall be in writing.
   B. Notices sent to the Landlord may be sent to the following:
      I. 1250 S. 51st St. Salt Lake City, UT, 84104
      II. Fax: 801-555-2345
      III. Email: landlord@domain.com
   D. Notice may be given by either party to the other in any of the following ways:
      I. Regular mail
      II. Personal delivery

Many leases go month-to-month after the initial lease term ends. This means that you can choose to move out with just one month's notice. It also means that your landlord can raise your rent or change your rental terms with one month's notice.

24. **Abandonment:**
If Tenant vacated the Leased Premises before the end of the Lease term without written permission from the Landlord, the Leased Premises is then considered to be abandoned and Tenant is in default of this Lease Agreement. Under these circumstances, Tenant may be responsible for damages and loses allowed by federal, state and local regulations.

25. **Landlord's Remedies:**
If Tenant violates any part of this Lease Agreement, including non-payment of rent, the Tenant is in default of this Lease Agreement. In the event of a default, the Landlord may initiate legal proceedings in accordance with local and state regulations to evict or have Tenant removed from the Leased Premises as well as seek judgment against Tenant for any monies owed to Landlord as a result of Tenant's default.
   A. The Tenant understands and agrees that if the Tenant files a petition of bankruptcy, it will not release Tenant from the fulfillment of the terms and conditions of the Lease Agreement.

26. **Subordination:**
This Lease Agreement is subject and subordinate to any lease, financing loans, other arrangements, or right to possession with regards to the building or land that the Landlord is obligated to now or in the future including existing and future financing, and/or loans or leases on the building and land.

27. **Condemnation:**
If the whole or any part of the Leased Premises is taken by any authority having power of condemnation, this Lease Agreement will end. Tenant shall peaceably vacate the Leased Premises and remove all personal property and the lease terms will no longer apply. The Tenant, however, is responsible for all rent and charges until such time that Tenant vacated the Leased Premises.

28. **Assignment or Sublease:**
Tenant agrees not to transfer, assign, or sub-lease the Leased Premises without the Landlord's written permission.

29. **Joint and Several Liability:**
The Tenant understands and agrees that if there is more than one Tenant that has signed the Lease Agreement, each Tenant is individually and completely responsible for all obligations under the terms of the Lease Agreement.

Usually, you may not sublet, or rent out, your apartment without first discussing it with your landlord. If you need to sublet your apartment, you will probably be responsible for finding the new tenant.

Apartment Lease

When you sign a lease, you agree to pay the rent for the amount of time specified, usually one year. If you move out or stop paying the rent before that period ends, you have broken the lease. If you break the lease, you will likely not get your security deposit back. Be sure to read your lease carefully to see the consequences involved in breaking the lease.

Page 4 of 4

30. Misrepresentation:
If any information provided by Tenant in application for this Lease is found to be knowingly incorrect, untruthful and/or misleading, it is a breach of this Lease.

31. Binding of Heirs and Assigns:
All provisions, terms and conditions of this Lease Agreement shall be binding to Tenant, Landlord, their Heirs, Assignees and Legal Successors.

32. Severability:
If any part of this Lease Agreement is not valid, enforceable, binding or legal, it will not cancel or void the rest of this Lease Agreement. The remainder of the Lease Agreement will continue to be valid and enforceable by the Landlord, to the maximum extent of the laws and regulations set forth by local, state and federal governments.

33. Governing Law:
This Agreement shall be governed, construed and interpreted by, through and under the Laws of the State of Utah.

34. Paragraph Headings:
Paragraph headings in this Lease Agreement are for convenient reference only and do not represent the rights or obligations of the Landlord or Tenant.

35. Entire Agreement:
A. Landlord and Tenant agree that this Lease Agreement and any attached Addendums, Rules and Regulations, and/or Special Terms and Conditions accurately represent all terms and agreements between the Landlord and Tenant regarding the Leased Premises.
B. Tenant acknowledges the receipt of any disclosures required by the State of Utah as well as any disclosures required by federal, state, and local jurisdictions.

Notice: This is an important LEGAL document.
- You may have an attorney review the Lease Agreement prior to signing it.
- You are giving up certain important rights.
- If the Landlord fails to enforce any provision of this Lease Agreement, it will not constitute a waiver of any default, future default or default of the remaining provisions.
- Time is of the essence in this Lease Agreement.

By signing this Lease Agreement, the Tenant certifies that he/she has read, understood and agrees to comply with all the terms, conditions, Rules and Regulations of this Lease Agreement including any addendums and that he/she has received the following:
1. Copies of all Addendums, Rules and Regulations, Special Terms, Conditions, and Applications.
2. All necessary Key(s), Garage Door Openers(s), Security Card(s), and/or Auto Sticker(s) to the Lease Premises.

Tenant's Signature: _Sandra Margoles_   Date: _10/1/11_

Tenant's Signature: _Benjamin Margoles_   Date: _10/1/11_

Landlord/Agent Signature: _____   Date: _____

Be sure that you have completely read and understood your lease before you sign it. By signing a lease, you are agreeing to all of its terms. Typically, you receive the keys to your apartment and other items when you sign your lease.

Don't withhold information on your apartment application! If your landlord finds out that you misrepresented certain information, he or she may choose to cancel your lease altogether.

Voter Registration Form

In order to vote in an election, you usually need to submit your voter registration form at least one month before the date of that election. Check with your state or county board of elections to find out the cut-off date for your area.

In many states, you can register to vote before you turn 18. You can do this as long as you will be 18 before the date of the election.

Voter Registration Application
Before completing this form, review the General, Application, and State-specific instructions.

Are you a citizen of the United States of America? ☒ Yes ☐ No

Will you be 18 years old on or before election day? ☒ Yes ☐ No

If you checked "No" in response to either of these questions, do not complete form.
(Please see state-specific instructions for rules regarding eligibility to register prior to age 18.)

This space for office use only.

1	(Circle one) (Mr.) Mrs. Miss Ms.	Last Name Sobol	First Name Derek	Middle Name(s) James	(Circle one) Jr Sr II III IV

2	Home Address 512 Main Street	Apt. or Lot #	City/Town Newport News	State VA	Zip Code 23605

3	Address Where You Get Your Mail If Different From Above	City/Town	State	Zip Code

4	Date of Birth 10/02/1990 Month Day Year	5	Telephone Number (optional) 757-555-2587	6	ID Number - (see item 6 in the instructions for your state) S512-886-3954

7	Choice of Party (see item 7 in the instructions for your State)	8	Race or Ethnic Group (see item 8 in the instructions for your State)	

9	I have reviewed my state's instructions and I swear/affirm that: ■ I am a United States citizen. ■ I meet the eligibility requirements of my state and subscribe to any oath required. ■ The information I have provided is true to the best of my knowledge under penalty of perjury. If I have provided false information, I may be fined, imprisoned, or (if not a U.S. citizen) deported from or refused entry to the United States.	*Derek F. Sobol* Please sign full name (or put mark) ▲ Date: 9 / 13 / 2011 Month Day Year

If you are registering to vote for the first time: please refer to the application instructions for information on submitting copies of valid identification documents with this form.

Please fill out the sections below if they apply to you.

If this application is for a **change of name**, what was your name before you changed it?

A	Mr. Mrs. Miss Ms.	Last Name	First Name	Middle Name(s)	(Circle one) Jr Sr II III IV

If you were **registered before but this is the first time you are registering from the address in Box 2**, what was your address where you were registered before?

B	Street (or route and box number)	Apt. or Lot #	City/Town/County	State	Zip Code

If you live in a rural area but do not have a street number, or if you have no address, please show on the map where you live.

■ Write in the names of the crossroads (or streets) nearest to where you live.

■ Draw an X to show where you live.

■ Use a dot to show any schools, churches, stores, or other landmarks near where you live, and write the name of the landmark.

C	Example

Route #2

● Grocery Store

Woodchuck Road

Public School ●

X

If you change your name or move to a new address, you will need to fill out a new voter registration form to update your information. You may also make these changes when you apply for a new driver's license.

If the applicant is unable to sign, who helped the applicant fill out this application? Give name, address and phone number (phone number optional).

D	

Mail this application to the address provided for your state.

Sample Ballot

Different states and municipalities record your vote in different ways. You may receive a paper ballot like this one, or you may vote using a touch-screen voting machine.

Some places allow you to vote for all Democratic or all Republican candidates by filling out just one line. You may choose to do this if voting for all of the candidates on one party's ticket.

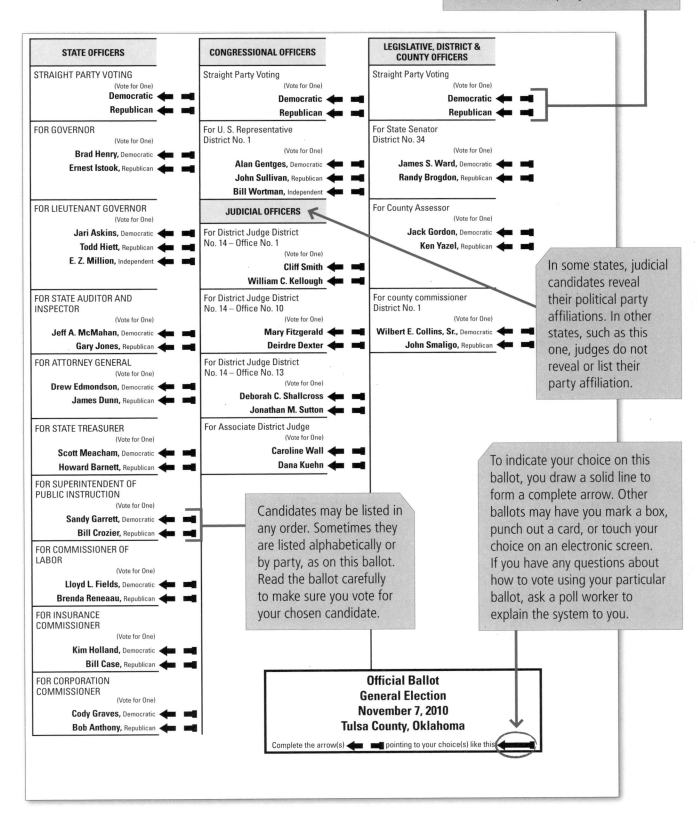

STATE OFFICERS

STRAIGHT PARTY VOTING
(Vote for One)
Democratic
Republican

FOR GOVERNOR
(Vote for One)
Brad Henry, Democratic
Ernest Istook, Republican

FOR LIEUTENANT GOVERNOR
(Vote for One)
Jari Askins, Democratic
Todd Hiett, Republican
E. Z. Million, Independent

FOR STATE AUDITOR AND INSPECTOR
(Vote for One)
Jeff A. McMahan, Democratic
Gary Jones, Republican

FOR ATTORNEY GENERAL
(Vote for One)
Drew Edmondson, Democratic
James Dunn, Republican

FOR STATE TREASURER
(Vote for One)
Scott Meacham, Democratic
Howard Barnett, Republican

FOR SUPERINTENDENT OF PUBLIC INSTRUCTION
(Vote for One)
Sandy Garrett, Democratic
Bill Crozier, Republican

FOR COMMISSIONER OF LABOR
(Vote for One)
Lloyd L. Fields, Democratic
Brenda Reneaau, Republican

FOR INSURANCE COMMISSIONER
(Vote for One)
Kim Holland, Democratic
Bill Case, Republican

FOR CORPORATION COMMISSIONER
(Vote for One)
Cody Graves, Democratic
Bob Anthony, Republican

CONGRESSIONAL OFFICERS

Straight Party Voting
(Vote for One)
Democratic
Republican

For U. S. Representative District No. 1
(Vote for One)
Alan Gentges, Democratic
John Sullivan, Republican
Bill Wortman, Independent

JUDICIAL OFFICERS

For District Judge District No. 14 – Office No. 1
(Vote for One)
Cliff Smith
William C. Kellough

For District Judge District No. 14 – Office No. 10
(Vote for One)
Mary Fitzgerald
Deirdre Dexter

For District Judge District No. 14 – Office No. 13
(Vote for One)
Deborah C. Shallcross
Jonathan M. Sutton

For Associate District Judge
(Vote for One)
Caroline Wall
Dana Kuehn

LEGISLATIVE, DISTRICT & COUNTY OFFICERS

Straight Party Voting
(Vote for One)
Democratic
Republican

For State Senator District No. 34
(Vote for One)
James S. Ward, Democratic
Randy Brogdon, Republican

For County Assessor
(Vote for One)
Jack Gordon, Democratic
Ken Yazel, Republican

For county commissioner District No. 1
(Vote for One)
Wilbert E. Collins, Sr., Democratic
John Smaligo, Republican

In some states, judicial candidates reveal their political party affiliations. In other states, such as this one, judges do not reveal or list their party affiliation.

Candidates may be listed in any order. Sometimes they are listed alphabetically or by party, as on this ballot. Read the ballot carefully to make sure you vote for your chosen candidate.

To indicate your choice on this ballot, you draw a solid line to form a complete arrow. Other ballots may have you mark a box, punch out a card, or touch your choice on an electronic screen. If you have any questions about how to vote using your particular ballot, ask a poll worker to explain the system to you.

Official Ballot
General Election
November 7, 2010
Tulsa County, Oklahoma

Complete the arrow(s)　pointing to your choice(s) like this

Chapter Recap

Using the list below, place a check mark next to the goals you achieved in Chapter 2.

▶ **In Lesson 1, you . . .**

- ☐ Learned about personal banking documents
- ☐ Considered how to set up a personal budget
- ☐ Discovered factors that contribute to your credit report
- ☐ Examined a payday loan application and terms

▶ **In Lesson 2, you . . .**

- ☐ Studied doctor's and hospital bills
- ☐ Reviewed the parts of a lab procedure bill
- ☐ Learned how to fill out a private health insurance application
- ☐ Examined a Medicaid insurance application

▶ **In Lesson 3, you . . .**

- ☐ Learned about common mailing documents
- ☐ Studied driver's permit and license applications
- ☐ Discovered how to apply for an apartment
- ☐ Examined a voter registration form and a ballot

Chapter Review

Name: _____   Date: _____

▶ Directions: Determine whether the following statements are true or false. If the statement is true, write T. If the statement is false, write F. Then rewrite the false statement to make it true.

Deductions	**Statutory**		
	Federal Income Tax	-45.22	2,351.44
	Social Security Tax	-29.83	1,551.67
	Medicare Tax	-6.98	363.89
	PA State Income Tax	-17.37	903.24
	City Income Tax	-8.23	427.96
	PA SUI/SDI Tax	-0.60	31.20

Vac Hrs Left		40.00
Sick Hrs Left		16.00
Title	Operator	

Other			
	401(K)	-28.85*	1,500.20
	Stock Plan	-15.00	50.00
	Loan	-30.00	150.00

*Excluded from federal taxable wages
Your federal taxable wages this period are $386.15

Important Notes
EFFECTIVE THIS PAY PERIOD YOUR REGULAR
HOURLY RATE HAS BEEN CHANGED FROM $8.00
TO $10.00 PER HOUR.
WE WILL BE STARTING OUR ANNUAL FUND
DRIVE SOON AND LOOK FORWARD TO YOUR
PARTICIPATION.

VERIFY AUTHENTICITY COLORED AREA MUST CHANGE IN TONE GRADUALLY AND EVENLY FROM DARK AT TOP TO LIGHT AT BOTTOM

G9 60-124433 464

Town Real Estate
455 Barnes Ave.
Wilkes-Barre, PA 18701

Payroll check number	02470383
Pay date:	10/12/2011
Social Security No.	XXX-XX-XXX

**Pay to the
order of:** KATHI COSTELLO

This amount: TWO HUNDRED THIRTY-TWO AND 95/100 DOLLARS $232.95

1085 NE 3rd St.
Wilkes-Barre, PA 18073

VOID AFTER 180 DAYS

Tomas B. Bunson
AUTHORIZED SIGNATURE

⑆ 02470283 ⑆ ⑇ 04331627 ⑇ 100844 8402 ⑆

1. Kathi's federal taxable wages for this period were $270.35.

   _____

   _____

2. As with Kathi's check, the check attached to your pay stub will be for an amount less than your federal taxable wages.

   _____

   _____

▶ Directions: Write your answers to the questions on the lines below.

Dr. Elaine Borsi
14409 W. Detroit Ave.
Suite 300
Lakewood, OH 44107

PATIENT NAME		ACCOUNT NUMBER
Deandra Lawson		**52199830**

STATEMENT DATE	TOTAL ACCOUNT BALANCE	PERSONAL BALANCE NOW DUE
9-15-11	**$52.27**	**$52.27**

TO INQUIRE ABOUT YOUR ACCOUNT CALL **(800) 555-4777**	INDICATE AMOUNT REMITTED $

IF YOU WISH TO PAY BY CREDIT CARD OR PROVIDE INSURANCE INFORMATION – SEE BACK

10.2.2403 1 AV 0.335 88449511.ps 1 - 1
Ilulululululullulllullulullullullullululul

Deandra Lawson
1409 W. 116th St.
Cleveland OH 44106

↑ INDICATE CHANGES IN ADDRESS DIRECTLY ABOVE ↑

↓ MAKE CHECKS PAYABLE TO AND MAIL TO ADDRESS BELOW ↓

Ilulululululullulllullulullullullullululul

Lakewood Medical Professionals
PO Box 123456
Cleveland OH 44101

↑ MAKE CHECKS PAYABLE TO AND MAIL TO ADDRESS ABOVE ↑

- - - - - - - - - - - - - - - PLEASE DETACH AND RETURN TOP PORTION WITH PAYMENT TO ADDRESS INDICATED ABOVE.

DATE	CPT CODE	DESCRIPTION OF SERVICES	PROFESSIONAL CHARGES	CREDITS
03/20/10 SERVICE RENDERED	99284	EXTENDED EXAM	$241.73	
04/12/10		INSURANCE PAYMENT		$189.46

3. For what portion of the $241.73 bill is Deandra responsible?

_____

CREDIT CARD INFORMATION	
ACCOUNT NUMBER	CARD VERIFICATION #
☐☐☐☐☐☐☐☐☐☐☐☐☐☐☐☐	☐☐☐

Expiration Date ___/___/___ Amount Paid $_____

Signature X _____

* The card verification # is the 3-digit number in the signature area on the back of your card. Please see an example on the back of this statement.

Please return this section with your payment.

PATIENTS NAME	ACCOUNT #	STATEMENT DATED
William Guzman	V12345678	10/17/11
DUE DATE	TOTAL DUE	PLEASE PAY THIS AMOUNT
11/6/07	$108.13	$108.13
		AMOUNT ENCLOSED

Pay online at
www.eugenecityhospital.com/billing

☐ **HAVE YOU MOVED? HAS YOUR INSURANCE CHANGED?**
Then check box and enter changes to your address or insurance on the reverse side of this bill.

To set up a payment plan, please call Patient Account Services 877-555-5555

4. What are two ways that you can pay this hospital bill?

_____

_____

Name: _____   Date: _____

▶ Directions: Review and complete the document below.

Page 1 of 4

5.

EXQUISITE HEALTH

Individual & Family Enrollment Application

PART I. Tell us who you are enrolling and select the product:
Application must be typed or completed in blue or black ink.
THE APPLICATION MUST BE COMPLETED BY THE APPLICANT.

Requested Effective Date
☐☐/☐☐/☐☐☐☐

A. Reason for Application

FAMILY TYPE
☐ Self   ☐ Self & Spouse/Domestic Partner
☐ Self & Child   ☐ Self & Children
☐ Self, Spouse/Domestic Partner and Child(ren)

☐ *Please check for Domestic Partner enrollment*

☐ Process as separate policies

ENROLLMENT TYPE
☐ New Enrollment   ☐ Change Plan*   ☐ Add Dependent*

*Member ID number (listed on your ID card): _____

B. Billing options (please choose for both medical and life)
First Premium Payment (select one)   **Monthly Premium Payments (select one)**

☐ Automated Bank Draft (Please complete the Simple Pay Option section)

☐ Pay by Check (Please include completed check and send with application. Amount must match monthly premium.)

☐ Credit card (Please complete the credit card section on application)

☐ Automated Bank Draft (Please complete the Simple Pay Option section)

☐ Monthly Bill ($5.00 administrative fee applies; **not available with Term Life**)

☐ Credit card (Please complete credit card section; **not available with Term Life**)

C. Choice of Coverage

PPO* – Exquisite Health Life Insurance Company: Available for 1st and 15th of the month effective dates

SimpleValue ☐ 30   ☐ 40   ☐ 50
with ☐ Generic Rx   *or* ☐ Combo Rx

HSA (Compatible Plans) ☐ SimpleChoice   ☐ SmartChoice

SimpleChoice ☐ 15   ☐ 25   ☐ 35   ☐ 40   ☐ 50
☐ FirstChoice PPO   ☐ ValueChoice 1500

*As a convenience to you, if you have applied for Individual PPO coverage and do not meet the underwriting requirements for preferred premiums for the PPO plan for which you applied, Exquisite Health may elect to offer you our Modified Issue PPO option. The Modified offer may be a plan that will have a rate that is 20% or 50% higher than the standard rate for which you applied. You will be automatically enrolled unless otherwise specified. Please check this box should you not wish to be automatically enrolled into the Modified Issue PPO option and the new rate.
☐ **NO, do not enroll me**

HMO – Exquisite Health of California: Only available for the 1st of the month effective dates ☐ HMO 15   ☐ HMO 40

Add – Term Life Insurance Coverage
(Part VI <u>must be completed</u>)
☐ $15,000   ☐ $30,000   ☐ $50,000

Add – Dental and Vision Plus
☐ Dental & Vision Plus
Primary Dentist Number (HMO plans only): _____

PART II. Applicant Information (Note: For the most favorable rate, make the younger spouse/domestic partner the primary applicant.)

Primary Applicant's Last Name	First Name	MI	☐ Male ☐ Female
Home Address			

City	State	ZIP	County applicant resides in

Home Phone Number ( )	Work Phone Number ( )	Email address

Primary Applicant's Birth Date (mo/day/year) ☐☐/☐☐/☐☐☐☐	Primary Applicant's Social Security Number ☐☐☐ ☐☐ ☐☐☐☐

Height	Weight (lbs)	Primary Care Physician ID # (if applicable)	Current Patient ☐ Yes ☐ No	Physician Group ID#

Type of Business: ☐ Self Employed/Consultant ☐ Unemployed (between jobs) ☐ Professional/Management ☐ Student ☐ Other: ☐ Employed (Non-managerial) ☐ Retired _____	Occupation:	Salary Range (optional): ☐ $18,000–30,000 ☐ $60,001–75,000 ☐ $30,001–45,000 ☐ $75,001–90,000 ☐ $45,001–60,000 ☐ $90,001+

Would you be interested in other Exquisite Health or affiliated entities, products and services ☐ Yes ☐ No May we contact you by email? ☐ Yes ☐ No *The release of your information may result in an Exquisite Health representative or Authorized Agent contacting you.*	In the past 6 months, have you been a resident of the United States? ☐ Yes ☐ No If no, where was your last residence? _____

How did you hear about Exquisite Health's Individual and Family coverage?
☐ Radio   ☐ Mail   ☐ Billboard   ☐ Newspaper   ☐ Yellow Pages   ☐ Broker   ☐ Internet

☐ Other:_____

EXQUISITE HEALTH

Primary's Social Security Number

☐☐☐ ☐☐ ☐☐☐☐

PART III. Family member(s) to be enrolled

List all eligible family members to be enrolled other than yourself. If a listed family member's last name is different from yours, please explain on a separate sheet of paper. For Domestic Partner coverage all requirements for eligibility, as required by the applicable laws of the State of California, must be met and a joint Declaration of Domestic Partnership must be filed with the California Secretary of State. **To be processed under one Subscriber, all family members must reside at the same address.** *HMO only*: If you are applying for HMO coverage, you must select a Physician Group and Primary Care Physician. You may choose the same or different Physician Group and Primary Care Physician for each family member you are enrolling. If you do not select a Primary Care Physician, one will be selected for you within your regional area.

Relation	Last Name First Name MI	Social Security No.	Date of Birth	Height	Weight (lbs)	Primary Care Physical ID#	Current Patient	Physician Group ID#
☐ Husband ☐ Wife	Spouse/Domestic Partner	— —					☐ Yes ☐ No	
☐ Son ☐ Daughter	Child 1	— —					☐ Yes ☐ No	
Full Time Student? ☐ Yes ☐ No	Units Carried	Name of School						
☐ Son ☐ Daughter	Child 2	— —					☐ Yes ☐ No	
Full Time Student? ☐ Yes ☐ No	Units Carried	Name of School						
☐ Son ☐ Daughter	Child 3	— —					☐ Yes ☐ No	
Full Time Student? ☐ Yes ☐ No	Units Carried	Name of School						
☐ Son ☐ Daughter	Child 4	— —					☐ Yes ☐ No	
Full Time Student? ☐ Yes ☐ No	Units Carried	Name of School						

For additional dependents please attach another sheet with the requested information.

PART IV. (a) Statement of health (All questions must be answered. Include information for yourself and each family member applying for coverage. Please answer all questions "Yes" or "No." (IF "YES," PLEASE CIRCLE THE SPECIFIC **CONDITIONS**.) Complete Part B on page 4.

Question	Yes	No
1) A. Is either the applicant or spouse/domestic partner or female dependent, whether or not listed on the application, currently pregnant?	☐	☐
B. If you are a male listed on this application, are you expecting a child with anyone, even if the mother is not listed on this application?	☐	☐
C. If you are a male listed on this application, has your spouse, even if not listed on this application, performed a home pregnancy test that has reacted positive during the previous 90 days?	☐	☐
D. During the previous 90 days, has any female applicant performed a home pregnancy test that has reacted positive?	☐	☐
2) Have you or any applying family member had an abnormal physical exam, laboratory results, EKG, X-ray(s), MRI, CT scan or other diagnostic test(s), or been advised to have diagnostic test(s), treatment(s), surgery or hospitalization(s), or are you waiting for the results of any diagnostic test(s)?	☐	☐
3) Have you or any applying family member been seen by a health care practitioner, been a patient in a hospital, clinic, surgicenter, sanatorium or other medical facility as an inpatient or outpatient?	☐	☐

Question	Yes	No
4) Are you or any applying family member eligible for Medicare benefits as a result of disability or chronic illness?	☐	☐
5) Have you or any applying family member ever had any signs, symptoms, diagnosis of, or consulted a health care practitioner, received advice from a health care practitioner, sought treatment from a health care practitioner, had treatment recommended by a health care practitioner, received treatment from a health care practitioner, or been hospitalized for any of the following:		
A. Chest pain, high or low blood pressure, heart disease, heart murmur, palpitations or irregular heart beat, peripheral vascular disease, blood clot, phlebitis, varicose veins, blood disorder, anemia, enlarged lymph nodes, or any other heart, cardiovascular, or circulatory disorder?	☐	☐
B. Headaches, dizziness, paralysis, stroke, loss of consciousness, seizure disorder, sleep apnea, multiple sclerosis, cerebral palsy, or any other disorder of the brain or nervous system?	☐	☐

Name: _____ Date: _____

EXQUISITE HEALTH

Primary's Social Security Number
☐☐☐ ☐☐ ☐☐☐☐

PART IV. (a) Statement of health (continued)

	Yes	No
5) C. Disorder of the mouth, throat or esophagus, tonsillitis, ulcer(s), colitis, ulcerative colitis, spastic colitis, Crohn's disease, gall bladder disorder, chronic diarrhea, hernia, hemorrhoids, hepatitis, pancreatitis, intestinal or rectal problems, liver disease, cirrhosis, stomach disorder, or any other disorder of the digestive system?	☐	☐
D. Allergy, sinusitis, bronchitis, emphysema, chronic obstructive pulmonary disease (COPD), pneumonia, tuberculosis, coughing up blood, or any other lung or respiratory disorder?	☐	☐
E. Asthma?	☐	☐
If "Yes," have you been hospitalized or been to an emergency room in the past 24 months?	☐	☐
Have you received any adrenaline or epinephrine injections?	☐	☐
F. Disorder of the kidney or bladder, infections, blood in urine, pyelonephritis, or any other disorder of the urinary tract?	☐	☐
G. Arthritis, rheumatoid arthritis, bursitis, gout, disorder of the back, spine, bone or joint, herniated, ruptured, or bulging disc, muscle or tendon pain, carpal tunnel syndrome, muscular dystrophy, fixation device or any other disorder of the musculoskeletal system?	☐	☐
H. Jaw problems, temporal mandibular joint syndrome (TMJ), pain or difficulty breathing, chewing or swallowing?	☐	☐
I. Diabetes, thyroid disorder, adrenal disorder, lupus, Raynaud's disease, chronic fatigue syndrome, Epstein-Barr virus, unintentional weight loss or any other disorder of the metabolic system?	☐	☐
J. Cancer, melanoma, tumor, cyst, growth, leukemia, Hodgkin's disease, or any other malignancy or any unbiopsied or undiagnosed tumor, cyst or growth?	☐	☐
K. Psoriasis, keratosis, herpes, burn(s), birthmark(s), warts, or any other disorder of the skin?	☐	☐
L. Disorder of the eyes or sight, glaucoma, cataracts, disorder of the ears or hearing, ear infection (otitis media), disorder of the nose or breathing, deviated nasal septum?	☐	☐
M. Nervous, mental, emotional or obsessive compulsive disorder, behavioral disorder, panic attack(s), anxiety, depression, manic depression, schizophrenia, attention deficit disorder, ADHD, or eating disorder?	☐	☐

	Yes	No
N. Alcohol or substance abuse/dependency, counseling, member of a support group?	☐	☐
(i) Do you consume alcoholic beverages?	☐	☐
If "yes", please indicate the number of alcoholic beverages you consume weekly (a beverage is 12 ounces of beer, 6 ounces of wine, 1 ounce of liquor). Applicant _____ Spouse/Domestic Partner _____		
O. Premature birth, developmental delay, congenital abnormalities, clubfoot, cleft lip or palate, or Down's syndrome?	☐	☐
P. Cosmetic or reconstructive surgery, including breast implants?	☐	☐
Q. Male reproductive system: disorder of the prostate, infections, impotency, sexual dysfunction, infertility, sexually transmitted disease or any other disorder of the reproductive system?	☐	☐
R. Female reproductive system: disorder of the breast, fibroid tumors, infertility, menstruation disorders, abnormal Pap test, infections, sexually transmitted disease, abnormal bleeding, endometriosis or any other disorder of the uterus or reproductive system?	☐	☐
6) Have you or any applying family member been diagnosed as having or been treated for AIDS (Acquired Immune Deficiency Syndrome) or ARC (AIDS-Related Complex)?	☐	☐
7) Have you or any applying family member consulted any health care practitioner for any condition or symptom(s) for which a diagnosis has not been established?	☐	☐
8) During the past 12 months, have you or any applying family member smoked cigarettes, cigars, pipes, or used chewing tobacco?	☐	☐
9) During the past three years, have you or any applying family member consulted any health care practitioner for any reason not listed on this form?	☐	☐
10) During the past 12 months, have you or any applying family member experienced symptoms for which any health care practitioner has not been consulted?	☐	☐
11) Is the applicant or any applying family member currently taking medication? If "Yes," please complete section IV (b).	☐	☐
12) Has the applicant or any applying family member taken a prescription medication during the past 12 months for a period of more than two weeks? If "Yes," please complete Part IV (b).	☐	☐

EXQUISITE HEALTH

Primary's Social Security Number

☐☐☐ ☐☐ ☐☐☐☐

PART IV. (a) Statement of health (continued)
Female applicants only (applicable to all females listed on the application). Attach another page if more than two females are listed on the application.

Applicant Name:			Applicant Name:		
13)A. Have you had a menstrual period in each of the last six months, including within the last 30 days? If "No," please explain:	Yes ☐	No ☐	13)A. Have you had a menstrual period in each of the last six months, including within the last 30 days? If "No," please explain:	Yes ☐	No ☐
B. (i) Have you had a pelvic exam? If yes, date of last pelvic exam (Mo/Dy/Yr):	Yes ☐	No ☐	B. (i) Have you had a pelvic exam? If yes, date of last pelvic exam (Mo/Dy/Yr):	Yes ☐	No ☐
(ii) Have you had a pap smear? If yes, date of last pap smear (Mo/Dy/Yr):	Yes ☐	No ☐	(ii) Have you had a pap smear? If yes, date of last pap smear (Mo/Dy/Yr):	Yes ☐	No ☐
(iii) Were the results of the exam(s) normal? If "No," please explain:	Yes ☐	No ☐	(iii) Were the results of the exam(s) normal? If "No," please explain:	Yes ☐	No ☐

PART IV. (b) Statement of health – If you answered "Yes" to any questions in Section IV (a), please identify the question number and explain in FULL DETAIL below. If additional space is necessary, please attach extra pages.

Question Number	Family member name and name used on doctor's records	Diagnosis, signs or symptoms, condition, treatment or recommendation	Still under treatment?	Dates of treatment or Hospitalization (Mo/Yr) Began Ended	Full name, address & telephone number of every health care practitioner, clinic, hospital or any other medical facility (include ZIP code)
			☐ Yes ☐ No		
			☐ Yes ☐ No		
			☐ Yes ☐ No		
			☐ Yes ☐ No		
			☐ Yes ☐ No		
			☐ Yes ☐ No		

DOCTOR'S VISITS – Please provide information regarding the last health care practitioner visit or physical examination for ALL family members you wish to cover.

Name of Individual	Date of Visit	Reason for visit	Result of Visit	Full name, address & telephone number of every health care practitioner, clinic, hospital or any other medical facility (include ZIP code)

Name: _____   Date: _____

► Directions: Review and complete the document below.

6.

NON-COMMERCIAL LEARNER'S PERMIT APPLICATION
PLEASE TYPE OR PRINT ALL INFORMATION IN BLUE OR BLACK INK

YOU MUST APPLY IN PERSON

THIS FORM IS VALID FOR 1 YEAR FROM THE DATE OF PHYSICAL EXAMINATION
The physical date may not be more than 6 months prior to your 16th birthday.

DRIVER'S LICENSE
NUMBER/I.D. NUMBER:_____

LAST NAME(S)				JR., ETC.

FIRST NAME		MIDDLE NAME	

DATE OF BIRTH	HEIGHT	SOCIAL SECURITY NUMBER	SEX	TELEPHONE (8 a.m. to 4:30 p.m.)
MONTH DAY YEAR	FEET INCHES			

EYE COLOR *(Please check one)*:   ☐ BLUE   ☐ BROWN   ☐ GREEN   ☐ HAZEL   ☐ PINK   ☐ BLACK   ☐ GRAY   ☐ DICHROMATIC   ☐ OTHER _____

STREET ADDRESS - A Post Office Box number may be used in addition to the actual residence address but cannot be used as the only address.	CITY	STATE	ZIP CODE

	PERMIT(S) DESIRED	FEE	ENTER FEE FOR EACH ITEM CHECKED
CHECK DESIRED PERMIT(S)	☐ CLASS A (Combination Vehicle over 26,000), ☐ CLASS B (Truck or Bus over 26,000), ☐ CLASS C (Automobile)	$5.00	
	☐ CLASS M (Motorcycle) MSEA Fee is included	$15.00	
MUST CHECK ONE	LICENSE REQUIRED	FEE	ENTER FEE FOR LICENSE CHECKED
	☐ 4-Year Photo	$28.00	
	☐ 2-Year Photo (Age 65 & Over)	$17.50	
	☐ Organ Donation Awareness Trust Fund (I wish to contribute $1.00)	$1.00	
PAID BY: ☐ Check ☐ Money Order Payable to PennDOT (Cash **CANNOT** be accepted)		TOTAL	$

► Directions: Write your answers to the questions on the lines below.

7. What are two pieces of personal information that you must provide when applying for a driver's permit?

_____

_____

8. What different types of vehicles might this application allow you to drive?

_____

_____

▶ Directions: Determine whether the following statement is true or false. If the statement is true, write T. If the statement is false, write F. Then rewrite the false statement to make it true.

SOCIAL SECURITY ADMINISTRATION
Application for a Social Security Card

Form Approved
OMB No. 0960-0066

		First	Full Middle Name	Last
1	**NAME** TO BE SHOWN ON CARD	Ana	Maria	Martinez
	FULL NAME AT BIRTH IF OTHER THAN ABOVE	First	Full Middle Name	Last
	OTHER NAMES USED ON YOUR SOCIAL SECURITY CARD			

2	Social Security number previously assigned to the person listed in item 1 ➡	☐☐☐ – ☐☐ – ☐☐☐☐

3	**PLACE OF BIRTH** (Do Not Abbreviate)	Albuquerque, New Mexico		Office Use Only	**4**	**DATE OF BIRTH**	02/02/2011
	City	State or Foreign Country		FCI			MM/DD/YYYY

5	**CITIZENSHIP** (Check One) ➡	☒ U.S. Citizen	☐ Legal Alien Allowed To Work	☐ Legal Alien **Not** Allowed To Work(See Instructions On Page 3)	☐ Other (See Instructions On Page 3)

6	**ETHNICITY** Are You Hispanic or Latino? (Your Response is Voluntary) ☒ Yes ☐ No	**7**	**RACE** Select One or More (Your Response is Voluntary)	☐ Native Hawaiian ☐ Alaska Native ☐ Asian	☐ American Indian ☐ Black/African American	☐ Other Pacific Islander ☒ White

8	**SEX** ➡	☐ Male	☒ Female

9	**A. MOTHER'S NAME AT HER BIRTH** ➡	First Martha	Full Middle Name Maria	Last Name At Her Birth Diaz
	B. MOTHER'S SOCIAL SECURITY NUMBER (See instructions for 9 B on Page 3) ➡	☒☒☒ – ☒☒ – ☒☒☒☒		☐ Unknown

10	**A. FATHER'S NAME** ➡	First Armando	Full Middle Name Pedro	Last Martinez
	B. FATHER'S SOCIAL SECURITY NUMBER (See instructions for 10B on Page 3) ➡	☒☒☒ – ☒☒ – ☒☒☒☒		☐ Unknown

11	Has the person listed in item 1 or anyone acting on his/her behalf ever filed for or received a Social Security number card before? ☐ Yes (If "yes" answer questions 12-13) ☒ No ☐ Don't Know (If "don't know," skip to question 14.)

12	Name shown on the most recent Social Security card issued for the person listed in item 1 ➡	First	Full Middle Name	Last Name

13	Enter any different date of birth if used on an earlier application for a card	_____ MM/DD/YYYY

14	**TODAY'S DATE** 05/15/2012 MM/DD/YYYY	**15**	**DAYTIME PHONE NUMBER**	505 Area Code	555-8912 Number

16	**MAILING ADDRESS** (Do Not Abbreviate)	Street Address, Apt. No., PO Box, Rural Route No. 24318 Canyon Way, #1	Albuquerque, NM	87107
		City	State/Foreign Country	ZIP Code

I declare under penalty of perjury that I have examined all the information on this form, and on any accompanying statements or forms, and it is true and correct to the best to my knowledge.

17	**YOUR SIGNATURE** ▶ *Martha Diaz*	**18**	**YOUR RELATIONSHIP TO THE PERSON IN ITEM 1 IS:** ☐ Self ☒ Natural Or Adoptive Parent ☐ Legal Guardian ☐ Other Specify _____

9. Only the applicant may submit an application for a Social Security number.

_____

_____

Name: _____ Date: _____

▶ Directions: **Select the choice that best answers the question below.**

4. **Term of Lease Agreement:**
   The Lease Agreement will begin on October 1, 2011 and will end on October 1, 2012.

5. **Use & Occupancy of Property:**
   A. The only person(s) living in the property is/are: Sandra Margoles, Benjamin Margoles.
   B. Any changes in the occupancy will require written consent of the Landlord.
   C. The Tenant will use the property only as a residence.

6. **Amount of Rent:**
   A. The amount of the Rent is $775.00, to be paid monthly.

7. **Date rent is due:**
   A. The rent is due in advance on or before the 5th day of each month. The rent due date is the date the Landlord must receive the Tenant's payment.
   B. Rental payments are made payable to: Best Properties.
   C. Rental payments may be delivered to the Landlord at: Best Properties, 1250 S. 51st St., Salt Lake City, UT 84104.

8. **Late Fee:**
   A. If the rent or any other charges are not received by the Landlord on or before 5 days after the rent due date, Tenant must pay a late fee of $25 in addition to the rent.
   B. Rental payments paid late 3 times within a 12-month period creates a default of the Lease Agreement.
   C. Payments received by Landlord when there are arrearages shall be credited first to any outstanding balance and then applied to the current amount due.

9. **Returned Payments:**
   A. A returned payment fee of $20 will be added for all returned payments. A personal check will not be accepted as payment to replace a returned payment.
   B. If there are more than 2 instances of returned payments, Tenant(s) agree that the Landlord may require all future payments to be made only by Certified Check or Money Order.
   C. If your financial institution returns your rental payment and causes the rental payment to be late, a later charge will apply.

10. **Security Deposit**
   A. The Tenant(s) have paid to the Landlord a Security Deposit of $775.00, to be held in an Escrow Account.
   B. The Security Deposit is intended to pay the cost of damages, cleaning, excessive wear and tear, and unreturned keys once the Lease Agreement has ended and/or for any unpaid charges or attorney fees suffered by the Landlord by reason of Tenant's default of this Lease Agreement.
   C. Tenant may be responsible for any unpaid charges or attorney fees, suffered by the Landlord by reason of Tenant's default of this Lease in accordance to state and local laws and regulations.
   D. Under no circumstance can the Security Deposit be used as a payment for rent and/or for charges due during the term of this Lease Agreement.
   E. The Leased Premises must be left in good, clean condition, with all trash, debris, and Tenant's personal property removed. The Leased Premises shall be left with all appliances and equipment in working order.
   F. Landlord's recover of damages will not be limited to the amount of the Security Deposit.

10. According to this lease, when will you receive your security deposit back?

   A. at the end of the initial lease term

   B. when you end the lease entirely

   C. if you need the money to pay your rent

   D. before the landlord completes any repairs

▶ Directions: **Choose the answer that best completes the statement below.**

---

12. **Appliances:**
    A. Landlord will supply and maintain: refrigerator, stove, heater
    B. Tenant must have written approval before installing any appliance. Landlord accepts no responsibility for the maintenance, repair or upkeep of any appliance supplied by the Tenant. Tenant agrees he/she is responsible for any damage that occurs to the Leased Premises resulting from the addition of any appliance that is supplied by the Tenant.

13. **Maintenance and Repairs:**
    Landlord shall be responsible for repairs in or about the Leased Premises unless caused by the negligence of the Tenant. Tenant will be responsible for any repairs caused by his/her negligence.
    A. It is the responsibility of the Tenant to promptly notify the Landlord of the need for any such repair of which the Tenant becomes aware.
    B. If any required repair is caused by the negligence of the Tenant and/or Tenant's guests, the Tenant will be fully responsible for the cost of the repair and/or replacement that may be needed.
    C. The Tenant must keep the Leased Premises clean and sanitary at all times and remove all rubbish, garbage, and other waste in a clean, tidy and sanitary manner.
    D. Tenant must abide by all local recycling regulations.
    E. The Tenant shall properly use and operate all electrical cooking and plumbing fixtures and keep them clean and sanitary.
    F. The Tenant is not permitted to paint, make any alterations, improvements or additions to the premises without first obtaining the written permission of the Landlord. The Landlord's permission to a particular painting, alteration, improvement, or addition shall not be deemed as consent to future painting, alterations, improvements, or additions.
    G. The Tenant is responsible for removing snow and ice from stairs and walkways.

14 **Condition of Property:**
    A. The Tenant acknowledges that the Tenant has inspected the Leased Premises and at the commencement of this Lease Agreement, the interior and exterior of the Leased Premises, as well as all equipment and any appliances are found to be in an acceptable condition and in good working order.
    B. The Tenant agrees that neither the Landlord nor his agent has made promises regarding the condition of the Leased Premises.
    C. The Tenant agrees to return the Leased Premises to Landlord at end of the Lease Agreement in the same condition it was at the beginning of the Lease Agreement.

15. **Pets:**
    Pets are not allowed.

16. **Parking**
    Parking is provided. Two assigned spaces.

17. **Rules and Regulations:**
    A. Late fees are strictly enforced and any unpaid fees will not be waived.
    B. The Tenant may not interfere with the peaceful enjoyment of the neighbors.
    C. The Tenant will be responsible for any fine and/or violation that is imposed on the Landlord due to the Tenant's negligence.
    D. The Tenant shall abide by Federal, State, and Local Laws.
    E. The Tenant agrees not to use the Leased Premises for any unlawful purpose, including but not limited to the sale, use or possession of illegal drugs on or around the Lease Premises.
    F. The Tenant must report any malfunction with smoke detector(s) immediately to the Landlord. The Tenant agrees not to remove, dismantle or take any action to interfere with the operation of any smoke detector(s) installed on the Leased Premises.

---

11. Under this lease agreement, the tenant is responsible for

    A. no repairs.

    B. all repairs.

    C. repairs needed due to the tenant's carelessness.

    D. repairs that the landlord does not want to do.

CHAPTER 3

Business Documents

▶ **LESSON 1:**

New Hire

pages 112–119

▶ **LESSON 2:**

Employment

pages 120–129

Chapter Recap	Chapter Review
☑ _____	_____
☑ _____	_____
☑ _____	_____

▶ **CHAPTER 3:**

Recap/Review

pages 130–140

BUSINESS DOCUMENTS

New Hire

CONTENTS

You may think that you fill out countless forms and applications when you're seeking a job, but there are still a few more to complete after you've landed it. Employers require certain documents in order to verify your right to work in the United States. Other documents ensure that employers hold back the correct amount of taxes from each of your paychecks.

After you're hired, you'll be required to fill out forms related to:

- taxes
- personal information
- payment of wages
- hours worked

Usually, someone from the company's Human Resources department will instruct you about how to complete this new-hire paperwork. However, if you work for a smaller company, your boss may oversee this paperwork.

Most forms associated with new-hire paperwork are legal documents. You may have to provide identification to be able to complete them. They often require a signature. Your taxes and paycheck are affected by the information on these documents. These documents are very important and may be complicated. To ensure that you understand these documents, feel free to ask your supervisor or human resources manager to explain them to you. Studying the examples in this chapter will help you interpret or complete the documents in the chapter review and in real life.

Online Time Sheets

Many companies use an online system to track their employees' work hours. If you work at a restaurant or store, you may clock in and out on a shared computer or cash register. Some offices have Web sites where employees log their time each day.

I-9 Form

The federal government requires employers to verify the employment eligibility of new employees. If you are hired for a temporary or permanent position, you most likely will fill out and sign an I-9 form.

Department of Homeland Security
U.S. Citizenship and Immigration Services

Form I-9, Employment Eligibility Verification

Read instructions carefully before completing this form. The instructions must be available during completion of this form.

ANTI-DISCRIMINATION NOTICE: It is illegal to discriminate against work-authorized individuals. Employers CANNOT specify which document(s) they will accept from an employee. The refusal to hire an individual because the documents have a future expiration date may also constitute illegal discrimination.

Section 1. Employee Information and Verification (To be completed and signed by employee at the time employment begins.)

Print Name: Last	First	Middle Initial	Maiden Name
Shah	Ahmed	A	

Address (Street Name and Number)	Apt. #	Date of Birth (month/day/year)
12565 Ford Rd.	14	05/02/1985

City	State	Zip Code	Social Security #
Dearborn	MI	48124	XXX-XX-XXXX

I am aware that federal law provides for imprisonment and/or fines for false statements or use of false documents in connection with the completion of this form.

I attest, under penalty of perjury, that I am (check one of the following):

[X] A citizen of the United States

[ ] A noncitizen national of the United States (see instructions)

[ ] A lawful permanent resident (Alien #)

[ ] An alien authorized to work (Alien # or Admission #) _____
until (expiration date, if applicable - month/day/year) _____

Employee's Signature *Ahmed A. Shah*   Date (month/day/year) 03/14/2012

> Although you don't need to be a U.S. citizen to work legally in the United States, you do need to be authorized to work in the country. The I-9 form verifies that you are a citizen or an approved immigrant.

Preparer and/or Translator Certification (To be completed and signed if Section 1 is prepared by a person other than the employee.) I attest, penalty of perjury, that I have assisted in the completion of this form and that to the best of my knowledge the information is true and correct.

Preparer's/Translator's Signature	Print Name

Address (Street Name and Number, City, State, Zip Code)	Date (month/day/year)

Section 2. Employer Review and Verification (To be completed and signed by employer. Examine one document from List A OR examine one document from List B and one from List C, as listed on the reverse of this form, and record the title, number, and expiration date, if any, of the document(s).)

List A	OR	List B	AND	List C
Document title:				
Issuing authority:				
Document #:				
Expiration Date (if any):				
Document #:				
Expiration Date (if any):				

CERTIFICATION: I attest, under penalty of perjury, that I have examined the document(s) presented by the above-named employee, that the above-listed document(s) appear to be genuine and to relate to the employee named, that the employee began employment on (month/day/year) _____ and that to the best of my knowledge the employee is authorized to work in the United States. (State employment agencies may omit the date the employee began employment.)

Signature of Employer or Authorized Representative	Print Name	Title

Business or Organization Name and Address (Street Name and Number, City, State, Zip Code)	Date (month/day/year)

Section 3. Updating and Reverification (To be completed and signed by employer.)

B. Date of Rehire (month/day/year) (if applicable)

> There are many different documents you can provide to prove your employment eligibility. Some documents, such as a U.S. passport, prove both your identity and your citizenship status. Other documents prove either your identity or your eligibility. For example, you may provide a driver's license or state ID card along with a Social Security card to prove your eligibility.

Date (month/day/year)

Form I-9 (Rev. 08/07/09) Y Page 4

W-4 Form

Employers use the W-4 form to determine the correct amount of tax to withhold from an employee's wages. Ideally, the amount you withhold will exactly equal the annual tax due.

Form W-4 (2010)

Purpose. Complete Form W-4 so that your employer can withhold the correct federal income tax from your pay. Consider completing a new Form W-4 each year and when your personal or financial situation changes.

Exemption from withholding. If you are exempt, complete **only** lines 1, 2, 3, 4, and 7 and sign the form to validate it. Your exemption for 2010 expires February 16, 2011. See Pub. 505, Tax Withholding and Estimated Tax.

Note. You cannot claim exemption from withholding if (a) your income exceeds $950 and includes more than $300 of unearned income (for example, interest and dividends) and (b) another person can claim you as a dependent on his or her tax return.

Basic instructions. If you are not exempt, complete the **Personal Allowances Worksheet** below. The worksheets on page 2 further adjust your withholding allowances based on itemized deductions, certain credits, adjustments to income, or two-earners/multiple jobs situations.

Complete all worksheets that apply. However, you may claim fewer (or zero) allowances. For regular wages, withholding must be based on allowances you claimed and may not be a flat amount or percentage of wages.

Head of household. Generally, you may claim head of household filing status on your tax return only if you are unmarried and pay more than 50% of the costs of keeping up a home for yourself and your dependent(s) or other qualifying individuals. See Pub. 501, Exemptions, Standard Deduction, and Filing Information, for information.

Tax credits. You can take projected tax credits into account in figuring your allowable number of withholding allowances. Credits for child or dependent care expenses and the child tax credit may be claimed using the **Personal Allowances Worksheet** below. See Pub. 919, How Do I Adjust My Tax Withholding, for information on converting your other credits into withholding allowances.

Nonwage income. If you have a large amount of nonwage income, such as interest or dividends, consider making estimated tax

payments using Form 1040-ES, Estimated Tax for Individuals. Otherwise, you may owe additional tax. If you have pension or annuity income, see Pub. 919 to find out if you should adjust your withholding on Form W-4 or W-4P.

> The numbers on each of these lines stand for one deduction on your income tax return. The more deductions you claim, the lower your paycheck withholdings will be. However, if you take too many deductions, you may owe taxes.

Personal Allowances Worksheet (Keep for your records.)

A	Enter "1" for **yourself** if no one else can claim you as a dependent	**A** 1
B	Enter "1" if: { • You are single and have only one job; or • You are married, have only one job, and your spouse does not work; or • Your wages from a second job or your spouse's wages (or the total of both) are $1,500 or less. }	**B** 0
C	Enter "1" for your **spouse**. But, you may choose to enter "-0-" if you are married and have either a working spouse or more than one job. (Entering "-0-" may help you avoid having too little tax withheld.)	**C** 0
D	Enter number of **dependents** (other than your spouse or yourself) you will claim on your tax return . . .	**D** 1
E	Enter "1" if you will file as **head of household** on your tax return (see conditions under **Head of household** above) .	**E** 0
F	Enter "1" if you have at least $1,800 of **child or dependent care expenses** for which you plan to claim a credit . .	**F** 0
	(**Note.** Do **not** include child support payments. See Pub. 503, Child and Dependent Care Expenses, for details.)	
G	**Child Tax Credit** (including additional child tax credit). See Pub. 972, Child Tax Credit, for more information.	
	• If your total income will be less than $61,000 ($90,000 if married), enter "2" for each eligible child; then **less** "1" if you have three or more eligible children.	
	• If your total income will be between $61,000 and $84,000 ($90,000 and $119,000 if married), enter "1" for each eligible child plus "1" **additional** if you have six or more eligible children.	**G** 0
H	Add lines A through G and enter total here. (**Note.** This may be different from the number of exemptions you claim on your tax return.) ▶ **H**	2
	For accuracy, complete all worksheets that apply. { • If you plan to **itemize or claim adjustments to income** and want to reduce your withholding, see the **Deductions and Adjustments Worksheet** on page 2. • If you have **more than one job** or are **married and you and your spouse both work** and the combined earnings from all jobs exceed $18,000 ($32,000 if married), see the **Two-Earners/Multiple Jobs Worksheet** on page 2 to avoid having too little tax withheld. • If **neither** of the above situations applies, **stop here** and enter the number from line H on line 5 of Form W-4 below. }	

- - - - - - - - - - - **Cut here and give Form W-4 to your employer. Keep the top part for your records.** - - - - - - - - - - -

Form W-4
Department of the Treasury
Internal Revenue Service

Employee's Withholding Allowance Certificate

▶ Whether you are entitled to claim a certain number of allowances or exemption from withholding is subject to review by the IRS. Your employer may be required to send a copy of this form to the IRS.

OMB No. 1545-0074
2010

1 Type or print your first name and middle initial.	Last name		2 Your social security number
Janelle	Powers		XXX XX XXXX

Home address (number and street or rural route)	3 ☐ Single ☐ Married ☒ Married, but withhold at higher Single rate.
423 W. Harding Rd., #5	Note. If married, but legally separated, or spouse is a nonresident alien, check the "Single" box.
City or town, state, and ZIP code	4 If your last name differs from that shown on your social security card,
Hoboken, NJ 07031	check here. You must call 1-800-772-1213 for a replacement card. ▶ ☐

5	Total number of allowances you are claiming (from line H above **or** from the applicable worksheet on page 2)	**5**	2
6	Additional amount, if any, you want withheld from each paycheck	**6** $	27.50
7	I claim exemption from withholding for 2010, and I certify that I meet **both** of the following conditions for exemption.		
	• Last year I had a right to a refund of **all** federal income tax withheld because I had **no** tax liability **and**		
	• This year I expect a refund of **all** federal income tax withheld because I expect to have **no** tax liability.		
	If you meet both conditions, write "Exempt" here . . . . ▶	**7**	

Under penalties of perjury, I declare that I have examined this certificate and to the best of my knowledge and belief, it is true, correct, and complete.

Employee's signature
(Form is not valid unless you sign it.) ▶ *Janelle Powers*

> Qualifying for certain tax credits, such as the Child Tax Credit, can significantly reduce the amount of taxes that you owe at the end of the year. If you qualify for the credits listed on this Personal Allowance Worksheet, be sure to claim the deduction on your W-4 form.

> If you have owed taxes in the past or have more than one job, you may wish to withhold additional money from each paycheck. The extra money you make from a second job may put you into a higher tax bracket, meaning that you might owe more in taxes.

W-4 Form

Your filing status can make a big difference in the amount of money that you owe in taxes. Be sure you identify the correct filing status [married filing jointly, head of household (single parent), or single]. This will help you determine the correct number of deductions to claim.

Page 2 of 2

Form W-4 (2010)   Page **2**

Deductions and Adjustments Worksheet

Note. Use this worksheet *only* if you plan to itemize deductions or claim certain credits or adjustments to income.

1	Enter an estimate of your 2010 itemized deductions. These include qualifying home mortgage interest, charitable contributions, state and local taxes, medical expenses in excess of 7.5% of your income, and miscellaneous deductions	1	$ 3500
2	Enter: $11,400 if married filing jointly or qualifying widow(er) / $8,400 if head of household / $5,700 if single or married filing separately	2	$ 11400
3	**Subtract** line 2 from line 1. If zero or less, enter "-0-"	3	$ 0
4	Enter an estimate of your 2010 adjustments to income and any additional standard deduction. (Pub. 919)	4	$ 74
5	**Add** lines 3 and 4 and enter the total. (Include any amount for credits from *Worksheet 6* in Pub. 919.)	5	$ 74
6	Enter an estimate of your 2010 nonwage income (such as dividends or interest)	6	$ 0
7	**Subtract** line 6 from line 5. If zero or less, enter "-0-"	7	$ 74
8	**Divide** the amount on line 7 by $3,650 and enter the result here. Drop any fraction	8	0
9	Enter the number from the **Personal Allowances Worksheet,** line H, page 1	9	2
10	**Add** lines 8 and 9 and enter the total here. If you plan to use the **Two-Earners/Multiple Jobs Worksheet,** also enter this total on line 1 below. Otherwise, **stop here** and enter this total on Form W-4, line 5, page 1	10	2

Two-Earners/Multiple Jobs Worksheet (See *Two earners or multiple jobs* on page 1.)

Note. Use this worksheet *only* if the instructions under line H on page 1 direct you here.

1	Enter the number from line H, page 1 (or from line 10 above if you used the **Deductions and Adjustments Worksheet**)	1	2
2	Find the number in **Table 1** below that applies to the **LOWEST** paying job and enter it here. **However,** if you are married filing jointly and wages from the highest paying job are $65,000 or less, do not enter more than "3."	2	3
3	If line 1 is **more than or equal to** line 2, subtract line 2 from line 1. Enter the result here (if zero, enter "-0-") and on Form W-4, line 5, page 1. **Do not** use the rest of this worksheet	3	
	Note. If line 1 is *less than* line 2, enter "-0-" on Form W-4, line 5, page 1. Complete lines 4–9 below to figure the additional withholding amount necessary to avoid a year-end tax bill.		
4	Enter the number from line 2 of this worksheet	4	3
5	Enter the number from line 1 of this worksheet	5	2
6	**Subtract** line 5 from line 4	6	1
7	Find the amount in **Table 2** below that applies to the **HIGHEST** paying job and enter it here	7	$ 550
8	**Multiply** line 7 by line 6 and enter the result here. This is the additional annual withholding needed	8	$ 550
9	Divide line 8 by the number of pay periods remaining in 2010. For example, divide by 26 if you are paid every two weeks and you complete this form in December 2009. Enter the result here and on Form W-4, line 6, page 1. This is the additional amount to be withheld from each paycheck	9	$ 27.50

Table 1

Married Filing Jointly		All Others	
If wages from LOWEST paying job are—	Enter on line 2 above	If wages from LOWEST paying job are—	Enter on line 2 above
$0 - $7,000	0	$0 - $6,000	0
7,001 - 10,000	1	6,001 - 12,000	1
10,001 - 16,000	2	12,001 - 19,000	2
16,001 - 22,000	3	19,001 - 26,000	3
22,001 - 27,000	4	26,001 - 35,000	4
27,001 - 35,000	5	35,001 - 50,000	5
35,001 - 44,000	6	50,001 - 65,000	6
44,001 - 50,000	7	65,001 - 80,000	7
50,001 - 55,000	8	80,001 - 90,000	8
55,001 - 65,000	9	90,001 -120,000	9
65,001 - 72,000	10	120,001 and over	10
72,001 - 85,000	11		
85,001 -105,000	12		
105,001 -115,000	13		
115,001 -130,000	14		
130,001 - and over	15		

Table 2

Married Filing Jointly		All Others	
If wages from HIGHEST paying job are—	Enter on line 7 above	If wages from HIGHEST paying job are—	Enter on line 7 above
$0 - $65,000	$550	$0 - $35,000	$550
65,001 - 120,000	910	35,001 - 90,000	910
120,001 - 185,000	1,020	90,001 - 165,000	1,020
185,001 - 330,000	1,200	165,001 - 370,000	1,200
330,001 and over	1,280	370,001 and over	1,280

You may have a working spouse or more than one job. In that case, use this worksheet to ensure that you claim the correct number of dependents for your tax withholding. Sometimes, combined incomes from two jobs can change your tax rate, giving you an unpleasant surprise when you file your taxes.

Personal Data Form

Employers need your personal information on file so that they may mail you important information, call you at home, or contact a friend or family member in the event of an emergency. You will likely need to fill out at least one personal information form when you are hired.

Human Resources Department

New Employee Personal Data Sheet

Instructions: The following data is needed to establish a personnel record for you as a new employee. Please complete all information and, if changes occur, be sure to notify the Human Resources Department. Forms for such changes are available through Human Resources. Forms are also available online.

Name: ___Tatelbaum,___ (Last)   ___Sarah___ (First)

Social Security #: ___XXX-XX-XXXX___   Preferred First Name: ___Sarah___

Address: ___8125 W. Taft Rd., Apt 4D___ (Street)

___Omaha___ (City)   ___NE___ (State)

Be sure to update your manager or human resources department (HR) if your personal information changes. This may include moving or changing your name, phone number, or emergency contact. HR can provide you with a new form.

Mailing Address: _____ (If different from shown above)

Home Phone #: ___402-555-1277___   Work Phone #: ___402-555-6200___

Home Email: ___saraht619@domain.com___   Work Email: ___tatelbaumsl@company.com___

Sex: ☐ Male   ☒ Female

☐ Hispanic (3) ☐ Asian (2) ☐ American Indian (1)

Although no one wants to think about getting sick or hurt at work, illnesses and accidents do occur. If something happens, your company will call your emergency contact.

Emergency Contact:

Name: ___Tatelbaum,___ (Last)   ___Eileen___ (First)   ___M___ (MI)

Address: ___4512 Gabbard Rd.___ (Street)

___Omaha___ (City)   ___NE___ (State)   ___68105___ (Zip)

Phone #: ___402-555-8614___   Relationship: ___mother___

___Sarah Tatelbaum___ (Employee Signature)   ___8/15/2011___ (Date signed)

Voluntary Disclosure Form

Employers collect voluntary disclosure forms to give to the federal government. These forms help show the diversity of employees working at a company. It will be your choice as to whether you fill out these forms.

> The federal government categorizes people of Hispanic origin as an ethnicity rather than a separate race. If you are of Hispanic or Latino heritage, check the "Hispanic or Latino" box under ethnicity. Then check the "White" box under race.

Voluntary Disclosure Form

The federal government under Executive Order 11246 requires the corporation to report sex and race/ethnic origin of applicants for employment. Submission of information is <u>voluntary</u>, and failure to provide it will not subject you to any adverse treatment. Your cooperation is appreciated.

Name: _____Gutierrez_____Victor_____J_____
(Last)   (First)   (MI)

Date of Application: _04_ / _18_ / _2012_

Position(s) Applied For: _Cable installation technician_____

Indicate Gender:
- ☒ Male
- ☐ Female
- ☐ Choose not to identify

Indicate Ethnic group:
- ☒ Hispanic or Latino
- ☐ Not Hispanic or Latino
- ☐ Choose not to identify

Indicate your Race:
- ☒ White
- ☐ Black or African American
- ☐ Asian
- ☐ Native Hawaiian or Other Pacific Islander
- ☐ American Indian or Alaskan Native
- ☐ Two or more Races
- ☐ Choose not to identify

> If you identify yourself as belonging to more than one race, select the "Two or More Races" option instead of marking the boxes for each race with which you identify.

Revised EEO-1 Race and Ethnicity Categories	Descriptions
Hispanic or Latino	A person of Cuban, Mexican, Puerto Rican, South or Central American, or other Spanish culture or origin regardless of race.
White	A person having origins in any of the original peoples of Europe, the Middle East, or North America
Black or African-American	A person having origins in any of the black racial groups of Africa.
Asian	A person with origins in any of the original peoples of the Far East, Southeast Asia, or the Indian subcontinent including, for example, Cambodia, China, India, Japan, Korea, Malaysia, Pakistan, the Philippine Islands, Thailand, and Vietnam.
Native Hawaiian or Other Pacific Islander	A person having origins in any of the people of Hawaii, Guam, Samoa, or other Pacific Islands.
American Indian or Alaskan Native	A person having origins in any of the original peoples of North and South America (including Central America), and who maintain tribal affiliation or community attachment.
Two or More Races	All persons who identify with more than one of the above races or ethnicity.

Brighter Cable is an equal opportunity corporation and does not discriminate on the basis of race, color, sex, national origin, religion, age, disability, or veteran status in admission or access to, or treatment or employment in, its programs and activities. Individuals who may have inquiries regarding the corporation's policy and procedures should contact Melissa Wear-Grimm @509-555-8000.

Direct Deposit Enrollment

Signing up for direct deposit allows you to have your paycheck deposited electronically into your bank account. This means that you will not receive a paper check that you must deposit with your bank in person.

Pax Group Effective September 2009	**Direct Deposit Application for Payroll**		**Office Use Only** Date Entered: _____ Initials: _____

Direct deposit information can be submitted electronically through Employee Self Service or by submitting this application form. To submit electronically, your career account and password is needed. New employees may need to complete this application until a career account and password has been established.

MAIN Account	Type of Account	Bank Information	
Indicate one: [X] Add ☐ Change	Indicate: [X] Checking ☐ Savings	ABA Transit Routing Number: 9 6 0 0 5 2 8 4 0 6 Account Number: 330571580 Bank Name: Stony Brook Federal Bank Bank City, State: Stony Brook, NY	**NET PAY**
2nd Account	**Type of Account**	**Bank Information**	**Dollar Amount**
Indicate one: [X] Add ☐ Change ☐ Delete	Indicate: ☐ Checking [X] Savings	ABA Transit Routing Number: 9 6 0 0 5 2 8 4 0 6 Account Number: 658412098 Bank Name: Stony Brook Federal Bank Bank City, State: Stony Brook, NY	Indicate: Stony Brook, NY Specified Dollar Amount: $50
3nd Account	**Type of Account**	**Bank Information**	**Dollar Amount**
Indicate one: ☐ Add ☐ Change ☐ Delete	Indicate: ☐ Checking ☐ Savings	ABA Transit Routing Number: ☐☐☐☐☐☐☐☐☐ Account Number: _____ Bank Name: _____ Bank City, State: _____	Indicate: _____ Specified Dollar Amount: _____

I hereby authorize Pax Group and the financial institution(s) listed above to initiate electronic credit entries and, if necessary, debit entries and adjustments for any credit entries made in error to my account(s). This authorization will remain in effect until I have cancelled or changed my account information in writing or electronically through Employee Self Service.

Stephanie Robie   7-14-12

Signature   Date

Often, you may choose to have your paycheck deposited into more than one account. Along with a checking account, choosing to have some money deposited into your savings account can be a good way to save money out of each paycheck. Be sure to fill out the correct routing number and account number for each account. Because the accounts themselves are different, so too are the account numbers.

Time Sheet

If you work in a job for which you receive hourly wages, you likely will need to fill out a time sheet each pay period so that you may be paid for the correct number of hours. Salaried employees also may have to complete time sheets. These employees may not have to clock in and out when they take lunch. Usually, salaried employees do not receive overtime pay.

If you are paid hourly, be sure to record any overtime that you may work. Often, overtime pay is higher than your regular pay, making those extra hours very valuable on your paycheck.

WEEKLY TIME SHEET

Week Ending: 11/18/11　　　　　**Name: Alicia Orozco**

	IN	OUT	IN	OUT	Hours	Overtime
MONDAY	7:58 a.m.	12:01 p.m.	1:03 p.m.	5:07 p.m.	8	
	8:02 a.m.	11:58 p.m.	1:01 p.m.	4:59 p.m.	8	
	7:31 a.m.	11:29 p.m.	12:02 p.m.	5:03 p.m.	9	1 hour
	8:01 a.m.	12:04 p.m.	1:08 p.m.	6:11 p.m.	9	1 hour
	8:04 a.m.	12:03 p.m.	1:02 p.m.	5:05 p.m.	8	
SATURDAY						
SUNDAY	8:32 a.m.	1:05 p.m.			4.5	4.5 hours

Employee Signature: _Alicia Orozco_

Employer's Signature: _S. A. Bahar_

When you fill out your time sheet, be sure to note the times that you clocked in and out for unpaid breaks, such as lunch. You may need to calculate your overall hours worked. Sometimes, an electronic time-keeping system will calculate hours for you.

As with other employment documents, you must sign your time sheet so that it may be considered official or approved. Ensure accuracy of your time sheet before signing and approving it. Fraudulent or incorrect information may be grounds for employee termination.

Companies often round time worked to certain increments, such as one-quarter hour, or 15 minutes. Here, although Alicia worked 8 hours and 2 minutes, she rounded it down to 8 hours.

BUSINESS DOCUMENTS

Employment

CONTENTS

After you're on the job, you will continue to encounter employment documents. You will want to review some documents before making decisions about your employee benefits or your employment agreement. Taking the time to review your company's policy manual will help you understand the expectations of your workplace. Perhaps you will have the opportunity to follow certain company procedures or even write a few yourself.

If you've been hired for part-time work or only for a specific project or period of time, you may be considered a contract employee. If so, it will be important to be familiar with the details of your contract before agreeing to its terms.

After some time on the job, you'll begin to see other work-related documents. You will probably start receiving regular performance reviews. Whether you are new on the job or you have been working at the same place for a long time, it's important to stay current on workplace benefits, procedures, and policies. Benefits, such as health insurance, change yearly. Employers may periodically update procedure and policy manuals. If your company changes its procedures or policies, be sure to read the updated documents.

The information in this chapter will help you become familiar with several types of workplace documents. Studying the examples in this lesson will help you interpret or complete the documents in the chapter review and in real life.

Online Trade Groups

If you practice a specific trade, you may be able to join a trade services group. For instance, a welder might join the American Welding Society. These groups may offer helpful services through their Web sites, such as contract review, networking, job opportunities, and continuing education.

Company Healthcare Benefits Plan

Many companies offer employees the opportunity to enroll in healthcare plans that the companies at least partially pay. Review your healthcare options carefully to decide the right option for you.

A deductible is the portion of an insurance claim that you must pay before your insurance company will cover any expenses.

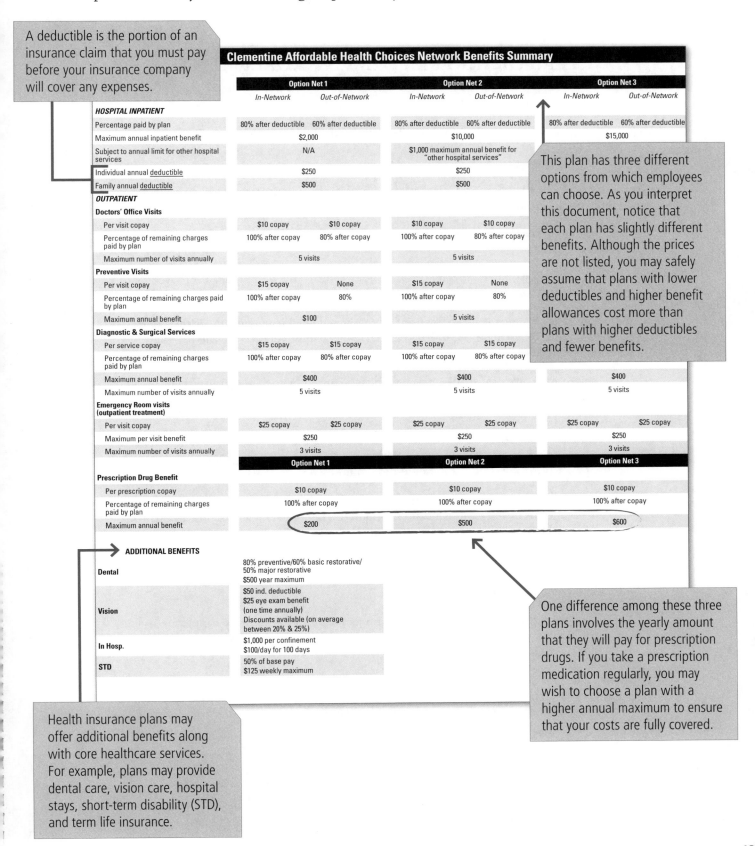

Clementine Affordable Health Choices Network Benefits Summary

	Option Net 1		Option Net 2		Option Net 3	
	In-Network	Out-of-Network	In-Network	Out-of-Network	In-Network	Out-of-Network
HOSPITAL INPATIENT						
Percentage paid by plan	80% after deductible	60% after deductible	80% after deductible	60% after deductible	80% after deductible	60% after deductible
Maximum annual inpatient benefit	$2,000		$10,000		$15,000	
Subject to annual limit for other hospital services	N/A		$1,000 maximum annual benefit for "other hospital services"			
Individual annual deductible	$250		$250			
Family annual deductible	$500		$500			
OUTPATIENT						
Doctors' Office Visits						
Per visit copay	$10 copay	$10 copay	$10 copay	$10 copay		
Percentage of remaining charges paid by plan	100% after copay	80% after copay	100% after copay	80% after copay		
Maximum number of visits annually	5 visits		5 visits			
Preventive Visits						
Per visit copay	$15 copay	None	$15 copay	None		
Percentage of remaining charges paid by plan	100% after copay	80%	100% after copay	80%		
Maximum annual benefit	$100		5 visits			
Diagnostic & Surgical Services						
Per service copay	$15 copay	$15 copay	$15 copay	$15 copay		
Percentage of remaining charges paid by plan	100% after copay	80% after copay	100% after copay	80% after copay		
Maximum annual benefit	$400		$400		$400	
Maximum number of visits annually	5 visits		5 visits		5 visits	
Emergency Room visits (outpatient treatment)						
Per visit copay	$25 copay	$25 copay	$25 copay	$25 copay	$25 copay	$25 copay
Maximum per visit benefit	$250		$250		$250	
Maximum number of visits annually	3 visits		3 visits		3 visits	
	Option Net 1		Option Net 2		Option Net 3	
Prescription Drug Benefit						
Per prescription copay	$10 copay		$10 copay		$10 copay	
Percentage of remaining charges paid by plan	100% after copay		100% after copay		100% after copay	
Maximum annual benefit	$200		$500		$600	

ADDITIONAL BENEFITS

Dental	80% preventive/60% basic restorative/50% major restorative $500 year maximum
Vision	$50 ind. deductible $25 eye exam benefit (one time annually) Discounts available (on average between 20% & 25%)
In Hosp.	$1,000 per confinement $100/day for 100 days
STD	50% of base pay $125 weekly maximum

This plan has three different options from which employees can choose. As you interpret this document, notice that each plan has slightly different benefits. Although the prices are not listed, you may safely assume that plans with lower deductibles and higher benefit allowances cost more than plans with higher deductibles and fewer benefits.

One difference among these three plans involves the yearly amount that they will pay for prescription drugs. If you take a prescription medication regularly, you may wish to choose a plan with a higher annual maximum to ensure that your costs are fully covered.

Health insurance plans may offer additional benefits along with core healthcare services. For example, plans may provide dental care, vision care, hospital stays, short-term disability (STD), and term life insurance.

Employee Contract

Sometimes, you may take a contract job, or a position for a specified period of time, rather than accepting a permanent staff position. The terms of contract jobs vary greatly. For example, a contract job may not offer any benefits, like paid time off.

TEMPORARY EMPLOYMENT AGREEMENT

This agreement serves to establish a temporary employment relationship between

Strunk Electrical Services, LLC (hereinafter referred to as "the Company")

AND

Virgilio Orta, 4534 Bird Street, Carlsbad, NM 88220 (hereinafter referred to as "the Temporary Employee")

1. This is not a permanent employment contract and under no circumstances may it be construed as such.

2. As per point 1 above, the Company is not liable to register the Temporary Employee for any statutory deductions normally related to permanent staff.

3. The Temporary Employee is hereby notified that should any payments under this contract be considered taxable income and that such payments will be reported to the Internal Revenue Service.

4. The Temporary Employee shall perform work as required by the Company either on odd days or weekends or full time and may be required to work overtime. This shall not be construed as a permanent relationship.

5. The Temporary Employee shall remain in the employ of the Company for a duration of three (3) months from the date of the execution of this agreement. <u>This agreement may also terminate when the job is done or should the requirements of the Company change.</u>

6. The Temporary Employee shall at all times abide by the safety rules, regulations, and working conditions of the Company and maintain the highest standard of professionalism and workmanship in accordance with Company Policy.

7. Should the Temporary Employee be found guilty of contravening the Company's Policies and Procedures, then the Temporary Employee will be disciplined accordingly and the agreement could be terminated immediately.

8. Any and all disputes or claims between the Company and the Temporary Employee arising out of this contract shall be resolved by submission of the same to a private mediation council of the Company's choice for resolution.

9. Should the labor requirement be reduced for any reason whatsoever, it will be at the employer's discretion as to how the work will be allocated and to whom. These decisions will be based on performance and not necessarily the length of service.

> If there isn't enough work for all employees (permanent and contract), the employer can take some of the promised work away from the contract employee. The employer has the right to decide who performs the available work.

> The employer has the right to end the contract early. This may occur if the job for which the employee has been hired finishes sooner than expected or if the company decides that it no longer needs the extra help.

Employee Contract

This contract gives the employer the right to end the employee's contract early. This can occur if the employer decides that the contracted worker has not performed the job well. However, the employer agrees to pay for any work that has already been completed.

11. Should the Temporary Employee wish to terminate this contract, he/she will only be entitled to receive pay for the hours that he/she has worked.

12. Should the Temporary Employee not perform his/her duties as described below and not meet the requirements and standards of the Company, the Company may terminate the contract with immediate effect and the Temporary Employee will be remunerated for the hours that he/she has worked.

13. Should the Temporary Employee withhold his/her services for whatever reason, a principle of "no work, no pay" shall apply.

The Temporary Employee agrees to perform the services described below (or in attachments):

Skilled electrical services, including but not limited to: the installation, maintenance, and repair of electrical wiring; evaluating existing electrical service for adherence to relevant building codes; maintenance of electrical systems, such as intercoms and control systems.

PAYMENT:

The Company shall compensate the Temporary Employee for the services at the rate of $22 per hour. By signing below, the Temporary Employee certifies under the penalty of perjury that the name and address given is the Temporary Employee's legal name and address.

The expected job responsibilities are clearly listed in this contract. Be sure that you enter into a contract only if you are certain of the kind of work that will be expected from you.

SIGNATURE _F. D. Strunk_
(for and on behalf of the Company)
James D. Strunk

SIGNATURE _Virgilio Orta_
(Temporary Employee)
Virgilio Orta

Non-Compete Agreement

Sometimes companies ask permanent and contract employees to sign non-compete agreements. These agreements limit the kind of other work that an employee can perform while the agreement is in effect.

NON-COMPETE AGREEMENT

1. During my employment with Maxx Auto Repairs, I will not independently accept, nor work on car repairs for payment, unless I have sought and received written approval from my supervisor or human resources.

2. Upon termination of employment with Maxx Auto Repairs for any cause whatsoever, I will not continue to work on assignments that I began at Maxx Auto Repairs unless I have sought and received written approval from an authorized representative of the company.

3. Within 180 days of termination of my employment with Maxx Auto Repairs for any cause whatsoever, I will not solicit nor accept work from any individual or firm that has been a client of the firm within the past year unless I have sought and received written approval from an authorized representative of the company.

4. Upon termination of my employment with Maxx Auto Repairs for any cause whatsoever, I will surrender to the company in good condition any and all records in my possession regarding the company's business, suppliers, prospects, and clients. Further, I will not make nor retain copies of these records.

This is a legally binding agreement. I understand that by signing it, I am agreeing to the terms set out within this document.

I understand and agree to the above mentioned employment requirements.

SIGNATURE *Keshawn A. Bell*

Keshawn A. Bell
Date: 07/18/2012

This agreement states that the employee cannot perform any other paying work that might compete with his work for the car repair company. This does not apply if he works for free. He may also receive written permission from his employer to do other work.

This agreement will not allow an employee to apply for or take any jobs from any clients of the car repair company. This restriction lasts for six months after leaving the company. This type of waiting period is common in non-compete agreements.

Performance Review

Nearly all employers provide regular performance reviews for their employees. These reviews allow workers and their managers to discuss what has been going well and what the employee can do to improve his or her performance.

> Categories such as "excellent," "good," "fair," or "poor" are often used by employers to measure employee performance. Different employers may use different categories.

EMPLOYEE PERFORMANCE REVIEW

EMPLOYEE INFORMATION

Employee Name:	Fatima Borden	Date:	04/05/2011
Department:	Accounting	Period of Review:	04/01/2010 – 04/01/2011
Reviewer:	Marilyn Mohr	Reviewer's Title:	Supervisor, Payroll Operations

PERFORMANCE EVALUATION	EXCELLENT	GOOD	FAIR	POOR	COMMENTS
Job Knowledge		✓			
Productivity		✓			
Work Quality		✓			
Technical Skills		✓			
Work Consistency	✓				
Enthusiasm		✓			
Cooperation		✓			
Attitude		✓			
Initiative			✓		Fatima does not usually seek out additional challenges in addition to her regular duties.
Work Relations	✓				Fatima is very well liked among the team and within the company at large.
Creativity			✓		Fatima's position offers relatively few opportunities to show creative problem-solving skills.
				✓	Fatima is often late, and this has not improved despite repeated discussions about the matter.
		✓			
	✓				If Fatima is assigned a task, it will be completed correctly and on time.
			✓		Fatima usually checks her e-mail once per day, and many matters go unaddressed for several hours as a result of this practice.
Overall Rating		✓			

> Typically, performance reviews are given once a year. Sometimes, a new employee may request a review after three or six months of employment. This allows the employee to get an early perspective on his or her performance.

> This employee has been performing well, but her employer has some suggestions to help her improve. Following these suggestions may help Fatima build new skills or earn a promotion.

OPPORTUNITIES FOR DEVELOPMENT

Fatima should work on arriving at the office on time and on checking her e-mail several times throughout the day. She should also seek out new challenges to grow her already strong payroll skills.

REVIEWERS COMMENTS

Fatima has performed generally good work throughout the year. She will receive a 3% pay increase effective the first pay period of April 2011.

By signing this form, you confirm that you have discussed this review in detail with your supervisor.

Fatima Borden	*4/5/2011*
Employee Signature	Date
Marilyn Mohr	*4/5/2011*
Reviewer's Signature	Date

> You may receive a pay increase following your performance review. It may be a small raise to cover increased cost-of-living. Outstanding employees may receive larger increases based on merit. However, the company will only give raises if it can afford to do so.

Union Contract

If you are a member of a labor union, then your employment is covered by the conditions of your union contract. Read your contract carefully and talk to your shop steward or union representative if you have any questions about its contents.

I.G. GRIEVANCE PROCEDURE

16. A grievance is defined as an allegation by an employee, a group of employees, or the Union that the City has violated, misapplied, or misinterpreted a term or condition of employment provided in this Agreement.

> Union contracts cover a variety of topics. This excerpt describes the procedure that the union and the employer have agreed to follow if an employee has a complaint about his or her workplace.

> This section describes the first section in the grievance process. Here, the employee simply discusses the problem with his or her supervisor. The employee may proceed with the next step in the grievance process if the first step fails to resolve the problem.

STEPS OF THE PROCEDURE

18. Except for grievances involving multiple employees, all grievances must be initiated at Step 1 of the grievance procedure.

19. A grievance affecting more than one employee shall be filed with the appointing officer or designee. Grievances affecting more than one department shall be filed with the Employee Relations Division. In the event the City disagrees with the level at which the grievance is filed, it may submit the matter to the Step it believes is appropriate for consideration of the dispute.

20. The grievant may have a Union representative present at all steps of the grievance procedure.

21. Step 1: An employee shall discuss the grievance informally with his/her immediate supervisor as soon as possible but in no case later than twenty-five (25) days from the date of the occurrence of the act or the date the grievant might reasonably have been expected to have learned of the alleged violation being grieved.

22. If the grievance is not resolved within seven (7) days after contact with the immediate supervisor, the grievant will submit the grievance in writing to the immediate supervisor on a mutually agreeable grievance form. The grievance will set forth the 4 facts of the grievance, the terms and conditions of employment claimed to have been violated, misapplied, or misinterpreted, and the remedy or solution being sought by the grievant.

23. The immediate supervisor shall respond in writing within ten (10) days following receipt of the Step 1 written grievance.

24. Step 2: A grievant dissatisfied with the immediate supervisor's response at Step 1 may appeal to the intermediate supervisor in writing within ten (10) days of receipt of the Step 1 answer. The intermediate supervisor must respond in writing within thirty (30) days of receipt of the Step 2 grievance.

25. Step 3: A grievant dissatisfied with the intermediate supervisor's response at Step 2 may appeal to the Appointing Officer or designee, in writing, within fifteen (15) days of receipt of the Step 2 answer. The Appointing Officer or designee shall respond in writing within thirty (30) days of receipt of the Step 3 grievance.

26. Step 4: A grievant dissatisfied with the Appointing Officer's response at Step 3 may appeal to the Director, Employee Relations, in writing, within twenty (20) days of receipt of the Step 3 answer. The Director shall respond to the appeal in writing within thirty-five (35) days of receipt of the Step 4 grievance.

Union Contract

Notice that even within one section of the contract, different topics are covered. This portion describes how an arbitrator—a person who helps resolve complaints—may be used as part of the formal grievance process.

ARBITRATION

27. If the Union is dissatisfied with the Step 4 response it may invoke arbitration by notifying the Director, Employee Relations, in writing within twenty (20) days of the date of the Step 4 decision.

Selection of the Arbitrator

28. When a matter is appealed to arbitration the parties shall first attempt to mutually agree upon an Arbitrator to hear the matter. In the event no agreement is reached within ten (10) working days or any extension of time mutually agreed upon, the parties shall request that the State Mediation and Conciliation Service provide the parties with a list of seven (7) potential arbitrators. The parties, by lot, shall alternately strike names from the list, and the name that remains shall be the arbitrator designated to hear the particular matter.

29. The parties may, by mutual agreement, agree to an alternate method of arbitrator selection and appointment, including the expedited appointment of an arbitrator from a list provided by the State Mediation and Conciliation Service.

Authority of the Arbitrator

30. The arbitrator shall have no authority to add to, subtract from, modify, or amend the terms of this Agreement. The decision of the Arbitrator shall be final and binding on all Parties.

Fees and Expenses of Arbitrator

31. Each party shall bear its own expenses in connection with the arbitration, including, but not limited to, witness and attorneys' fee, and any fees for preparation of the case. Transcripts shall not be required except that either party may request a transcript, provided that the party making such a request shall be solely responsible for the cost: All fees and expenses of the arbitrator and the court reporter, if any, shall be split equally between the parties.

Hearing Dates and Date of Award

32. The parties shall make their best efforts to schedule hearings within forty (40) days of selection of an arbitrator. Awards shall be due within forty (40) days following the receipt of closing arguments. As a condition of appointment, arbitrators shall be advised of this requirement and shall certify their willingness to abide by these time limits.

33. Any claim for monetary relief shall not extend more than twenty (20) days prior to the filing of a grievance, unless considerations of equity or bad faith justify a greater entitlement. The arbitrator shall be required to deduct from any monetary awards all income derived from any subsequent employment or unemployment compensation received by the employee.

34. In the event a grievance is not filed or appealed in a timely manner, it shall be dismissed. Failure of the City to timely reply to a grievance shall authorize appeal to the next grievance step.

Notice that this contract places an informal time limit on the filing of a complaint. Read your union contract to find out whether stricter time limits or other restrictions are part of your agreement.

Company Policy Manual

Most employers provide new employees with a company policy manual. Take the time to read this manual to learn about your company's policies, and keep a copy in case you need to refer to it.

Dress Code Policy

At Waverly Real Estate, it is our policy to present a professional image to the clients we serve. All staff members must be dressed appropriately at the office every day. We follow a business casual dress code. Casual clothing deserves the same attention to detail as a traditional corporate wardrobe. Creating a look that is professional and comfortable sets the right tone. The following represents some guidelines relative to the policy.

Appropriate attire for men:

- Business suits
- Dress pants
- Khakis or other slacks
- Sport coat or sweater
- Dress shirt or polo-type shirt
- Clean and well-kept shoes with socks

> This company policy explains that employees should wear professional or business casual clothing to work. This includes suits, dresses, khakis, and button-down shirts.

Appropriate attire for women:

- Pant or skirt suits
- Dresses
- Skirts and skorts
- Blazer or sweater
- Blouse or polo-type shirt
- Clean and well-kept shoes with socks or nylons

> The dress code policy also lists the kinds of clothes that employees should *not* wear to work. If you worked at this company and wore one of these articles of clothing to your job, you might be sent home to change clothes.

Inappropriate attire:

- Jeans
- Wrinkled, stained, or dirty clothing
- Sleeveless shirts and tank tops
- Undershirts or shirts meant to be worn as undergarments
- Flashy, "loud" clothing
- T-shirts with printed messages
- Overly revealing outfits
- Garments that are transparent or too tight
- Casual clothing such as jogging suits or pajamas

> Maintaining a clean, neat, professional appearance at work is always a good practice. For example, most workplaces discourage visible piercings and tattoos. Male employees should keep any facial hair well groomed. Women should avoid wearing heavy amounts of makeup.

In addition to proper dress, employees are expected to present a clean, neat, and like appearance. For example, male employees are expected to have neatly combed hair and to be clean-shaven or to have neatly trimmed mustaches and/or beards. Female employees are expected to have neatly combed hair and to not wear excessive make-up. All employees are prohibited from wearing extreme or eccentric hairstyles, clothing or jewelry that do not present a professional appearance. Reasonable accommodations will be made for employees' religious beliefs consistent with business necessity to present a professional appearance to the public.

If an employee dresses inappropriately, he or she will be counseled by a supervisor or manager. If the clothing is unduly distracting or unsafe, the employee may be sent home without pay to change clothes. Repeated disregard for the dress policy may result in disciplinary action up to and including discharge.

Company Procedure Manual

Whether you work in a shop, an office, or some other type of workplace, your company probably has set procedures for some of the tasks you do at work. It's important to read and fully follow your company's procedures.

> This procedure manual explains that keeping files ordered and consistent helps the office maintain patient information. It also ensures that anyone in the office is able to find them.

DES MOINES FAMILY PHYSICIANS	Page 1 of 1

Category: Medical records/transcription Policy #: 4510

Title: Storage and retrieval of medical records

Carla Pacheco, MD

Authorized Signature	Authorized Signature	Authorized Signature
Review Date: 07/18/2011	Review Date:	Review Date:

Policy: Storage and retrieval of medical records.

To ensure consistency and accessibility of medical records, specific procedures will be followed at Des Moines Family Physicians.

Procedures:

1. Storage

    A. Files are stored in alphabetical order by patient's last name. Although we have several physicians on site, charts will not be separated by physician.

    B. Return all charts to the main filing area by the end of the day. Do not keep charts outside of the main filing area for any reason except immediate use or hospitalization. For example, do not keep charts outside of the main filing area to track tasks that need to be completed, such as the ordering of tests.

    C. Do not remove charts from the Des Moines Family Physicians practice office for any reason.

2. Retrieval

    When removing a patient's chart, place a red "Out" chart locator in its place to alert other staff members that the chart has been removed intentionally and is not lost or misfiled. This practice will also make it easier to refile the chart.

> This section of the company procedure manual explains how to store the files at a medical office. Notice that it explains exactly how the files should be ordered and calls for all files to be returned at the end of each day.

Chapter Recap

Using the list below, place a checkmark next to the goals you achieved in Chapter 3.

▶ **In Lesson 1, you . . .**

☐ Learned how to fill out tax documents related to work

☐ Studied common new-hire paperwork

☐ Examined a direct deposit enrollment form

☐ Reviewed a sample time sheet

▶ **In Lesson 2, you . . .**

☐ Examined contracts and non-compete agreements

☐ Considered the parts of a performance review

☐ Studied an employee contract and a union contract

☐ Reviewed the information in company policy and procedure manuals

Chapter Review

Name: _____ Date: _____

▶ Directions: Review and complete the document below.

1.

OMB No. 1615-0047; Expires 08/31/12

Department of Homeland Security
U.S. Citizenship and Immigration Services

Form I-9, Employment Eligibility Verification

Read instructions carefully before completing this form. The instructions must be available during completion of this form.

ANTI-DISCRIMINATION NOTICE: It is illegal to discriminate against work-authorized individuals. Employers CANNOT specify which document(s) they will accept from an employee. The refusal to hire an individual because the documents have a future expiration date may also constitute illegal discrimination.

Section 1. Employee Information and Verification *(To be completed and signed by employee at the time employment begins.)*

Print Name: Last	First	Middle Initial	Maiden Name

Address *(Street Name and Number)*	Apt. #	Date of Birth *(month/day/year)*

City	State	Zip Code	Social Security #

I am aware that federal law provides for imprisonment and/or fines for false statements or use of false documents in connection with the completion of this form.

I attest, under penalty of perjury, that I am (check one of the following):

☐ A citizen of the United States
☐ A noncitizen national of the United States (see instructions)
☐ A lawful permanent resident (Alien #)
☐ An alien authorized to work (Alien # or Admission #) _____ until (expiration date, if applicable - *month/day/year*) _____

Employee's Signature _____ Date *(month/day/year)* _____

Preparer and/or Translator Certification *(To be completed and signed if Section 1 is prepared by a person other than the employee.)* I attest, under penalty of perjury, that I have assisted in the completion of this form and that to the best of my knowledge the information is true and correct.

Preparer's/Translator's Signature	Print Name

Address *(Street Name and Number, City, State, Zip Code)*	Date *(month/day/year)*

Section 2. Employer Review and Verification *(To be completed and signed by employer. Examine one document from List A OR examine one document from List B and one from List C, as listed on the reverse of this form, and record the title, number, and expiration date, if any, of the document(s).)*

	List A	OR	List B	AND	List C
Document title:	_____		_____		_____
Issuing authority:	_____		_____		_____
Document #:	_____		_____		_____
Expiration Date *(if any)*:	_____		_____		_____
Document #:	_____				
Expiration Date *(if any)*:	_____				

CERTIFICATION: I attest, under penalty of perjury, that I have examined the document(s) presented by the above-named employee, that the above-listed document(s) appear to be genuine and to relate to the employee named, that the employee began employment on *(month/day/year)* _____ and that to the best of my knowledge the employee is authorized to work in the United States. (State employment agencies may omit the date the employee began employment.)

Signature of Employer or Authorized Representative	Print Name	Title

Business or Organization Name and Address *(Street Name and Number, City, State, Zip Code)*	Date *(month/day/year)*

Section 3. Updating and Reverification *(To be completed and signed by employer.)*

A. New Name *(if applicable)*	B. Date of Rehire *(month/day/year)* *(if applicable)*

C. If employee's previous grant of work authorization has expired, provide the information below for the document that establishes current employment authorization.

Document Title:	Document #:	Expiration Date *(if any)*:

I attest, under penalty of perjury, that to the best of my knowledge, this employee is authorized to work in the United States, and if the employee presented document(s), the document(s) I have examined appear to be genuine and to relate to the individual.

Signature of Employer or Authorized Representative	Date *(month/day/year)*

Form I-9 (Rev. 08/07/09) Y Page 4

▶ Directions: Write your answer to the questions on the lines below.

Personal Allowances Worksheet (Keep for your records.)

A   Enter "1" for **yourself** if no one else can claim you as a dependent . . . .   **A**   1

B   Enter "1" if: {   • You are single and have only one job; or
  • You are married, have only one job, and your spouse does not work; or
  • Your wages from a second job or your spouse's wages (or the total of both) are $1,500 or less.   }   . .   **B**   0

C   Enter "1" for your **spouse.** But, you may choose to enter "-0-" if you are married and have either a working spouse or
  more than one job. (Entering "-0-" may help you avoid having too little tax withheld.) . . . .   **C**   0

D   Enter number of **dependents** (other than your spouse or yourself) you will claim on your tax return . . . . . .   **D**   1

E   Enter "1" if you will file as **head of household** on your tax return (see conditions under **Head of household** above) .   **E**   0

F   Enter "1" if you have at least $1,800 of **child or dependent care expenses** for which you plan to claim a credit . .   **F**   0
  (**Note.** Do **not** include child support payments. See Pub. 503, Child and Dependent Care Expenses, for details.)

G   **Child Tax Credit** (including additional child tax credit). See Pub. 972, Child Tax Credit, for more information.
  • If your total income will be less than $61,000 ($90,000 if married), enter "2" for each eligible child; then **less** "1" if you have three or more eligible children.
  • If your total income will be between $61,000 and $84,000 ($90,000 and $119,000 if married), enter "1" for each eligible
  child plus "1" **additional** if you have six or more eligible children.   **G**   0

H   Add lines A through G and enter total here. (**Note.** This may be different from the number of exemptions you claim on your tax return.) ▶ **H**   2

For accuracy,   {   • If you plan to **itemize or claim adjustments to income** and want to reduce your withholding, see the **Deductions**
complete all   **and Adjustments Worksheet** on page 2.
worksheets   • If you have **more than one job** or are **married and you and your spouse both work** and the combined earnings from all jobs exceed
that apply. $18,000 ($32,000 if married), see the **Two-Earners/Multiple Jobs Worksheet** on page 2 to avoid having too little tax withheld.
    • If **neither** of the above situations applies, **stop here** and enter the number from line H on line 5 of Form W-4 below.

- - - - - - - - - - - - - - - - - -   Cut here and give Form W-4 to your employer. Keep the top part for your records.   - - - - - - - - - - - - - - -

Form **W-4**
Department of the Treasury
Internal Revenue Service

Employee's Withholding Allowance Certificate

▶ Whether you are entitled to claim a certain number of allowances or exemption from withholding is
subject to review by the IRS. Your employer may be required to send a copy of this form to the IRS.

OMB No. 1545-0074

20 10

1 Type or print your first name and middle initial.	Last name	2 Your social security number
Janelle	Powers	XXX XX XXXX

Home address (number and street or rural route)	3 ☐ Single ☐ Married ☒ Married, but withhold at higher Single rate.
423 W. Harding Rd., #5	Note. If married, but legally separated, or spouse is a nonresident alien, check the "Single" box.

City or town, state, and ZIP code	4 If your last name differs from that shown on your social security card,
Hoboken, NJ 07031	check here. You must call 1-800-772-1213 for a replacement card. ▶ ☐

5   Total number of allowances you are claiming (from line **H** above **or** from the applicable worksheet on page 2) | **5** | 2 |

6   Additional amount, if any, you want withheld from each paycheck . . . . | **6** | $ 27.50 |

7   I claim exemption from withholding for 2010, and I certify that I meet **both** of the following conditions for exemption.
  • Last year I had a right to a refund of **all** federal income tax withheld because I had **no** tax liability **and**
  • This year I expect a refund of **all** federal income tax withheld because I expect to have **no** tax liability.
  If you meet both conditions, write "Exempt" here . . . . ▶ | 7 |

Under penalties of perjury, I declare that I have examined this certificate and to the best of my knowledge and belief, it is true, correct, and complete.

Employee's signature
(Form is not valid unless you sign it.) ▶ *Janelle Powers*   Date ▶ 9/11/10

8 Employer's name and address (Employer: Complete lines 8 and 10 only if sending to the IRS.)	9 Office code (optional)	10 Employer identification number (EIN)

For Privacy Act and Paperwork Reduction Act Notice, see page 2.   Cat. No. 10220Q   Form **W-4** (2010)

---

2.   Can anyone else claim Janelle as a dependent? How do you know?

_____

_____

3.   Has Janelle chosen to have more than the standard deduction withheld from each paycheck?
  If so, how much extra will be witheld?

_____

_____

Name: _____ Date: _____

▶ Directions: Write your answer to the questions on the lines below.

WEEKLY TIME SHEET

Week Ending: 11/18/11   Name: Alicia Orozco

	IN	OUT	IN	OUT	Hours	Overtime
MONDAY	7:58 a.m.	12:01 p.m.	1:03 p.m.	5:07 p.m.	8	
TUESDAY	8:02 a.m.	11:58 p.m.	1:01 p.m.	4:59 p.m.	8	
WEDNESDAY	7:31 a.m.	11:29 p.m.	12:02 p.m.	5:03 p.m.	9	1 hour
THURSDAY	8:01 a.m.	12:04 p.m.	1:08 p.m.	6:11 p.m.	9	1 hour
FRIDAY	8:04 a.m.	12:03 p.m.	1:02 p.m.	5:05 p.m.	8	
SATURDAY						
SUNDAY	8:32 a.m.	1:05 p.m.			4.5	4.5 hours

Employee Signature: *Alicia Orozco*

Employer's Signature: *S. A. Bahar*

4. How many total hours of overtime did Alicia work in the week ending 11/18/11?

_____

_____

5. Does Alicia get a paid lunch? How do you know?

_____

_____

_____

► Directions: Determine whether each of the following statements is true or false. If the statement is true, write T. If the statement is false, write F. Then rewrite the false statement to make it true.

BENEFITS SUMMARY	Option Net 1		Option Net 2		Option Net 3	
	In-Network	Out-of-Network	In-Network	Out-of-Network	In-Network	Out-of-Network
HOSPITAL INPATIENT						
Percentage paid by plan	80% after deductible	60% after deductible	80% after deductible	60% after deductible	80% after deductible	60% after deductible
Maximum annual inpatient benefit	$2,000		$10,000		$15,000	
Subject to annual limit for other hospital services	N/A		$1,000 maximum annual benefit for "other hospital services"		$1,500 maximum annual benefit for "other hospital services"	
Individual annual deductible	$250		$250		$250	
Family annual deductible	$500		$500		$500	

Clementine Affordable Health Choices Network Benefits Summary

6. The three different options for this plan offer essentially the same levels of coverage.

_____

_____

7. On this company healthcare benefits plan, Option Net 3 offers the best level of hospital inpatient coverage.

_____

_____

► Directions: Select the choice that best answers the question below.

BENEFITS SUMMARY	Option Net 1		Option Net 2		Option Net 3	
	In-Network	Out-of-Network	In-Network	Out-of-Network	In-Network	Out-of-Network
OUTPATIENT						
Doctors' Office Visits						
Per visit copay	$10 copay	$10 copay	$10 copay	$10 copay	$10 copay	$10 copay
Percentage of remaining charges paid by plan	100% after copay	80% after copay	100% after copay	80% after copay	100% after copay	80% after copay
Maximum number of visits annually	5 visits		5 visits		5 visits	
Preventive Visits						
Per visit copay	$15 copay	None	$15 copay	None	$15 copay	None
Percentage of remaining charges paid by plan	100% after copay	80%	100% after copay	80%	100% after copay	80%

8. Under these plans, how much will you pay out-of-pocket when you visit an in-network doctor because you are sick?

   A. $10

   B. $15

   C. 80% of the total cost

   D. 100% of the total cost

Name: _____ Date: _____

► Directions: Write your answer to each question on the lines below.

	Option Net 1	Option Net 2	Option Net 3
Prescription Drug Benefit			
Per prescription copay	$10 copay	$10 copay	$10 copay
Percentage of remaining charges paid by plan	100% after copay	100% after copay	100% after copay
Maximum annual benefit	$200	$500	$600

9. Which of these three healthcare plans offers the best prescription drug coverage? Why?

_____

_____

_____

10. How much will these healthcare benefits plans pay for prescription drugs after the co-pay amount?

_____

► Directions: Select the choice that best answers the question below.

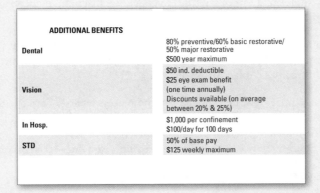

ADDITIONAL BENEFITS	
Dental	80% preventive/60% basic restorative/ 50% major restorative $500 year maximum
Vision	$50 ind. deductible $25 eye exam benefit (one time annually) Discounts available (on average between 20% & 25%)
In Hosp.	$1,000 per confinement $100/day for 100 days
STD	50% of base pay $125 weekly maximum

11. How much will these healthcare plans pay the insured person if he or she suffers from short-term disability?

A. $1,000

B. $2,500

C. $20,000

D. half of the person's base pay up to $125 a week

Chapter Review

▶ Directions: Write your answers to the questions on the lines below.

1. This is not a permanent employment contract and under no circumstances may it be construed as such.

2. As per point 1 above, the Company is not liable to register the Temporary Employee for any statutory deductions normally related to permanent staff.

3. The Temporary Employee is hereby notified that should any payments under this contract be considered taxable income and that such payments will be reported to the Internal Revenue Service.

4. The Temporary Employee shall perform work as required by the Company either on odd days or weekends or full time and may be required to work overtime. This shall not be construed as a permanent relationship.

5. The Temporary Employee shall remain in the employ of the Company for a duration of three (3) months from the date of the execution of this agreement. This agreement may also terminate when the job is done or should the requirements of the Company change.

6. The Temporary Employee shall at all times abide by the safety rules, regulations, and working conditions of the Company and maintain the highest standard of professionalism and workmanship in accordance with Company Policy.

7. Should the Temporary Employee be found guilty of contravening the Company's Policies and Procedures, then the Temporary Employee will be disciplined accordingly and the agreement could be terminated immediately.

8. Any and all disputes or claims between the Company and the Temporary Employee arising out of this contract shall be resolved by submission of the same to a private mediation council of the Company's choice for resolution.

9. Should the labor requirement be reduced for any reason whatsoever, it will be at the employer's discretion as to how the work will be allocated and to whom. These decisions will be based on performance and not necessarily the length of service.

12. How long is this employee contract in effect?

_____

_____

13. Who has more rights under this contract: the employer or the employee? Explain your answer.

_____

_____

_____

_____

Name: _____   Date: _____

▶ Directions: Determine whether each of the following statements is true or false. If the statement is true, write T. If the statement is false, write F. Then rewrite the false statement to make it true.

STEPS OF THE PROCEDURE

18.   Except for grievances involving multiple employees, all grievances must be initiated at Step 1 of the grievance procedure.

19.   A grievance affecting more than one employee shall be filed with the appointing officer or designee. Grievances affecting more than one department shall be filed with the Employee Relations Division. In the event the City disagrees with the level at which the grievance is filed, it may submit the matter to the Step it believes is appropriate for consideration of the dispute.

20.   The grievant may have a Union representative present at all steps of the grievance procedure.

21.   Step 1: An employee shall discuss the grievance informally with his/her immediate supervisor as soon as possible but in no case later than twenty-five (25) days from the date of the occurrence of the act or the date the grievant might reasonably have been expected to have learned of the alleged violation being grieved.

22.   If the grievance is not resolved within seven (7) days after contact with the immediate supervisor, the grievant will submit the grievance in writing to the immediate supervisor on a mutually agreeable grievance form. The grievance will set forth the 4 facts of the grievance, the terms and conditions of employment claimed to have been violated, misapplied, or misinterpreted, and the remedy or solution being sought by the grievant.

23.   The immediate supervisor shall respond in writing within ten (10) days following receipt of the Step 1 written grievance.

24.   Step 2: A grievant dissatisfied with the immediate supervisor's response at Step 1 may appeal to the intermediate supervisor in writing within ten (10) days of receipt of the Step 1 answer. The intermediate supervisor must respond in writing within thirty (30) days of receipt of the Step 2 grievance.

25.   Step 3: A grievant dissatisfied with the intermediate supervisor's response at Step 2 may appeal to the Appointing Officer or designee, in writing, within fifteen (15) days of receipt of the Step 2 answer. The Appointing Officer or designee shall respond in writing within thirty (30) days of receipt of the Step 3 grievance.

---

14. This portion of the union contract describes the process for handling an employee complaint.

_____

_____

15. The first step of the grievance process is to file a formal written complaint with the employee's direct supervisor.

_____

_____

▶ Directions: Determine whether each of the following statements is true or false. If the statement is true, write T. If the statement is false, write F. Then rewrite the false statement to make it true.

ARBITRATION

27. If the Union is dissatisfied with the Step 4 response it may invoke arbitration by notifying the Director, Employee Relations, in writing within twenty (20) days of the date of the Step 4 decision.

Selection of the Arbitrator

28. When a matter is appealed to arbitration the parties shall first attempt to mutually agree upon an Arbitrator to hear the matter. In the event no agreement is reached within ten (10) working days or any extension of time mutually agreed upon, the parties shall request that the State Mediation and Conciliation Service provide the parties with a list of seven (7) potential arbitrators. The parties, by lot, shall alternately strike names from the list, and the name that remains shall be the arbitrator designated to hear the particular matter.

29. The parties may, by mutual agreement, agree to an alternate method of arbitrator selection and appointment, including the expedited appointment of an arbitrator from a list provided by the State Mediation and Conciliation Service.

---

16. According to this contract, only the Union may select an arbitrator.

_____

_____

Hearing Dates and Date of Award

32. The parties shall make their best efforts to schedule hearings within forty (40) days of selection of an arbitrator. Awards shall be due within forty (40) days following the receipt of closing arguments. As a condition of appointment, arbitrators shall be advised of this requirement and shall certify their willingness to abide by these time limits.

33. Any claim for monetary relief shall not extend more than twenty (20) days prior to the filing of a grievance, unless considerations of equity or bad faith justify a greater entitlement. The arbitrator shall be required to deduct from any monetary awards all income derived from any subsequent employment or unemployment compensation received by the employee.

34. In the event a grievance is not filed or appealed in a timely manner, it shall be dismissed. Failure of the City to timely reply to a grievance shall authorize appeal to the next grievance step.

---

17. According to this contract, if a grievance is not filed in a timely manner, it will be referred to an arbitrator.

_____

_____

Name: _____ Date: _____

▶ Directions: Determine whether each of the following statements is true or false. If the statement is true, write T. If the statement is false, write F. Then rewrite the false statement to make it true.

Dress Code Policy

At Waverly Real Estate, it is our policy to present a professional image to the clients we serve. All staff members must be dressed appropriately at the office every day. We follow a business casual dress code. Casual clothing deserves the same attention to detail as a traditional corporate wardrobe. Creating a look that is professional and comfortable sets the right tone. The following represents some guidelines relative to the policy.

Appropriate attire for men:
- Business suits
- Dress pants
- Khakis or other slacks
- Sport coat or sweater
- Dress shirt or polo-type shirt
- Clean and well-kept shoes with socks

Appropriate attire for women:
- Pant or skirt suits
- Dresses
- Skirts and skorts
- Blazer or sweater
- Blouse or polo-type shirt
- Clean and well-kept shoes with socks or nylons

Inappropriate attire:
- Jeans
- Wrinkled, stained, or dirty clothing
- Sleeveless shirts and tank tops

---

18. The purpose of this dress code policy is to ensure employees dress in a manner that presents a professional image to clients.

_____

_____

19. An employee would not be in violation of the dress code is he wore nice jeans and a polo shirt to work.

_____

_____

▶ Directions: **Choose the answers that best complete the statements below.**

DES MOINES FAMILY PHYSICIANS   Page 1 of 1

Category: Medical records/transcription   Policy #: 4510

Title: Storage and retrieval of medical records

Carla Pacheco, MD

| Authorized Signature | Authorized Signature | Authorized Signature |
| Review Date: 07/18/2011 | Review Date: | Review Date: |

Policy: Storage and retrieval of medical records.

To ensure consistency and accessibility of medical records, specific procedures will be followed at Des Moines Family Physicians.

Procedures:

1. Storage

   A. Files are stored in alphabetical order by patient's last name. Although we have several physicians on site, charts will not be separated by physician.

   B. Return all charts to the main filing area by the end of the day. Do not keep charts outside of the main filing area for any reason except immediate use or hospitalization. For example, do not keep charts outside of the main filing area to track tasks that need to be completed, such as the ordering of tests.

   C. Do not remove charts from the Des Moines Family Physicians practice office for any reason.

---

20. The main purpose of this company policy is to

    A. ensure files are stored alphabetically.
    B. help the doctor determine how to read charts.
    C. maintain files so that they are easy to find.
    D. keep the office clean and tidy.

21. This policy states that patient files may be taken outside of the main filing area

    A. when they are needed for immediate use.
    B. to keep track of tasks that need to be completed.
    C. if an employee needs to order tests for a patient.
    D. at the request of the nurse practitioner.

Financial Documents

CHAPTER **4**

▶ **LESSON 1:**

Home Finance
pages 142–153

▶ **LESSON 2:**

Saving, Borrowing, and Investing
pages 154–181

▶ **LESSON 3:**

Taxes
pages 182–197

Chapter Recap	Chapter Review
☑ ___	___
☑ ___	___
☑ ___	___

▶ **CHAPTER 4:**

Recap/Review
pages 198–208

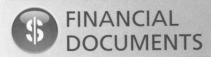

FINANCIAL DOCUMENTS

Home Finance

CONTENTS

Whether you rent or own your home, you must pay certain regular bills each month. For example, most people pay their mortgage or rent on a monthly basis. You also may receive monthly or quarterly bills for your utilities, such as electric, gas, water, telephone, and cable television services. If you live in an apartment, some of these bills may be included in your monthly rent payment. Owners of condominiums and some homes must pay homeowner's association fees for shared services, such as landscaping or snow removal.

No matter the type of home you have, paying your bills on time will help you feel secure in knowing that you have the essential services you need. For extra peace of mind, you may wish to take out special insurance plans that cover damages or loss to your home and belongings. Learning to read documents in this lesson will make managing your home finances and services much easier. Studying the examples in this lesson will help you interpret or complete the documents in the chapter review and in real life.

E-bills

Most utility companies and service providers now offer the option of receiving your monthly bill online. If you sign up for this service, you will receive an e-mail when your latest bill is available.

Electric Bill

Devices that you plug into the wall use electricity that you purchase from a regional electric company. The company tracks your electricity use with a meter outside your home or apartment building.

> By examining the summary of charges, you can see the amount of electricity you used. On this bill, you can see that the customer used 268 kWh, or kilowatt hours, in the 24 days of the billing period. The electric company determines your kWh usage by subtracting the hours from your previous reading.

New England Electric

SERVICE FOR	BILLING PERIOD		
Lena Wahler	Aug 5, 2011 to Aug 29, 2011		
462 Bay State Blvd., #3	ACCOUNT NUMBER	PLEASE PAY BY	AMOUNT DUE
Brockton, MA 02301	999990 – 99999	September 29, 2011	**$70.54**

Account Balance:

Total Amount Due at Last Billing	55.65
	−55.65
	0.00
	70.54
Balance Due ▶	**$70.54**

> Some states allow you to shop around to select the cheapest power-generating company. For instance, one company may have a lower generation charge than its competitor. You are automatically signed up with the primary power company when you set up your service. However, you may be able find a better deal with another company. Your electric service will otherwise remain the same.

Details of Current Charges:

Service Period	No. of days	Current Reading	Previous Reading	Total Usage
Aug 5 – Aug 29	24	32097	31811	268 kWh

Meter Number   33333333

> Several different charges contribute to your total electric bill. The electric company charges you for transmission, distribution, and transition of your electricity. You also pay a charge for energy efficiency and renewable energy. You pay the electric company for the power you use and for the services it provides.

Delivery Service
RATE Residential Regular R-1

Transmission Charge	0.0266 x 286 kWh	7.61
Distribution Charge	0.0233 x 286 kWh	6.66
Transition Charge	0.0137 x 286 kWh	3.92
Energy Efficiency	0.0266 x 286 kWh	7.61
Renewable Energy	0.0025 x 286 kWh	.72

Total Delivery Services ▶ **$26.52**

Supplier Services
Basic-Fixed

Generation Charge	0.1539 x 286 kWh	44.02

Total Supplier Services ▶ **$44.02**

Account Balance ▶ **$70.54**

Water Bill

Most city water departments bill you for your actual consumption of water. Your water bill may also contain charges for other city services such as trash pickup. You can save water by taking shorter showers and running fuller loads of laundry. Both will help reduce your water bill.

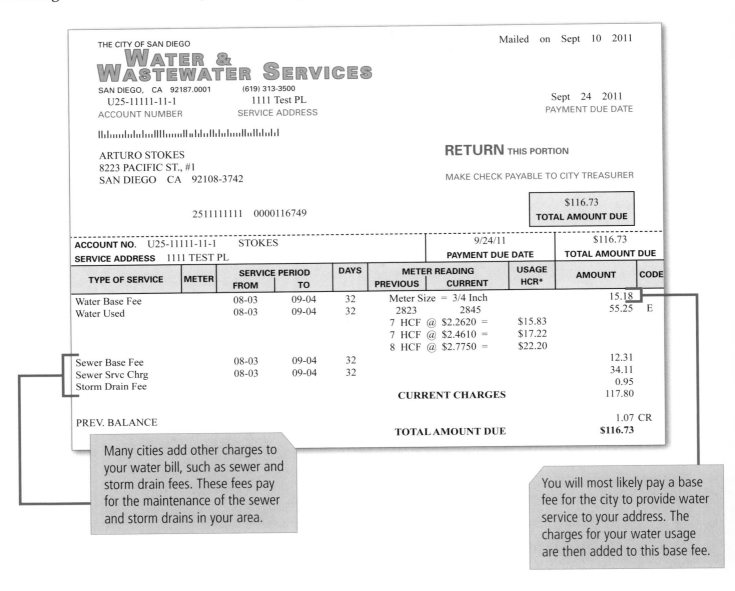

THE CITY OF SAN DIEGO

WATER & WASTEWATER SERVICES

SAN DIEGO, CA 92187.0001
U25-11111-11-1
ACCOUNT NUMBER

(619) 313-3500
1111 Test PL
SERVICE ADDRESS

Mailed on Sept 10 2011

Sept 24 2011
PAYMENT DUE DATE

ARTURO STOKES
8223 PACIFIC ST., #1
SAN DIEGO CA 92108-3742

RETURN THIS PORTION

MAKE CHECK PAYABLE TO CITY TREASURER

2511111111   0000116749

$116.73
TOTAL AMOUNT DUE

| ACCOUNT NO. U25-11111-11-1 STOKES | 9/24/11 | $116.73 |
| SERVICE ADDRESS 1111 TEST PL | PAYMENT DUE DATE | TOTAL AMOUNT DUE |

TYPE OF SERVICE	METER	SERVICE PERIOD FROM	SERVICE PERIOD TO	DAYS	METER READING PREVIOUS	METER READING CURRENT	USAGE HCR*	AMOUNT	CODE
Water Base Fee		08-03	09-04	32	Meter Size = 3/4 Inch			15.18	
Water Used		08-03	09-04	32	2823	2845		55.25	E
					7 HCF @ $2.2620 =	$15.83			
					7 HCF @ $2.4610 =	$17.22			
					8 HCF @ $2.7750 =	$22.20			
Sewer Base Fee		08-03	09-04	32				12.31	
Sewer Srvc Chrg		08-03	09-04	32				34.11	
Storm Drain Fee								0.95	
					CURRENT CHARGES			117.80	
PREV. BALANCE								1.07 CR	
					TOTAL AMOUNT DUE			**$116.73**	

Many cities add other charges to your water bill, such as sewer and storm drain fees. These fees pay for the maintenance of the sewer and storm drains in your area.

You will most likely pay a base fee for the city to provide water service to your address. The charges for your water usage are then added to this base fee.

Gas Bill

While some homes use electricity to power appliances and heating systems, others use natural gas. That gas powers appliances such as stoves, ovens, and clothes dryers. Some furnaces also rely on natural gas as a power source.

> Your gas furnace usage may vary depending on the time of year. Many gas companies offer you the option of signing up for budget or level billing. This allows you to spread over the course of the year high charges that you may incur during the cold winter months. You then pay one flat rate each month.

Greenbriar Gas

For more information about your bill, see reverse
Or call **1-800-555-5555**

Name	AUTUMN GIBSON
Service Location	422 E. 27TH ST., #14
	CHARLESTON, WV 25303

Residental

Natural Gas Account Number

1 09 33 555 498775 0
Please Use When Calling or Writing

Rate Code 201   Check digit 0533   Page 1 or 1

Your Gas Usage

ACTUAL READING   ESTIMATED

Your average cost per day for this bill is $0.68.

Your next meter reading is schedule for OCT 22, 2012

Meter Reading Information   #T4546450

Present SEP 23, 2012 – Estimated Reading	5
Previous AUG 22, 2012 – Actual Reading	4
Total MCF Used for 32 Days	1

Your Last Bill

Account Balance Last Bill	38.50
Automatic Payment Received – SEP 04, 2012	38.50 CR
Account Balance Remaining	$0.00

Your Current Greenbriar Gas Charges

$14.9970 per MCF	
Charge for 1 MCF	14.99
Customer Charge	8.50
Current Billing Charges	$21.49
Account Balance	$21.49
TOTAL PAYMENT DUE	**$21.49**

** $21.49 WILL BE DEDUCTED AUTOMATICALLY ON OCT 06, 2012 **

General Information

Greenbriar Gas has a new phone number. For natural gas service emergencies, call 1-800-555-5555. For Customer Service, call the same number between 8:00am and 8:00pm weekdays and 8:00am and 4:30pm on weekends.

You can pay on the internet or by phone. Visit www.paymybill.com/greenbriargas or call 1-800-555-5555. Service fees apply.

> Some utility companies offer automatic payment plans. If you sign up for this plan, the amount of your most recent gas bill will automatically be taken out of the checking account or credit card that you select. This means that your payments will always be on time.

Billing Date	Total Payment Due After Due Date	Late Payment Charge if Paid After Due Date	Due Date
SEP 24, 2012	**$21.49**	**$0.00**	**OCT 14, 2012**

Greenbriar Gas

▲ Detach ▲
Here

PO BOX 5099
CHARLESTON WV 25301

Total Payment Due After Due Date	Deduct Date
$21.49	**OCT 06, 2012**

"X" if changes on back   Greenbriar Gas Account Amount Paid

IІІІııІІІ..ІІІІ..ІІ..ІІІІ..ІІ..ІІ..ІІ..ІІ..ІІ..ІІ..ІІ..ІІ..ІІ

7 20 20 206 208201 5 T5
AUTUMN GIBSON
422 E. 27TH ST., #14
CHARLESTON, WV 25303

IІІІ..ІІ..ІІ..ІІІІІ..ІІ..ІІ..ІІ..ІІ..ІІ..ІІ..ІІ..ІІ..ІІ..ІІ
GREENBRIAR GAS
PO BOX 5099
CHARLESTON WV 25301

000000000   9   053372020206209201   00002149   9   0002149   01

Cable Bill

You can choose many different levels of service when you sign up for cable. The most basic, and cheapest, package usually consists of about 13 network channels. You can pay more for cable channels and even more for premium channels, such as HBO.

ACCOUNT NUMBER	ACCOUNT NAME	CLOSING DATE
AKJN509748	KENNY FREEMAN	08/01/2011

ADDRESS AT WHICH SERVICE PROVIDED	SERVICE PERIOD FROM TO	BILLING PHONE #	REPAIR PHONE #	SERVICE PHONE #
725 10TH ST.	07/01/2011 07/31/2011	859–555–9214	859–555–1111	859–555–2222

DATE	DESCRIPTION	AMOUNT
	BALANCE FORWARD	71.89
01/01/11	PAYMENT – THANK YOU	–72.00
02/01/11	BASIC CABLE SERVICE	19.90
02/01/11	PREMIUM-EXPANDED BASIC	33.60
02/01/11	SA DIG BAS-PACKAGE	14.95
02/01/11	FCC FEES	0.08
02/01/11	STATE EXCISE-CABLE TV	2.05
02/01/11	MULTI-VIDEO TV CABLE	1.64

State and federal governments levy special taxes on cable television services. If you are shopping for a new plan, keep in mind that you pay a little bit more than the stated price each month due to these taxes.

Cable providers typically offer different programming packages. Cheaper packages offer fewer channels but normally lack HD-quality broadcast signals. Expensive packages offer HD viewing and more channels. If you watch just a few channels regularly, you may be able to save money with a smaller package.

YOUR ONLINE BILL-PAY PASSWORD: XXX-XXXXXX

PRIOR BALANCE	CHARGES	CREDIT	AMOUNT DUE
71.89	72.22	-$72.00	$72.11

BLUEGRASS CABLE
PO BOX 0295
LEXINGTON KY 40501

RETURN SERVICE REQUESTED

ACCOUNT NUMBER	SERVICE PERIOD
AKJN509748	07/01/2011 TO 07/31/2011

CLOSING DATE	DUE DATE	AMOUNT DUE
08/01/2011	08/16/2011	$72.11

SERVICE ADDRESS	AMOUNT ENCLOSED
	$

KENNY FREEMAN
725 10TH ST.
LEXINGTON KY 40502

00160160950202000000228

If you overpay your balance owed, you will receive a credit on your next month's bill.

Bundled Cable Bill

Many cable companies now offer telephone and Internet service, just as many phone companies now offer television programming through their own wired services. Choosing a bundled plan may help you save money if you use all of these services.

To avoid a late fee, you may wish to write the due dates of all of your bills on a calendar where you can easily refer to them. This will help you remember to pay them on time.

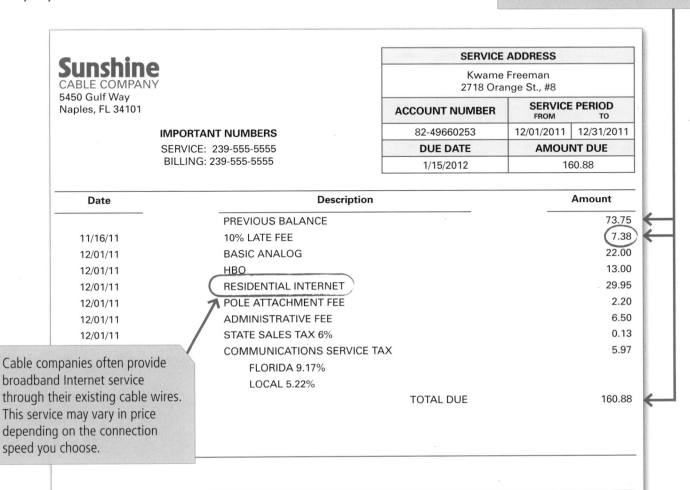

Sunshine
CABLE COMPANY
5450 Gulf Way
Naples, FL 34101

IMPORTANT NUMBERS
SERVICE: 239-555-5555
BILLING: 239-555-5555

SERVICE ADDRESS		
Kwame Freeman 2718 Orange St., #8		
ACCOUNT NUMBER	**SERVICE PERIOD** FROM	TO
82-49660253	12/01/2011	12/31/2011
DUE DATE	**AMOUNT DUE**	
1/15/2012	160.88	

Date	Description	Amount
	PREVIOUS BALANCE	73.75
11/16/11	10% LATE FEE	7.38
12/01/11	BASIC ANALOG	22.00
12/01/11	HBO	13.00
12/01/11	RESIDENTIAL INTERNET	29.95
12/01/11	POLE ATTACHMENT FEE	2.20
12/01/11	ADMINISTRATIVE FEE	6.50
12/01/11	STATE SALES TAX 6%	0.13
	COMMUNICATIONS SERVICE TAX	5.97
	FLORIDA 9.17%	
	LOCAL 5.22%	
	TOTAL DUE	160.88

Cable companies often provide broadband Internet service through their existing cable wires. This service may vary in price depending on the connection speed you choose.

Accounts paid after the 15th of each month are delinquent and will be charged a 10% late fee. Failure to keep your account current can jeopardize your standing and may result in disconnection. To avoid unnecessary charges, please notify Sunshine Cable Company 30 days in advance of any changes to your service including disconnection.

- - - - PLEASE DETACH AT PERFORATION AND RETURN THE BOTTOM PORTION WITH MAILED PAYMENT, USE ENCLOSED ENVELOPE TO ENSURE PROPER ROUTING. - - - -

Sunshine
CABLE COMPANY
5450 Gulf Way
Naples, FL 34101

Remember to include your account number on the check if you mail one to pay your bill. Always include this portion of the bill with your check or money order to ensure prompt processing of your payment.

SERVICE ADDRESS		
Kwame Freeman 2718 Orange St., #8		
ACCOUNT NUMBER	**SERVICE PERIOD** FROM	TO
82-49660253	12/01/2011	12/31/2011
DUE DATE	**AMOUNT DUE**	
1/15/2012	160.88	

MAKES CHECKS PAYABLE TO: Sunshine Cable

PLEASE INDICATE AMOUNT ENCLOSED $

Ilhluuuluululuullllumulululdlhluuulhldlulul
**********AUTO**5-DIGIT 32580 11## -1
KWAME FREEMAN
2718 ORANGE ST., #8
NAPLES, FL 34101

lulullullluuulululluluullluullllulululuull
SUNSHINE CABLE COMPANY
5450 GULF WAY
NAPLES, FL 34101

Home Mortgage Statement

When you buy a home, you will probably pay for it over the course of 15 or 30 years. Choosing a 30-year mortgage will help keep your monthly payment low. However, keep in mind that you will pay a great deal more interest and make many more payments.

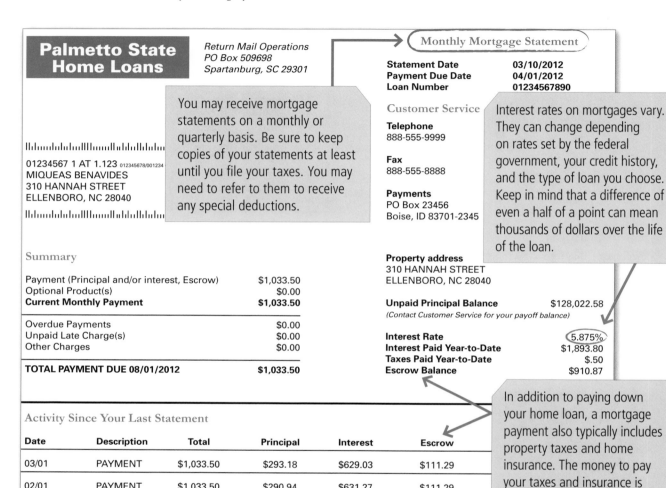

Palmetto State Home Loans

Return Mail Operations
PO Box 509698
Spartanburg, SC 29301

You may receive mortgage statements on a monthly or quarterly basis. Be sure to keep copies of your statements at least until you file your taxes. You may need to refer to them to receive any special deductions.

01234567 1 AT 1.123 012345678/001234
MIQUEAS BENAVIDES
310 HANNAH STREET
ELLENBORO, NC 28040

Summary

Payment (Principal and/or interest, Escrow)	$1,033.50
Optional Product(s)	$0.00
Current Monthly Payment	**$1,033.50**
Overdue Payments	$0.00
Unpaid Late Charge(s)	$0.00
Other Charges	$0.00
TOTAL PAYMENT DUE 08/01/2012	**$1,033.50**

Monthly Mortgage Statement

Statement Date	03/10/2012
Payment Due Date	04/01/2012
Loan Number	01234567890

Customer Service

Telephone
888-555-9999

Fax
888-555-8888

Payments
PO Box 23456
Boise, ID 83701-2345

Interest rates on mortgages vary. They can change depending on rates set by the federal government, your credit history, and the type of loan you choose. Keep in mind that a difference of even a half of a point can mean thousands of dollars over the life of the loan.

Property address
310 HANNAH STREET
ELLENBORO, NC 28040

Unpaid Principal Balance $128,022.58
(Contact Customer Service for your payoff balance)

Interest Rate	5.875%
Interest Paid Year-to-Date	$1,893.80
Taxes Paid Year-to-Date	$.50
Escrow Balance	$910.87

In addition to paying down your home loan, a mortgage payment also typically includes property taxes and home insurance. The money to pay your taxes and insurance is estimated and held in an escrow account. When those bills are due, usually once a year, your mortgage company pays them for you from the escrow account.

Activity Since Your Last Statement

Date	Description	Total	Principal	Interest	Escrow
03/01	PAYMENT	$1,033.50	$293.18	$629.03	$111.29
02/01	PAYMENT	$1,033.50	$290.94	$631.27	$111.29
01/01	PAYMENT	$1,033.50	$288.70	$633.50	$111.29

In the early years of your mortgage, most of each payment you make will go toward interest on your loan. As time goes on, each payment will contribute more and more to paying off the principal—the actual loan amount—of your mortgage.

Home Mortgage Bill/Statement

When you take out a home mortgage, you may decide to automatically deduct your payment from your checking account. Otherwise, you will typically receive a monthly bill.

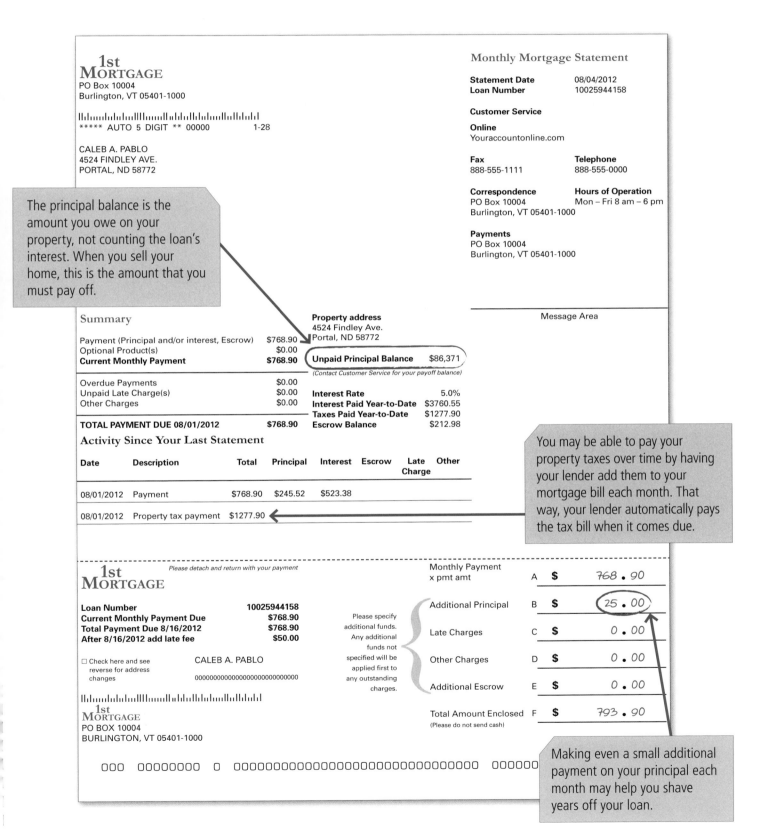

1st MORTGAGE
PO Box 10004
Burlington, VT 05401-1000

\|\|\|..\|\|.\|\|..\|\|\|\|\|\|..\|\|..\|\|.\|\|\|.\|\|\|.\|..\|\|\|.\|\|.\|\|.\|\|.\|
***** AUTO 5 DIGIT ** 00000   1-28

CALEB A. PABLO
4524 FINDLEY AVE.
PORTAL, ND 58772

Monthly Mortgage Statement

Statement Date	08/04/2012
Loan Number	10025944158

Customer Service

Online
Youraccountonline.com

Fax	**Telephone**
888-555-1111	888-555-0000

Correspondence	**Hours of Operation**
PO Box 10004	Mon – Fri 8 am – 6 pm
Burlington, VT 05401-1000	

Payments
PO Box 10004
Burlington, VT 05401-1000

Message Area

> The principal balance is the amount you owe on your property, not counting the loan's interest. When you sell your home, this is the amount that you must pay off.

Summary

Payment (Principal and/or interest, Escrow)	$768.90
Optional Product(s)	$0.00
Current Monthly Payment	**$768.90**
Overdue Payments	$0.00
Unpaid Late Charge(s)	$0.00
Other Charges	$0.00
TOTAL PAYMENT DUE 08/01/2012	**$768.90**

Property address
4524 Findley Ave.
Portal, ND 58772

Unpaid Principal Balance	**$86,371**

(Contact Customer Service for your payoff balance)

Interest Rate	5.0%
Interest Paid Year-to-Date	$3760.55
Taxes Paid Year-to-Date	$1277.90
Escrow Balance	$212.98

Activity Since Your Last Statement

Date	Description	Total	Principal	Interest	Escrow	Late Charge	Other
08/01/2012	Payment	$768.90	$245.52	$523.38			
08/01/2012	Property tax payment	$1277.90					

> You may be able to pay your property taxes over time by having your lender add them to your mortgage bill each month. That way, your lender automatically pays the tax bill when it comes due.

1st MORTGAGE   *Please detach and return with your payment*

Loan Number	10025944158
Current Monthly Payment Due	$768.90
Total Payment Due 8/16/2012	$768.90
After 8/16/2012 add late fee	$50.00

☐ Check here and see reverse for address changes

CALEB A. PABLO

00000000000000000000000000000

\|\|.\|..\|.\|.\|..\|\|\|\|\|..\|.\|.\|.\|\|.\|..\|.\|\|.\|.\|.\|

1st MORTGAGE
PO BOX 10004
BURLINGTON, VT 05401-1000

Please specify additional funds. Any additional funds not specified will be applied first to any outstanding charges.

Monthly Payment x pmt amt	A	$	768.90
Additional Principal	B	$	25.00
Late Charges	C	$	0.00
Other Charges	D	$	0.00
Additional Escrow	E	$	0.00
Total Amount Enclosed	F	$	793.90

(Please do not send cash)

☐☐☐   ☐☐☐☐☐☐☐   ☐   ☐☐☐☐☐☐☐☐☐☐☐☐☐☐☐☐☐☐☐☐☐☐☐☐☐☐☐☐☐   ☐☐☐☐☐☐

> Making even a small additional payment on your principal each month may help you shave years off your loan.

Homeowner's Association Bill

If you own a condominium or house, you may pay a special homeowner's association, or HOA, fee. This fee will be in addition to your mortgage and property taxes. It covers services and items that are shared among all of the units, such as roof repair or lawn maintenance.

**THE ARMITAGE CONDOMINIUM
UNIT OWNERS ASSOCIATION**

Kelley Mickel, Treasurer
1834 Pacific Drive
Portland, OR 97752

June 1, 2011

Depending on the bylaws of your homeowner's association, you may be responsible for paying HOA fees on a monthly, quarterly, semi-annual, or even annual basis. You can ask your homeowner's association president or treasurer for more details.

TO: Condo Owner

RE: SEMI-ANNUAL ASSESSMENT for The Armitage Condominium Unit Owners Association for the period July 1, 2011 thru December 31, 2011

In accordance with the bylaws of The Armitage Condominium Association, and as approved by The Armitage Board of Directors, an assessment of $310 per month is payable on a semi-annual basis.

Therefore, for the period of July 1, 2011 thru December 31, 2011 an assessment of $1860.00 is due and payable by July 1, 2011. Please note late fees will be assessed in accordance with Rules and Regulations. Please make your check payable to THE ARMITAGE CONDOMINIUM ASSOCIATION and remit to:

The Armitage Condominium Association
Kelley Mickel, Treasurer
1834 Pacific Drive
Portland, OR 97752

Thank you,

Kelley Mickel

Kelley Mickel, Treasurer
The Armitage Condominium Unit Owners Association

The amount of an HOA fee can vary greatly depending on your area, the size and age of the units, and the types of services provided by the homeowner's association. Keep in mind that HOA fees can increase on a yearly basis. When you shop for a condo or any home with a HOA, be sure to ask about the HOA fee to avoid any unpleasant surprises.

Please cut off this portion and return with your payment.

Condo Owner Name: _____

Unit Address: _____

Amount enclosed: _____

Flood Insurance Plan

If you live near a coastline or river bed at risk of flooding, you may be required by your lender to carry flood insurance. Regular homeowner's or renter's insurance does not normally cover water damage in the event of a flood.

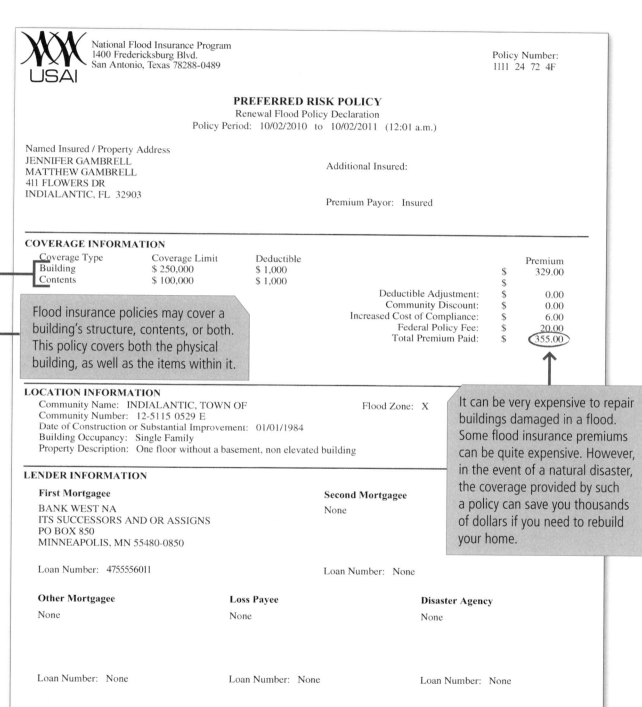

National Flood Insurance Program
1400 Fredericksburg Blvd.
San Antonio, Texas 78288-0489

USAI

Policy Number:
1111 24 72 4F

PREFERRED RISK POLICY
Renewal Flood Policy Declaration
Policy Period: 10/02/2010 to 10/02/2011 (12:01 a.m.)

Named Insured / Property Address
JENNIFER GAMBRELL
MATTHEW GAMBRELL
411 FLOWERS DR
INDIALANTIC, FL 32903

Additional Insured:

Premium Payor: Insured

COVERAGE INFORMATION

Coverage Type	Coverage Limit	Deductible		Premium
Building	$ 250,000	$ 1,000	$	329.00
Contents	$ 100,000	$ 1,000	$	

Deductible Adjustment:	$	0.00
Community Discount:	$	0.00
Increased Cost of Compliance:	$	6.00
Federal Policy Fee:	$	20.00
Total Premium Paid:	$	355.00

> Flood insurance policies may cover a building's structure, contents, or both. This policy covers both the physical building, as well as the items within it.

LOCATION INFORMATION
Community Name: INDIALANTIC, TOWN OF
Community Number: 12-5115 0529 E
Date of Construction or Substantial Improvement: 01/01/1984
Building Occupancy: Single Family
Property Description: One floor without a basement, non elevated building

Flood Zone: X

> It can be very expensive to repair buildings damaged in a flood. Some flood insurance premiums can be quite expensive. However, in the event of a natural disaster, the coverage provided by such a policy can save you thousands of dollars if you need to rebuild your home.

LENDER INFORMATION

First Mortgagee

BANK WEST NA
ITS SUCCESSORS AND OR ASSIGNS
PO BOX 850
MINNEAPOLIS, MN 55480-0850

Second Mortgagee
None

Loan Number: 4755556011

Loan Number: None

Other Mortgagee
None

Loss Payee
None

Disaster Agency
None

Loan Number: None

Loan Number: None

Loan Number: None

THIS IS NOT A BILL

SEE POLICY CONTRACT FOR SPECIFIC TERMS, CONDITIONS AND EXCLUSIONS

A COPY OF THIS DOCUMENT IS AVAILABLE ON USA1.COM

Contact USAI at 1-800-555-USAI (8724) between 7:30 a.m. and 6:00 p.m. CST Monday – Friday or 8:00 a.m. to 4:30 p.m. CST on Saturday

Renter's Insurance

Renter's insurance provides coverage for the goods you own inside a rental house or apartment. This means that you can make a claim if you are the victim of a burglary or a fire that results in the loss of some of your possessions.

This policy details the limits of liability. For example, this insurance company would pay up to $100,000 in family liability protection. A deductible refers to the portion of a loss you would pay before your insurance would kick in. In this policy, for example, you must pay the first $500 of any camera loss.

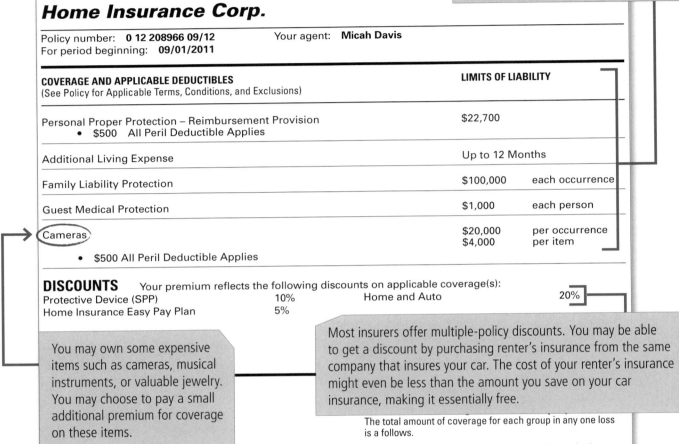

Home Insurance Corp.

Policy number: **0 12 208966 09/12**   Your agent: **Micah Davis**
For period beginning: **09/01/2011**

COVERAGE AND APPLICABLE DEDUCTIBLES (See Policy for Applicable Terms, Conditions, and Exclusions)	LIMITS OF LIABILITY	
Personal Proper Protection – Reimbursement Provision • $500 All Peril Deductible Applies	$22,700	
Additional Living Expense	Up to 12 Months	
Family Liability Protection	$100,000	each occurrence
Guest Medical Protection	$1,000	each person
Cameras • $500 All Peril Deductible Applies	$20,000 $4,000	per occurrence per item

DISCOUNTS   Your premium reflects the following discounts on applicable coverage(s):

Protective Device (SPP)   10%   Home and Auto   20%
Home Insurance Easy Pay Plan   5%

You may own some expensive items such as cameras, musical instruments, or valuable jewelry. You may choose to pay a small additional premium for coverage on these items.

Most insurers offer multiple-policy discounts. You may be able to get a discount by purchasing renter's insurance from the same company that insures your car. The cost of your renter's insurance might even be less than the amount you save on your car insurance, making it essentially free.

Property We Cover Under Coverage C:

1. Personal property owned or used by an insured person anywhere in the world. When personal property is located at a residence other than the **residence premises**, coverage is limed to 10% of **Coverage C – Personal Property Protection**. This limitation does not apply to personal property in a newly acquired principal residence for the 30 days immediately after you begin to move property there or to personal property in student dormitory, fraternity, or sorority housing.

2. At **your** option, personal property owned by a guest or **residence employee** while the property is in a residence **you** are occupying.

Limitation On Certain Personal Property:

Limitations apply to the following groups of personal property if the personal property can reasonably be considered a part

The total amount of coverage for each group in any one loss is a follows.

1. $200 – Money, bullion, bank notes, coins and other numismatic property.

2. $200 – Property used or intended for use in a **business** while the property is away from the **residence premises**.

   This does not include electronic data processing equipment or the recording or storage media used with that equipment.

3. $1,000 – Property used or intended for use in a **business**, including property held as samples or for sale or delivery after sale, while the property is on the **residence premises**. This does not include electronic data processing equipment or the recording or storage media used with that equipment.

4. $1,000 – Trading cards, subject a maximum amount of $250 per card.

Renter's Insurance

Some categories of goods have coverage limits. You may need to take out another policy to cover expensive items. For example, this policy only covers jewelry worth up to $1,000.

5. $1,000 – Accounts, bills, deeds, evidences of debt, letters of credit, notes other than bank notes, passports, securities, tickets, and stamps, including philatelic property.

6. $1,000 – Manuscript including documents stored on electronic media.

7. $1,000 – Watercraft, including their attached or unattached trailers, furnishings, equipment, parts and motors.

8. $1,000 – Trailers not used with watercraft.

9. $1,000 – Theft of jewelry, watches, precious and semi-precious stones, gold other than goldware, silver other than silverware, platinum and furs, including any item containing fur that represents its principal value.

10. $1,000 – Any motorized land vehicle parts, equipment, or accessories not attached to or located in or upon any motorized land vehicle.

11. $2,000 – Theft of firearms.

12. $2,500 – Theft of silverware, pewterware, or goldware.

13. $5,000 – Electronic data processing equipment and the recording or storage media used with that equipment whether or not the equipment is used in a business. Recording or storage media will be covered only up to:

    a) the retail value of the media, if pre-programmed, or

    b) the retail value of the media in clank or unexposed form, if blank or self-programmed.

14. $10,000 – Theft of rugs, including, but not limited to any handwoven silk or wool rug, carpet, tapestry, wall-hanging or other similar article whose principal value is determined by its color, design, quality of wool or silk, quality of weaving, condition or age, subject to a maximum amount of $2,500 per item.

Property We Do Not Cover Under Coverage C:

1. Personal property specifically described and insured by this or any other insurance.

2. Animals.

3. Motorized land vehicles, including, but not limited to any land vehicle powered or assisted by a motor or engine. **We** do not over any motorized land vehicle parts, equipment or accessories attached to or located in or upon any motorized land vehicle. **We** do not cover motorized land vehicles designed for assisting the handicapped or used solely for the service of the **insured premises** and not licensed for use on the public roads.

4. Aircraft and aircraft parts. This does not include model or hobby craft not designed to carry people or cargo.

5. Property of roomers, boarders, tenants not related to an **insured person**.

6. Property located away from the **residence premises** and rented or held for rental to others.

7. Any device, cellular communication system, radar signal reception system, accessory, or antenna designed for reproducing, detecting, receiving, transmitting, recording or playing back data, sound, or picture that may be powered by electricity from a motorized land vehicle or watercraft and while in or upon a motorized land vehicle or watercraft.

Losses We Cover Under Coverage C

We will cover sudden and accidental direct physical loss to the property described in **Coverage C – Personal Property Protection**, except as limited or excluded in this policy, caused by:

Some goods cannot be insured under renter's insurance. For example, this policy does not cover animals. You could not claim the value of your pet if it were lost or stolen.

    a) loss to covered property inside a building, caused by rain, snow, sleet, sand or dust unless the wind or hail first damages the roof or walls and the wind forces rain, snow, sleet, sand or dust through the damaged roof or wall.

    b) loss to watercraft and their trailers, furnishings, equipment and motors unless inside a fully enclosed building. However, we do cover canoes and rowboats on the **residence premises**.

3. Explosion.

4. Riot or Civil Commotion, including pillage and looting during, and at the site of, the riot or civil commotion.

5. Aircraft, including self-propelled missiles and spacecraft.

6. Vehicles.

7. Smoke.

    We do not cover loss caused by smoke from the manufacturing of controlled substances, agricultural smudging or industrial operations.

8. Vandalism and Malicious Mischief.

    We do not cover vandalism or malicious mischief **if your residence premises** has been vacant or unoccupied for more than 30 consecutive days immediately prior to the vandalism or malicious mischief.

Most home and renter's insurance policies do not cover vandalism to your home if it is unoccupied for a long period of time. For example, you may rent a share of a beach house. Your policy would not cover vandalism if the house were unoccupied during the winter months.

FINANCIAL DOCUMENTS

Saving, Borrowing, and Investing

CONTENTS

Tech TIP

Online Lenders

Some Web sites allow you to submit just one mortgage application online and receive pre-approval offers from several lenders. This may help you develop an idea of the types of loans for which you may qualify or even help you find a mortgage that works for you.

Rob and Maya were excited to discover that they were going to become parents. They decided that it was time to buy a home in which to raise their new family. After a few weeks of looking, they found the perfect townhouse. They couldn't wait to move in.

First, though, Rob and Maya had to fill out many legal documents. They applied for a mortgage with their bank and reviewed numerous forms explaining their loan options and costs. When they finally closed on their new home, they were left with a huge stack of important paperwork. Luckily, their real estate agent helped them read and understand all of these documents.

Like Rob and Maya, you may decide to buy a home. If so, understanding the type of paperwork you will see may help prepare you for the process. This lesson will help you become familiar with paperwork related to saving for retirement and buying a car or a home. Studying the examples in this lesson will help you interpret or complete the documents in the chapter review and in real life.

Personal Financial Statement

A stock is a share, or portion, of a particular company or corporation. A mutual fund is a collection of professionally managed investments, mostly in the form of stocks. You will receive a monthly or quarterly statement of your account if you invest in stocks or mutual funds.

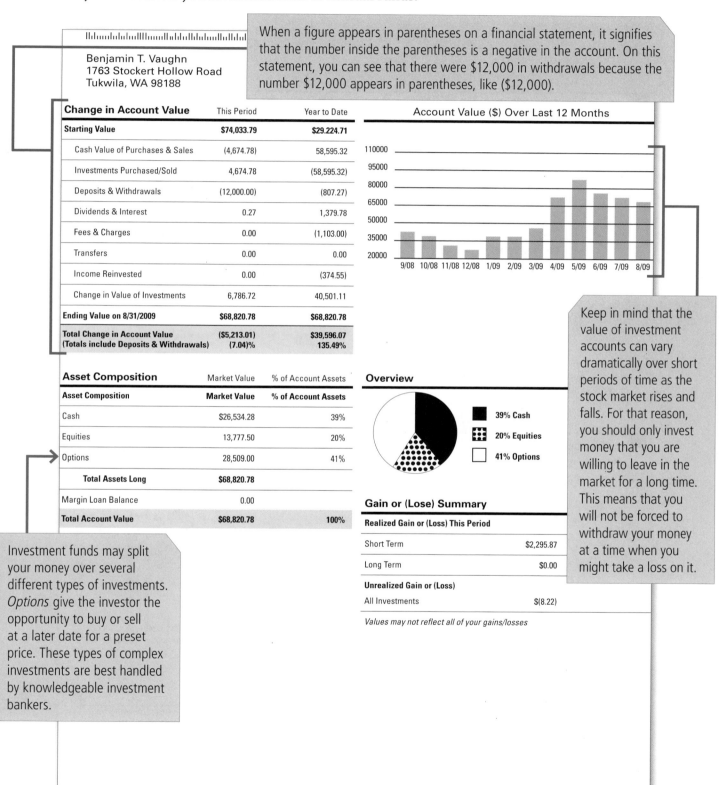

When a figure appears in parentheses on a financial statement, it signifies that the number inside the parentheses is a negative in the account. On this statement, you can see that there were $12,000 in withdrawals because the number $12,000 appears in parentheses, like ($12,000).

Benjamin T. Vaughn
1763 Stockert Hollow Road
Tukwila, WA 98188

Change in Account Value

Change in Account Value	This Period	Year to Date
Starting Value	$74,033.79	$29.224.71
Cash Value of Purchases & Sales	(4,674.78)	58,595.32
Investments Purchased/Sold	4,674.78	(58,595.32)
Deposits & Withdrawals	(12,000.00)	(807.27)
Dividends & Interest	0.27	1,379.78
Fees & Charges	0.00	(1,103.00)
Transfers	0.00	0.00
Income Reinvested	0.00	(374.55)
Change in Value of Investments	6,786.72	40,501.11
Ending Value on 8/31/2009	$68,820.78	$68,820.78
Total Change in Account Value (Totals include Deposits & Withdrawals)	($5,213.01) (7.04)%	$39,596.07 135.49%

Account Value ($) Over Last 12 Months

Keep in mind that the value of investment accounts can vary dramatically over short periods of time as the stock market rises and falls. For that reason, you should only invest money that you are willing to leave in the market for a long time. This means that you will not be forced to withdraw your money at a time when you might take a loss on it.

Asset Composition

Asset Composition	Market Value	% of Account Assets
Cash	$26,534.28	39%
Equities	13,777.50	20%
Options	28,509.00	41%
Total Assets Long	$68,820.78	
Margin Loan Balance	0.00	
Total Account Value	$68,820.78	100%

Overview

- 39% Cash
- 20% Equities
- 41% Options

Gain or (Lose) Summary

Realized Gain or (Loss) This Period	
Short Term	$2,295.87
Long Term	$0.00
Unrealized Gain or (Loss)	
All Investments	$(8.22)

Values may not reflect all of your gains/losses

Investment funds may split your money over several different types of investments. *Options* give the investor the opportunity to buy or sell at a later date for a preset price. These types of complex investments are best handled by knowledgeable investment bankers.

401(k) Plan Enrollment Form

Employers may allow employees the opportunity to invest some of their earnings into a long-term retirement savings account called a 401(k). Non-profit organizations, such as charities and hospitals, may offer similar accounts called 403(b) accounts.

Enrollment Form
401(k) PLAN

Instructions

Please print using blue or black ink. Please keep a copy for your records and send completed form to the following address or fax it to **1-888-555-1000**. If faxing, please keep original for your records. Please ensure the 'Your Authorization' section is included when you return the form.

401 Processing Center
PO Box 5094
Chapel Hill, NC 27510

About You

Plan number

`7 2 0 4 5 8`

Who is your employer?

City of Asheville
(Please print entire employer name)

> Your employer works with an investment company to select your 401(k) plan options. Expect to see slightly different plans at different employers. However, all plans function essentially the same way. You will have the amount of money you choose to invest automatically deducted from each paycheck and invested in your plan of choice.

Have you recently changed employers? ☐ Yes ☒ No

Previous Employer Name: _____

Are you a sworn Law Enforcement Officer? ☐ Yes ☒ No

Social Security number

`X X X - X X - X X X X`

Daytime telephone number

`8 2 8 - 5 5 5 - 6 4 2 5`
area code

First name

`Q u i n c y`

MI `D`

Last name

`S h e r m a n`

Address

`2 2 4 3   H i d d e n   P o n d   R o a d   A p t . 5`

City

`A s h v i l l e`

State `N C` ZIP code `2 8 8 1 0`

Date of birth

`0 1   1 1   1 9 8 1`
month   day   year

Gender

`X` M ☐ F

Original date employed

`0 3   0 2   2 0 1 1`
month   day   year

Contribution Information

I wish to contribute the following from my salary per pay period:

☒ **Before-Tax Contribution Election.**

☐ $ `_ _ _ _ , _ _ 8 0` .00 (please provide whole dollars only)

OR

☐ `_ _ _ _` % (please fill in % from 1-80%, in whole percentages)

☐ **Roth 401(k) Contribution Election.**

☐ $ `_ _ _ _ , _ _ _ _` .00 (please provide whole dollars only)

OR

☐ `_ _ _ _` % (please fill in % from 1-80%, in whole percentages)

> If you choose to withdraw money from your 401(k) before retirement, you will pay extra taxes on that income. You may pay up to an additional 10 percent tax on any money withdrawn from a 401(k) account before your 60th birthday.

My yearly salary is $ _$31500_ . My pay frequency is _2/mo._ . Please note that if the contribution amount provided is not in the correct format (dollar vs. percentage), Prudential will use your salary information to calculate your contribution in accordance with what your payroll requires.

> You can invest money in a 401(k) without paying taxes on it. The federal government allows you to invest tax-free up to a certain limit. In 2011, for example, this limit was $16,500. Even a small contribution can add up to big retirement savings over time. You will eventually pay taxes on the money when you withdraw it during retirement.

Important information and signature is required on the following page.
The signature page must be provided in order for your enrollment to be processed.

401(k) Plan Enrollment Form

Investment Allocation
(Please fill out Part I, II or Part III. Do not fill out more than one section.)

Fill out Part I, II or Part III. **Please complete only _one_ section.**

Part I RetirementPlus with Automatic Age Adjustment:

By completing this section, you enroll in RetirementPlus, Investment Corp.'s asset allocation program, and you direct Investment Corp. to invest your contribution(s) according to a RetirementPlus model portfolio that is based on your risk tolerance and time horizon. You also direct Investment Corp to automatically rebalance your account according to the model portfolio chosen on a quarterly basis. Enrollment in RetirementPlus can be canceled at any time.

Choose Your Risk Tolerance ☐ Conservative ☒ Moderate ☐ Aggressive

RetirementPlus also automatically adjusts your allocations over time based on your current age and the expected retirement age. To ensure that your allocations are updated correctly, please confirm your expected retirement age below. If an Expected Retirement Age is not provided, age 65 will be used.

Expected Retirement Age: ⌊6⌋5⌋

OR

Part II GoalMaker _without_ Automatic Age Adjustment

By completing this section, I confirm that I do not want to take advantage of RetirementPlus' Age-Adjustment Feature. Please invest my contributions according to the model portfolios selected below.

Please refer to the Retirement Planning Guide for more information.

RetirementPlus without Automatic Age Adjustment:

Time Horizon (years until retirement)	RetirementPlus Model Portfolio (check one box only)		
	Conservative	Moderate	Aggressive
0 to 5 Years	☐ C01	☐ M01	☐ R01
6 to 10 Years	☐ C02	☐ M02	☐ R02
11 to 15 Years	☐ C03	☐ M03	☐ R03
16 Plus Years	☐ C04	☐ M04	☐ R04

OR

Part III Design your own investment allocation

If you would like to design your own asset allocation instead of selecting a RetirementPlus model portfolio, designate the percentage of your contribution to be invested in each of the available investment options. (Please use whole percentages. The total must equal 100%.)

I wish to allocate my contributions to the Plan as follows:

Percent Allocated	Codes	Investment Options
⌊_⌋_⌋_⌋%	NK	Prudential Stable Value Fund
⌊_⌋_⌋_⌋%	WJ	Fidelity Intermediate Bond Fund
⌊_⌋_⌋_⌋%	BR	Goldman Sachs Mid Cap Value A
⌊_⌋_⌋_⌋%	TU	Van Kampen Equity and Income
⌊_⌋_⌋_⌋%	DV	Van Kampen Growth & Income
⌊_⌋_⌋_⌋%	NL	Vanguard Equity Index Portfolio
⌊_⌋_⌋_⌋%	P2	Growth Fund of America
⌊_⌋_⌋_⌋%	P0	Oppenheimer Main Street Small Cap
⌊_⌋_⌋_⌋%	P5	EuroPacific Growth Fund
⌊1⌋0⌋0⌋%	**Total**	

This form must be completed accurately and received by Investment Corp. Retirement before Investment Corp. Retirement receives contributions on your behalf. If a completed form is not received, Investment Corp. will invest contributions in the Plan's default investment option, the Stable Value Fund. Upon receipt of your completed enrollment form, all **future** contributions will be allocated according to your investment selection. You must contact Investment Corp. Retirement to transfer any **existing** funds from the Stable Value Fund used to invest your defaulted contributions.

Your Authorization

This section must be completed in order to process your enrollment.

I direct my employer to make payroll deductions as I have indicated. I understand that upon enrollment, if my Plan allows, I will have telephone and/or Internet privileges to perform transactions via Investment Corp.'s Interactive Voice Response service and Online Retirement Center.

I agree that Investment Corp. Retirement, the Plan's trustees, or the state of North Carolina will not be liable for any loss, liability, cost, or expense for implementing my instructions via the Internet or by telephone. I understand that Investment Corp. Retirement will execute on my instructions only when proper identification is simultaneously provided. This identification may consist of information that Investment Corp. Retirement may reasonably deem necessary to establish my identity. I hereby give Investment Corp. Retirement the right to tape record the telephone conversation of any telephone instructions received by Investment Corp. Retirement.

X _Quincy D. Sherman_ Date _04 | 15 | 2012_
Participant's signature

Social Security Number_____

If you wish, you may decide how to divide your 401(k) investment funds. This may be a good choice if you have an existing investment fund or stock portfolio that you would like to maintain.

When you sign up for a 401(k) plan, you may choose to have your funds invested along a risk-tolerance level. If you are young, you may wish to choose a high or aggressive risk level that offers the potential for greater gains over the long term. But this also means that you could face a greater risk of loss in the short term.

401(k) Plan Statement

Just like any other investment account, 401(k) accounts generate regular statements that detail how your investments have been performing. Reviewing these statements will allow you to monitor your investments.

La Croix Investments
PO Box 50669
New York NY 10001
www.lacroixinvestments.com

LA CROIX
Statement of Retirement Account

January 01, 2011 – June 30, 2011

0117688 02 MB 0 534 **AUTO T4 0 0 721 45504.110618 11

Alia Harb
2934 Zimmerman Lane, Apt. 14
Los Angeles, CA 90057

For Assistance Contact:
La Croix Administrative Services
www.lacroixinvestments.com
1–800–555–0204   Customer Service Representatives
1–800–555–7777   Automated Telephone (TOPS)

Your Retirement Account At A Glance

Employer name:	Southern Edge Waterworks	Participant Program: La Croix Investments
Contract Number:	91 664754	Participant Number: 50698810

Opening Balance as of 01/01/2011   **$25,721.76**

Your Contributions

SALARY DEFERRAL	$1,483.07	
Total Your Contributions		$1,483.07

Employer Contributions

EMPLOYER MATCHING*	$266.99	
Total Employer Contributions		$266.99
Investment Results		$591.57
Closing Balance as of 06/30/2011		**$28,063.39**

> Some employers match a certain portion of employee 401(k) contributions. This occurs as part of their benefits package. If your employer matches contributions, consider contributing as much as you can afford. The more you contribute, the more matching dollars you will receive.

*Source is subject to vesting.
Please contact your Employer for questions regarding your plan's vesting schedule.

Your Current Asset Allocation

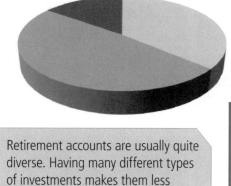

Money Market*	**21.01%**
Money Market Portfolio	21.01%
Domestic Bonds	**30.26%**
Guaranteed Interest Option	18.06%
Franklin Custodian Funds – US Govt Securities Series	12.20%
Large Company Stocks	**48.73%**
Alliance Growth & Income	20.26%
Janice Growth and Income Fund	19.11%
Janice Mercury Fund	9.36%

> Retirement accounts are usually quite diverse. Having many different types of investments makes them less vulnerable to changes in the stock market. It also allows them many opportunities to grow.

401(k) Plan Statement

LA CROIX INVESTMENTS   Statement of Retirement Account 01/01/2011 – 06/30/2011

| Employer name: | Southern Edge Waterworks | Participant Name: | Alia Harb |
| Contract Number: | 91 664754 | Participant Number: | 50698810 |

Transaction Summary By Investment Option (continued)

Activity	TOTAL
Opening Balance	$25,721.76
Contributions	$1,750.06
Withdrawals	$0.00
Net Transfers	$0.00
Investment Results	$591.57
Closing Balance	$28,063.39

> This account grew by more than $2,000 in just six months, thanks to new contributions and sound investing. Experts recommend beginning your 401(k) contributions as soon as you begin working. This will give your account plenty of time to grow.

Transaction Summary By Source

Activity	PROFIT SHARING	PRIOR PLAN ROLLOVER	EMPLOYER 401K	SALARY DEFERRAL
Opening Balance	$320.75	$944.01	$501.56	$29,092.55
Contributions	$0.00	$0.00	$0.00	$1,463.07
Withdrawals	$0.00	$0.00	$0.00	$0.00
Investment Results	$7.33	$21.16	$11.68	$462.77
Closing Balance	$328.08	$965.17	$513.24	$31,018.39

Activity	EMPLOYEE MATCHING	TOTAL
Opening Balance	$3,853.89	$25,721.76
Contributions	$266.99	$1,750.06
Withdrawals	$0.00	$0.00
Investment Results	$88.63	$591.57
Closing Balance	$4,209.51	$28,063.39

> When you leave a job, you will probably want to roll over, or move, your existing 401(k) account. You may put it into an account with your new employer or into a different type of retirement account. Your investment company can help you transfer funds correctly.

Roth IRA Plan

Individual retirement accounts, or IRAs, are private retirement savings funds. They share some features with 401(k) accounts. Roth IRAs differ from 401(k) accounts or traditional IRAs. They are funded by post-tax dollars from your paycheck.

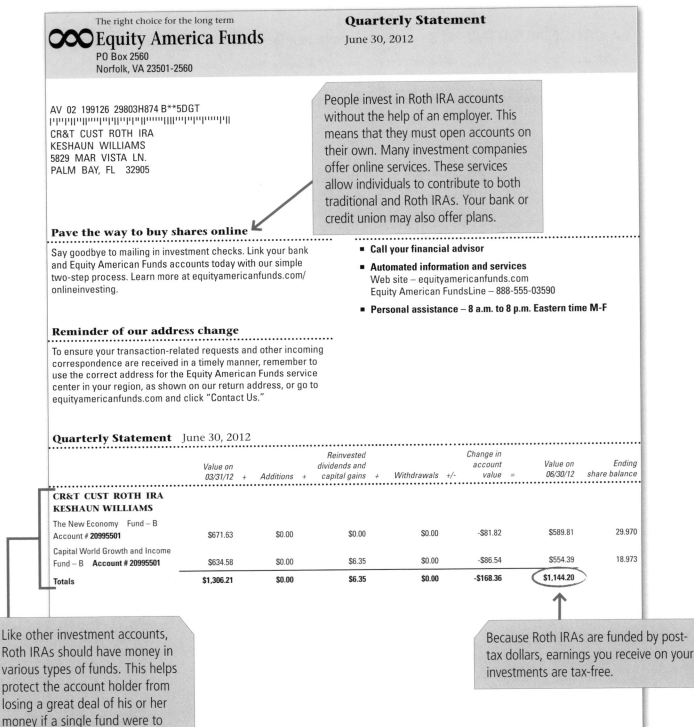

Roth IRA Plan

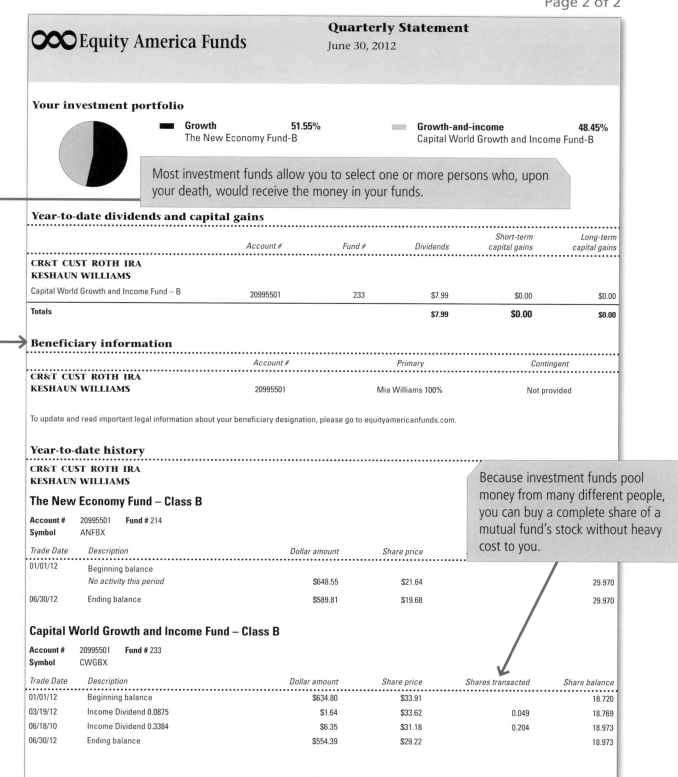

∞ Equity America Funds

Quarterly Statement
June 30, 2012

Your investment portfolio

Growth	51.55%	
The New Economy Fund-B		
Growth-and-income	48.45%	
Capital World Growth and Income Fund-B		

Most investment funds allow you to select one or more persons who, upon your death, would receive the money in your funds.

Year-to-date dividends and capital gains

	Account #	Fund #	Dividends	Short-term capital gains	Long-term capital gains
CR&T CUST ROTH IRA **KESHAUN WILLIAMS**					
Capital World Growth and Income Fund – B	20995501	233	$7.99	$0.00	$0.00
Totals			**$7.99**	**$0.00**	**$0.00**

Beneficiary information

	Account #	Primary	Contingent
CR&T CUST ROTH IRA **KESHAUN WILLIAMS**	20995501	Mia Williams 100%	Not provided

To update and read important legal information about your beneficiary designation, please go to equityamericanfunds.com.

Year-to-date history

CR&T CUST ROTH IRA
KESHAUN WILLIAMS

The New Economy Fund – Class B

Account # 20995501 **Fund #** 214
Symbol ANFBX

Trade Date	Description	Dollar amount	Share price	
01/01/12	Beginning balance			
	No activity this period	$648.55	$21.64	29.970
06/30/12	Ending balance	$589.81	$19.68	29.970

Because investment funds pool money from many different people, you can buy a complete share of a mutual fund's stock without heavy cost to you.

Capital World Growth and Income Fund – Class B

Account # 20995501 **Fund #** 233
Symbol CWGBX

Trade Date	Description	Dollar amount	Share price	Shares transacted	Share balance
01/01/12	Beginning balance	$634.80	$33.91		18.720
03/19/12	Income Dividend 0.0875	$1.64	$33.62	0.049	18.769
06/18/10	Income Dividend 0.3384	$6.35	$31.18	0.204	18.973
06/30/12	Ending balance	$554.39	$29.22		18.973

Automobile Loan Application

If you buy a new or used car, you will probably take out a loan to pay for it. You will fill out a loan application with your auto dealer or bank to begin the process. Many dealers have agreements with car companies or banks to help arrange your loan.

> Even though the car cost $13,000, Eugene only financed $12,075. That's because he put down $1,000 on the loan. He also traded his old vehicle to the dealership for $1,175. After financing an additional $1,250 in fees and charges, Eugene took out a car loan for $12,075.

CREDIT APPLICATION ☒ STANDARD RETAIL ☐ LEASE ☐ FIXED VALUE

DEALERSHIP NAME **COOPER CARS**   FAX **602-555-5555**

READ THESE DIRECTIONS BEFORE COMPLETING THIS APPLICATION ➤

If applying for individual credit in your own name and relying only on your own income or assets for repayment of the credit requested, complete Section B.
If applying for joint credit with another person, complete Sections B and C.
Sign here to indicate that you intend to apply for joint credit: X _____ APPLICANT (SIGN OR INITIAL)   X _____ CO-APPLICANT (SIGN OR INITIAL)
If applying for individual credit but are relying on income from alimony, child support, separate maintenance, or on the income or assets of another person as the basis for repayment of the credit requested, complete Section B and provide information in Section C about the other person.
Wisconsin residents must complete Section D.

SECTION A: VEHICLE

☐ NEW ☐ AUCTION ☒ USED VEHICLE MILEAGE **74,886** VEHICLE IDENTIFICATION NO. **1G1FP22PXS2100001**

YR. **2005** MAKE **Delt** MODEL **Adventure** ENGINE **V6**

☐ AC ☒ P.S./P.B. ☐ A/T ☐ LIST OTHER EQUIP.

TRADE IN YR. **2001** MAKE **Tia** MODEL **Maxion** ENGINE **4-cyl.**

☐ AC ☒ P.S./P.B. ☐ A/T ☐ LIST OTHER EQUIP.

OTHER CHARGES LIFE/A & HI – $ SERV. CONT. – $ OTHER – $

INSURANCE INFORMATION INSURANCE COMPANY

Cash Price		$ **$13,000**
Cash down $ + Rebate $ =		$ **$1,000**
Trade-in Allowance	$	$ **$1,175**
Owing on trade	$	$ **$0**
Net Trade-In		$
Total Down Payment		$
Unpaid Balance of Cash Price		$
Total of Other charges to be Financed		$ **$1,250**
Total Amount to be **Financed** for (**36 months**) mos.		$ **$12,075**

AGENTS NAME   PHONE NO.

SECTION B: APPLICANT

HAVE YOU EVER FILED FOR BANKRUPTCY? ☐ YES ☒ NO IF YES, WHEN?

> The length of car loans vary. Often, used cars are financed for three years, while new cars may be paid for over a period of five or six years. Taking out the shortest loan with payments that you can afford will help reduce the total amount of interest you pay on the loan.

APPLICANT NAME (FIRST, LAST, MIDDLE INT.) **Eugene Su**

ADDRESS **563 Coplin Avenue**

CITY, STATE, ZIP **Phoenix, AZ 85034**

HOME PHONE NO. **(602) 555-9221** EMAIL **hsu@pax.com**

MORTGAGE COMPANY/LANDLORD **Jane Redman** MARKET VALUE $ MORTGAGE BALANCE $

TIME AT RES. YRS **3** MOS **2** ☐ OWNING/BUYING ☒ RENTING ☐ OTHER RENT/MORT. **$875**

PREVIOUS ADDRESS, CITY, STATE, ZIP TIME AT PREV RES. YRS? MOS?

EMPLOYMENT EMPLOYER'S NAME AND ADDRESS **Phoenix Library, 101 1st St., Phoenix AZ 85001** BUSINESS PHONE NO. OCCUPATION **library technician** TIME ON JOB YRS? **5** MOS? **4**

MONTHLY INCOME $ **3125** PREVIOUS EMPLOYER NAME AND ADDRESS **South West University Library, 7500 Learning Way, Phoenix AZ 85012** OCCUPATION **student library assistant** TIME ON JOB YRS? **3** MOS? **10**

OTHER INCOME Source(s) of other income: alimony, child support or separate maintenance income need not be disclosed if you do not wish to have it considered a basis for repaying this obligation.

ADDITIONAL MONTHLY INCOME $ SOURCE(S):

PRINCIPALS (To be completed if a Corporation or Partnership) TYPE OF BUSINESS

STATE OF INCORPORATION NAME OF PRINCIPAL/APPLICANT TITLE YEARS % OF OWNERSHIP

DATE OF INCORPORATION NAME OF PRINCIPAL/APPLICANT TITLE YEARS % OF OWNERSHIP

CREDIT REFERENCES — Includes finance companies, banks, credit card, charge accounts, suppliers. Indicate any other name(s) under which credit references and credit history may be verified. OTHER NAME(S)

NAME OF CREDITOR/CREDIT CARD CO.	ADDRESS, BRANCH, PHONE, OR CREDIT CARD NUMBER	OPEN	CLOSED	DATE OPEN	HIGH	TERM	PAYMENTS	BALANCE ($)
Student First Card	6666 4156 3333 6747	☒	☐	05/01/2001	$1250		$0	$0
Points Plus Credit Card	5555 4023 8888 1439	☒	☐	08/15/2008	$775		$50	$500
PREV CAR FINANCED OR LEASED WITH Best Car Loans, 7500 10th St., Chicago IL 60601	PREVIOUS ACCOUNT WITH CREDITOR ☐ YES ☒ NO	☐	☒	01/15/2006	$5,025	36 mos.	$155	$0

BANK, SAVINGS BANK, OR CREDIT UNION **Bank of Arizona** BRANCH ADDRESS **Downtown branch** TYPE OF ACCT. ☒ CHECKING ☒ SAVINGS

Debts: List all debts including alimony, child support, separate maintenance. Use separate page if needed $ **300** PER MO DEBTS **student loan, credit cards**

By signing this application:
1. You authorized Dealer, Cooper Cars, and any finance company, bank, or other financial institution to which the Dealer or Cooper Cars submits your application, to investigate your application, to investigate your credit and employment history, obtain credit reports, and release information about your credit experience as the law permits.
2. If an account is created, you authorized Cooper Cars, and any finance company, bank, or financial institution to which the Dealer or Cooper Cars submits your credit application to obtain credit reports for the purpose of retrieving or taking collection action on your account or for other legitimate purposes associated with your records.
3. You certify that you have read and agree to the terms of this application and that the information in it is complete and true, and you certify that the vehicle for which you are applying for financing is for the applicant or the joint applicants own use.
4. You authorize a credit investigation of you credit based on the information, which you provide voluntarily; the information is true and correct and reflects all your current debts. In addition, you authorize the release of federal and state records of employment and income history, including State Employment Security Agency ("SESA") records. The SESA authorization is for this transaction only and continues in effect for one (1) year unless limited by state law, in which case the authorization continues in effect for the maximum periods, not to exceed one (1) year as allowed by law. A bankruptcy proceeding is neither in progress nor expected. If the attached application is submitted in the name of a business, a current and year-end financial statement, including P&L statement, and balance sheet may be required, audited if possible.
5. To the extent permitted by law, you give Cooper Cars and any financial institution to which the dealer or Cooper Cars submits you application ("us") permission to a) monitor and record any telephone conversation between you and us b) to contact you on your wireless telephone (including text messaging) through manual, autodial, and prerecorded means and you acknowledge that you may incur wireless telephone charges resulting from such contact.
6. IN EXCHANGE FOR THE TIME, EFFORT, AND EXPENSE IN REVIEWING YOUR APPLICATION AND FOR OTHER VALUABLE CONSIDERATION, WHICH IS HEREBY ACKNOWLEDGED, YOU AGREE TO ALL OF THE TERMS OF THE IMPORTANT CONTRACT OF ARBITRATION CONTAINED ON THE REVERSE SIDE OF THIS APPLICATION AND ACKNOWLEDGE THAT YOU HAVE READ AND UNDERSTAND ITS TERMS.

SIGNATURE OF APPLICATION X **Eugene Su** DATE X **03/15/2011**

> Expect a dealership or bank to check your credit report when you apply for an automobile loan. A better credit score will help you qualify for loans with better terms, such as lower interest rates.

Realtor's Home Listing

Real estate agents provide informative sheets about properties for sale. These sheets give you details about a property's price, size, and other features.

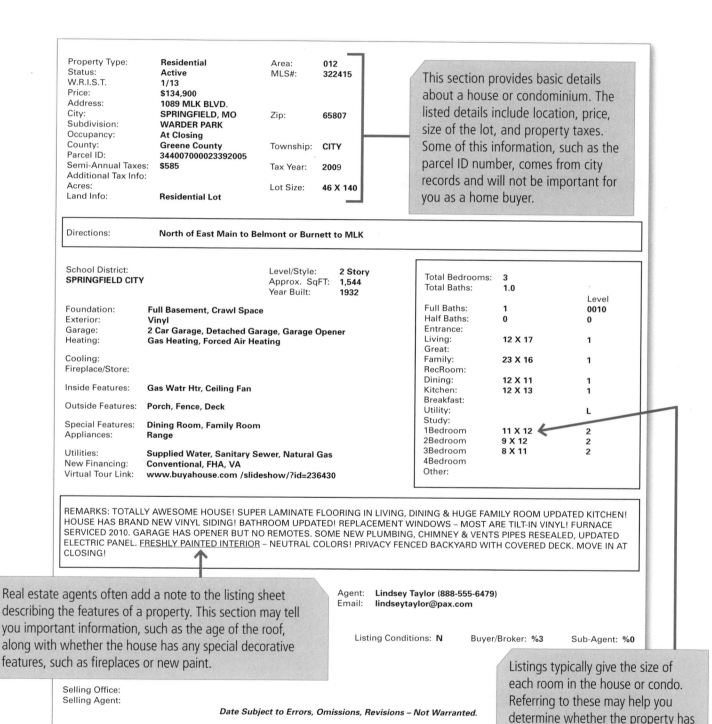

Property Type:	**Residential**	Area:	**012**	
Status:	**Active**	MLS#:	**322415**	
W.R.I.S.T.	**1/13**			
Price:	**$134,900**			
Address:	**1089 MLK BLVD.**			
City:	**SPRINGFIELD, MO**	Zip:	**65807**	
Subdivision:	**WARDER PARK**			
Occupancy:	**At Closing**			
County:	**Greene County**	Township:	**CITY**	
Parcel ID:	**344007000023392005**			
Semi-Annual Taxes:	**$585**	Tax Year:	**2009**	
Additional Tax Info:				
Acres:		Lot Size:	**46 X 140**	
Land Info:	**Residential Lot**			

This section provides basic details about a house or condominium. The listed details include location, price, size of the lot, and property taxes. Some of this information, such as the parcel ID number, comes from city records and will not be important for you as a home buyer.

Directions:	**North of East Main to Belmont or Burnett to MLK**

School District:
SPRINGFIELD CITY

Level/Style:	**2 Story**
Approx. SqFT:	**1,544**
Year Built:	**1932**

Foundation:	**Full Basement, Crawl Space**	
Exterior:	**Vinyl**	
Garage:	**2 Car Garage, Detached Garage, Garage Opener**	
Heating:	**Gas Heating, Forced Air Heating**	
Cooling:		
Fireplace/Store:		
Inside Features:	**Gas Watr Htr, Ceiling Fan**	
Outside Features:	**Porch, Fence, Deck**	
Special Features:	**Dining Room, Family Room**	
Appliances:	**Range**	
Utilities:	**Supplied Water, Sanitary Sewer, Natural Gas**	
New Financing:	**Conventional, FHA, VA**	
Virtual Tour Link:	**www.buyahouse.com /slideshow/?id=236430**	

Total Bedrooms:	**3**	
Total Baths:	**1.0**	
		Level
Full Baths:	**1**	**0010**
Half Baths:	**0**	**0**
Entrance:		
Living:	**12 X 17**	**1**
Great:		
Family:	**23 X 16**	**1**
RecRoom:		
Dining:	**12 X 11**	**1**
Kitchen:	**12 X 13**	**1**
Breakfast:		
Utility:		**L**
Study:		
1Bedroom	**11 X 12**	**2**
2Bedroom	**9 X 12**	**2**
3Bedroom	**8 X 11**	**2**
4Bedroom		
Other:		

REMARKS: TOTALLY AWESOME HOUSE! SUPER LAMINATE FLOORING IN LIVING, DINING & HUGE FAMILY ROOM UPDATED KITCHEN! HOUSE HAS BRAND NEW VINYL SIDING! BATHROOM UPDATED! REPLACEMENT WINDOWS – MOST ARE TILT-IN VINYL! FURNACE SERVICED 2010. GARAGE HAS OPENER BUT NO REMOTES. SOME NEW PLUMBING, CHIMNEY & VENTS PIPES RESEALED, UPDATED ELECTRIC PANEL. FRESHLY PAINTED INTERIOR – NEUTRAL COLORS! PRIVACY FENCED BACKYARD WITH COVERED DECK. MOVE IN AT CLOSING!

Real estate agents often add a note to the listing sheet describing the features of a property. This section may tell you important information, such as the age of the roof, along with whether the house has any special decorative features, such as fireplaces or new paint.

Agent:	**Lindsey Taylor (888-555-6479)**
Email:	**lindseytaylor@pax.com**

Listing Conditions:	**N**	Buyer/Broker: **%3**	Sub-Agent: **%0**

Listings typically give the size of each room in the house or condo. Referring to these may help you determine whether the property has enough space for your family and personal items. You will want to pay particular attention if you have large pieces of furniture, such as a king-size bed.

Selling Office:
Selling Agent:

Date Subject to Errors, Omissions, Revisions – Not Warranted.

Home Loan Application

Before you can buy a home, you must first be approved for a loan. Typically, you complete a home loan application with a representative from your bank or lending company. That person can help you fill out the application completely and accurately.

Uniform Residential Loan Application

This application is designed to be completed by the applicant(s) with the Lender's assistance. Applicants should complete this form as "Borrower" or "Co-Borrower," as applicable. Co-Borrower information must also be provided (and the appropriate box checked) when ☐ the income or assets of a person other than the Borrower (including the Borrower's spouse) will be used as a basis for loan qualification or ☐ the income or assets of the Borrower's spouse or other person who has community property rights pursuant to state law will not be used as a basis for loan qualification, but his or her liabilities must be considered because the spouse or other person has community property rights pursuant to applicable law and Borrower resides in a community property state, the security property is located in a community property state, or the Borrower is relying on other property located in a community property state as a basis for repayment of the loan.

If this is an application for joint credit, Borrower and Co-Borrower each agree that we intend to apply for joint credit (sign below):

_____   _____
Borrower   Co-Borrower

I. TYPE OF MORTGAGE AND TERMS OF LOAN

Mortgage Applied for:	☐ VA ☒ FHA	☐ Conventional ☐ USDA/Rural Housing Service	☐ Other (explain):	Agency Case Number	Lender Case Number

Amount $ 110,800	Interest Rate 5.25 %	No. of Months 360	Amortization Type:	☒ Fixed Rate ☐ GPM	☐ Other (explain): ☐ ARM (type):

II. PROPERTY INFORMATION AND PURPOSE OF LOAN

Subject Property Address (street, city, state & ZIP)
1664 Modoc Alley

No. of Units: 1

Legal Description of Subject Property (attach description if necessary)
SE¼ 31 T125N R87W

Year Built: 1964

Purpose of Loan: ☒ Purchase ☐ Refinance ☐ Construction ☐ Construction-Peramanent ☐ Other (explain):

Property will be: ☒ Primary Residence ☐ Secondary Residence ☐ Investment

(b) Cost of Improvement $

Describe Improvement

Cost: $

> There are several different types of home loans available to consumers. The federal government's Federal Housing Administration writes special FHA loans that require low down payments. However, not all properties are approved to receive FHA loans. Talk to your loan officer or real estate agent if you are planning to take out this type of mortgage.

> With a fixed rate loan, the interest rate on your loan will not change. However, an adjustable rate mortgage (ARM) has a rate that can change after a certain period. The rate might start out low but rise over time. Changes in the interest rate will affect your monthly payment.

Title will be held in what Name(s)
Delicia Melgar Briones

Manner in which Title will be held

Source of Down Payment, Settlement Charges, and/or Subordinate Financing (explain)
savings

III. BORROWER INFORMATION

	Borrower	Co-Borrower

Borrower's Name (include Jr. or Sr. if applicable)
Delicia Melgar Briones

Co-Borrower's Name (include Jr. or Sr. if applicable)

Social Security Number XXX-XX-XXXX	Home Phone (incl. area code) 208-555-7969	DOB (mm/dd/yyyy) 05/08/1972	Yrs. School 14	Social Security Number	Home Phone (incl. area code)	DOB (mm/dd/yyyy)	Yrs. School

☐ Married ☒ Unmarried (include single, divorced, widowed) ☐ Separated

Dependents (not listed by Co-Borrower) no. 1 ages

☐ Married ☐ Unmarried (include single, divorced, widowed) ☐ Separated

Dependents (not listed by Borrower) no. ages

Present Address (street, city, state, ZIP) ☐ Own ☒ Rent 6 No. Yrs.
404 Lakeland Park Drive, Apt. 3C

Present Address (street, city, state, ZIP) ☐ Own ☐ Rent ___ No. Yrs.

Mailing Address, if different from Present Address

Mailing Address, if different from Present Address

Complete this line if this is a refinance loan.

Former Address (street, city, state, ZIP) ☐ Own ☐ Rent ___ No. Yrs.

Former Address (street, city, state, ZIP) ☐ Own ☐ Rent ___ No. Yrs.

IV. EMPLOYMENT INFORMATION

	Borrower	Co-Borrower

Name & Address of Employer ☐ Self Employed
Loganville General Hospital
100 Main St.
Loganville, GA 30249

Yrs. on this job: 4

Yrs. employed in this line of work/profession: 12

Name & Address of Employer

Position/Title/Type of Business
Radiology technician

Business Phone (incl. area code)
770-555-5000

Position/Title/Type of Business

If employed in current position for less than two years or if currently employed in more than one position, complete the following:

> As part of the home loan process, you will need to provide basic identifying information to begin the application, such as your name, current address, and Social Security number. You may be applying for a loan with your spouse or another co-borrower. If so, that person will also need to provide his or her information.

Home Loan Application

You do not need to report all types of income if you do not plan to use them to pay your mortgage.

Borrower		IV. EMPLOYMENT INFORMATION (cont'd)		Co-Borrower	
Name & Address of Employer ☐ Self Employed		Dates (from – to)	Name & Address of Employer ☐ Self Employed		Dates (from – to)
		Monthly Income $			Monthly Income $
Position/Title/Type of Business	Business Phone (incl. area code)		Position/Title/Type of Business	Business Phone (incl. area code)	
Name & Address of Employer ☐ Self Employed		Dates (from – to)	Name & Address of Employer ☐ Self Employed		Dates (from – to)
		Monthly Income $			Monthly Income $
Position/Title/Type of Business	Business Phone (incl. area code)		Position/Title/Type of Business	Business Phone (incl. area code)	

V. MONTHLY INCOME AND COMBINED HOUSING EXPENSE INFORMATION

Gross Monthly Income	Borrower	Co-Borrower	Total	Combined Monthly Housing Expense	Present	Proposed
Base Empl. Income*	$ 3800	$	$	Rent	$ $750	
Overtime				First Mortgage (P&I)		$
Bonuses				Other Financing (P&I)		
Commissions				Hazard Insurance	$45	
Dividends/Interest				Real Estate Taxes	$300	
Net Rental Income				Mortgage Insurance		
Other (before completing, see the notice in "describe other income," below)				Homeowner Assn. Dues		
				Other:		
Total	$ 3800	$	$	Total	$ $1095	$

* Self-Employed Borrower(s) may be required to provide additional documentation such as tax returns and financial statements.

Describe Other Income   Notice: Alimony, child support, or separate maintenance income need not be revealed if the Borrower (B) or Co-Borrower (C) does not choose to have it considered for repaying this loan.

B/C		Monthly Amount
		$

VI. ASSETS AND LIABILITIES

This Statement and any applicable supporting schedules may be completed jointly by both married and unmarried Co-Borrowers if their assets and liabilities are sufficiently joined so that the Statement can be meaningfully and fairly presented on a combined basis; otherwise, separate Statements and Schedules are required. If the Co-Borrower section was completed about a non-applicant spouse or other person, this Statement and supporting schedules must be completed about that spouse or other person also.

Completed ☐ Jointly ☐ Not Jointly

ASSETS	Cash or Market Value	Liabilities and Pledged Assets. List the creditor's name, address, and account number for all outstanding debts, including automobile loans, revolving charge accounts, real estate loans, alimony, child support, stock pledges, etc. Use continuation sheet, if necessary. Indicate by (*) those liabilities, which will be satisfied upon sale of real estate owned or upon refinancing of the subject property.		
Description				
Cash deposit toward purchase held by:	$ 22,000			

List checking and savings accounts below		LIABILITIES	Monthly Payment & Months Left to Pay	
Name and address of Bank, S&L, or Credit Union Loganville Bank 100 1st St., Loganville, GA 30249		Name and address of Company Automotive Lender, Inc. 1000 45th St. New York NY 10001	$ Payment/Months 275/mo	
Acct. no. 125502189	$ 2,500	Acct. no.		
Name and address of Bank, S&L, or Credit Union Loganville Bank 100 1st St., Loganville, GA 30249		Name and address of Company Mastercharge PO Box 1234 New York NY 10010	$ Payment/Months 75/mo	
Acct. no. 9054121	$ 23,500	Acct. no.		
			$ Payment/Months	$

In recent years, lenders have again begun requiring large down payments for mortgages. A down payment of 20 percent of the purchase price may help you qualify for a loan more easily.

This application requires you to list your assets and your liabilities. Assets are things you own. For example, a paid-off car might be an asset of $10,000. A liability is something you owe. For example, if you owe $3,000 to a credit card company, you'd list that amount as a liability.

Home Loan Application

VI. ASSETS AND LIABILITIES (cont'd)

Name and address of Bank, S&L, or Credit Union		Name and address of Company	$ Payment/Months	$
Acct. no.	$	Acct. no.		
Stocks & Bonds (Company name/ number & description)	$	Name and address of Company	$ Payment/Months	$
		Acct. no.		
Life insurance net cash value	$	Name and address of Company	$ Payment/Months	$
Face amount: $				
Subtotal Liquid Assets	$			
Real estate owned (enter market value from schedule of real estate owned)	$			
Vested interest in retirement fund	$			
Net worth of business(es) owned (attach financial statement)	$	Acct. no.		
Automobiles owned (make and year)	$	Alimony/Child Support/Separate Maintenance Payments Owed to:		
Other Assets (itemize) 2007 Delt	$ 9500	Job-Related Expense (child care, union dues, etc.)		
	$	**Total Monthly Payments**	$ 350	
Total Assets a.	$ 33645	Net Worth (a minus b) ▶ $ 23800	**Total Liabilities b.**	$ 9845

> Lenders consider your debt-to-income ratio when determining the amount of a monthly mortgage you can afford. Experts recommend that your house payment be no more than 28 to 33 percent of your total monthly income.

Schedule of Real Estate Owned (If additional properties are owned, use continuation sheet.)

Property Address (enter S if sold, PS if pending sale or R if rental being held for income) ▼	Type of Property	Present Market Value	Amount of Mortgages & Liens	Gross Rental Income	Mortgage Payments	Insurance, Maintenance, Taxes & Misc.	Net Rental Income
		$	$	$	$	$	$
Totals		$	$	$			

List any additional names under which credit has previously been received and indicate appropriate creditor name(s) and account

Alternate Name	Creditor Name

> When you buy a house, you must pay costs in addition to the actual purchase price of the property. These "closing costs" and other expenses may include prepaid property taxes. These costs will add a few thousand dollars to your total loan amount.

VII. DETAILS OF TRANSACTION

a.	Purchase price	$ 130,000
b.	Alterations, improvements, repairs	
c.	Land (if acquired separatelys)	
d.	Refinance (incl. debts to be paid off)	
e.	Estimated prepaid items	750
f.	Estimated closing costs	2500
g.	PMI, MIP, Funding Fee	
h.	Discount (if Borrower will pay)	
i.	Total costs (add items a through h)	133250

VIII. DECLARATIONS

If you answer "Yes" to any questions a through i, please use continuation sheet for explanation.

		Borrower		Co-Borrower	
		Yes	No	Yes	No
a.	Are there any outstanding judgments against you?	☐	☒	☐	☐
b.	Have you been declared bankrupt within the past 7 years?	☐	☒	☐	☐
c.	Have you had property foreclosed upon or given title or deed in lieu thereof in the last 7 years?	☐	☒	☐	☐
d.	Are you a party to a lawsuit?	☐	☒	☐	☐
e.	Have you directly or indirectly been obligated on any loan which resulted in foreclosure, transfer of title in lieu of foreclosure, or judgment?	☐	☒	☐	☐

(This would include such loans as home mortgage loans, SBA loans, home improvement loans, educational loans, manufactured (mobile) home loans, any mortgage, financial obligation, bond, or loan guarantee. If "Yes," provide details, including date, name, and address of Lender, FHA or VA case number, if any, and reasons for the action.)

Home Loan Application

As part of your purchase contract, the seller may agree to pay part of your costs at closing, or the stage at which the title of the property transfers from the seller to the buyer. This can save you cash at closing, even if you do not receive any money off the original sale price.

Page 4 of 4

VII. DETAILS OF TRANSACTION		
j.	Subordinate financing	
k.	Borrower's closing costs paid by Seller	2000
l.	Other Credits (explain)	
m.	Loan amount (exclude PMI, MIP, Funding Fee financed)	110,000
n.	PMI, MIP, Funding Fee financed	0
o.	Loan amount (add m & n)	110,000
p.	Cash from Borrower (subtract j, k, l & o from i)	21,250

VIII. DECLARATIONS

If you answer "Yes" to any questions a through i, please use continuation sheet for explanation.

	Borrower		Co-Borrower	
	Yes	No	Yes	No
f. Are you presently delinquent or in default on any Federal debt or any other loan, mortgage, financial obligation, bond, or loan guarantee? If "Yes," give details as described in the preceding question.	☐	☒	☐	☐
g. Are you obligated to pay alimony, child support, or separate maintenance?	☐	☒	☐	☐
h. Is any part of the down payment borrowed?	☐	☒	☐	☐
i. Are you a co-maker or endorser on a note?	☐	☒	☐	☐
j. Are you a U.S. citizen?	☒	☐	☐	☐
k. Are you a permanent resident alien?	☐	☒	☐	☐
l. Do you intend to occupy the property as your primary residence? If "Yes," complete question m below.	☒	☐	☐	☐
m. Have you had an ownership interest in a property in the last three years?	☐	☒	☐	☐

(1) What type of property did you own—principal residence (PR), second home (SH), or investment property (IP)? _____

(2) How did you hold title to the home—solely by yourself (S), jointly with your spouse (SP), or jointly with another person (O)? _____

IX. ACKNOWLEDGEMENT AND AGREEMENT

Each of the undersigned specifically represents to Lender and to Lender's actual or potential agents, brokers, processors, attorneys, insurers, servicers, successors and assigns and agrees and acknowledges that: (1) the information provided in this application is true and correct as of the date set forth opposite my signature and that any intentional or negligent misrepresentation of this information contained in this application may result in civil liability, including monetary damages, to any person who may suffer any loss due to reliance upon any misrepresentation that I have made on this application, and/or in criminal penalties including, but not limited to, fine or imprisonment or both under the provisions of Title 18, United States Code, Sec. 1001, et seq.; (2) the loan requested pursuant to this application (the "Loan") will be secured by a mortgage or deed of trust on the property described in this application; (3) the property will not be used for any illegal or prohibited purpose or use; (4) all statements made in this application are made for the purpose of obtaining a residential mortgage loan; (5) the property will be occupied as indicated in this application; (6) the Lender, its servicers, successors or assigns may retain the original and/or an electronic record of this application, whether or not the Loan is approved; (7) the Lender and its agents, brokers, insurers, servicers, successors, and assigns may continuously rely on the information contained in the application, and I am obligated to amend and/or supplement the information provided in this application if any of the material facts that I have represented herein should change prior to closing of the Loan; (8) in the event that my payments on the Loan become delinquent, the Lender, its servicers, successors or assigns may, in addition to any other rights and remedies that it may have relating to such delinquency, report my name and account information to one or more consumer reporting agencies; (9) ownership of the Loan and/or administration of the Loan account may be transferred with such notice as may be required by law; (10) neither Lender nor its agents, brokers, insurers, servicers, successors or assigns has made any representation or warranty, express or implied, to me regarding the property or the condition or value of the property; and (11) my transmission of this application as an "electronic record" containing my "electronic signature," as those terms are defined in applicable federal and/or state laws (excluding audio and video recordings), or my facsimile transmission of this application containing a facsimile of my signature, shall be as effective, enforceable and valid as if a paper version of this application were delivered containing my original written signature.

Acknowledgement. Each of the undersigned hereby acknowledges that any owner of the Loan, its servicers, successors and assigns, may verify or reverify any information contained in this application or obtain any information or data relating to the Loan, for any legitimate business purpose through any source, including a source named in this application or a consumer reporting agency.

Borrower's Signature x *Delicia Melgar Brisnes*	Date 11/05/2010	Co-Borrower's Signature Signature x	Date

X. INFORMATION FOR GOVERNMENT MONITORING PURPOSES

The following information is requested by the Federal Government for certain types of loans related to a dwelling in order to monitor the lender's compliance with equal credit opportunity, fair housing and home mortgage disclosure laws. You are not required to furnish this information, but are encouraged to do so. The law provides that a lender may not discriminate either on the basis of this information, or on whether you choose to furnish it. If you furnish the information, please provide both ethnicity and race. For race, you may check more than one designation. If you do not furnish ethnicity, race, or sex, under Federal regulations, this lender is required to note the information on the basis of visual observation and surname if you have made this application in person. If you do not wish to furnish the information, please check the box below. (Lender must review the above material to assure that the disclosures satisfy all requirements to which the lender is subject under applicable state law for the particular type of loan applied for.)

BORROWER ☐ I do not wish to furnish this information

Ethnicity: ☒ Hispanic or Latino ☐ Not Hispanic or Latino

Race: ☐ American Indian or Alaska Native ☐ Asian ☐ Black or African American
☐ Native Hawaiian or Other Pacific Islander ☐ White

Sex: ☒ Female ☐ Male

CO-BORROWER ☐ I do not wish to furnish this information

Ethnicity: ☐ Hispanic or Latino ☐ Not Hispanic or Latino

Race: ☐ American Indian or Alaska Native ☐ Asian ☐ Black or African American
☐ Native Hawaiian or Other Pacific Islander ☐ White

Sex: ☐ Female ☐ Male

To be Completed by Interviewer	Interviewer's Name (print or type)	Name and Address of Interviewer's Employer
This application was taken by: ☐ Face-to-face interview ☐ Mail ☐ Telephone ☐ Internet	Interviewer's Signature ___ Date	
	Interviewer's Phone Number (incl. area code)	

You are not required to provide information about your race and ethnicity on home loan applications. Doing so will not affect your likelihood of receiving a loan.

Good Faith Estimate

Mortgage lenders must provide a Good Faith Estimate (GFE) to the borrower, as required by the Real Estate Settlement Procedures Act. This document provides estimates of monthly mortgage costs and closing costs. Usually, the final amount won't differ much from the GFE.

RESPA
GOOD FAITH ESTIMATE

Applicant(s): BRYAN MONAHAN   Date: 01/23/2011
Property Address: 240 W. MURRAY RD.

			Loan Type	Estimated Monthly Payments	
Sales Price/Payoff	$	96,800.00	☒ FHA	Mortgage Principal & Interest	$ 527.46
Closing Costs (if financed) +	$		☐ VA	Real Estate Taxes Estimate	$ 40.33
Total Acquisition	$	96,800.00	☐ CONV	Hazard Insurance Estimate	$ 37.50
Less: Down Payments	$	2,904.00		Flood Insurance Estimate	$
Initial Mortgage Amount	$	93,896.00		PMI/FHA Insurance Premium	$ 38.87
FHA MIP or VA Funding Fee	$	1,408.00	Rate 5.270 %	Other	$ 22.99
Adjusted Mortgage Amount	$	95,304.00	Term 360 Months	Est. Total Monthly Payments	$ 667.15

Note Type: Fixed Rate ☒   Adjustable Rage ☐
Loan Product Name: _____

The information provided below reflect estimates of the charges, which you are likely to incur at the settlement of your loan. The fees listed are estimates–the actual charges may be more or less. Your transaction may not involve a fee for every item listed. The numbers listed beside the estimates generally correspond to the numbered lines contained in the HUD-1 or HUD-1A settlement statement that you will be receiving at settlement. The HUD-1 or HUD-1A settlement statement will show you the actual cost for items paid at settlement.

Estimates Closing Costs

			Buyer		Seller
801	Loan Origination Fee (%)		$	801	$ 938.96
802	Loan Discount Fee (Points) (%)		$	802	$
803	Appraisal Fee	P.O.C.	$	803	$
804	Credit Report	P.O.C.	$	804	
805	Lender's Inspection Fee		$	805	
808	Flat Application/Closing Cost		$	808	
809	Mortgage Broker Fee		$	809	
810	Loan Documentation Preparation Fee		$	810	
811	Underwriting Fee		$	811	
8__	Tax Related Service Fee		$	8__	
8__	Loan Commitment Fee		$	8__	
8__	Flood Certification Fee	P.O.C.	$	8__	
8__	Draw Fees		$	8__	
8__	Other: __		$	8__	
8__	Other: __		$	8__	
1101	Settlement or Closing Fee		$	1101	
1102	Abstract or Title Search		$	1102	
1103	Title Examination	P.O.C.	$	1103	
1104	Title Insurance Binder		$	1104	
1105	Documentation Preparation Fee (deeds, mortgage, notes, etc.)		$	105	
1107	Attorney Feeds		$	1107	
1108	Title Insurance		$	1108	
1111	EPA Endorsement/ARM Endorsement		$	1111	
1201	Recording Fee		$	1201	
1204	Assignment Fee		$	1204	
1301	Survey		$	1201	
1302	Pest Inspection		$	1203	$ 170.00
1303	Courier Fee		$	1303	$
13__	Other: OHFA FEES		$	13__	$ 170
13__	Other:		$	13__	$
	Total Estimated Closing Costs		$		$ 2,966.46

ESTIMATED PREPAID ITEMS

901	Interest for 15 days at 13.76 per day		$ 206.40	
902	Mortgage Ins. Premium/Funding Fee – (Annual) (FHA/VA)		$ 1,408.00	
903	Hazard Insurance Premium – (Annual)		$ 450.00	
904	Flood Insurance Premium – (Annual)		$	
1001	Months of Hazard Insurance Reserve 2 @ $ 37.50		$ 75.00	
1002	Months of PMI Reserve @ $ 38.87		$	
1004	Months of Tax Reserve 2 @ $ 40.33		$ 80.66	
1006	Months of Flood Insurance Reserve @ $		$	
			$ 2,220.06	

TOTAL ESTIMATED INCITEMENT

Down Payment	$ 2,904.00
Estimated Closing Cost	$ 2,966.46
Estimated Prepaid Items	$ 2,220.06
Other: Seller Paid Closing	$ 2,966.46
Less: Seller Paid Prepaids	$ 812.06
Less: OHFA 2ND	$ 2,904.00
Less: Contract Deposit	$
Less: Financed MIP/	$
Less: Funding Fee	$ 1,408.00
TOTAL	$

ACKNOWLEDGEMENT

This Good Faith Estimate is being provided by Union Savings Bank. It is not an approval of your application nor a commitment to make the loan. These estimates are provided pursuant to the Real Estate Settlement Procedures Act of 1974, as amended (RESPA). Additional information can be found in the HUD Special Information Booklet, which is to be provided to you by your mortgage broker or lender, if you r application is to purchase residential real property and the Lender will take a first lien on the property. I/We acknowledge receipt of the documents listed below in connection with the loan application to refinance ro finance the purchase of the above listed property.

1. "A Homebuyers Guide to Settlement Costs" (Purchases Only); and the "Consumer Handbook on ARM Mortgages" (if applicable)
2. A copy of this "Good Faith Estimate" & Supplement to the Good Faith Estimate
3. Adjustable Rate Mortgage Loan Disclosure (if applicable)

I/We Understand that a non-refundable fee of $ _____ is given for the processing of the loan application. This will be applied to the cost at the time of closing.

Bryan Monahan   11/05/2010
Applicant's Signature   Date

_____   _____
Applicant's Signature   Date

Your total monthly house payment may include more than just your mortgage. Depending on the size of your down payment, you may need to pay PMI, or private mortgage insurance, until you have a certain level of equity in your home. Many home buyers also choose to pay part of their property taxes and home insurance each month to spread out the costs.

This section details the estimated costs that you will pay when you close on your home. It includes your down payment, closing costs, and other fees associated with your mortgage. Usually, you must pay cash for your closing costs. Some closing costs may be paid by the seller.

Mortgage Application

There any many different ways to obtain a mortgage. The documents to fill out are just as varied. If you wish to purchase a home but do not have enough money for a down payment, you may be able to take out a second mortgage to cover that amount.

Page 1 of 4

APPLICANT EVALUATION FORM

Address of Home You Want To Buy: _1750 S. 52rd St._

Where You Heard About the Availability of the Home: _sign in yard_ ←

> Some information on mortgage applications may not relate to your chances for approval. This question, for example, exists to help the developer judge the effectiveness of its different types of advertising.

TO BE COMPLETED BY DEVELOPER:

Sales Price of Unit: $_____

Lender Providing First Mortgage Loan:_____

PHOP:_____ Yes _____No   Non PHOP: _____ Yes _____ No

First Mortgage Loan Amount Required $_____

Estimate of Closing Costs $_____   To Be Financed? _____ Yes _____ No

Total Amount of Applicant Down Payment $_____

I.   GENERAL INFORMATION

__Applicant__	__Co-Applicant__
Name: _Daniel C. Wright_	_Michelle R. Wright_
Address: _2076 Scott Street_	_2076 Scott Street_
Pittsburgh, PA Zip _15222_	_Pittsburgh, PA_ Zip _15222_
Phone (Home/Work) _878-555-4225_	_878-555-4225_
Date of Birth: _2/18/85_	_11/12/86_
Social Security No: _XXX-XX-XXXX_	_XXX-XX-XXXX_
Single _____ Married _X_ Separated ____Divorced _____	Single _____ Married _X_ Separated _____Divorced _____
Race (for data purposes only): _African-American_	Race (for data purposes only): _African-American_

II.   HOUSEHOLD INFORMATION ←

Total Number of Household Members (include Applicant and Co-Applicant): _____2_____

Provide information in chart below for each household member:

Name	Relationship to Applicant	Age

> If you have children or other people who are part of your household, include information about them in this section. You do not need to include their incomes as part of your application.

Mortgage Application

Lenders often want to know about your current housing situation. This helps them gauge your ability to make mortgage payments. Being a first-time homebuyer does not necessarily make it harder for you to get a loan.

III. BANKING/DEPOSIT INFORMATION

Provide information for Applicant and Co-Applicant.

Name of Institution	Address	Type of Account	Account Number	Balance
Steel Mill Bank	115 2nd St.	Checking	10984266	$ 3572
Steel Mill Bank	115 2nd St.	Savings	05129874	$ 4075
				$
				$

IV. CURRENT HOUSING INFORMATION

A. Applicant:

Do you currently rent?   Yes_____   No__X__Total Rent Per Month: $_____

Do you currently own a home? Yes__X__   No_____Mortgage Payment Per Month: $ $672

   If yes, please provide address: 8564 Glen Trail_____   Year Purchased: 2008

B. Co-Applicant:

Do you currently live with Applicant?   Yes__X__No_____Total Rent Per Month: $_____

If no:
Do you currently rent?   Yes_____No_____Total Rent Per Month: $_____
Do you current own a home?   Yes_____No_____Mortgage Payment Per Month: $_____

If yes, please provide address: _____Year Purchased: _____

V. OBLIGATION/EXPENSES

Provide information for Applicant <u>and</u> Co-Applicant:

Obligation/Expense	Creditor	Monthly Payment	Balance
Auto Loan	Bridge City Car Loans	$ 265	$ 7500
Auto Loan	Bridge City Bank	$ 328	$ 12,500
Credit Card	Mastercharge, 1111 5021 3333 1098	$ 45	$ 1345
Credit Card		$	$
Credit Card			
Personal Loan			
Alimony/Child Support			
Credit Union (Please Circle)	Saving Loan		
Other	Student Loans	$ 75	$ 3500
Total		$ 713	$ 24845

Lenders need to know about your current monthly expenses to determine how much mortgage you can afford to pay. They will also access your credit report. Make sure you do not intentionally omit any expenses in an attempt to improve your application's chance for success.

Mortgage Application

VI.   EMPLOYMENT INFORMATION

Applicant	**Co-Applicant**

Employer: _West's Tool & Die_   _Franklin Elementary_

Address: _2500 W. Ohio Ave._   _123 School St._

Pittsburgh, PA   Zip _15220_   _Pittsburgh, PA_   Zip _15202_

Month/Year Employed: From: _02/06_ To: _present_   From: _09/2007_ To: _present_

Yearly Gross Salary: $ _38,000_ $ _23,000_

Position Held: _branch manager_   _Classroom aide_

If Employed Less Than Three Years with Current Employer: ←

Previous Employer:_____   _____

Address:_____   _____

Month/Year Employed: From: _____ To: _____   From: _____

> Changing jobs in the past three years will probably not negatively affect your chances of getting a mortgage. Lenders simply want to get a sense of your employment history.

VII.   OTHER SOURCES OF INCOME

> Do you receive regular income from Social Security, investments, or other sources? If so, you should include it here to give a more complete picture of your monthly income.

Applicant	**Co-Applicant**
$_____ per month	$_____ per month
$_____ per month	$_____ per month
$_____ per month	$_____ per month
$_____ per month	$ _____ per month
$_____ per month	$ _____ per month

Total Rent Income:

Other Income (Specify Sources):

_____ $_____ per month $ _____ per month

_____ $_____ per month $ _____ per month

_____ $_____ per month $ _____ per month

_____ $_____ per month $ _____ per month

Mortgage Application

VIII. CREDIT AND LEGAL:

Have you ever been or are you presently involved in any of the following? Check all that apply:

Bankruptcy _____   Judgment _____

Lawsuits _____   Liens on Property _____

Other (Please specify): _____

> Have you declared bankruptcy or been a party to a lawsuit? If so, that will not necessarily prevent you from obtaining a mortgage. However, a recent bankruptcy or property lien may make mortgage approval difficult.

IX. OTHER ASSETS

Stocks, Bonds, Other Investments: $ _700_____
Market Value of Real Estate Owned: $ _____
Other: _____ $ _____

TOTAL: $ _____

X. CERTIFICATION & AUTHORIZATION

I (We) certify that the statements contained in this application for credit are true and accurate concerning my (our) financial condition. This information is given for the purpose of obtaining credit, and I (we) authorize the Urban Redevelopment Authority of Pittsburgh (URA) to investigate my (our) credit.

I (We) also hereby authorize the URA to discuss with _____3rd Bank East_____ (Developer/Lender) any information relating to my (our) Lease/Purchase Agreement and my application for a Mortgage Loan.

_____Daniel C. Wright_____   _____08/01/2012_____
Applicant's Signature   Date

_____Michelle R. Wright_____   _____08/01/2012_____
Co-Applicant's Signature   Date

***** **PLEASE ATTACH THE FOLLOWING:******

1. **Signed copies of your IRS financial income tax returns from the previous two years.**

2. **Copies of your <u>most recent consecutive</u> pay stubs for one (1) month**

3. **A copy of your signed Sales Agreement.**

> Lenders will verify your income by reviewing previous income tax returns or copies of recent pay stubs. If you are planning to apply for a mortgage, be sure to keep copies of your pay stubs and tax returns. You will then be able to easily provide this information.

Offer Letter

When you make a formal offer to purchase a property, your real estate agent will prepare an offer letter like this one. This letter details the terms of your offer to the seller.

> You may wish to include certain existing appliances with the property when you buy it. These may include the refrigerator, stove, and washer and dryer. If so, your offer letter should specify these items.

Contract to Purchase Real Estate

(Form approved by the Dayton Area Board of Realtors®. This is a legally binding contract If the provisions are not understood, legal advise should be obtained.)

Dayton, Ohio ___2-11-12___ Date

1.
2. **OFFER.** The undersigned Purchaser offers to buy through _First Bank of Dayton_
3. Broker(s), on the terms and conditions set forth below, the real property (the "Property") located in _Cedarville_
4. County of _____Greene_____, State of Ohio, described as follows: _2241 Millburn St. 45314_
5.

(Street and number, Zip Code, Legal Description)

6. The Property shall include the land, all appurtenant rights, privileges and easements, and all building, improvements and fixtures, including, but not limited to, such
7. of the following as are now on the Property; all electrical, heating, plumbing and bathroom fixtures; all window and door shades, blinds, awnings and screens; storm
8. windows and doors; television antenna; curtain rods; garage door opener and control(s); all landscaping; and _refrigerator, stove,_
9. _garbage disposal, all attached fixtures, dishwasher_
10.
11. Any personal property items listed above are owned by Seller and will be free and clear of liens and security interest
12. **2. PRICE.** Purchaser agrees to pay for the Property the sum of $ _69,000_
13. payable in cash at closing. Purchaser's obligations under this Contract are conditioned upon Purchaser's ability to obtain prior to closing a mortgage loan of
14. $ _____70,000_____ (Conventional) (FHA) (VA) at rates and terms generally prevailing in the Dayton, Ohio area.
15. Mortgage discount points/origination fees/prepaid items permitted by lender/Purchaser's closing costs not to exceed _____$2000_____ are to be paid by Seller
16. Seller shall have the option to cancel this Contract if Purchaser fails to either (a) make a complete mortgage loan application, including ordering an appraisal, within
17. __3__ days after the date of acceptance of this offer, or (b) obtain mortgage loan approval within __10__ days after the date of acceptance of this offer.
18. **3. DEED.** Seller shall furnish a transferable and recordable general warranty deed conveying to Purchaser, or nominee, a marketable title to the Property (as determined
19. with reference to the Ohio State Bar Association Standards of Title Examinations) with dower rights, if any released, free and clear of all liens, rights to take liens,
20. and encumbrances whatsoever, except (a) legal highways, (b) any mortgage assumed by Purchaser, (s) all installments of taxes and assessments becoming due and
21. payable after closing, (d) rights of tenants in possession, (e) zoning and other laws and (f) easements and restrictions of record which would not prevent Purchaser
22. from using the Property for the following purpose: _____residence_____ If title to all or part
23. of the Property is unmarketable or is subject to matters not excepted as provided above, Seller at Seller's sole cost shall cure any title defects and/or remove such
24. matters within 10 days after receipt of written notice from Purchaser, and if necessary the closing date may be extended to permit Seller the full 10 days to clear title.
25. **TITLE INSURANCE.** Purchasers are encouraged to inquire about the benefits of title insurance from the closing agent or other title insurance provider. A lender's pol-
26. icy of title insurance does not provide protection to the purchaser. It is recommended that purchasers obtain an owner's policy of title insurance to insure their own interests.
27. **4. TAXES.** At closing, Seller shall pay or credit on the purchase price (a) all real estate taxes and assessments, including penalties and interest, which became
28. due and payable prior to the closing, (b) a pro rate share, calculated as of the closing date in the manner set forth below, of the taxes and assessments becoming
29. due and payable after the closing, and (c) the amount of any agricultural tax savings accrued as of the closing date which would be subject to recoupment if the
30. Property were converted to a non-agricultural use (whether or not such conversion actually occurs), unless Purchaser has indicated in paragraph 3 that Purchaser
31. is acquiring the Property for agricultural purposes. If the Property is located in Montgomery County, the tax proration shall b made in accordance with the
32. Montgomery Country "short proration" method, in which Seller's share is based upon the numbers of days from the date of the immediately preceding semi-
33. annual installment to the date of closing. If the Property is located outside of Montgomery County, the tax proration shall be made in accordance with (check one);
34. _____ the Montgomery County "short proration" method or _____ the "long proration" method, in which Seller's share is based upon the taxes and assessments
35. which are a lien for the year of the closing. (If neither method is checked, the short proration shall apply.) If the short proration method is used, any special assessments
36. which are payable in a single annual installment shall nevertheless be prorated on the long proration method. All prorations shall be based upon the most recent avail-
37. able tax rates, assessments and valuations.
38. **5. SELLER'S REPRESENTATIONS.** Seller represents that those signing the Contract constitute all of the owners of the title to the Property, together with their
39. respective spouses. Seller further represents that with respect to the Property (c) no orders of any public authority are pending, (b) no work has been performed or
40. improvements constructed that may result in future assessments,(a) no notices have been received from any public agency with respect to condemnation or appropria-
41. tion, change in zoning, proposed future assessments, correction of conditions, or other similar matters, and (d) to the best of Seller's knowledge, no toxic, explosive
42. or other hazardous substances having stored, disposed of concealed within or release on or from the Property and no other adverse environmental conditions
43. affect the Property. These representations shall survive the closing.
44. **6. POSSESSION.** Rentals, interest on any assumed mortgages, water and other utility bills, and any current operating expenses shall be prorated as of the date of
45. closing. If the Property is owner-occupied, possession is to be given __2__ days after closing at __2__ A.M. (P.M.) and utilities shall not be prorated as above but
46. paid for by Seller until delivery of possession. Seller shall be responsible to Purchaser for any damages caused by Seller's failure to deliver possession on the stated date.
47. **7. DAMAGE TO BUILDINGS.** If any buildings or other improvements are substantially managed or destroyed prior to the closing. Purchaser shall have the option
48. (a) to proceed with the closing and receive the proceeds of any insurance payable in connection therewith, or (b) to terminate this Contract. Seller shall keep the
49. Property adequately insured against fire and extended coverage perils prior to closing. Seller agrees to maintain the Property in its present condition until delivery
50. of possession, subject to ordinary wear and tear, and the provisions of this paragraph. Purchaser shall have the right to conduct a walk-through inspection to verify the
51. condition of the property prior to the closing.
52. **8. ACCEPTANCE; CLOSING.** This offer shall remain open for acceptance until _____2-13-12_____ (Date), at 11:59 p.m. The closing for delivery of the
53. deed and payment of the balance of the purchase price shall be held on or before _____3-10-12_____ (Date), at a time and place mutually agreed upon by Seller and
54. Purchaser. In the event of both parties to agree, the closing shall be held on the last day designated in the paragraph, and the Selling Broker shall designate
55. the time and place of closing.
56. **9. EARNEST MONEY; DEFAULT.** Upon acceptance of this offer, Purchaser has delivered to _____First Bank of Dayton_____, Broker
57. the sum of $ _____500.00_____ as earnest money, to be (1) deposited in the Broker's trust account promptly after acceptance of this offer or (2)
59. closing does not occur because of Seller's default or because any condition of this Contract is not satisfied or waived, Purchaser shall be entitled to the earnest money.
60. The parties acknowledge, however, that the Broker will not make a determination as to which party is entitled to the earnest money. Instead, the Broker shall release the
61. earnest money from the trust account only (a) in accordance with the joint written instructions of Seller and Purchaser, or (b) in accordance with the following proce-
62. dure; if the closing does not occur for any reason (including the default of either party), the Broker holding the earnest money may notify Seller in writing that the earnest
63. money will be returned to Purchaser unless Seller makes a written demand for the earnest money within 20 days after the date of the Broker's notice. If the Broker does
64. not receive a written demand from the Seller within the 20-day period, the Broker shall return the earnest money to Purchaser. If a written demand from Seller is received
65. by the Broker within the 20-day period, the Broker shall retain the earnest money until (i) Seller and Purchaser have settled the dispute; (ii) disposition has been ordered
66. by a final court order; or (iii) the Broker deposits the earnest money with the court pursuant to applicable court procedures. Payment or refund of the earnest money
67. shall not prejudice the rights of the Broker(s) or the non-defaulting party in an action for damages or specific performance against the defaulting party.
68. **10. GENERAL PROVISIONS.** Upon acceptance, this offer shall become a complete agreement binding upon and inuring to benefit of Purchaser and Seller and
69. their respective heirs, personal representatives, successors, and assigns, and shall be deemed to contain all the terms and conditions agreed upon, there being no oral
70. conditions, representations, warranties, or agreements. Any subsequent conditions, representations, warranties, or agreements shall not be valid and binding upon the
71. parties unless in writing signed by both parties. Purchaser has examined the Property and, except as otherwise provided in this Contract, is purchasing it "as is"
72. in its present condition, relying upon such examination as to the condition, character, size, utility, and zoning of the Property. Time is of the essence of all provisions
73. of this Contract. Any word used in this Contract shall be construed to mean either singular or plural as indicated by the number of signatures below.
74. **11. INSPECTIONS AND OTHER ADDENDA.** The following Addenda and attachments are attached to and shall be considered an integral part of this Contract:
75. ☒ Inspection Addendum ☐ Land Contract Addendum ☐ Other (Describe) _____
76. **WITNESS:** _Kristin Sharrod_   **Purchaser** _Karen Mixon_
77. **MAKE DEED TO:** _Karen Mixon_   **Purchaser** _____
78. _____   **Address** _589 S. Collier St., Xenia, OH 45385_

> After the seller accepts the borrower's offer on a house, the contract enters what is commonly called the "inspection period." During this time, the borrower will pay a certified home inspector to inspect the home. The inspector examines the main components of the house (roof, air conditioning, heating elements, plumbing, electrical wiring, etc.), for problems or potential issues. The borrower receives a report of the inspector's findings. During the inspection period, the borrower may choose not to buy the home without losing his or her deposit. The borrower may also choose to renegotiate certain terms of the offer based on findings from the home inspection.

> Once you make an offer, the owner will have a set period of time in which to accept, decline, or make a counter offer. After you have reached an agreement, you will normally close on the property within 30 days.

HUD Application

HUD, or the U.S. Department of Housing and Urban Development, oversees loans offered by the Federal Housing Administration and Veterans Administration. Talk to your loan officer to see whether either of these types of loans may be right for you.

HUD/VA Addendum to Uniform Residential Loan Application

OMB Approval No.   VA: 2900-0144
HUD: 2502-0059 (exp (11/30/2010)

Part I - Identifying Information (mark the type of application)

1. ☐ **VA** Application for Home Loan Guaranty   ☒ **HUD/FHA** Application for Insurance under the National Housing Act

2. Agency Case No. (include any suffix)   555-4056410-001

3. Lender's Case No.

4. Section of the Act (for HUD cases)   203(b)

5. Borrower's Name & Present Address (include zip code)
Collette Foster
163 W. Charles St.
Hammond, LA 70401

6. Property Address (including name of subdivision, lot & block no. & zip code)
4502 S. Olive St.
Hammond, LA 70401

7. Loan Amount (include the UFMIP if for HUD or Funding Fee if for VA) $ 100424

8. Interest Rate   5.350 %

9. Proposed Maturity   30 yrs.   mos.

10. Discount Amount (only if borrower is permitted to pay)

11. Amount of Up Front Premium $ 1484.10

12a. Amount of Monthly Premium $ 40.97 / mo.

12b. Term of Monthly Premium   128 months

13. Lender's I.D. Code   5550125899

14. Sponsor / Agent I.D. Code

15. Lender's Name & Address (include zip code)
Bayou Bank
4799 Prentiss Ave.
New Orleans, LA 70130

16. Name & Address of Sponsor / Agent

17. Lender's Telephone Number   504-555-5011

Type or Print all entries clearly

VA: The veteran and the lender hereby apply to the Secretary of Veterans Affairs for Guaranty of the loan described here under Section 3710, Chapter 37, Title 38, United States Code, to the full extent permitted by the veteran's entitlement and severally agree that the Regulations promulgated pursuant to Chapter 37, and in effect on the date of the loan shall govern the rights, duties, and liabilities of the parties.

18. First Time Homebuyer?
a. ☒ Yes
b. ☐ No

19. VA Only
Title will be Vested in:
☐ Veteran
☐ Veteran & Spouse
☐ Other (specify)

20. Purpose of Loan (blocks 9 - 12 are for VA loans only)

> Because FHA loans require only a 3 percent down payment, you likely will pay additional private mortgage insurance (PMI). You'll pay PMI until you have acquired 10- to 20-percent equity in your home. This loan requires a PMI payment of about $41 per month for nearly 11 years.

Part II - Lender's Certification

21. The undersigned lender makes the following certifications to induce the Department of Veterans Affairs to issue a certificate of commitment to guarantee the subject loan or a Loan Guaranty Certificate under Title 38, U.S. Code, or to induce the Department of Housing and Urban Development - Federal Housing Commissioner to issue a firm commitment for mortgage insurance or a Mortgage Insurance Certificate under the National Housing Act.

A. The loan terms furnished in the Uniform Residential Loan Application and this Addendum are true, accurate and complete.

> Veterans qualify for special loans under the Veterans Administration's loan program. Unlike FHA loans, VA loans can be used to purchase or refinance manufactured homes. They can also be used to buy traditionally constructed homes.

E. The Uniform Residential Loan Application and this Addendum were signed by the borrower after all sections were completed.

F. This proposed loan to the named borrower meets the income and credit requirements of the governing law in the judgment of the undersigned.

G. To the best of my knowledge and belief, I and my firm and its principals: **(1)** are not presently debarred, suspended, proposed for debarment, declared ineligible, or voluntarily excluded from covered transactions by any Federal department or agency; **(2)** have not, within a three-year period preceding this proposal, been convicted of or had a civil judgment rendered against them for (a) commission of fraud or a criminal offense in connection with obtaining, attempting to obtain, or performing a public (Federal, State or local) transaction or contract under a public transaction; (b) violation of Federal or State antitrust statutes or commission of embezzlement, theft, forgery, bribery, falsification or destruction of records, making false statements, or receiving stolen property; **(3)** are not presently indicted for or otherwise criminally or civilly charged by a governmental entity (Federal, State or local) with commission of any of the offenses enumerated in paragraph G(2) of this certification; and **(4)** have not, within a three-year period preceding this application/proposal, had one or more public transactions (Federal, State or local) terminated for cause or default.

Items "H" through "J" are to be completed as applicable for VA loans only.

H. The names and functions of any duly authorized agents who developed on behalf of the lender any of the information or supporting credit data submitted are as follows:
Name & Address

Function (e.g., obtained information on the Uniform Residential Loan Application, ordered credit report, verifications of employment, deposits, etc.)

If no agent is shown above, the undersigned lender affirmatively certifies that all information and supporting credit data were obtained directly by the lender.

I. The undersigned lender understands and agrees that it is responsible for the omissions, errors, or acts of agents identified in item H as to the functions with which they are identified.

J. The proposed loan conforms otherwise with the applicable provisions of Title 38, U.S. Code, and of the regulations concerning guaranty or insurance of loans to veterans.

Signature of Officer of Lender   Title of Officer of Lender   Date (mm/dd/yyyy)

Part III - Notices to Borrowers. Public reporting burden for this collection of information is estimated to average 6 minutes per response, including the time for reviewing instructions, searching existing data sources, gathering and maintaining the data needed, and completing and reviewing the collection of information. This agency may not conduct or sponsor, and a person is not required to respond to, a collection information unless that collection displays a valid OMB control number can be located on the OMB Internet page at http://www.whitehouse.gov/omb/library/OMBINV.LIST.OF.AGENCIES. html#LIST_OF_AGENCIES. **Privacy Act Information.** The information requested on the Uniform Residential Loan Application and this Addendum is authorized by 38 U.S.C. 3710 (if for DVA)and 12 U.S.C. 1701 et seq. (if for HUD/FHA). The Debt Collection Act of 1982, Pub. Law 97-365, and HUD's Housing and Community Development Act of 1987, 42 U.S.C. 3543, require persons applying for a federally insured or guaranteed loan to furnish his/her social security number (SSN). You must provide all the requested information, including your SSN. HUD and/or VA may conduct a computer match to verify the information you provide. HUD and/or VA may disclose certain information to Federal, State and local agencies when relevant to civil, criminal, or regulatory investigations and prosecutions. It will not otherwise be disclosed or released outside of HUD or VA, except as required and permitted by law. The information will be used to determine whether you qualify as a mortgagor. Any disclosure of information outside VA or HUD/FHA will be made only as permitted by law. Failure to provide any of the requested information, including SSN, may

HUD Application

Unlike a rental unit, purchased homes require that payments be made on them even if you no longer live there. If you decide to move out of your home, you must continue to make mortgage payments until you sell it and pay off the loan entirely.

result in disapproval of your loan application. This is notice to you as required by the Right to Financial Privacy Act of 1978 that VA or HUD/FHA has a right of access to financial records held by financial institutions in connection with the consideration or administration of assistance to you. Financial records involving your transaction will be available to VA and HUD/FHA without further notice or authorization but will not be disclosed or released by this institution to another Government Agency or Department without your consent except as required or permitted by law. Caution. Delinquencies, defaults, foreclosures and abuses of mortgage loans involving programs of the Federal Government can be costly and detrimental to your credit, now and in the future. The lender in this transaction, its agents and assigns as well as the Federal Government, its agencies, agents and assigns, are authorized to take any and all of the following actions in the event loan payments become delinquent on the mortgage loan described in the attached application: (1) Report your name and account information to a credit bureau; (2) Assess additional interest and penalty charges for the period of time that payment is not made; (3) Assess charges to cover additional administrative costs incurred by the Government to service your account; (4) Offset amounts owed to you under other Federal programs; (5) Refer your account to a private attorney, collection agency or mortgage servicing agency to collect the amount due, foreclose the mortgage, sell the property and seek judgment against you for any deficiency; (6) Refer your account to the Department of Justice for litigation in the courts; (7) If you are a current or retired Federal employee, take action to offset your salary, or civil service retirement benefits; (8) Refer your debt to the Internal Revenue Service for offset against any amount owed to you as an income tax refund; and (9) Report any resulting written-off debt of yours to the Internal Revenue Service as your taxable income. All of these actions can and will be used to recover any debts owed when it is determined to be in the interest of the lender and/or the Federal Government to do so.

Part IV - Borrower Consent for Social Security Administration to Verify Social Security Number

I authorize the Social Security Administration to verify my Social Security number to the Lender identified in this document and HUD/FHA, through a computer match conducted by HUD/FHA.

I understand that my consent allows no additional information from my Social Security records to be provided to the Lender, and HUD/FHA and that verification of my Social Security number does not constitute confirmation of my identity. I also understand that my Social Security number may not be used for any other purpose than the one stated above, including resale or redisclosure to other parties. The only other redisclosure permitted by this authorization is for review purposes to ensure that HUD/FHA complies with SSA's consent requirements.

I am the individual to whom the Social Security number was issued or that person's legal guardian. I declare and affirm under the penalty of perjury that the information contained herein is true and correct. I know that if I make any representation that I know is false to obtain information from Social Security records, I could be punished by a fine or imprisonment or both.

This consent is valid for 180 days from the date signed, unless indicated otherwise by the individual(s) named in this loan application.

Read consent carefully. Review accuracy of social security number(s) and birth dates provided on this application.

Signature(s) of Borrower(s)	Date Signed	Signature(s) of Co - Borrower(s)	Date Signed
Collette Foster	11/4/12		/ /

Part V - Borrower Certification

22. **Complete the following for a HUD/FHA Mortgage .**

22a. Do you own or have you sold **other** real estate within the past 60 months on which there was a HUD/FHA mortgage? ☐ Yes ☐ No

Is it to be sold? ☐ Yes ☐ No 22b. Sales Price $ 22c. Original Mortgage Amt $

22d. Address

22e. If the dwelling to be covered by this mortgage is to be rented, is it a part of, adjacent or contiguous to any project subdivision or group of concentrated rental properties involving eight or more dwelling units in which you have any financial interest? ☐ Yes ☐ No If "Yes" give details.

22f. Do you own more than four dwellings ? ☐ Yes ☐ No If "Yes" submit form HUD-92561.

23. **Complete for VA-Guaranteed Mortgage** . Have you ever had a VA home Loan? ☐ Yes ☐ No

24. **Applicable for Both VA & HUD.** As a home loan borrower, you will be legally obligated to make the mortgage payments called for by your mortgage loan contract. The fact that you dispose of your property after the loan has been made **will not relieve you of liability for making these payments. Payment of the loan in full is ordinarily the way liability on a mortgage note is ended.** Some home buyers have the mistaken impression that if they sell their homes when they move to another locality, or dispose of it for any other reasons, they are no longer liable for the mortgage payments and that liability for these payments is solely that of the new owners. Even though the new owners may agree in writing to assume liability for your mortgage payments, this assumption agreement will not relieve you from liability to the holder of the note which you signed when you obtained the loan to buy the property. Unless you are able to sell the property to a buyer who is acceptable to VA or to HUD/FHA and who will assume the payment of your obligation to the lender, you will not be relieved from liability to repay any claim which VA or HUD/FHA may be required to pay your lender on account of default in your loan payments. **The amount of any such claim payment will be a debt owed by you to the Federal Government.** This debt will be the object of established collection procedures.

It is against the law for a lender or borrower to refuse to give someone a loan on the basis of his or her race, national origin, age, religion, or other personal factors. If you believe that you have been denied a loan for one of these reasons, you may be able to take legal action.

Note: If box 2b or 2d is checked, the veteran's spouse must also sign below.

(3) Mark the applicable box (not applicable for Home Improvement or Refinancing Loan) I have been informed that ($) is :

☐ the reasonable value of the property as determined by VA or;

☒ the statement of appraised value as determined by HUD / FHA.

Note: If the contract price or cost exceeds the VA "Reasonable Value" or HUD/FHA "Statement of Appraised Value", mark either item (a) or item (b), whichever is applicable.

☐ (a) I was aware of this valuation when I signed my contract and I have paid or will pay in cash from my own resources at or prior to loan closing a sum equal to the difference between the contract purchase price or cost and the VA or HUD/FHA established value. I do not and will not have outstanding after loan closing any unpaid contractual obligation on account of such cash payment;

☐ (b) I was not aware of this valuation when I signed my contract but have elected to complete the transaction at the contract purchase price or cost. I have paid or will pay in cash from my own resources at or prior to loan closing a sum equal to the difference between contract purchase price or cost and the VA or HUD/FHA established value. I do not and will not have outstanding after loan closing any unpaid contractual obligation on account of such cash payment.

(4) Neither I, nor anyone authorized to act for me, will refuse to sell or rent, after the making of a bona fide offer, or refuse to negotiate for the sale or rental of, or otherwise make unavailable or deny the dwelling or property covered by his/her loan to any person because of race, color, religion, sex, handicap, familial status or national origin. I recognize that any restrictive covenant on this property relating to race, color, religion, sex, handicap, familial status or national origin is illegal and void and civil action for preventive relief may be brought by the Attorney General of the United States in any appropriate U.S. District Court against any person responsible for the violation of the applicable law.

(5) All information in this application is given for the purpose of obtaining a loan to be insured under the National Housing Act or guaranteed by the Department of Veterans Affairs and the information in the Uniform Residential Loan Application and this Addendum is true and complete to the best of my knowledge and belief. Verification may be obtained from any source named herein.

(6) **For HUD Only** (for properties constructed prior to 1978) I have received information on lead paint poisoning. ☐ Yes ☐ Not Applicable

(7) **I am aware that neither HUD / FHA nor VA warrants the condition or value of the property**

Signature(s) of Borrower(s) -- **Do not sign** unless this application is fully completed. Read the certifications carefully & review accuracy of this application.

Signature(s) of Borrower(s)	Date Signed	Signature(s) of Co - Borrower(s)	Date Signed
Collette Foster	11/4/12		/ /

(**Borrowers Must Sign Both Parts IV & V**) Federal statutes provide severe penalties for any fraud, intentional misrepresentation, or criminal connivance or conspiracy purposed to influence the issuance of any guaranty or insurance by the VA Secretary or the HUD/FHA Commissioner.

HUD Application

When you apply for a mortgage, your approval is only good for a set period of time. This means that if you apply before you have an accepted house offer, your mortgage approval might expire before you complete your purchase. You would then need to reapply.

Direct Endorsement Approval for a HUD/FHA-Insured Mortgage

U.S. Department of Housing and Urban Development

Part I - Identifying Information (mark the type of application)

1. [X] **HUD/FHA** Application for Insurance under the National Housing Act

2. Agency Case No. (include any suffix)   555-4056410-001

3. Lender's Case No.

4. Section of the Act (for HUD cases)   203(b)

5. Borrower's Name & Present Address (include zip code)
Collette Foster
163 W. Charles St.
Hammond, LA 70401

6. Property Address (including name of subdivision, lot & block no. & zip code)
4502 S. Olive St.
Hammond, LA 70401

7. Loan Amount (include the UFMIP) $ 100424

8. Interest Rate   5.350 %

9. Proposed Maturity   30 yrs.   mos.

10. Discount Amount (only if borrower is permitted to pay)

11. Amount of Up Front Premium $ 1484.10

12a. Amount of Monthly Premium $ 40.97 /mo.

12b. Term of Monthly Premium   128 months

13. Lender's I.D. Code   5550125899

14. Sponsor / Agent I.D. Code

15. Lender's Name & Address (include zip code)
Bayou Bank
4799 Prentiss Ave.
New Orleans, LA 70130

16. Name & Address of Sponsor / Agent

17. Lender's Telephone Number   504-555-5011

Type or Print all entries clearly

[X] **Approved:** Approved subject to the additional conditions stated below, if any.

Date Mortgage Approved   3/2/2011

Date Approval Expires   9/6/2011

[ ] **Modified & Approved as follows:**

Loan Amount (include UFMIP)	Interest Rate	Proposed Maturity	Monthly Payment	Amount of Up Front Premium	Amount of Monthly Premium	Term of Monthly Premium
$	%	Yrs. Mos	$	$	$	months

Additional Conditions:

[ ] If this is proposed construction, the builder has certified compliance with HUD requirements on form HUD-92541.

[ ] If this is new construction, the lender certifies that the property is 100% complete (both on site and off site improvements) **and** the property meets HUD's minimum property standards and local building codes.

[ ] Form HUD-92544, Builder's Warranty is required.

[ ] The property has a 10-year warranty.

[ ] Owner-Occupancy **Not** required (item (b) of the Borrower's Certificate does not apply).

[ ] The mortgage is a high loan-to-value ratio for non-occupant mortgagor in military.

[ ] Other: (specify)

Your FHA or VA loan may be subject to certain modifications or conditions. Be sure to review any of these additional conditions. Make sure that you follow all the rules associated with your new mortgage.

[ ] This mortgage was rated as an "accept" or "approve" by FHA's Total Mortgage Scorecard. As such, the undersigned representative of the mortgagee certifies to the integrity of the data supplied by the lender used to determine the quality of the loan, that a Direct Endorsement Underwriter reviewed the appraisal (if applicable) and further certifies that this mortgage is eligible for HUD mortgage insurance under the Direct Endorsement program. I hereby make all certifications required for this mortgage as set forth in HUD Handbook 4000.4

Mortgagee Representative _____

[X] This mortgage was rated as a "refer" by a FHA's Total Mortgage Scorecard, and/or was manually underwritten by a Direct Endorsement underwriter. As such, the undersigned Direct Endorsement underwriter certifies that I have personally reviewed the appraisal report (if applicable), credit application, and all associated documents and have used due diligence in underwriting this mortgage. I find that this mortgage is eligible for HUD mortgage insurance under the Direct Endorsement program and I hereby make all certifications required for this mortgage as set forth in HUD Handbook 4000.4

Direct Endorsement Underwriter _T. Harrison Ford_   DE's CHUMS ID Number _____

The Mortgagee, its owners, officers, employees or directors [ ] do [X] do not **have a financial interest in or a relationship, by affiliation or ownership, with the builder or seller involved in this transaction.**

Truth-in-Lending Statement

A truth-in-lending statement provides information about the actual costs associated with your mortgage. Reviewing this statement will help you better understand the amount you will pay over the life of your loan.

FEDERAL TRUTH-IN-LENDING DISCLOSURE STATEMENT
(MADE IN COMPLIANCE WITH FEDERAL LAW)

Lender: **RICHMOND CREDIT UNION**
Loan No.: **33-550154-0**   Date: **05/15/12**
Borrower(s): **DARLENE RICKMAN, DARIUS RICKMAN**

Property Address: **50123 N. 24TH ST.**
RICHMOND, VA 23220

☐ Initial Disclosure estimated at time of application   ☒ Final Disclosure based on contract terms

ANNUAL PERCENTAGE RATE	FINANCE CHARGE	AMOUNT FINANCED	TOTAL OF PAYMENTS
The cost of your credit as a yearly rate.	The dollar amount the credit will cost you assuming the annual percentage rate does not change.	The amount of credit provided to you or on your behalf as of loan closing.	The amount you will have paid after you have made all payments as scheduled assuming the annual percentage rate does not change.
5.855 %	$ **108077.07**	$ **98616.07**	$ **206693.14**

YOUR PAYMENT SCHEDULE WILL BE:

NUMBER OF PAYMENTS	* AMOUNT OF PAYMENTS	MONTHLY PAYMENTS ARE DUE BEGINNING	NUMBER OF PAYMENTS	* AMOUNT OF PAYMENTS	MONTHLY PAYMENTS ARE DUE BEGINNING
12	601.76	05/01/2006			
12	601.17	05/01/2007			
12	600.55	05/01/2008			
12	599.90	05/01/2009			
12	599.22	05/01/2010			
12	598.49	05/01/2011			
12	597.73	05/01/2012			
12	596.92	05/01/2013			
12	596.07	05/01/2014			
12	595.18	05/01/2015			
8	594.23	05/01/2016			
231	560.79	01/01/2017			
1	552.93	04/01/2036			

* Includes mortgage insurance

> Most likely, you will pay off your home loan over the course of 15 or 30 years. If so, you'll end up paying much more than the original loan amount. For example, this loan is for $98,616.07. However, the borrowers pay interest for 30 years. As a result, the borrowers will actually pay $206,693.14 to the lender over the life of the loan.

> Note that this loan includes payments that decrease for the first several years as the homeowner pays less private mortgage insurance (PMI). The interest rate and principal paid on the mortgage itself does not change over time.

☐ **DEMAND FEATURE:**   This loan transaction has a demand feature.
☒ **REQUIRED DEPOSIT:**   The annual percentage rate does not take into account your required deposit.
☐ **VARIABLE RATE FEATURE:**   The annual percentage rate may increase during the term of your loan if the index used to set the Note interest rate increases. A new index may be substituted under certain circumstances, and substitution of the new index may also increase the rate. The index at the beginning of your loan is described below:

SECURITY INTEREST: You are giving a security interest in:
☒ the goods or property being purchased.   ☐ real property you already own.

FILING OR RECORDING FEES: $ **150.00**
LATE CHARGE: If a payment is more than **15** days late, you will be charged $ **30.50** / **4.00** % of the total payment past due.

PREPAYMENT: If you pay off your loan early, you
☐ may   ☒ will not   have to pay a penalty.
☐ may   ☒ will not   be entitled to a refund of part of the finance charge.

INSURANCE: Credit life, accident, health or loss of income insurance is not required in connection with this loan. This loan transaction requires the following insurance:
☒ Hazard Insurance   ☐ Flood Insurance   ☐ Private Mortgage Insurance   ☒ Mutual Mortgage Insurance
Borrower(s) may obtain hazard and flood insurance through any person of his/her choice, provided said carrier meets the requirements of the Lender. If Borrower desires Property Insurance to be obtained through the Lender's designated agency, the cost will be set forth in a separate insurance statement furnished by the Lender.

ASSUMPTION: Someone buying your house
☐ may   ☒ may, subject to conditions,   ☐ may not assume the remainder of your loan on the original terms.
See your contract documents for additional information regarding nonpayment, default, right to accelerate the maturity of the obligation, prepayment rebates and penalties, and the Lender's policy regarding assumption of the obligation.
☐ all dates and numerical disclosures except late payment disclosures are estimates.   means an estimate.

The undersigned hereby acknowledge receiving and reading a completed copy of this disclosure along with copies of the documents provided. The delivery and signing of this disclosure does not constitute an obligation on the part of the lender to make, or the Borrower(s) to accept, the loan as identified.

Read, acknowledged and accepted this **15th** day of **May, 2012**

Darlene Rickman _____(Borrower)   _____(Borrower)
DARLENE RICKMAN
Darius Rickman _____(Borrower)   _____(Borrower)
DARIUS RICKMAN

> Just like utility and credit card bills, mortgage payments must be made on time or you may incur a late fee. This fee may vary depending on the amount of your mortgage.

Settlement Statement

When you close on, or purchase, a property, you will receive a settlement statement. This document explains all of the closing costs associated with the transfer of the property. This statement shows your costs as either a buyer or as a seller.

A.		B. TYPE OF LOAN:		
U.S. DEPARTMENT OF HOUSING & URBAN DEVELOPMENT		1. [X] FHA 2. [ ] FmHA 3. [ ] CONV. UNINS. 4. [ ] VA 5. [ ] CONV. INS.		
SETTLEMENT STATEMENT		6. FILE NUMBER: 55501255	7. LOAN NUMBER: 005659932004	
		8. MORTGAGE INS CASE NUMBER: 555-1105685-559		

C. NOTE: This form is furnished to give you a statement of actual settlement costs. Amounts paid to and by the settlement agent are shown.
Items marked "[POC]" were paid outside the closing; they are shown here for informational purposes and are not included in the totals.
1.0 3/96 (091303.PFD/091303/20)

D. NAME AND ADDRESS OF BORROWER:	E. NAME AND ADDRESS OF SELLER:
John Prentice	Mario Hernandez
G. PROPERTY LOCATION: 55012 Nahiolea St. Apt. 389 Halawa, HI 96701	**H. SETTLEMENT AGENT:** 55-5065014 Halston's Title Agency, Inc. **PLACE OF SETTLEMENT** 9011 Kaonohi St., Suite 3, Halawa, HI 96701

> The value of your home may rise or fall in the time after you purchase it. If you sell it for less than the amount of your original mortgage, you must pay the difference between the sale price and the mortgage amount. This means that a seller might have to take a financial loss if he or she needs to sell a property that has declined in value.

J. SUMMARY OF BORROWER'S TRANSACTION		K. SUMMARY OF SELLER'S TRANSACTION	
100. GROSS AMOUNT DUE FROM BORROWER:		**400. GROSS AMOUNT DUE TO SELLER:**	
101. Contract Sales Price	98,500.00	401. Contract Sales Price	98,500.00
102. Personal Property		402. Personal Property	
103. Settlement Charges to Borrower (Line 1400)	1,901.60	403.	
104.		404.	
105.		405.	
Adjustments For Items Paid By Seller in advance		*Adjustments For Items Paid By Seller in advance*	
106. County Assessments to		406. County Assessments to	
107. County Taxes to		407. County Taxes to	
108. Assessments to		408. Assessments to	
109.		409.	
110.		410.	
111.		411.	
112.		412.	
120. GROSS AMOUNT DUE FROM BORROWER	100,401.60	**420. GROSS AMOUNT DUE TO SELLER**	98,500.00
200. AMOUNTS PAID BY OR IN BEHALF OF BORROWER:		**500. REDUCTIONS IN AMOUNT DUE TO SELLER:**	
201. Deposit/earnest money $250.00 RETURNED		501. Excess Deposit (See Instructions)	
202. Principal Amount of New Loan(s)	96,715.00	502. Settlement Charges to Seller (Line 1400)	10,174.25
203. Existing loan(s) taken subject to		503. Existing loan(s) taken subject to	
204.		504. Payoff of first Mortgage to U. S. Home Mortgage	102,786.82
205.		505. Payoff of second Mortgage	
206.		506.	
207.		507. Courier Docs & Wire Payoff fee to Safemark Title A	85.00
208.		508.	
209.		509.	
Adjustments For Items Unpaid By Seller		*Adjustments For Items Unpaid By Seller*	
210. County Assessments to		510. County Assessments to	
211. County Taxes 01/01/09 to 04/30/09	541.07	511. County Taxes 01/01/09 to 04/30/09	541.07
212. Assessments to		512. Assessments to	
213.		513.	
214.		514.	
215.		515.	
216.		516.	
217.		517.	
218.		518.	
219.		519.	
220. TOTAL PAID BY/FOR BORROWER	97,256.07	**520. TOTAL REDUCTION AMOUNT DUE SELLER**	113,587.14
300. CASH AT SETTLEMENT FROM/TO BORROWER:		**600. CASH AT SETTLEMENT TO/FROM SELLER:**	
301. Gross Amount Due From Borrower (Line 120)	100,401.60	601. Gross Amount Due To Seller (Line 420)	98,500.00
302. Less Amount Paid By/For Borrower (Line 220)	(97,256.07)	602. Less Reductions Due Seller (Line 520)	(113,587.14)
303. CASH (X FROM) (TO) BORROWER	3,145.53	*603. CASH (TO) (X FROM) SELLER*	15,087.14

Substitute Form 1099-S:

SELLER'S TAX ID SOLICITATION: THE INFORMATION IN BLOCKS E, G, H, I AND ON LINES 401, 406, 407 and 408 IS IMPORTANT TAX INFORMATION AND IS BEING FURNISHED TO THE INTERNAL REVENUE SERVICE. IF YOU ARE REQUIRED TO FILE A RETURN, A NEGLIGENCE PENALTY OR OTHER SANCTION MAY BE IMPOSED ON YOU IF THIS ITEM IS REQUIRED TO BE REPORTED AND THE IRS DETERMINES THAT IT HAS NOT BEEN REPORTED. YOU ARE REQUIRED BY LAW TO PROVIDE THE SETTLEMENT AGENT WITH YOUR CORRECT TAXPAYER IDENTIFICATION NUMBER. IF YOU DO NOT PROVIDE THE SETTLEMENT AGENT WITH YOUR CORRECT TAXPAYER IDENTIFICATION NUMBER, YOU MAY BE SUBJECT TO CIVIL OR CRIMINAL PENALTIES IMPOSED BY LAW.

For sales or exchanges of certain real estate, the person responsible for closing a real estate transaction must report the real estate proceeds to the Internal Revenue Service and must furnish this statement to you. To determine if you have to report the sale or exchange of your main home on your tax return, see the 2009 Schedule D (Form 1040) instructions. If the real estate was not your main home, report the transaction on Form 4797, Sales of Business Property, Form 6252, Installment Sale Income, and/or Schedule D (Form 1040). Capital Gains and Losses. You may have to recapture (pay back) all or part of a Federal mortgage subsidy if all the following apply: a) You received a loan provided from the proceeds of a qualified mortgage bond or you received a mortgage credit certificate; b) Your original mortgage loan was provided after 1990; and c) You sold or disposed of your home at a gain during the first 9 years after you received the Federal mortgage subsidy. This will increase your tax. See Form 8828, Recapture of Federal Mortgage Subsidy, and Pub. 523, Selling Your Home.

If you have already paid the real estate tax for the period that includes the sale date, subtract the amounts on Lines 406, 407 & 408 from the amount already paid to determine your deductible real estate tax. But if you have already deducted the real estate tax in a prior year, generally report this amount as income on the "Other Income" line of Form 1040. For more information, see Pub. 523.

For Paperwork Reduction Act Notice, see the 2009 Instructions for Forms 1099, 1098, 5498, and W-G2.
Department of the Treasury - Internal Revenue Service

UNDER PENALTIES OF PERJURY, I CERTIFY THAT THE NUMBER SHOWN BELOW ON THIS STATEMENT

Mario Hernandez

Seller's Signature   Seller's Signature
TaxID/SSN: TaxID/SSN:

> The seller must pay this amount in order to clear his or her original mortgage debt in addition to the sale price of the home. If a home has declined steeply in value, this amount could be much more.

Settlement Statement

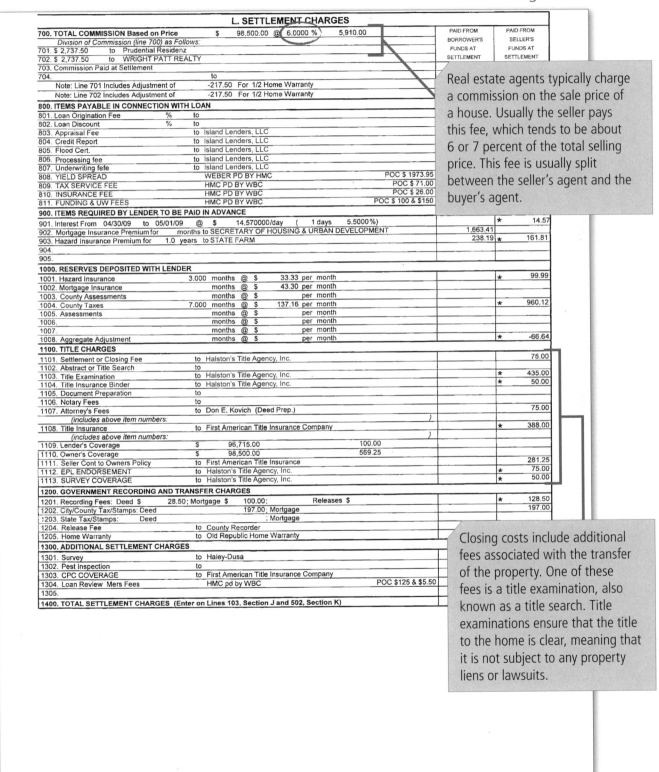

L. SETTLEMENT CHARGES

		PAID FROM BORROWER'S FUNDS AT SETTLEMENT	PAID FROM SELLER'S FUNDS AT SETTLEMENT
700. TOTAL COMMISSION Based on Price $ 98,500.00 @ 6.0000 % 5,910.00			
Division of Commission (line 700) as Follows:			
701. $ 2,737.50 to Prudential Residenz			
702. $ 2,737.50 to WRIGHT PATT REALTY			
703. Commission Paid at Settlement			
704. to			
Note: Line 701 Includes Adjustment of -217.50 For 1/2 Home Warranty			
Note: Line 702 Includes Adjustment of -217.50 For 1/2 Home Warranty			
800. ITEMS PAYABLE IN CONNECTION WITH LOAN			
801. Loan Origination Fee % to			
802. Loan Discount % to			
803. Appraisal Fee to Island Lenders, LLC			
804. Credit Report to Island Lenders, LLC			
805. Flood Cert. to Island Lenders, LLC			
806. Processing fee to Island Lenders, LLC			
807. Underwriting fefe to Island Lenders, LLC			
808. YIELD SPREAD WEBER PD BY HMC	POC $ 1973.95		
809. TAX SERVICE FEE HMC PD BY WBC	POC $ 71.00		
810. INSURANCE FEE HMC PD BY WBC	POC $ 26.00		
811. FUNDING & UW FEES HMC PD BY WBC	POC $ 100 & $150		
900. ITEMS REQUIRED BY LENDER TO BE PAID IN ADVANCE			
901. Interest From 04/30/09 to 05/01/09 @ $ 14.570000/day (1 days 5.5000%)		* 14.57	
902. Mortgage Insurance Premium for months to SECRETARY OF HOUSING & URBAN DEVELOPMENT		1,663.41	
903. Hazard Insurance Premium for 1.0 years to STATE FARM		238.19 * 161.81	
904.			
905.			
1000. RESERVES DEPOSITED WITH LENDER			
1001. Hazard Insurance 3.000 months @ $ 33.33 per month		* 99.99	
1002. Mortgage Insurance months @ $ 43.30 per month			
1003. County Assessments months @ $ per month			
1004. County Taxes 7.000 months @ $ 137.16 per month		* 960.12	
1005. Assessments months @ $ per month			
1006. months @ $ per month			
1007. months @ $ per month			
1008. Aggregate Adjustment months @ $ per month		* -66.64	
1100. TITLE CHARGES			
1101. Settlement or Closing Fee to Halston's Title Agency, Inc.		75.00	
1102. Abstract or Title Search to			
1103. Title Examination to Halston's Title Agency, Inc.		* 435.00	
1104. Title Insurance Binder to Halston's Title Agency, Inc.		* 50.00	
1105. Document Preparation to			
1106. Notary Fees to			
1107. Attorney's Fees to Don E. Kovich (Deed Prep.)		75.00	
(includes above item numbers:)			
1108. Title Insurance to First American Title Insurance Company		* 388.00	
(includes above item numbers:)			
1109. Lender's Coverage $ 96,715.00 100.00			
1110. Owner's Coverage $ 98,500.00 569.25			
1111. Seller Cont to Owners Policy to First American Title Insurance		281.25	
1112. EPL ENDORSEMENT to Halston's Title Agency, Inc.		* 75.00	
1113. SURVEY COVERAGE to Halston's Title Agency, Inc.		* 50.00	
1200. GOVERNMENT RECORDING AND TRANSFER CHARGES			
1201. Recording Fees: Deed $ 28.50; Mortgage $ 100.00; Releases $		* 128.50	
1202. City/County Tax/Stamps: Deed 197.00; Mortgage		197.00	
1203. State Tax/Stamps: Deed ; Mortgage			
1204. Release Fee to County Recorder			
1205. Home Warranty to Old Republic Home Warranty			
1300. ADDITIONAL SETTLEMENT CHARGES			
1301. Survey to Haley-Dusa			
1302. Pest Inspection to			
1303. CPC COVERAGE to First American Title Insurance Company			
1304. Loan Review Mers Fees HMC pd by WBC	POC $125 & $5.50		
1305.			
1400. TOTAL SETTLEMENT CHARGES (Enter on Lines 103, Section J and 502, Section K)			

Real estate agents typically charge a commission on the sale price of a house. Usually the seller pays this fee, which tends to be about 6 or 7 percent of the total selling price. This fee is usually split between the seller's agent and the buyer's agent.

Closing costs include additional fees associated with the transfer of the property. One of these fees is a title examination, also known as a title search. Title examinations ensure that the title to the home is clear, meaning that it is not subject to any property liens or lawsuits.

Home Equity Loan Application

After you have made payments for a while on your home, you likely will have some equity, or stored value, in it. You may wish to borrow against this to pay for home improvements or other expenses. Remember that this loan must be repaid when you sell your house.

HOME EQUITY LOAN APPLICATION
PLEASE TYPE OR PRINT

You may use a home equity loan to pay for anything you wish. However, responsible borrowers tend to use these funds to make improvements that increase the value of their homes.

Check one to indicate the type of account you are requesting. Note: Married applicants may apply for separate accounts.

☒ Joint Account
☐ Individual Account - Relying solely on my income and assets.
☐ Individual Account - Relying on my income and assets as well as income or assets of another.

INFORMATION FOR GOVERNMENT MONITORING PURPOSES

The following information is requested by the Federal Government if this loan is related to a dwelling, in order to monitor the lender's compliance with equal credit opportunity and fair housing laws. You are not required to furnish this information, but are encouraged to do so. The law provides that a lender may neither discriminate on the basis of this information, nor on whether you choose to furnish it. However, if you choose not to furnish it, under Federal regulations this lender is required to note race and sex on the basis of visual observation or surname. If you do not wish to furnish the above information, please initial below.

Home equity loans normally only cover a portion of the total value of your home. They must be repaid in a shorter period of time than traditional mortgages.

CO-APPLICANT: I do not wish to furnish this information (initials) _____
RACE/NATIONAL ORIGIN: ☒ Black ☐ Hispanic ☐ White
☐ American Indian, Alaskan Native ☐ Asian, Pacific Islander
☐ Other (specify) _____
SEX: ☐ Male ☒ Female **AGE** _____ yrs.
MARITAL STATUS: ☒ Married ☐ Separated
☐ Unmarried (includes single, divorced, widowed)

TERMS REQUESTED

Amount	Length of Account Term	Periodic Payment Date	Purpose
$ 15,000	10 years	15th	Home improvements

COLLATERAL PROPERTY

Address	Year Built	Date Purchased	Present Value	Balance Owing
1934 Horner Street, Killeen, TX 76540	1982	07/2009	145,000	105,000

Title in Name(s) of:	Address of Title Holder	Name and Address of Mortgage Holder
Anthony E. Swallow	1934 Horner Street, Killeen, TX 76540	Bank of Texas Phone No. 888-555-9899 Acct. No. B550294001555

INDIVIDUAL APPLICANT INFORMATION

Name	Birthdate	Social Security No.
Anthony E. Swallow	3 / 23 / 74	XXX-XX-XXXX

Address	County	Drivers License No.
1934 Horner Street, Killeen, TX 76540	Bell	AA22000813

Home Phone	Business Phone	Number of Dependants	Age of Dependants
254-555-6127	254-555-3600	1	12

Employer/Self Employed	Position	Years Employed	Employer's Address
U.S. Army	Traffic coordinator	4	12500 King St., Killeen TX 76545

Previous Employer	Position	Years Employed	Previous Employer's Address
On Time Arrivals	Delivery person	2	5675 E. 35th St., Killeen TX 76451

Name and Address of Applicant's Nearest Relative	Relationship
Dina Swallow, 857 S. Ranch Dr., Killeen TX 76544	mother

Wages, Salary, Commissions		How Often Paid
Gross $ 2800 /month Net $ 1960 /month		biweekly

Alimony, child support, or separate maintenance income need not be revealed if you do not wish to have it considered. Alimony, child support, or separate maintenance received pursuant to: ☐ Court Order ☐ Written Agreement ☐ Oral Understanding.

Other Income: Source _____ Amount/Month _____

Marital Status ☒ Married ☐ Separated ☐ Unmarried (includes single, divorced, and widowed)

TYPE OF ACCOUNT REQUESTED

Provide the information in this section for a joint applicant, another party that will use or contribute assets or income toward repayment on the account, or for your spouse if you live in, or the collateral property is located in, AZ, CA, ID, LA, NM, NV, TX, WA or WI.

Name	Birthdate	Social Security No.
Keara Swallow	7 / 18 / 75	XXX-XX-XXXX

Address	County	Drivers License No.
1934 Horner Street, Killeen, TX 76540	Bell	AA28800544

Home Phone	Business Phone	Number of Dependants	Age of Dependants
254-555-6127	254-555-1850	2	12, 17

Employer/Self Employed	Position	Years Employed	Employer's Address
First Employment Services	Traffic coordinator	4	6598 Rose Trail, Killeen TX 76548

Previous Employer	Position	Years Employed	Previous Employer's Address
On Time Arrivals	Human resources associate	2	5675 E. 35th St., Killeen TX 76451

Name and Address of Joint Applicant's or Other Party's Nearest Relative	Relationship
Keith Harrison, 3571 E. 18th St., Killeen TX 76542	

Wages, Salary, Commissions		How Often Paid
Gross $ 2500 /month Net $ 1750 /month		biweekly

Alimony, child support, or separate maintenance income need not be revealed if you do not wish to have it considered. Alimony, child support, or separate maintenance received pursuant to: ☐ Court Order ☐ Written Agreement ☐ Oral Understanding.

Other Income: Source _____ Amount/Month _____

Marital Status ☒ Married ☐ Separated ☐ Unmarried (includes single, divorced and widowed)

Home Equity Loan Application

Your ability to qualify for a home equity loan will depend on your personal assets and debts. Lenders will look favorably on borrowers who have higher assets and lower debts.

Different states may have different laws regarding these types of loans. Review the conditions at the end of your loan application to see whether your state has any special amendments about which you should be aware.

Page 2 of 2

ASSET AND DEBT INFORMATION

If "Joint Applicant or Other Party Information" section was completed above, this section should be completed giving information about both the Applicant and the Joint Applicant or Other Party. Please identify the Applicant-related information with an "*". Attach additional sheets if necessary.

ASSETS

DESCRIPTION OF ASSETS	NAME(S) OF OWNER(S)	SUBJECT TO DEBT: YES/NO	VALUE
Checking Account Number(s) (where) 00-555-98212-23	Bank of Texas	no	$ 1415
Savings Account Number(s) (where) 555-0059-523	Bank of Texas	no	3450
Automobiles (Make, Model, Year) 2004 Delt 501/2008 Mia Takeoff		yes/yes	8000/16,000
Marketable Securities (Issuer, Type, No. of Shares)			
Life Insurance (cash value)			
Other Real Estate (Location, when acquired)			
Other Assets (Describe)			
Total Assets 28865			$

OUTSTANDING DEBTS (Include charge accounts, installment contracts, credit cards, rent, mortgages and other obligations.)

CREDITOR	ACCOUNT NUMBER	NAME IN WHICH THE ACCOUNT IS CARRIED	ORIGINAL AMOUNT	PRESENT BALANCE	MONTHLY PAYMENTS
Landlord or Mortgage Holder on other Real Estate					
Auto Loan	0255128902	Keara Swallow	$20,000	$5235	$395
Auto Loan					
Credit or Charge Card Mastercharge	6500 5555 4012 3333	Anthony Swallow		$750	$35
Credit or Charge Card Office Warehouse	1200 2222 4650 7777	Keara Swallow		$212	$20
TOTAL DEBTS $6005			$ 20,000	$ 6,197	$ 450

Credit References

			Date Paid
1. Auto Loans Inc.	$ 18,500		08/2009
2. Mastercharge	$ 1250		Date Paid 09/2010

GENERAL INFORMATION

If you or a joint applicant or other party answers "yes" to any of the following questions, please explain in the space provided.

Are you a guarantor or co-maker of any leases, contracts or debts? ☐ Yes ☒ No

Are there any suits or judgments pending against you? ☐ Yes ☒ No
(Include amount)

Have you been declared bankrupt in the last 10 years? ☐ Yes ☒ No

Illinois Residents: If the home equity account requested may be accessed by a credit card, the following statement applies. Residents of Illinois may contact the Illinois Commissioner of Banks and Trust Companies for comparative information on interest rates, charges, fees, and grace periods. State of Illinois, CIP, P.O. Box 10181, Springfield, Illinois 62791 (800) 634-5452

New York Residents: A consumer report may be ordered in connection with your application. Upon your request, we will inform you whether or not a report was ordered. If a report was ordered we will tell you the name and address of the consumer reporting agency that provided the report. Subsequent reports may be ordered or utilized in connection with an update, renewal or extension of credit for which you have applied.

Ohio Residents: The Ohio laws against discrimination require all creditors make credit equally available to all credit worthy customers, and that credit reporting agencies maintain separate credit histories on each individual upon request. The Ohio Civil Rights Commission administers compliance with this law.
Any person who, with intent to defraud or knowing that he is facilitating a fraud against an insurer, submits an application or files a claim containing a false or deceptive statement is guilty of insurance fraud.

Married Wisconsin Residents: No provision of any marital property agreement, unilateral statement under Wisc. Statutes §766.59 or a court decree under Wisc. Statutes §766.70 adversely affects the interest of the lender unless the lender, prior to the time the credit is granted, is furnished a copy of the agreement, statement or decree or has actual knowledge of the adverse provision when the obligation to the lender is incurred.

I certify that everything I have stated in this application and on any attachments is correct. You may keep this application whether or not it is approved. By signing below I authorize you to check my credit and employment history and to answer questions others may ask you about my credit record with you. I understand that I must update this credit information at your request and if my financial condition changes.

I acknowledge receipt of the Home Equity Brochure and the lender's Home Equity disclosure statement on today's date.

Applicant X _Anthony Swallow_ Date _1/04/12_   Joint-Applicant X _Keara Swallow_   Date _1/04/12_

CREDITOR USE ONLY		
Date Application Received:	Received By:	Amount Requested $
Approved By:	Approved By:	Amount Approved $
Rescindable? ☐ Yes ☐ No	Funding Date:	Initial Advance $

FINANCIAL DOCUMENTS

Taxes

CONTENTS

You **must pay income taxes if you work in the United States.** Depending on where you live, you may pay state and local income tax in addition to federal income and payroll taxes. Some localities have school district taxes in addition to local income tax, and some states and cities charge no income tax at all.

Federal taxes are due each year on April 15 or the next business day if April 15 falls on a Saturday or Sunday. However, you may file your taxes as soon as you have all of the required paperwork. Employers must send W-2 forms (forms that state your income and taxes you've paid) by the end of January.

Whether you owe taxes or are due a return depends on the amount of money you earned, the amount your employer withheld from your paycheck, and the number of your exemptions or write-offs. Be sure to file your taxes even if you owe money. If you owe but cannot pay right away, contact the tax office to set up a payment plan.

The government has additional taxes for different types of income. If you earned income as an independent contractor, you must pay self-employment tax. This covers Social Security and Medicare taxes that would normally be deducted from your paycheck. Studying the examples in this lesson will help you interpret or complete the documents in the chapter review and in real life.

E-filing

The federal government and some states and cities allow you to submit your taxes electronically through the Internet. Tax preparation software such as TurboTax can help you complete your own taxes correctly and submit them online. Often, you can do all of this for less money than it would cost you to use a tax preparation service.

W-2 Form

Each employer from which you earned taxed wages in the past year must send you a W-2 form. You may receive multiple copies of the form, which would allow you to include them with your state, local, school district, and/or federal tax return. You need the information from these forms in order to complete your tax return.

FORM **W-2 Wage and Tax Statement**
Copy C For EMPLOYEE'S RECORDS (See notice on back of copy B)

Dept. of the Treasury • Internal Revenue Service
This information is being furnished to the Internal Revenue Service. If you are required to file a tax return, a negligence penalty or other sanction may be imposed on you if this income is taxable and you fail to report it.

These substitute W-2 Wage and Tax Statements are acceptable for filing with your Federal, State and Local Income Tax Returns.
If you worked in multiple locations, or had several forms of special compensation, you may receive more than one of these documents.

	Federal Box 1	Soc. Sec. Box 3 & 7	Medicare Box 5	State Box 16	Local Box 18
Gross	35048.26	35048.26	35048.26	35048.26	35048.26
Sect. 125 Plan	657.54-	657.54-	657.54-	657.54-	657.54-
W-2 Wages	34390.72	34390.72	34390.72	34390.72	34390.72

All four copies of your W-2 are on this page, separated by perforations. The white copies are for your tax returns; the blue copy is for your records. General instructions for these forms, including an explanation of the letter codes used in box 12, are on the other side of the page.

To the right is an explanation of the contents of the wage boxes on your W-2. Please note that the Gross amount shown may include adjustments.

A. CONTROL NUMBER 3052008289	This information is being furnished to the Internal Revenue Service	2005	OMB NO. 1545-0008	1 WAGES, TIPS, OTHER COMPENSATION 34390.72	2 FEDERAL INCOME TAX WITHHELD 3259.11
B. EMPLOYER IDENTIFICATION NUMBER 42-5559782		D. EMPLOYEE'S SOCIAL SECURITY NUMBER XXX XX XXXX		3 SOCIAL SECURITY WAGES 34390.72	4 SOCIAL SECURITY TAX WITHHELD 2132.22
C. EMPLOYER'S NAME, ADDRESS, AND ZIP CODE				5 MEDICARE WAGES AND TIPS 34390.72	6 MEDICARE TAX WITHHELD 498.67

MAZER
6680 POE AVE
DAYTON   OH 45414

13	Statutory Employee [ ]	Retirement Plan [X]	Third-Party Sick Pay [ ]

7 SOCIAL SECURITY TIPS	8 ALLOCATED TIPS
9 ADVANCE EIC PAYMENT	10 DEPENDENT CARE BENEFITS

E. EMPLOYEE'S FIRST NAME AND INITIAL   LAST NAME
RON L   YEARLING
APT 23
166 LORETTA AVENUE
FAIRBORN, OH 45324

11 NONQUALIFIED PLANS	12 a-d
14 OTHER	

15 STATE OH	EMPLOYER'S STATE I.D. NO. 51-087895 2	16 STATE WAGES, TIPS, ETC. 34390.72	17 STATE INCOME TAX 1099.05	18 LOCAL WAGES, TIPS, ETC. 34390.72	19 LOCAL INCOME TAX 601.82	20 LOCALITY NAME VANDALIA

If you work for a large company, the name and address that you see here may differ from the address at which you work. Don't worry; your employer has still withheld the necessary taxes for you.

Employers typically withhold a certain amount of money from each of your paychecks and send it to the government throughout the year. Your W-2 form lists the amount of money that has been withheld on your behalf.

Federal Income Tax Tables

Federal income tax tables show you exactly how much federal income tax you owe based on your taxable income. You will need to refer to these tables if you complete your taxes by hand.

2009 Tax Table—Continued

If line 43 (taxable income) is—		And you are—			
At least	But less than	Single	Married filing jointly *	Married filing separately	Head of a household
		Your tax is—			

23,000

At least	But less than	Single	Married filing jointly	Married filing separately	Head of a household
23,000	23,050	3,036	2,619	3,036	2,856
23,050	23,100	3,044	2,626	3,044	2,864
23,100	23,150	3,051	2,634	3,051	2,871
23,150	23,200	3,059	2,641	3,059	2,879
23,200	23,250	3,066	2,649	3,066	2,886
23,250	23,300	3,074	2,656	3,074	2,894
23,300	23,350	3,081	2,664	3,081	2,901
23,350	23,400	3,089	2,671	3,089	2,909
23,400	23,450	3,096	2,679	3,096	2,916
23,450	23,500	3,104	2,686	3,104	2,924
23,500	23,550	3,111	2,694	3,111	2,931
23,550	23,600	3,119	2,701	3,119	2,939
23,600	23,650	3,126	2,709	3,126	2,946
23,650	23,700	3,134	2,716	3,134	2,954
23,700	23,750	3,141	2,724	3,141	2,961
23,750	23,800	3,149	2,731	3,149	2,969
23,800	23,850	3,156	2,739	3,156	2,976
23,850	23,900	3,164	2,746	3,164	2,984
23,900	23,950	3,171	2,754	3,171	2,991
23,950	24,000	3,179	2,761	3,179	2,999

24,000

At least	But less than	Single	Married filing jointly	Married filing separately	Head of a household
					3,006
					3,014
					3,021
					3,029
					3,036
					3,044
					3,051
					3,059
					3,066
					3,074
					3,081
					3,089
24,600	24,650	3,276	2,859	3,276	3,096
24,650	24,700	3,284	2,866	3,284	3,104
24,700	24,750	3,291	2,874	3,291	3,111
24,750	24,800	3,299	2,881	3,299	3,119
24,800	24,850	3,306	2,889	3,306	3,126
24,850	24,900	3,314	2,896	3,314	3,134
24,900	24,950	3,321	2,904	3,321	3,141
24,950	25,000	3,329	2,911	3,329	3,149

25,000

At least	But less than	Single	Married filing jointly	Married filing separately	Head of a household
25,000	25,050	3,336	2,919	3,336	3,156
25,050	25,100	3,344	2,926	3,344	3,164
25,100	25,150	3,351	2,934	3,351	3,171
25,150	25,200	3,359	2,941	3,359	3,179
25,200	25,250	3,366	2,949	3,366	3,186
25,250	25,300	3,374	2,956	3,374	3,194
25,300	25,350	3,381	2,964	3,381	3,201
25,350	25,400	3,389	2,971	3,389	3,209
25,400	25,450	3,396	2,979	3,396	3,216
25,450	25,500	3,404	2,986	3,404	3,224
25,500	25,550	3,411	2,994	3,411	3,231
25,550	25,600	3,419	3,001	3,419	3,239
25,600	25,650	3,426	3,009	3,426	3,246
25,650	25,700	3,434	3,016	3,434	3,254
25,700	25,750	3,441	3,024	3,441	3,261
25,750	25,800	3,449	3,031	3,449	3,269
25,800	25,850	3,456	3,039	3,456	3,276
25,850	25,900	3,464	3,046	3,464	3,284
25,900	25,950	3,471	3,054	3,471	3,291
25,950	26,000	3,479	3,061	3,479	3,299

26,000

At least	But less than	Single	Married filing jointly	Married filing separately	Head of a household
26,000	26,050	3,486	3,069	3,486	3,306
26,050	26,100	3,494	3,076	3,494	3,314
26,100	26,150	3,501	3,084	3,501	3,321
26,150	26,200	3,509	3,091	3,509	3,329
26,200	26,250	3,516	3,099	3,516	3,336
26,250	26,300	3,524	3,106	3,524	3,344
26,300	26,350	3,531	3,114	3,531	3,351
26,350	26,400	3,539	3,121	3,539	3,359
26,400	26,450	3,546	3,129	3,546	3,366
26,450	26,500	3,554	3,136	3,554	3,374
26,500	26,550	3,561	3,144	3,561	3,381
26,550	26,600	3,569	3,151	3,569	3,389
26,600	26,650	3,576	3,159	3,576	3,396
26,650	26,700	3,584	3,166	3,584	3,404
26,700	26,750	3,591	3,174	3,591	3,411
26,750	26,800	3,599	3,181	3,599	3,419
26,800	26,850	3,606	3,189	3,606	3,426
26,850	26,900	3,614	3,196	3,614	3,434
26,900	26,950	3,621	3,204	3,621	3,441
26,950	27,000	3,629	3,211	3,629	3,449

27,000

At least	But less than	Single	Married filing jointly	Married filing separately	Head of a household
27,000	27,050	3,636	3,219	3,636	3,456
27,050	27,100	3,644	3,226	3,644	3,464
27,100	27,150	3,651	3,234	3,651	3,471
27,150	27,200	3,659	3,241	3,659	3,479
27,200	27,250	3,666	3,249	3,666	3,486
27,250	27,300	3,674	3,256	3,674	3,494
27,300	27,350	3,681	3,264	3,681	3,501
27,350	27,400	3,689	3,271	3,689	3,509
27,400	27,450	3,696	3,279	3,696	3,516
27,450	27,500	3,704	3,286	3,704	3,524
27,500	27,550	3,711	3,294	3,711	3,531
27,550	27,600	3,719	3,301	3,719	3,539
27,600	27,650	3,726	3,309	3,726	3,546
27,650	27,700	3,734	3,316	3,734	3,554
27,700	27,750	3,741	3,324	3,741	3,561
27,750	27,800	3,749	3,331	3,749	3,569
27,800	27,850	3,756	3,339	3,756	3,576
27,850	27,900	3,764	3,346	3,764	3,584
27,900	27,950	3,771	3,354	3,771	3,591
27,950	28,000	3,779	3,361	3,779	3,599

28,000

At least	But less than	Single	Married filing jointly	Married filing separately	Head of a household
28,000	28,050	3,786	3,369	3,786	3,606
28,050	28,100	3,794	3,376	3,794	3,614
28,100	28,150	3,801	3,384	3,801	3,621
28,150	28,200	3,809	3,391	3,809	3,629
28,200	28,250	3,816	3,399	3,816	3,636
28,250	28,300	3,824	3,406	3,824	3,644
28,300	28,350	3,831	3,414	3,831	3,651
28,350	28,400	3,839	3,421	3,839	3,659
28,400	28,450	3,846	3,429	3,846	3,666
28,450	28,500	3,854	3,436	3,854	3,674
28,500	28,550	3,861	3,444	3,861	3,681
28,550	28,600	3,869	3,451	3,869	3,689
28,600	28,650	3,876	3,459	3,876	3,696
28,650	28,700	3,884	3,466	3,884	3,704
28,700	28,750	3,891	3,474	3,891	3,711
28,750	28,800	3,899	3,481	3,899	3,719
28,800	28,850	3,906	3,489	3,906	3,726
28,850	28,900	3,914	3,496	3,914	3,734
28,900	28,950	3,921	3,504	3,921	3,741
28,950	29,000	3,929	3,511	3,929	3,749

29,000

At least	But less than	Single	Married filing jointly	Married filing separately	Head of a household
29,000	29,050	3,936	3,519	3,936	3,756
29,050	29,100	3,944	3,526	3,944	3,764
29,100	29,150	3,951			
29,150	29,200	3,959			
29,200	29,250	3,966			
29,250	29,300	3,974			
29,300	29,350	3,981			
29,350	29,400	3,989			
29,400	29,450	3,996			
29,450	29,500	4,004			
29,500	29,550	4,011			
29,550	29,600	4,019			
29,600	29,650	4,026			
29,650	29,700	4,034			
29,700	29,750	4,041			
29,750	29,800	4,049			
29,800	29,850	4,056			
29,850	29,900	4,064			
29,900	29,950	4,071			
29,950	30,000	4,079			

30,000

At least	But less than	Single	Married filing jointly	Married filing separately	Head of a household
30,000	30,050	4,086	3,669	4,086	3,906
30,050	30,100	4,094	3,676	4,094	3,914
30,100	30,150	4,101	3,684	4,101	3,921
30,150	30,200	4,109	3,691	4,109	3,929
30,200	30,250	4,116	3,699	4,116	3,936
30,250	30,300	4,124	3,706	4,124	3,944
30,300	30,350	4,131	3,714	4,131	3,951
30,350	30,400	4,139	3,721	4,139	3,959
30,400	30,450	4,146	3,729	4,146	3,966
30,450	30,500	4,154	3,736	4,154	3,974
30,500	30,550	4,161	3,744	4,161	3,981
30,550	30,600	4,169	3,751	4,169	3,989
30,600	30,650	4,176	3,759	4,176	3,996
30,650	30,700	4,184	3,766	4,184	4,004
30,700	30,750	4,191	3,774	4,191	4,011
30,750	30,800	4,199	3,781	4,199	4,019
30,800	30,850	4,206	3,789	4,206	4,026
30,850	30,900	4,214	3,796	4,214	4,034
30,900	30,950	4,221	3,804	4,221	4,041
30,950	31,000	4,229	3,811	4,229	4,049

31,000

At least	But less than	Single	Married filing jointly	Married filing separately	Head of a household
31,000	31,050	4,236	3,819	4,236	4,056
31,050	31,100	4,244	3,826	4,244	4,064
31,100	31,150	4,251	3,834	4,251	4,071
31,150	31,200	4,259	3,841	4,259	4,079
31,200	31,250	4,266	3,849	4,266	4,086
31,250	31,300	4,274	3,856	4,274	4,094
31,300	31,350	4,281	3,864	4,281	4,101
31,350	31,400	4,289	3,871	4,289	4,109
31,400	31,450				
31,450	31,500				
31,500	31,550				
31,550	31,600				
31,600	31,650				
31,650	31,700				
31,700	31,750				
31,750	31,800				
31,800	31,850				
31,850	31,900	4,364	3,946	4,364	4,184
31,900	31,950	4,371	3,954	4,371	4,191
31,950	32,000	4,379	3,961	4,379	4,199

> The amount of tax you pay depends on your filing status. Your filing status is indicated on your income tax return. It simply states whether you are filing as a single person, as part of a married couple, or as the head of household (a single parent).

> You will pay a little more in taxes each time your income increases by $50. Be sure to carefully read the tax table to find the correct amount, and double-check your math before writing the amount of your total owed tax.

> For example, if Dante is filing as head of household and made $28,575, he would owe $3,689 in federal taxes.

Federal Income Tax Tables

2009 Tax Table—*Continued*

These tax tables are for 2009 only. Because tax rates may change from year to year, be sure to use the most current tax tables when you file your taxes. These are typically included as part of your paper income tax return.

| If line 43 (taxable income) is— | | And you are— | | | |
At least	But less than	Single	Married filing jointly *	Married filing separately	Head of a household
					Your tax is—
32,000					
32,000	32,050	4,386	3,969	4,386	4,206
32,050	32,100	4,394	3,976	4,394	4,214
32,100	32,150	4,401	3,984	4,401	4,221
32,150	32,200	4,409	3,991	4,409	4,229
32,200	32,250	4,416	3,999	4,416	4,236
32,250	32,300	4,424	4,006	4,424	4,244
32,300	32,350	4,431	4,014	4,431	4,251
32,350	32,400	4,439	4,021	4,439	4,259
32,400	32,450	4,446	4,029	4,446	4,266
32,450	32,500	4,454	4,036	4,454	4,274
32,500	32,550	4,461	4,044	4,461	4,281
32,550	32,600	4,469	4,051	4,469	4,289
32,600	32,650	4,476	4,059	4,476	4,296
32,650	32,700	4,484	4,066	4,484	4,304
32,700	32,750	4,491	4,074	4,491	4,311
32,750	32,800	4,499	4,081	4,499	4,319
32,800	32,850	4,506	4,089	4,506	4,326
32,850	32,900	4,514	4,096	4,514	4,334
32,900	32,950	4,521	4,104	4,521	4,341
32,950	33,000	4,529	4,111	4,529	4,349
33,000					
33,000	33,050	4,536	4,119	4,536	4,356
33,050	33,100	4,544	4,126	4,544	4,364
33,100	33,150	4,551	4,134	4,551	4,371
33,150	33,200	4,559	4,141	4,559	4,379
33,200	33,250	4,566	4,149	4,566	4,386
33,250	33,300	4,574	4,156	4,574	4,394
33,300	33,350	4,581	4,164	4,581	4,401
33,350	33,400	4,589	4,171	4,589	4,409
33,400	33,450	4,596	4,179	4,596	4,416
33,450	33,500	4,604	4,186	4,604	4,424
33,500	33,550	4,611	4,194	4,611	4,431
33,550	33,600	4,619	4,201	4,619	4,439
33,600	33,650	4,626	4,209	4,626	4,446
33,650	33,700	4,634	4,216	4,634	4,454
33,700	33,750	4,641	4,224	4,641	4,461
33,750	33,800	4,649	4,231	4,649	4,469
33,800	33,850	4,656	4,239	4,656	4,476
33,850	33,900	4,664	4,246	4,664	4,484
33,900	33,950	4,671	4,254	4,671	4,491
33,950	34,000	4,681	4,261	4,681	4,499
34,000					
34,000	34,050	4,694	4,269	4,694	4,506
34,050	34,100	4,706	4,276	4,706	4,514
34,100	34,150	4,719	4,284	4,719	4,521
34,150	34,200	4,731	4,291	4,731	4,529
34,200	34,250	4,744	4,299	4,744	4,536
34,250	34,300	4,756	4,306	4,756	4,544
34,300	34,350	4,769	4,314	4,769	4,551
34,350	34,400	4,781	4,321	4,781	4,559
34,400	34,450	4,794	4,329	4,794	4,566
34,450	34,500	4,806	4,336	4,806	4,574
34,500	34,550	4,819	4,344	4,819	4,581
34,550	34,600	4,831	4,351	4,831	4,589
34,600	34,650	4,844	4,359	4,844	4,596
34,650	34,700	4,856	4,366	4,856	4,604
34,700	34,750	4,869	4,374	4,869	4,611
34,750	34,800	4,881	4,381	4,881	4,619
34,800	34,850	4,894	4,389	4,894	4,626
34,850	34,900	4,906	4,396	4,906	4,634
34,900	34,950	4,919	4,404	4,919	4,641
34,950	35,000	4,931	4,411	4,931	4,649

| If line 43 (taxable income) is— | | And you are— | | | |
At least	But less than	Single	Married filing jointly *	Married filing separately	Head of a household
					Your tax is—
35,000					
35,000	35,050	4,944	4,419	4,944	4,656
35,050	35,100	4,956	4,426	4,956	4,664
35,100	35,150	4,969	4,434	4,969	4,671
35,150	35,200	4,981	4,441	4,981	4,679
35,200	35,250	4,994	4,449	4,994	4,686
35,250	35,300	5,006	4,456	5,006	4,694
35,300	35,350	5,019	4,464	5,019	4,701
35,350	35,400	5,031	4,471	5,031	4,709
35,400	35,450	5,044	4,479	5,044	4,716
35,450	35,500	5,056	4,486	5,056	4,724
35,500	35,550	5,069	4,494	5,069	4,731
35,550	35,600	5,081	4,501	5,081	4,739
35,600	35,650	5,094	4,509	5,094	4,746
35,650	35,700	5,106	4,516	5,106	4,754
35,700	35,750	5,119	4,524	5,119	4,761
35,750	35,800	5,131	4,531	5,131	4,769
35,800	35,850	5,144	4,539	5,144	4,776
35,850	35,900	5,156	4,546	5,156	4,784
35,900	35,950	5,169	4,554	5,169	4,791
35,950	36,000	5,181	4,561	5,181	4,799
36,000					
36,000	36,050	5,194	4,569	5,194	4,806
36,050	36,100	5,206	4,576	5,206	4,814
36,100	36,150	5,219	4,584	5,219	4,821
36,150	36,200	5,231	4,591	5,231	4,829
36,200	36,250	5,244	4,599	5,244	4,836
36,250	36,300	5,256	4,606	5,256	4,844
36,300	36,350	5,269	4,614	5,269	4,851
36,350	36,400	5,281	4,621	5,281	4,859
36,400	36,450	5,294	4,629	5,294	4,866
36,450	36,500	5,306	4,636	5,306	4,874
36,500	36,550	5,319	4,644	5,319	4,881
36,550	36,600	5,331	4,651	5,331	4,889
36,600	36,650	5,344	4,659	5,344	4,896
36,650	36,700	5,356	4,666	5,356	4,904
36,700	36,750	5,369	4,674	5,369	4,911
36,750	36,800	5,381	4,681	5,381	4,919
36,800	36,850	5,394	4,689	5,394	4,926
36,850	36,900	5,406	4,696	5,406	4,934
36,900	36,950	5,419	4,704	5,419	4,941
36,950	37,000	5,431	4,711	5,431	4,949
37,000					
37,000	37,050	5,444	4,719	5,444	4,956
37,050	37,100	5,456	4,726	5,456	4,964
37,100	37,150	5,469	4,734	5,469	4,971
37,150	37,200	5,481	4,741	5,481	4,979
37,200	37,250	5,494	4,749	5,494	4,986
37,250	37,300	5,506	4,756	5,506	4,994
37,300	37,350	5,519	4,764	5,519	5,001
37,350	37,400	5,531	4,771	5,531	5,009
37,400	37,450				
37,450	37,500				
37,500	37,550				
37,550	37,600				
37,600	37,650				
37,650	37,700				
37,700	37,750				
37,750	37,800				
37,800	37,850				
37,850	37,900				
37,900	37,950				
37,950	38,000				

| If line 43 (taxable income) is— | | And you are— | | | |
At least	But less than	Single	Married filing jointly *	Married filing separately	Head of a household
					Your tax is—
38,600	38,650	5,844	4,959	5,844	5,196
38,650	38,700	5,856	4,966	5,856	5,204
38,700	38,750	5,869	4,974	5,869	5,211
38,750	38,800	5,881	4,981	5,881	5,219
38,800	38,850	5,894	4,989	5,894	5,226
38,850	38,900	5,906	4,996	5,906	5,234
38,900	38,950	5,919	5,004	5,919	5,241
38,950	39,000	5,931	5,011	5,931	5,249
39,000					
39,000	39,050	5,944	5,019	5,944	5,256
39,050	39,100	5,956	5,026	5,956	5,264
39,100	39,150	5,969	5,034	5,969	5,271
39,150	39,200	5,981	5,041	5,981	5,279
39,200	39,250	5,994	5,049	5,994	5,286
39,250	39,300	6,006	5,056	6,006	5,294
39,300	39,350	6,019	5,064	6,019	5,301
39,350	39,400	6,031	5,071	6,031	5,309
39,400	39,450	6,044	5,079	6,044	5,316
39,450	39,500	6,056	5,086	6,056	5,324
39,500	39,550	6,069	5,094	6,069	5,331
39,550	39,600	6,081	5,101	6,081	5,339
39,600	39,650	6,094	5,109	6,094	5,346
39,650	39,700	6,106	5,116	6,106	5,354
39,700	39,750	6,119	5,124	6,119	5,361
39,750	39,800	6,131	5,131	6,131	5,369
39,800	39,850	6,144	5,139	6,144	5,376
39,850	39,900	6,156	5,146	6,156	5,384
39,900	39,950	6,169	5,154	6,169	5,391
39,950	40,000	6,181	5,161	6,181	5,399
40,000					
40,000	40,050	6,194	5,169	6,194	5,406
40,050	40,100	6,206	5,176	6,206	5,414
40,100	40,150	6,219	5,184	6,219	5,421
40,150	40,200	6,231	5,191	6,231	5,429
40,200	40,250	6,244	5,199	6,244	5,436
40,250	40,300	6,256	5,206	6,256	5,444
40,300	40,350	6,269	5,214	6,269	5,451
40,350	40,400	6,281	5,221	6,281	5,459
		6,294	5,229	6,294	5,466
		6,306	5,236	6,306	5,474
		6,319	5,244	6,319	5,481
		6,331	5,251	6,331	5,489
		6,344	5,259	6,344	5,496
		6,356	5,266	6,356	5,504
		6,369	5,274	6,369	5,511
		6,381	5,281	6,381	5,519
		6,394	5,289	6,394	5,526
		6,406	5,296	6,406	5,534
		6,419	5,304	6,419	5,541
		6,431	5,311	6,431	5,549

Single people and married people filing separately pay higher taxes on the same amount of income than a married couple filing together with the same combined income. A person filing as head of household pays an amount between the other categories.

1040EZ Income Tax Return

You can use the 1040EZ income tax return to file your taxes if your earnings and deductions are fairly simple. Single or married people with no dependents, self-employment income, or special deductions may find this simple form easy to complete and file.

Department of the Treasury—Internal Revenue Service

Income Tax Return for Single and Joint Filers With No Dependents (99) **2009**

Form **1040EZ**

OMB No. 1545-0074

Label
(See page 9.)
Use the IRS label.
Otherwise, please print or type.

Presidential Election Campaign (see page 9)

Your first name and initial	Last name	Your social security number
James M.	Grubbs	XXX-XX-XXXX

If a joint return, spouse's first name and initial | Last name | Spouse's social security number
Elisha K. | Grubbs | XXX-XX-XXXX

Home address (number and street). If you have a P.O. box, see page 9. | Apt. no.
852 Meadow Lane | 10

▲ You **must** enter your SSN(s) above. ▲

City, town or post office, state, and ZIP code. If you have a foreign address, see page 9.
San Rafael CA 94901

Checking a box below will not change your tax or refund.

Check here if you, or your spouse if a joint return, want $3 to go to this fund . . ▶ [X] **You**   [X] **Spouse**

Income

Attach Form(s) W-2 here.

Enclose, but do not attach, any payment.

You may benefit from filing Form 1040A or 1040. See Before You Begin on page 4.

1. Wages, salaries, and tips. This should be shown in box 1 of your Form(s) W-2. Attach your Form(s) W-2.

2. Taxable interest. If the total is over $1,500, you cannot use Form 1040EZ.

3. Unemployment compensation in excess of $2,400 per recipient and Alaska Permanent Fund dividends (see page 11).

4. Add lines 1, 2, and 3. This is your **adjusted gross income**.

5. If someone can claim you (or your spouse if a joint return) as a dependent, check the applicable box(es) below and enter the amount from the worksheet on back.

   [ ] **You**   [ ] **Spouse**

   If no one can claim you (or your spouse if a joint return), enter $9,350 if **single**; $18,700 if **married filing jointly**. See back for explanation. | 5 | 18700 | 00

6. Subtract line 5 from line 4. If line 5 is larger than line 4, enter -0-. This is your **taxable income**. ▶ | 6 | 23896 | 21

> Be sure to claim the correct standard deduction on this line. Choosing the deduction for single people if you are married may cause you to accidentally pay higher taxes.

Payments, Credits, and Tax

7. Federal income tax withheld from Form(s) W-2 and 1099. | 7 | 3614 | 00

8. Making work pay credit (see worksheet on back). | 8 | 800 | 00

9a. **Earned income credit (EIC)** (see page 13). | 9a | 0 | 00

b. Nontaxable combat pay election. | 9b

10. Add lines 7, 8, and 9a. These are your **total payments and credits**. ▶ | 10 | 4414 | 00

11. **Tax.** Use the amount on **line 6 above** to find your tax in the tax table on pages 27 through 35 of the instructions. Then, enter the tax from the table on this line. | 11 | 2746 | 00

Refund

Have it directly deposited! See page 18 and fill in 12b, 12c, and 12d or Form 8888.

12a. If line 10 is larger than line 11, subtract line 11 from line 10. This is your **refund**. If Form 8888 is attached, check here ▶ [ ] | 12a | 1668 | 00

▶ b. Routing number | 1 0 6 8 2 2 2 2 | ▶c. Type: [X] Checking [ ] Savings

▶ d. Account number | 0 0 9 5 4 1 2 2 0 5 5 5

Amount you owe

13. If line 11 is larger than line 10, subtract line 10 from line 11. This is the **amount you owe**. For details on how to pay, see page 19. ▶ | 13 | 0 | 00

Third party designee

Do you want to allow another person to discuss this return with the IRS (see page 20)? [ ] **Yes.** Complete the following. [X] **No**

Designee's name ▶ | Phone no. ▶ | Personal identification number (PIN) ▶ [ ][ ][ ][ ][ ]

Sign here

Under penalties of perjury, I declare that I have examined this return, and to the best of my knowledge and belief, it is true, correct, and accurately lists all amounts and sources of income I received during the tax year. Declaration of preparer (other than the taxpayer) is based on all information of which the preparer has any knowledge.

Joint return? See page 6.

Keep a copy for your records.

Your signature	Date	Your occupation	Daytime phone number
James M. Grubbs	3/23/10	kitchen manager	415-555-1500

Spouse's signature. If a joint return, **both** must sign. | Date | Spouse's occupation
Elisha K. Grubbs | 3/23/10 | medical billing clerk

Paid preparer's use only

Preparer's signature ▶ | Date | Check if self-employed [ ] | Preparer's SSN or PTIN

Firm's name (or yours if self-employed), address, and ZIP code ▶ | EIN

For Disclosure, Privacy Act, and Paperwork Reduction Act Notice,

> If you overpaid your taxes throughout the year, you will be entitled to a tax refund when you file. Having this refund deposited directly into your checking or savings account helps you receive your refund quickly.

1040EZ Income Tax Return

> If you are an adult living on your own, you probably can claim yourself as a dependent. If you are attending school and living at home, however, your parents may still claim you as a dependent. Completing this worksheet will help you determine the proper personal deduction on your taxes.

Page 2 of 2

Form 1040EZ (2009)   Page **2**

Worksheet for Line 5 — Dependents who checked one or both boxes

Use this worksheet to figure the amount to enter on line 5 if someone can claim you (or your spouse if married filing jointly) as a dependent, even if that person chooses not to do so. To find out if someone can claim you as a dependent, see Pub. 501.

A. Amount, if any, from line 1 on front . . . . . .

     + _____ 300.00 _ Enter total ▶   **A** . _____

B. Minimum standard deduction . . . . **B** . ___950____

C. Enter the **larger** of line A or line B here . . . . **C** . _____

D. Maximum standard deduction. If **single,** enter $5,700; if **married filing jointly,** enter $11,400   **D** . _____

E. Enter the **smaller** of line C or line D here. This is your standard deduction . . . . . . **E** . _____

F. Exemption amount.

     ● If single, enter -0-.

     ● If married filing jointly and —

         —both you and your spouse can be claimed as dependents, enter -0-.

         —only one of you can be claimed as a dependent, enter $3,650.

     F . _____

G. Add lines E and F. Enter the total here and on line 5 on the front . . . . . . **G** . _____

(keep a copy for your records)

If you did not check any boxes on line 5, enter on line 5 the amount shown below that applies to you.

● Single, enter $9,350. This is the total of your standard deduction ($5,700) and your exemption ($3,650).

● Married filing jointly, enter $18,700. This is the total of your standard deduction ($11,400), your exemption ($3,650), and your spouse's exemption ($3,650).

Worksheet for Line 8 — Making work pay credit

> Sometimes the federal government approves special tax credits. This credit reduces the amount of tax that taxpayers owe by either $400 or $800. Be sure to investigate whether you can claim any special credits.

Before you begin: √   If you can be claimed as a dependent on someone else's return, you **do not** qualify for this credit.

       √   If married filing jointly, include your spouse's amounts with yours when completing this worksheet.

1a. **Important.** See the instructions on page 12 if **(a)** you received a taxable scholarship or fellowship grant not reported on a Form W-2, **(b)** your wages include pay for work performed while an inmate in a penal institution, or **(c)** you received a pension or annuity from a nonqualified deferred compensation plan or a nongovernmental section 457 plan.

     Do you (and your spouse if filing jointly) have 2009 wages of more than $6,451 ($12,903 if married filing jointly)?

     ☒ **Yes.**   Skip lines 1a through 3. Enter $400 ($800 if married filing jointly) on line 4 and go to line 5.

     ☐ **No.**   Enter your earned income (see instructions) . . . . . **1a.** _____

b. Nontaxable combat pay included on line 1a (see instructions) . . . **1b.** _____

2. Multiply line 1a by 6.2% (.062) . . . . **2.** _____

3. Enter $400 ($800 if married filing jointly) . . . . **3.** _____

4. Enter the **smaller** of line 2 or line 3 (unless you checked "Yes" on line 1a) . . . . . . **4.** ___800____

5. Enter amount from Form 1040EZ, line 4 (on front) . . . . . **5.** _____

6. Enter $75,000 ($150,000 if married filing jointly) . . . . . **6.** _____

7. Is the amount on line 5 more than the amount on line 6?

     ☐ **No.**   Skip line 8. Enter the amount from line 4 on line 9 below.

     ☐ **Yes.**   Subtract line 6 from line 5. . . . . **7.** _____

8. Multiply line 7 by 2% (.02) . . . . **8.** _____

9. Subtract line 8 from line 4. If zero or less, enter -0- . . . . **9.** _____

10. Did you (or your spouse, if filing jointly) receive an economic recovery payment in 2009? You may have received this payment if you received social security benefits, supplemental security income, railroad retirement benefits, or veterans disability compensation or pension benefits (see instructions).

     ☐ **No.**   Enter -0- on line 10.

     ☐ **Yes.**   Enter the total of the economic recovery payments received by you (and your spouse, if filing jointly). **Do not** enter more than $250 ($500 if married filing jointly) . . **10.** _____

11. **Making work pay credit.** Subtract line 10 from line 9. If zero or less, enter -0-. Enter the result here and on Form 1040EZ, line 8. . . . . **11.** _____

(keep a copy for your records)

Mailing return

Mail your return by **April 15, 2010.** Use the envelope that came with your booklet. If you do not have that envelope or if you moved during the year, see the back cover for the address to use.

1040 Income Tax Return

The 1040 income tax form is the longest and most thorough of the federal government's three main tax forms. If you need to complete a 1040 form, you may wish to research free seminars in your community on completing it correctly.

Page 1 of 3

Certain Cash Contributions for Haiti Relief Can Be Deducted on Your 2009 Tax Return

A new law allows you to choose to deduct certain charitable contributions of money on your 2009 tax return instead of your 2010 return. The contributions must have been made after January 11, 2010, and before March 1, 2010, for the relief of victims in areas affected by the January 12, 2010, earthquake in Haiti. Contributions of money include contributions made by cash, check, money order, credit card, charge card, debit card, or via cell phone.

The new law was enacted after the 2009 forms, instructions, and publications had already been printed. When preparing your 2009 tax return, you may complete the forms as if these contributions were made on December 31, 2009, instead of in 2010. To deduct your charitable contributions, you must itemize deductions on Schedule A (Form 1040) or Schedule A (Form 1040NR).

The contribution must be made to a qualified organization and meet all other requirements for charitable contribution deductions. However, if you made the contribution by phone or text message, a telephone bill showing the name of the donee organization, the date of the contribution, and the amount of the contribution will satisfy the recordkeeping requirement. Therefore, for example, if you made a $10 charitable contribution by text message that was charged to your telephone or wireless account, a bill from your telecommunications company containing this information satisfies the recordkeeping requirement.

Charitable organizations normally provide receipts of donations. This provides people with proof of their donations. In this case, the government chose to accept additional types of proof.

Although taxpayers can normally deduct charitable contributions over a certain portion of their incomes, the government sometimes allows other contributions to be removed from your taxable income. In 2009, for example, the government allowed donations to Haiti relief to be deducted, regardless of the amount.

1040 Income Tax Return

> You may claim children who live with you as dependents. You may also claim children who do not live with you as dependents if you are divorced or separated from the other parent. However, both parents may not claim the same child as a dependent if the parents file separate tax returns.

Form **1040** Department of the Treasury—Internal Revenue Service
U.S. Individual Income Tax Return 20**09** (99) IRS Use Only—Do not write or staple in this space.

For the year Jan. 1–Dec. 31, 2009, or other tax year beginning , 2009, ending , 20 OMB No. 1545-0074

Label
(See instructions on page 14.)
Use the IRS label.
Otherwise, please print or type.

Your first name and initial: David S. Last name: Kendrick Your social security number: XXX XX XXXX

If a joint return, spouse's first name and initial Last name Spouse's social security number

Home address (number and street). If you have a P.O. box, see page 14. 658 Davis Lane Apt. no. 1

You **must** enter your SSN(s) above.

City, town or post office, state, and ZIP code. If you have a foreign address, see page 14. Centennial, CO 80112

Checking a box below will not change your tax or refund.

Presidential Election Campaign ► Check here if you, or your spouse if filing jointly, want $3 to go to this fund (see page 14) ► ☒ You ☐ Spouse

Filing Status
Check only one box.

1 ☒ Single
2 ☐ Married filing jointly (even if only one had income)
3 ☐ Married filing separately. Enter spouse's SSN above and full name here. ►
4 ☐ Head of household (with qualifying person). (See page 15.) If the qualifying person is a child but not your dependent, enter this child's name here. ►
5 ☐ Qualifying widow(er) with dependent child (see page 16)

Exemptions

6a ☒ **Yourself.** If someone can claim you as a dependent, **do not** check box 6a
b ☐ **Spouse**

Boxes checked on 6a and 6b: 1

c **Dependents:**

(1) First name Last name	(2) Dependent's social security number	(3) Dependent's relationship to you	(4) ✔ if qualifying child for child tax credit (see page 17)
Rhiannon Kendrick	XXX XX XXXX	daughter	☐
			☐
			☐
			☐

If more than four dependents, see page 17 and check here ► ☐

No. of children on 6c who:
• lived with you: 1
• did not live with you due to divorce or separation (see page 18): 0

Dependents on 6c not entered above

d Total number of exemptions claimed

Add numbers on lines above ►: 2

7	Wages, salaries, tips, etc. Attach Form(s) W-2	7	39059 46
8a	**Taxable** interest. Attach Schedule B if required	8a	0 00
b	**Tax-exempt** interest. **Do not** include on line 8a	8b	0 00
9a	Ordinary dividends. Attach Schedule B if required	9a	0 00
b	Qualified dividends (see page 22)	9b	0 00
10	Taxable refunds, credits, or offsets of state and local income taxes (see page 23)	10	0 00
11	Alimony received	11	0 00
12	Business income or (loss). Attach Schedule C or C-EZ	12	0 00
13	Capital gain or (loss). Attach Schedule D if required. If not required, check here ► ☐	13	0 00
14	Other gains or (losses). Attach Form 4797	14	0 00
15a	IRA distributions 15a b Taxable amount (see page 24)	15b	0 00
16a	Pensions and annuities 16a b Taxable amount (see page 25)	16b	0 00
17	Rental real estate, royalties, partnerships, S corporations, trusts, etc. Attach Schedule E	17	0 00
18	Farm income or (loss). Attach Schedule F	18	0 00
19	Unemployment compensation in excess of $2,400 per recipient (see page 27)	19	3262 00
20a	Social security benefits 20a b Taxable amount (see page 27)	20b	0 00
21	Other income. List type and amount (see page 29)	21	0 00
22	Add the amounts in the far right column for lines 7 through 21. This is your **total income** ►	22	42321 46

Enclose, but do not attach, any payment. Also, please use **Form 1040-V.**

> Unemployment compensation is only subject to federal taxes if you received more than $2,400 in a single year. States and cities may tax the entire amount.

Adjusted Gross Income

23	Educator expenses (see page 29)	23	0 00
24	Certain business expenses of reservists, performing artists, and fee-basis government officials. Attach Form 2106 or 2106-EZ	24	0 00
25	Health savings account deduction. Attach Form 8889	25	600 00
26	Moving expenses. Attach Form 3903	26	0 00
27	One-half of self-employment tax. Attach Schedule SE	27	0 00
28	Self-employed SEP, SIMPLE, and qualified plans	28	0 00
29	Self-employed health insurance deduction (see page 30)	29	0 00
30	Penalty on early withdrawal of savings	30	0 00
31a	Alimony paid b Recipient's SSN ► XXX XX XXXX	31a	1200 00
32	IRA deduction (see page 31)	32	0 00
33	Student loan interest deduction (see page 34)	33	0 00
34	Tuition and fees deduction. Attach Form 8917	34	0 00
35	Domestic production activities deduction. Attach Form 8903	35	0 00
36	Add lines 23 through 31a and 32 through 35	36	1942 25
37	Subtract line 36 from line 22. This is your **adjusted gross income** ►	37	40379 21

> Certain types of savings or payments are deductible from your income. For example, you may put money tax-free into a health savings account to pay for medical bills and expenses.

For Disclosure, Privacy Act, and Paperwork Reduction Act Notice, see page 97. Cat. No. 11320B Form **1040** (2009)

1040 Income Tax Return

Certain tax credits may save you thousands of dollars. The first-time homebuyer tax credit mentioned on this form allowed new home buyers to take a tax credit of up to $8,000. Be sure to find out whether the government has instituted any tax credits that may apply to you.

Form 1040 (2009)   Page **2**

Tax and Credits	38	Amount from line 37 (adjusted gross income)	38	40379	21
	39a	Check if: ☐ **You** were born before January 2, 1945, ☐ Blind. ☐ **Spouse** was born before January 2, 1945, ☐ Blind. } **Total boxes checked ▶ 39a**			
Standard Deduction for—	b	If your spouse itemizes on a separate return or you were a dual-status alien, see page 35 and check here ▶ 39b☐			
	40a	**Itemized deductions** (from Schedule A) **or** your **standard deduction** (see left margin)	40a	1240.7	71
• People who check any box on line 39a, 39b, or 40b **or** who can be claimed as a dependent, see page 35.	b	If you are increasing your standard deduction by certain real estate taxes, new motor vehicle taxes, or a net disaster loss, attach Schedule L and check here (see page 35) . ▶ 40b☐			
	41	Subtract line 40a from line 38	41		
	42	**Exemptions.** If line 38 is $125,100 or less and you did not provide housing to a Midwestern displaced individual, multiply $3,650 by the number on line 6d. Otherwise, see page 37 . .	42		
	43	**Taxable income.** Subtract line 42 from line 41. If line 42 is more than line 41, enter -0-	43		
• All others:	44	**Tax** (see page 37). Check if any tax is from: **a** ☐ Form(s) 8814 **b** ☐ Form 4972 .	44		
Single or Married filing separately, $5,700	45	**Alternative minimum tax** (see page 40). Attach Form 6251	45		
	46	Add lines 44 and 45 . . . . . . ▶	46		
Married filing jointly or Qualifying widow(er), $11,400	47	Foreign tax credit. Attach Form 1116 if required . . .	47	0	00
	48	Credit for child and dependent care expenses. Attach Form 2441	48	0	00
	49	Education credits from Form 8863, line 29 . . .	49	0	00
Head of household, $8,350	50	Retirement savings contributions credit. Attach Form 8880	50	0	00
	51	Child tax credit (see page 42)	51	0	00
	52	Credits from Form: **a** ☐ 8396 **b** ☐ 8839 **c** ☐ 5695	52	0	00
	53	Other credits from Form: **a** ☐ 3800 **b** ☐ 8801 **c** ☐	53	0	00
	54	Add lines 47 through 53. These are your **total credits** . .	54		
	55	Subtract line 54 from line 46. If line 54 is more than line 46, enter -0- . . ▶	55	2684	00
Other Taxes	56	Self-employment tax. Attach Schedule SE . . .	56	0	00
	57	Unreported social security and Medicare tax from Form: **a** ☐ 4137 **b** ☐ 8919	57	0	00
	58	Additional tax on IRAs, other qualified retirement plans, etc. Attach Form 5329 if required . .	58	0	00
	59	Additional taxes: **a** ☐ AEIC payments **b** ☐ Household employment taxes. Attach Schedule H	59	0	00
	60	Add lines 55 through 59. This is your **total tax** . . . ▶	60	2684	00
Payments	61	Federal income tax withheld from Forms W-2 and 1099	61	4972	83
	62	2009 estimated tax payments and amount applied from 2008 return	62	0	00
	63	Making work pay and government retiree credits. Attach Schedule M	63	400	00
If you have a qualifying child, attach Schedule EIC.	64a	**Earned income credit (EIC)**	64a	0	00
	b	Nontaxable combat pay election ☐ 64b			
	65	Additional child tax credit. Attach Form 8812 . . .	65	0	00
	66	Refundable education credit from Form 8863, line 16 . .	66	0	00
	67	First-time homebuyer credit. Attach Form 5405 . . .	67	8000	00
	68	Amount paid with request for extension to file (see page 72)	68	0	00
	69	Excess social security and tier 1 RRTA tax withheld (see page 72)	69	0	00
	70	Credits from Form: **a** ☐ 2439 **b** ☐ 4136 **c** ☐ 8801 **d** ☐ 8885	70	0	00
	71	Add lines 61, 62, 63, 64a, and 65 through 70. These are your **total payments** . . ▶	71	13372	83
Refund	72	If line 71 is more than line 60, subtract line 60 from line 71. This is the amount you **overpaid**	72	10688	83
Direct deposit? See page 73 and fill in 73b, 73c, and 73d, or Form 8888.	73a	Amount of line 72 you want **refunded to you.** If Form 8888 is attached, check here . ▶ ☐	73a	10688	83
	b	Routing number 5 9 1 0 0 2 3 2 ▶ **c** Type: ☒ Checking ☐ Savings			
	d	Account number 4 5 2 2 0 9 9 2 3 8 0 4 5 4			
	74	Amount of line 72 you want **applied to your 2010 estimated tax** ▶ 74		0	00
Amount You Owe	75	**Amount you owe.** Subtract line 71 from line 60. For details on how to pay, see page 74 ▶	75	0	00
	76	Estimated tax penalty (see page 74) . . . 76		0	00

The government levies additional taxes on certain types of income. If you worked as an independent contractor, for example, you must pay self-employment tax to cover the Social Security and Medicare taxes that otherwise normally would be deducted from your paycheck.

Third Party Designee	Do you want to allow another person to discuss this return with the IRS (see page 75)? ☐ **Yes. Complete the following.** ☒ **No**
	Designee's name ▶ Phone no. ▶ Personal identification number (PIN) ▶

Sign Here Joint return? See page 15. Keep a copy for your records.	Under penalties of perjury, I declare that I have examined this return and accompanying schedules and statements, and to the best of my knowledge and belief, they are true, correct, and complete. Declaration of preparer (other than taxpayer) is based on all information of which preparer has any knowledge.
	Your signature *David S. Kendrick* Date 3/10/10 Your occupation truck driver Daytime phone number 303-555-8946
	Spouse's signature. If a joint return, **both** must sign. Date Spouse's occupation

Paid Preparer's Use Only	Preparer's signature ▶ Date Check if self-employed ☐ Preparer's SSN or PTIN
	Firm's name (or yours if self-employed), address, and ZIP code ▶ EIN Phone no.

Form **1040** (2009)

Mortgage Interest Paid Statement

The government allows you to write off the interest on your primary home's mortgage. You may choose to do this instead of taking the standard deduction. If you own a home, you will receive a statement (form 1098) from your lender each year stating how much mortgage interest you paid.

This box identifies the total amount that the borrower paid in mortgage interest. This person, for example, paid almost $8,200 in mortgage interest.

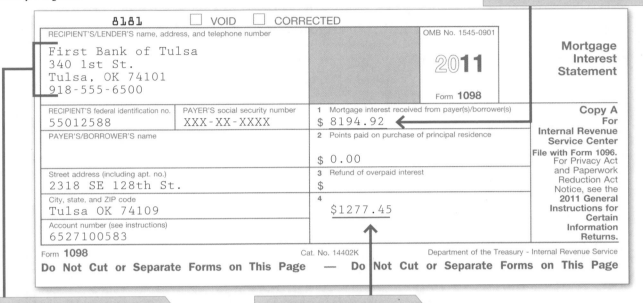

Your mortgage interest statement will come from your lender. If you have chosen to receive online statements, you may have to download your statement online rather than receive a paper copy in the mail.

This box shows the amount of mortgage insurance premiums the taxpayer paid.

State Income Tax Return

Forty-one states require residents to pay income taxes. If you live in a state that taxes your income, make sure you complete your federal taxes first. You'll need that information to complete any state, local, or school district taxes.

M1 MINNESOTA·REVENUE 2009 Individual Income Tax 200911

Please print. Leave unused boxes blank. Do not use staples on anything you submit.

Please print

Place an X if a foreign address:

Your first name and initial: Lisa A.
Last name: Cisneros

If a joint return, spouse's first name and initial | Last name

Current home address (street, apartment number, route): 1687 Little Lane, Apt. 6

City: Minnetonka
State: MN
Zip code: 55345

Many states and the federal government allow you to designate a few dollars from your taxes to help fund political campaigns. Choosing to donate these funds will not affect your refund or the amount of tax that you pay.

Filing status

2009 federal filing status (place an X in one oval box):
[X] (1) Single
[ ] (2) Married filing joint
[ ] (3) Married filing separate: Enter spouse's name and Social Security number here
[ ] (4) Head of Household
[ ] (5) Qualifying widow(er)

Fund

State Elections Campaign Fund
If you want $5 to go to help candidates for state offices pay campaign expenses, you may each enter the code number for the party of your choice. This will not increase your tax or reduce your refund.

Political party and code number:
Democratic Farmer-Labor . 11   Green 14
Independence 12   General Campaign
Republican 13   Fund 15

Your code: 15   Spouse's code:

Federal

From your federal return (for line references see instructions, page 9), enter the amount of:

A Wages, salaries, tips, etc.: $28,250 .00
B IRA, Pensions and annuities: 0 .00
C Unemployment: $2,564 .00
D Federal adjusted gross income: (If a negative number, place an X in oval box.) $30,814 .00

1 **Federal taxable income** (from line 43 of federal Form 1040, line 27 of Form 1040A or line 6 of Form 1040EZ) . . . . 1 ■ | 21464 .00
  If a negative number, place an X in oval box.

2 **State income tax or sales tax addition.** If you itemized deductions on federal Form 1040, complete the worksheet on page 9 of the instructions . . . . 2 ■ | 0 .00

3 Other additions to income, including non-Minnesota bond interest, standard deductions for real estate taxes and motor vehicle sales tax and excluded unemployment compensation (see instructions, page 10, enclose Schedule M1M) . 3 ■ | 0 .00

4 Add lines 1 through 3 (if a negative number, place an X in the oval box) . . . . 4 | 21464 .00
  If a negative number, place an X in oval box.

5 State income tax refund from line 10 of federal Form 1040 . . . . 5 ■

On this tax form, all numbers are rounded to the nearest whole dollar amount. When filling out some tax forms, you may need to round up to the next dollar (if the "change" is more than .50) or round down (if the "change" is less than .50).

6 Net interest or mutual fund dividends from U.S. bonds (see instructions, page 10) 6 ■
7 Education expenses you paid for your qualifying children in grades K–12 (see instructions, page 10). Enter the name and grade of each child: 7 ■

8 Other subtractions (see instructions, page 12, and enclose Schedule M1M) . . . . . . 8 ■

9 Total subtractions. Add lines 5 through 8 9

10 **Minnesota taxable income.** Subtract line 9 from line 4 10

11 **Tax** from the table on pages 22–27 of the M1 instructions 11

Some states use flat tax rates calculated as a percentage of your income. Others, such as Minnesota, calculate taxes using a sliding scale. For these states, you will need to refer to a tax table in order to determine the amount of tax to pay.

12 Alternative minimum tax (enclose Schedule M1MT) . . . . 12 ■

13 Add lines 11 and 12 13

14 **Full-year residents:** Enter the amount from line 13 on line 14. Skip lines 14a and 14b.
   Part-year residents and nonresidents: From Schedule M1NR, enter the tax from line 27 on line 14, from line 23 on line 14a, and from line 24 on line 14b (enclose Schedule M1NR) 14
   If a negative number, place an X in oval box.

a. M1NR: line 23
b. M1NR: line 24

15 Tax on lump-sum distribution (enclose Schedule M1LS) . . . . 15 ■ | 0 .00

16 Tax before credits. Add lines 14 and 15 . . . . 16 | 1293 .00

Do not send W-2s. Enclose Schedule M1W to claim Minnesota withholding.

Tax before credits

0 — Stock No. 1009010

State Income Tax Return

200912

Nonrefundable credits	17	Tax before credits. Amount from line 16	17	1293 .00
	18	Marriage credit for joint return when both spouses have taxable earned income or taxable retirement income *(determine from instructions, page 14)*	18 ■	0 .00
	19	Credit for taxes paid to another state *(enclose Schedule M1CR)*	19 ■	0 .00
	20	Other nonrefundable credits *(enclose Schedule M1C)*.	20 ■	0 .00
	21	Total nonrefundable credits. Add lines 18 through 20	21	0 .00

Tax	22	Subtract line 21 from line 17 *(if result is zero or less, leave blank)*	22	1293 .00
	23	Nongame Wildlife Fund contribution *(see instructions, page 15)* This will reduce your refund or increase amount owed	23 ■	0 .00
	24	Add lines 22 and 23	24	1293 .00

Total payments	25	**Minnesota income tax withheld.** Complete and enclose Schedule M1W to report Minnesota withholding from W-2, 1099 and W-2G forms *(do not send in W-2s, 1099s, W-2Gs)* .	25 ■	(1148) .00
	26	Minnesota estimated tax and extension *(Form M13)* payments made for 2009	26 ■	0 .00
	27	Child and dependent care credit *(enclose Schedule M1CD)*. Enter number of qualifying persons here: ▶	27 ■	
	28	Minnesota working family credit *(enclose Schedule M1WFC)*. Enter number of qualifying children here: ▶	28 ■	
	29	K–12 education credit *(enclose Schedule M1ED)*. Enter number of qualifying children here: ▶	29 ■	
	30	Lower income motor fuels tax credit *(see instructions, page 17; cannot exceed $25)* .	30 ■	
	31	Job Opportunity Building Zone *(JOBZ)* jobs credit *(enclose Schedule JOBZ)*	31 ■	
	32	Credit for tuberculosis testing on cattle. If you own cattle and had your cattle tested for bovine tuberculosis, see instructions, page 17	32 ■	0 .00
	33	Total payments. Add lines 25 through 32	33	1148 .00

> Just as employers withhold federal taxes, they also withhold state taxes. If you live in one state and work in another, you may receive a credit for the tax you paid to the state in which you work.

Refund or amount due	34	**REFUND.** If line 33 is more than line 24, subtract line 24 from line 33 *(see instructions, page 17)*. For direct deposit, complete line 35	34 ■	.00
	35	FAST REFUNDS! For direct deposit of the full refund on line 34, enter: Account type: ◯ Checking ◯ Savings Routing number _____ Account number _____		
	36	**AMOUNT YOU OWE.** If line 24 is more than line 33, subtract line 33 from line 24 *(see instructions, page 18)* . . . . . . **Make check out to Minnesota Revenue and send with Form M60**	36 ■	145 .00
	37	Penalty amount from Schedule M15 *(see instructions, page 18)*. Also subtract this amount from line 34 or add it to line 36 *(enclose Schedule M15)*	37 ■	0 .00
		IF YOU PAY ESTIMATED TAX and you want part of your refund credited to estimated tax, enter lines 38 and 39.		.00
	38	Amount from line 34 you want sent to you ◀	38 ■	
	39	Amount from line 34 you want applied to your 2010 estimated tax	39 ■	0 .00

Sign here

I declare that this return is correct and complete to the best of my knowledge and belief.

Your signature *Lisa A. Cisneros* Date 03/15/2010

Spouse's signature (if filing jointly) Daytime phone

Paid preparer: You must sign below.

Paid preparer's signature Date

Daytime phone

Include a copy of your 2009 federal return and schedules.
Mail to: Minnesota Individual Income Tax
St. Paul, MN 55145-0010
To check on the status of your refund, visit **www.taxes.state.mn.us**

◯ I authorize the Minnesota Department of Revenue to discuss this return with my preparer or the third-party designee indicated on my federal return.

> If you are self-employed or do not have state taxes withheld from your paycheck, you may pay estimated tax. If you are eligible for a tax refund, you may choose to have that refund applied to the next year's taxes.

Local Income Tax Return

Most of the nation's largest cities do not levy a local income tax. However, many smaller cities and towns do tax their citizens. If your city requires residents to pay a local income tax, be sure to submit the form each year along with your state and federal taxes.

> Did you move during the calendar year to a city with a local income tax. If so, you need only pay taxes on money you earned while living in that city.

Page 1 of 2

GR-1040 R

CITY OF GRAND RAPIDS INCOME TAX
INDIVIDUAL RETURN - RESIDENT - DUE April 30. 2010

2009 R

PLEASE TYPE OR PRINT

Your social security number	Your first name	Initial	Last name	Your occupation
XXX XX XXXX	William	J.	Carlisle	HVAC technician
Spouse's soc sec number	If joint return, spouse's first name	Initial	Last name	Spouse's occupation
XXX XX XXXX	Keisha	R	Carlisle	graphic designer

If married, is spouse filing a separate return? ☐ YES ☐ NO

Present home address (Number and street including apartment number): 2711 E. Lake Dr., #2

City, town or post office, state and zip code: Grand Rapids, MI 49839

Enter name and address used on 2008 return. If same as this year, print "Same." (If none filed, give reason.): Same

☐ PART-YEAR RESIDENT MO. DAY YR. FROM __/__/__ TO __/__/__   FORMER ADDRESS

☐ Check box if you DO NOT need a return form mailed next year.

EXEMPTIONS

1a. ☒ Yourself ☐ 65 or over ☐ Blind   1b. ☒ Spouse ☐ 65 or over ☐ Blind | Number of boxes checked. 1 | 2 |

2. List first names of your dependent children who live with you: Jonathan, Coco, Mia | Number of children listed. 2 | 3 |

3. Number of other dependents. (Same as federal) GO TO PAGE 2, LINE 23e | Number of other dependents. 3 | 0 |

4. Total number of exemptions. Add lines 1, 2, and 3 | Total number of exemptions. 4 | 5 |

INCOME

5. ENTER WAGES, TIPS AND OTHER COMPENSATION (DEFERRED COMPENSATION DISTRIBUTIONS, SICK PAY, ETC.) EARNED IN AND OUTSIDE OF GRAND RAPIDS. PART-YEAR RESIDENTS INCLUDE ALL WAGES EARNED DURING RESID

ATTACH COPY OF PAGE 1 OF FEDERAL FORM 1040 TO THIS RETURN

	EMPLOYER'S FED ID #	EMPLOYER'S NAME	ADDRESS OF ACTUAL WORK STATION		GRAND RAPIDS TAX WITHHELD		WAGES, ETC. (W-2 FORM, BOX 1)	
5a.	444-556666	A1 Heating and Air Conditioning	100 N. Main St.	5a		00	$34,277	00
5b.	555667777	Design Plus	7500 W. Erie Rd.	5b		00	$16,334	00
5c.				5c		00		00
5d.				5d		00		00
5e.	Totals for additional employers from page 2, line 24e.			5e		00		00
						00	6b	00
					7		$82	00
					8			00
					9a			00
					9b			00
					9c			00
					9d			00

> Tax deductions generally reduce the amount of income on which you want pay taxes. You may get tax deductions for owning a home, having children, spending money on a personal business, paying alimony, or other expenses. For example, if you made $25,600, but you had two children, you would be eligible for $2,000 in tax deductions ($1,000 for each child).

GRW-2 OR W-2 HERE

| 10. | Total income. Add lines 6b through 9d | 10 | $50,693 | 00 |

DEDUCTIONS   See instructions (PART-YEAR RESIDENTS ALLOCATE DEDUCTIONS FOR PERIOD OF RESIDENCY.)

11a. Individual Retirement Account deduction. (ATTACH PG. 1 OF FEDERAL RETURN & EVIDENCE OF PAYMENT)	11a	$2400	00
11b. Employee business expenses. (SEE INSTRUCTIONS AND ATTACH FEDERAL 2106 OR LIST)	11b		00
11c. Moving expenses. (Into Grand Rapids area only) (ATTACH FEDERAL 3903 OR LIST)	11c		00
11d. Alimony Paid. DO NOT INCLUDE CHILD SUPPORT (ATTACH COPY PAGE 1 OF FEDERAL RETURN)	11d		00
11e. Renaissance Zone Deduction. (ATTACH SCHEDULE RZ OF GR-1040R OR GR-1040NR)	11e		00
11f. Total deductions. Add lines 11a through 11e	11f	$2400	00
12. Total income after deductions. Subtract line 11f from line 10	12	$48,293	00
13. Amount for exemptions. (Number of exemptions from line 4 above ___5___ times $750)			
14. Total income subject to tax. Subtract line 13 from line 12			
15. City of Grand Rapids Tax at 1.3%. (MULTIPLY LINE 14 BY .013)			

PAYMENTS AND CREDITS   (If line 17 exceeds $100 see instructions for making estimated tax

16a. Tax withheld by your employer from line 6a above. (A COPY OF EACH W-2 FORM MUST BE ATTACHED)	16a	
16b. Payments on 2009 Declaration of Estimated Income Tax, payments with an extension and credits forward.	16b	
16c. Credit for tax paid to another city, by a partnership or S corporation. (ATTACH COPY OF OTHER CITY'S RETURN)	16c	
16d. Total payments and credits. Add lines 16a through 16c		

> Local income tax forms may allow you to donate part of your refund to area charitable organizations. These funds reduce of your total refund amount.

ENCLOSE CHECK OR MONEY ORDER FOR TAX DUE (DO NOT STAPLE TO RETURN)

TAX DUE — 17. If tax (line 15) is larger than payments (line 16d) you owe tax. ENTER TAX DUE and PAY WITH RETURN. Enclose check or money order payable to the Grand Rapids City Treasurer. Or pay with an electronic funds withdrawal: mark Pay Tax Due box on line 22, enter effective date and complete line 22 a, b & c. | 17 | | 00 |

OVERPAYMENT — 18. If payments (line 16d) are larger than tax (line 15) ENTER OVERPAYMENT. | 18 | $79 | 00 |

CREDIT TO 2010 — 19. Overpayment to be HELD and APPLIED TO YOUR 2010 ESTIMATED TAX. | 19 | | 00 | CREDIT TO 2010 |

DONATION — 20. Overpayment donation. All or any portion of overpayment may be donated to any fund.
a. ☒ American flags for veterans' graves in Grand Rapids. | 20a | $3 | 00 | DONATION 1
b. ☒ Grand Rapids Children's Fund. | 20b | $3 | 00 | DONATION 2
c. ☒ Grand Rapids Parks' Fund. | 20c | $3 | 00 | DONATION 3

REFUND — 21. Overpayment refund. For direct deposit mark Refund box on line 22 and complete 22 a, b & c. | 21 | $70 | 00 | REFUND

ELECTRONIC REFUND OR PAYMENT INFORMATION — 22. Mark one: ☒ Refund - Direct deposit ☐ Pay tax due - Electronic funds withdrawal >> Electronic funds withdrawal effective date: (If blank, default is date return processed.)
a. Routing number: 5 0 1 2 9 8 4 6
b. Account number: 1 2 0 4 5 5 9 3 0   c. Account type: ☒ Checking ☐ Savings

MAIL TO: GRAND RAPIDS INCOME TAX DEPARTMENT, PO BOX 2528, GRAND RAPIDS, MI 49501-2528

2009 GR-1040R PAGE 1

Local Income Tax Return

If you are self-employed or own a business, write the income you earned from your business here. You must provide copies of your documentation from your federal tax return to back up your claims.

Page 2 of 2

Name(s) as shown on page 1	Your social security number

FAILURE TO ATTACH DOCUMENTATION OR ATTACHING INCORRECT OR INCOMPLETE DOCUMENTATION WILL DELAY PROCESSING OF RETURN AND MAY RESULT IN DEDUCTIONS AND LOSSES BEING DISALLOWED

23. OTHER DEPENDENTS (Same as Federal)

	NAME OF OTHER DEPENDENT	RELATIONSHIP OF OTHER DEPENDENT	MONTHS OTHER DEPENDENT LIVED IN YOUR HOME
23a.			
23b.			
23c.			
23d.			
23e.	Number of other dependents listed on lines 23a through 23d. ENTER NUMBER HERE AND ON PAGE 1, LINE 3		

24. ADDITIONAL WAGES FROM EMPLOYERS NOT INCLUDED ON PAGE 1, LINES 5a THROUGH 5d

ENTER WAGES, TIPS AND OTHER COMPENSATION (DEFERRED COMPENSATION, SICK PAY, ETC.) EARNED IN AND OUTSIDE OF GRAND RAPIDS THAT ARE NOT INCLUDED ON PAGE 1, LINES 5a THROUGH 5d. PART-YEAR RESIDENTS INCLUDE WAGES EARNED DURING RESIDENCY.

EMPLOYER'S NAME	ADDRESS OF ACTUAL WORK STATION		GRAND RAPIDS TAX WITHHELD	WAGES, ETC. (FORM W-2, BOX 1)
24a.		24a	00	$0 00
24b.		24b	00	$0 00
24c.		24c	00	$0 00
24d.		24d	00	$0 00
24e. Total. Add lines 24a through 24d ENTER TOTALS HERE AND ON PAGE 1, LINE 5e		24e	00	$0 00

25. BUSINESS AND FARMING INCOME

25a. Net profit (or loss) from business or profession. (ATTACH FEDERAL SCHEDULE C)	25a	$0	00
25b. Net profit (or loss) from farming. (ATTACH FEDERAL SCHEDULE F)	25b	$0	00
25c. Applicable portion of net operating loss carryover. (ATTACH SCHEDULE)	25c	$0	00
25d. Retirement plan deduction. Check type of plan ☐KEOGH ☐SEP ☐SIMPLE (ATTACH FEDERAL SCHEDULE)	25d	$0	00
25e. Total. Add lines 25a and 25b and subtract lines 25c and 25d ENTER HERE AND ON PAGE 1, LINE 9a	25e	$0	00

26. SALES AND EXCHANGES OF PROPERTY

THE GRAND RAPIDS INCOME TAX ORDINANCE FOLLOWS THE INTERNAL REVENUE CODE IN ITS TREATMENT OF CAPITAL GAINS. ALL CAPITAL GAINS RECEIVED BY A RESIDENT OF GRAND RAPIDS ARE TAXABLE EXCEPT THE PORTION OF THE GAIN (OR LOSS) OCCURRING PRIOR TO JULY 1, 1967. IF THE AMOUNT OF CAPITAL GAINS REPORTED TO GRAND RAPIDS IS DIFFERENT FROM THE FEDERAL AMOUNT, ATTACH A SCHEDULE SHOWING THE COMPUTATION OF THE GRAND RAPIDS TAXABLE PORTION.

26a. Capital Gains from federal Schedule D. (ATTACH FEDERAL SCHEDULE D) Check box if no federal Sch. D filed ☐	26a	$0	00
26b. Other Gains from federal Form 4797. (ATTACH FEDERAL FORM 4797)	26b	$0	00
26c. Total. Add lines 26a and 26b. ENTER HERE AND ON PAGE 1, LINE 9b	26c	$0	00

27. RENTAL REAL ESTATE, ROYALTIES, PARTNERSHIPS, TRUSTS, ETC.

THE FEDERAL RULES CONCERNING PASSIVE LOSSES ARE APPLICABLE TO LOSSES DEDUCTED ON THIS RETURN.

27a. Income or loss from rental real estate and royalties from federal Schedule E, Part I. (ATTACH FEDERAL SCHEDULE E AND FORM 8582)	27a	$0	00
27b. Income or loss from partnerships and S corporations from federal Schedule E, Part II. (ATTACH FEDERAL SCH. E, SCH. K-1's AND FORM 8582)	27b	$0	00
27c. Income or loss from estates, trusts from federal Schedule E, Part III. (ATTACH FEDERAL SCHEDULE E, SCHEDULE K-1's AND FORM 8582)	27c	$0	00
27d. Income or loss from from real estate mortgage investment conduits (REMICs) from federal Schedule E, Part IV. (ATTACH A COPY OF FED. SCH. E)	27d	$0	00
27e. Net farm rental income or loss from federal Schedule E, Part V, line 40. (ATTACH A COPY OF FEDERAL SCHEDULE E)	27e	$0	00
27f. Total. Add lines 27a, 27b, 27c, 27d and 27e. ENTER HERE AND ON PAGE 1, LINE 9c	27f	$0	00

28. OTHER INCOME

OTHER INCOME INCLUDES: GAMBLING AND LOTTERY WINNINGS, INDIAN GAMING PROCEEDS, ALIMONY RECEIVED, PROFIT SHARING PLAN DISTRIBUTIONS, PREMATURE IRA AND PENSION DISTRIBUTIONS, ETC. ATTACH COPIES OF ALL APPLICABLE FED. SCHEDULES AND FORMS 1099.

RECEIVED FROM	KIND OF INCOME		AMOUNT	
28a.		28a	$0	00
28b.		28b	$0	00
28c. Total. Add lines 28a and 28b ENTER HERE AND ON PAGE 1, LINE 9d		28c	$0	00

29. THIRD-PARTY DESIGNEE

Do you want to allow another person to discuss this return with the Income Tax Department? ☐ Yes. Complete the following. ☒ No

Designee's name	Phone No. ( )	Personal identification number (PIN)

I declare that I have examined this return (including accompanying schedules and statements) and to the best of my knowledge and belief it is true, correct and complete. If prepared by a person other than taxpayer, the preparer's declaration is based on all information of which preparer has any knowledge.

	TAXPAYER'S SIGNATURE - If joint return, both husband and wife must sign.	DATE	SIGNATURE OF PREPARER OTHER THAN TAXPAYER	DATE
SIGN HERE ====>	*William F. Carlisle*	2|26|10		/ /
	SPOUSE'S SIGNATURE	DATE	FIRM'S NAME (OR YOURS IF SELF EMPLOYED), ADDRESS AND ZIP CODE	
====>	*Keisha R. Carlisle*	2|26|10		
	DAYTIME PHONE NUMBER (616) 555-2387		PHONE NUMBER ( )	
	E-MAIL ADDRESS willc@pax.com		E-MAIL ADDRESS	

Do you receive alimony? Did you win some money from a scratch-off lottery ticket? You must pay taxes on that income just as though you earned it at a job.

School District Income Tax Return

Some places require residents to pay an income tax that directly supports school districts in their area. This tax may be levied in place of or in addition to local income taxes.

If you pay school district income tax, be sure to file a separate school district income tax return. These taxes are not included on your regular state or local tax forms.

Ohio | Department of Taxation

Please use only black ink.

09020102

Taxable year beginning in **2009**

SD 100 Rev. 8/09
School District Income Tax Return

Enter school district # for this return (see pages 9-10).

SD# ▶▶ 3 9 0 1

File a separate Ohio form SD 100 for each taxing school district in which you lived during the taxable year.

Taxpayer Social Security no. (required) ▶▶ If deceased

X X X   X X   X X X X

Use UPPERCASE letters.

check box

Spouse's Social Security no. (only if joint return) ▶▶ If deceased

check box

Your first name   M.I.   Last name

M a r g u e r i t e   L. R a m u n d o

Spouse's first name (only if married filing jointly)   M.I.   Last name

Mailing address (for faster processing, use a street address)

5 2   O a k   S t . , U p p e r

City

State   ZIP code   County (first four letters)

O H   4 4 8 7 0   S A N D

ZIP code   County (first four letters)

Foreign postal code

If you didn't live in this school district for the entire year, the school district taxes you owe will be adjusted. You may still owe school district taxes if you lived in another district for part of the year.

School District Residency – File a separate Ohio form SD 100 for each taxing school district in which you lived during the taxable year.

Check applicable box

[X] Full-year resident   [ ] Part-year resident of SD# above   [ ] Full-year nonresident of SD# above

Enter date of nonresidency _____ to _____

Check box applicable for spouse (only if married filing jointly)

[ ] Full-year resident   [ ] Part-year resident of SD# above   [ ] Full-year nonresident of SD# above

Enter date of nonresidency _____ to _____

Filing Status – Check one (must match Ohio income tax return):

[X] Single or head of household or qualifying widow(er)

[ ] Married filing jointly

[ ] Married filing separately ▶▶ Enter spouse's SS#

Tax Type – Check one (for an explanation, see page 2 of the instructions)

I am filing this return because during the taxable year I lived in a(n):

[X] "Traditional" tax base school district. You must start with line 1 below.

[ ] "Earned income only" tax base school district. You must start with Schedule A, line 19 on page 2 of this return.

Please do not use staples, tape or glue. Place your W-2(s), check (payable to School District Income Tax) and Ohio form SD 40P on top of your return. Place any other supporting documents or statements after the last page of your return.

Go paperless. It's FREE!
Try I-File or Ohio eForms
by visiting tax.ohio.gov.

Most electronic filers receive their refunds in 5-7 business days by direct deposit!

INCOME INFORMATION – If the amount on line 1 is negative, shade the negative sign ("–") in the box provided.

1. "Traditional" tax base school district filer. Enter on this line your Ohio taxable income reported on line 5 of Ohio form IT 1040 or IT 1040EZ.

   "Earned income only" tax base school district filer. Complete Schedule A on page 2 of this return and then enter on this line the amount you show on page 2, line 22 of this return.

2. The amount of Ohio taxable income, if any, you earned while **not** a resident of the "traditional" tax base school district whose number you entered above. "Earned income only" school district filers must leave this line blank ....

3. School district taxable income (line 1 minus line 2; if less than zero, enter -0-) ....

Like state or federal taxes, you may be able to file your school district income tax form online. Electronic filing is free. It may help you receive your refund more quickly than through paper filing.

NO Payment Enclosed – **Mail to:**
School District Income Tax
P.O. Box 182197
Columbus, OH 43218-2197

If you have a federal extension of time to file, please include a copy or the confirmation number of the extension.

Payment Enclosed – **Mail to:**
School District Income Tax
P.O. Box 182389
Columbus, OH 43218-2389

2009 SD 100   pg. 1 of 2   **2009 SD 100**

School District Income Tax Return

Ohio | **Department of Taxation**

09020202

Taxable year beginning in **2009**

SD 100 Rev. 8/09
School District Income Tax Return

SS#

SD#

4. Amount from line 3, page 1 .... 4.

5. School district tax rate (enter the applicable decimal rate from pages 9-10 of the instructions) ....5. . **0 5**

> Your school district tax rate may vary depending on the school district in which you live. Check the tables enclosed with your school district tax return to find the correct rate.

6. Line 4 multiplied by line 5 .... 6.

7. Senior citizen credit (**limit $50 per return**). You must be 65 or older to claim this credit .... 7.

8. Total due before withholding and payments (line 6 minus line 7; if less than zero, enter -0-) .... **TOTAL TAX ▸ 8.**   **1 4 9 | 0 0**

9. School district income tax withheld (school district number on W-2(s) must agree with SD number in the upper right-hand corner on page 1 of this return) .... 9.   **1 5 0 | 0 0**

10. Add your 2009 Ohio form SD 100ES payment(s) ($ **1**), your 2009 Ohio form SD 40P extension payment(s) ($ **0**) and your 2008 school district overpayment credited to 2009 ($ **1**) .... 10.   **2 | 0 0**

11. Add lines 9 and 10 .... **TOTAL PAYMENTS ▸ 11.**   **1 5 2 | 0 0**

If line 11 is MORE THAN line 8, go to line 12. If line 11 is LESS THAN line 8, skip to line 15.

12. If line 11 is more than line 8, subtract line 8 from line 11 and enter the .... **AMOUNT OVERPAID ▸ 12.**   **3 | 0 0**

13. Enter the amount of school district overpayment on line 12 that you want .... **CREDITED TO 2010 ▸ 13.**   **3 | 0 0**

14. Line 12 minus line 13 .... **YOUR REFUND ▸ 14.**   **0 0**

> Depending on how much tax was withheld for your school district throughout the year, you may owe taxes or receive a refund.

15. If line 11 is less than line 8, subtract line 11 from line 8 .... 15.

16. Interest penalty on underpayment of estimated tax. Enclose Ohio form IT/SD 2210 and the appropriate worksheet if you annualize .... 16.

17. Interest and penalty due on late-paid tax and/or late-filed return .... 17.

18. Add lines 15, 16 and 17. If payment is enclosed, make check payable to School District Income Tax and include Ohio form SD 40P (see page 7 in the instructions) .... **AMOUNT YOU OWE ▸ 18.**   **0 0**

If your refund is less than $1.01, no refund will be issued. If you owe less than $1.01, no payment is necessary.

SCHEDULE A – "EARNED INCOME ONLY" TAX BASE SCHOOL DISTRICT AMOUNTS (See page 6 of the instructions.)

Complete this schedule only if you entered an "earned income only" tax base school district number in the upper right-hand corner on page 1 of this return.

19. Wages and other compensation described on page 6 of the instructions 19.   **0 0**

20. Net earnings from self-employment described on page 6 of the instructions. Shade the negative sign ("–") at right if the amount is less than -0- 20.   **0 0**

21. Depreciation expense adjustment, if any, described on page 6 of the instructions 21.   **0 0**

22. Add lines 19, 20 and 21. Enter the total here and on line 1 of this return 22.   **0 0**

SIGN HERE (required) — See page 1 of this return for mailing information.

I have read this return. Under penalties of perjury, I declare that, to the best of my knowledge and belief, the return and all enclosures are true, correct and complete.

▸ *Marguerite L. Ramundo*   04/01/2010
Your signature   Date

For Department Use Only

▸
Spouse's signature (see page 4 in the instructions)   Phone number (optional)

Preparer's name (please print; see page 4 in the instructions)   Phone number

Do you authorize your preparer to contact us regarding this return?   Yes   No

Code

● **2009 SD 100**   pg. 2 of 2   **2009 SD 100** ●

Chapter Recap

Using the list below, place a checkmark next to the goals you achieved in Chapter 4.

▶ **In Lesson 1, you . . .**

❏ Learned how to read utility bills

❏ Reviewed cable and bundled cable bills

❏ Studied mortgage statements

❏ Examined sample flood and renter's insurance policies

▶ **In Lesson 2, you . . .**

❏ Examined investment and retirement account statements

❏ Learned how to fill out an application for a car loan

❏ Reviewed a realtor's home listing sheet

❏ Studied different types of home loan applications

▶ **In Lesson 3, you . . .**

❏ Reviewed a W-2 form

❏ Examined a federal income tax table

❏ Studied different federal income tax returns

❏ Learned how to fill out state, local, and school district income tax returns

Chapter Review

Name: _____   Date: _____

▶ Directions: Choose the answer that best completes the statement below.

Account Balance:

Total Amount Due at Last Billing	55.65
Payment 7/18/11 – Thank You	−55.65

Balance Forward:	**0.00**
Current Charges:	70.54

Balance Due ▶ $70.54

Details of Current Charges:

Service Period	No. of days	Current Reading	Previous Reading	Total Usage
Aug 5 – Aug 29	24	32097	31811	268 kWh

Meter Number   33333333

Delivery Service
RATE Residential Regular R-1

Transmission Charge	0.0266 x 286 kWh	7.61
Distribution Charge	0.0233 x 286 kWh	6.66
Transition Charge	0.0137 x 286 kWh	3.92
Energy Efficiency	0.0266 x 286 kWh	7.61
Renewable Energy	0.0025 x 286 kWh	.72

Total Delivery Services ▶ $26.52

Supplier Services
Basic-Fixed

Generation Charge	0.1539 x 286 kWh	44.02

Total Supplier Services ▶ $44.02
Account Balance ▶ $70.54

---

1. You can find any overdue charges in the _____ section.

   A. current charges
   B. distribution charge
   C. balance forward
   D. supplier services

▶ Directions: Determine whether each of the following statements is true or false. If the statement is true, write T. If the statement is false, write F. Then rewrite the false statement to make it true.

THE CITY OF SAN DIEGO

WATER & WASTEWATER SERVICES

SAN DIEGO, CA 92187.0001   (619) 313-3500

| U25-11111-11-1 | 1111 Test PL |
| ACCOUNT NUMBER | SERVICE ADDRESS |

Mailed on Sept 10 2011

Sept 24 2011
PAYMENT DUE DATE

ARTURO STOKES
8223 PACIFIC ST., #1
SAN DIEGO   CA   92108-3742

RETURN THIS PORTION

MAKE CHECK PAYABLE TO CITY TREASURER

2511111111   0000116749

$116.73
TOTAL AMOUNT DUE

| ACCOUNT NO. U25-11111-11-1   STOKES | | | | | | 9/24/11 | $116.73 |
| SERVICE ADDRESS   1111 TEST PL | | | | | | **PAYMENT DUE DATE** | **TOTAL AMOUNT DUE** |

TYPE OF SERVICE	METER	SERVICE PERIOD FROM	TO	DAYS	METER READING PREVIOUS	CURRENT	USAGE HCR*	AMOUNT	CODE
Water Base Fee		08-03	09-04	32	Meter Size = 3/4 Inch			15.18	
Water Used		08-03	09-04	32	2823	2845		55.25	E
					7 HCF @ $2.2620 =	$15.83			
					7 HCF @ $2.4610 =	$17.22			
					8 HCF @ $2.7750 =	$22.20			
Sewer Base Fee		08-03	09-04	32				12.31	
Sewer Srvc Chrg		08-03	09-04	32				34.11	
Storm Drain Fee								0.95	
					CURRENT CHARGES			117.80	
PREV. BALANCE								1.07 CR	
					TOTAL AMOUNT DUE			**$116.73**	

2. This bill only has charges for the water that Arturo used.

_____

_____

3. The period for the bill above is three months.

_____

_____

4. This bill carries a credit from the previous period.

_____

_____

Name: _____   Date: _____

▶ Directions: Write your answer to each question on the lines below.

Sunshine
CABLE COMPANY
5450 Gulf Way
Naples, FL 34101

IMPORTANT NUMBERS
SERVICE: 239-555-5555
BILLING: 239-555-5555

SERVICE ADDRESS		
Kwame Freeman 2718 Orange St., #8		

| ACCOUNT NUMBER | SERVICE PERIOD | |
	FROM	TO
82-49660253	12/01/2011	12/31/2011
DUE DATE	**AMOUNT DUE**	
1/15/2012	160.88	

Date	Description	Amount
	PREVIOUS BALANCE	73.75
11/16/11	10% LATE FEE	7.38
12/01/11	BASIC ANALOG	22.00
12/01/11	HBO	13.00
12/01/11	RESIDENTIAL INTERNET	29.95
12/01/11	POLE ATTACHMENT FEE	2.20
12/01/11	ADMINISTRATIVE FEE	6.50
12/01/11	STATE SALES TAX 6%	0.13
	COMMUNICATIONS SERVICE TAX	5.97
	FLORIDA 9.17%	
	LOCAL 5.22%	
	TOTAL DUE	160.88

5. Other than cable, this bill includes charges for what other services?

_____

_____

6. Why did this consumer pay an additional $7.38 on top of his regular bill?

_____

_____

▶ Directions: Write your answer to each question on the lines below.

Uniform Residential Loan Application

This application is designed to be completed by the applicant(s) with the Lender's assistance. Applicants should complete this form as "Borrower" or "Co-Borrower," as applicable. Co-Borrower information must also be provided (and the appropriate box checked) when ☐ the income or assets of a person other than the Borrower (including the Borrower's spouse) will be used as a basis for loan qualification or ☐ the income or assets of the Borrower's spouse or other person who has community property rights pursuant to state law will not be used as a basis for loan qualification, but his or her liabilities must be considered because the spouse or other person has community property rights pursuant to applicable law and Borrower resides in a community property state, the security property is located in a community property state, or the Borrower is relying on other property located in a community property state as a basis for repayment of the loan.

If this is an application for joint credit, Borrower and Co-Borrower each agree that we intend to apply for joint credit (sign below):

_____   _____
Borrower   Co-Borrower

I. TYPE OF MORTGAGE AND TERMS OF LOAN				
Mortgage Applied for: ☐ VA ☒ FHA	☐ Conventional ☐ USDA/Rural Housing Service	☐ Other (explain):	Agency Case Number	Lender Case Number
Amount $ 110,000	Interest Rate 5.25 %	No. of Months 360	**Amortization Type:** ☒ Fixed Rate ☐ GPM	☐ Other (explain): ☐ ARM (type):

7. For what different types of mortgages can a potential home buyer use this application?

_____

_____

8. What is the interest rate on this loan?

_____

_____

9. Will the applicant's interest rate rise over time? Why or why not?

_____

_____

_____

Name: _____ Date: _____

▶ Directions: Select the choice that best answers each question below.

Uniform Residential Loan Application

VII. DETAILS OF TRANSACTION			VIII. DECLARATIONS					
			If you answer "Yes" to any questions a through i, please use continuation sheet for explanation.		Borrower		Co-Borrower	
					Yes	No	Yes	No
a.	Purchase price	$ 130,000	a.	Are there any outstanding judgments against you?	☐	☒	☐	☐
b.	Alterations, improvements, repairs		b.	Have you been declared bankrupt within the past 7 years?	☐	☒	☐	☐
c.	Land (if acquired separatelys)		c.	Have you had property foreclosed upon or given title or deed in lieu thereof in the last 7 years?	☐	☒	☐	☐
d.	Refinance (incl. debts to be paid off)		d.	Are you a party to a lawsuit?	☐	☒	☐	☐
e	Estimated prepaid items	750	e.	Have you directly or indirectly been obligated on any loan which resulted in foreclosure, transfer of title in lieu of foreclosure, or judgment?	☐	☒	☐	☐
f	Estimated closing costs	2500	(This would include such loans as home mortgage loans, SBA loans, home improvement loans, educational loans, manufactured (mobile) home loans, any mortgage, financial obligation, bond, or loan guarantee. If "Yes," provide details, including date, name, and address of Lender, FHA or VA case number, if any, and reasons for the action.)					
g	PMI, MIP, Funding Fee							
h	Discount (if Borrower will pay)							
i	Total costs (add items a through h)	133250						

10. Why is the total price slightly higher than the purchase price?

   A. The buyer must pay special taxes on her home purchase.

   B. Certain improvements and repairs are included in the price.

   C. Prepaid items and closing costs are added to the total.

   D. The borrower must pay extra because of her credit score.

11. The buyer for this home

   A. declared bankruptcy in the past 7 years.

   B. is party to a lawsuit.

   C. will not have to pay any closing costs.

   D. has no outstanding judgments against them.

▶ Directions: Write your answer to the question on the lines below.

Contract to Purchase Real Estate

43.   affect the Property. These representations shall survive the closing.
44. **6. POSSESSION.** Rentals, interest on any assumed mortgages, water and other utility bills, and any current operating expenses shall be prorated as of the date of
45.   closing. If the Property is owner-occupied, possession is to be given ___2___ days after closing at ___2___ A.M.(P.M.)and utilities shall not be prorated as above but
46.   paid for by Seller until delivery of possession. Seller shall be responsible to Purchaser for any damages caused by Seller's failure to deliver possession on the stated date.
47. **7. DAMAGE TO BUILDINGS.** If any buildings or other improvements are substantially managed or destroyed prior to the closing. Purchaser shall have the option
48.   (a) to proceed with the closing and receive the proceeds of any insurance payable in connection therewith, or (b) to terminate this Contract. Seller shall keep the
49.   Property adequately insured against fire and extended coverage perils prior to closing. Seller agrees to maintain the Property in its present condition until delivery
50.   of possession, subject to ordinary wear and tear, and the provisions of this paragraph. Purchaser shall have the right to conduct a walk-through inspection to verify the
51.   condition of the property prior to the closing.
52. **8. ACCEPTANCE; CLOSING.** This offer shall remain open for acceptance until _____2-13-12_____ (Date), at 11:59 p.m. The closing for delivery of the
53.   deed and payment of the balance of the purchase price shall be held on or before _____3-10-12_____ (Date), at a time and place mutually agreed upon by Seller and
54.   Purchaser. In the event of a failure of both parties to agree, the closing shall be held on the last day designated in the paragraph, and the Selling Broker shall designate
55.   the time and place of closing.
56. **9. EARNEST MONEY; DEFAULT.** Upon acceptance of this offer, Purchaser has delivered to _____First Bank of Dayton_____, Broker
57.   the sum of $ _____500.00_____ as earnest money, to be (1) deposited in the Broker's trust account promptly after acceptance of this offer or (2)
59.   closing does not occur because of Seller's default or because any condition of this Contract is not satisfied or waived, Purchaser shall be entitled to the earnest money.
60.   The parties acknowledge, however, that the Broker will not make a determination as to which party is entitled to the earnest money. Instead, the Broker shall release the
61.   earnest money from the trust account only (a) in accordance with the joint written instructions of Seller and Purchaser, or (b) in accordance with the following proce-
62.   dure; if the closing does not occur for any reason (including the default of either party), the Broker holding the earnest money may notify Seller in writing that the earnest
63.   money will be returned to Purchaser unless Seller makes a written demand for the earnest money within 20 days after the date of the Broker's notice. If the Broker does
64.   not receive a written demand from the Seller within the 20-day period, the Broker shall return the earnest money to Purchaser. If a written demand from Seller is received
65.   by the Broker within the 20-day period, the Broker shall retain the earnest money until (i) Seller and Purchaser have settled the dispute; (ii) disposition has been ordered
66.   by a final court order; or (iii) the Broker deposits the earnest money with the court pursuant to applicable court procedures. Payment or refund of the earnest money
67.   shall not prejudice the rights of the Broker(s) or the non-defaulting party in an action for damages or specific performance against the defaulting party.
68. **10. GENERAL PROVISIONS.** Upon acceptance, this offer shall become a complete agreement binding upon and inuring to benefit of Purchaser and Seller and
69.   their respective heirs, personal representatives, successors, and assigns, and shall be deemed to contain all the terms and conditions agreed upon, there being no oral
70.   conditions, representations, warranties, or agreements. Any subsequent conditions, representations, warranties, or agreements shall not be valid and binding upon the
71.   parties unless in writing signed by both parties. Purchaser has examined the Property and, except as otherwise provided in this Contract, is purchasing it "as is"
72.   in its present condition, relying upon such examination as to the condition, character, size, utility, and zoning of the Property. Time is of the essence of all provisions
73.   of this Contract. Any word used in this Contract shall be construed to mean either singular or plural as indicated by the number of signatures below.
74. **11. INSPECTIONS AND OTHER ADDENDA.** The following Addenda and attachments are attached to and shall be considered an integral part of this Contract:
75. ☒ Inspection Addendum   ☐ Land Contract Addendum   ☐ Other (Describe) _____
76. **WITNESS:** _Kristin Sharrod_   **Purchaser** _Karen Mixon_
77. **MAKE DEED TO:** _Karen Mixon_   **Purchaser**
78. _____   **Address** _589 S. Collier St., Xenia, OH 45385_

12. What time limits apply to this offer letter?

_____

_____

_____

_____

Name: _____   Date: _____

▶ Directions: Determine whether each of the following statements is true or false. If the statement is true, write T. If the statement is false, write F. Then rewrite the false statement to make it true.

FEDERAL TRUTH-IN-LENDING DISCLOSURE STATEMENT
(MADE IN COMPLIANCE WITH FEDERAL LAW)

Lender: **RICHMOND CREDIT UNION**
Loan No.: **33-550154-0**   Date: **05/15/12**
Borrower(s): **DARLENE RICKMAN, DARIUS RICKMAN**

Property Address: **50123 N. 24TH ST.**
RICHMOND, VA 23220

☐ Initial Disclosure estimated at time of application   ☒ Final Disclosure based on contract terms

ANNUAL PERCENTAGE RATE The cost of your credit as a yearly rate.	FINANCE CHARGE The dollar amount the credit will cost you assuming the annual percentage rate does not change.	AMOUNT FINANCED The amount of credit provided to you or on your behalf as of loan closing.	TOTAL OF PAYMENTS The amount you will have paid after you have made all payments as scheduled assuming the annual percentage rate does not change.
5.855 %	$ **108077.07**	$ **98616.07**	$ **206693.14**

13. If the borrowers make all the payments as scheduled, they will have paid $108,077.77 for their house.

_____

_____

SECURITY INTEREST: You are giving a security interest in:
☒ the goods or property being purchased.   ☐ real property you already own.

FILING OR RECORDING FEES: $ 150.00

LATE CHARGE: If a payment is more than   15   days late, you will be charged $ 30.50   /   4.00   % of the total payment past due.

PREPAYMENT: If you pay off your loan early, you
☐ may   ☒ will not   have to pay a penalty.
☐ may   ☒ will not   be entitled to a refund of part of the finance charge.

INSURANCE: Credit life, accident, health or loss of income insurance is not required in connection with this loan. This loan transaction requires the following insurance:
☒ Hazard Insurance   ☐ Flood Insurance   ☐ Private Mortgage Insurance   ☒ Mutual Mortgage Insurance
Borrower(s) may obtain hazard and flood insurance through any person of his/her choice, provided said carrier meets the requirements of the Lender. If Borrower desires Property Insurance to be obtained through the Lender's designated agency, the cost will be set forth in a separate insurance statement furnished by the Lender.

ASSUMPTION: Someone buying your house
☐ may   ☒ may, subject to conditions,   ☐ may not assume the remainder of your loan on the original terms.

See your contract documents for additional information regarding nonpayment, default, right to accelerate the maturity of the obligation, prepayment rebates and penalties, and the Lender's policy regarding assumption of the obligation.
☐ all dates and numerical disclosures except late payment disclosures are estimates.   means an estimate.

14. The borrower must pay a 3 percent fee if the payment is more than 15 days late.

_____

_____

▶ Directions: Choose the answer that best completes each statement below.

SETTLEMENT STATEMENT

J. SUMMARY OF BORROWER'S TRANSACTION		K. SUMMARY OF SELLER'S TRANSACTION	
100. GROSS AMOUNT DUE FROM BORROWER:		**400. GROSS AMOUNT DUE TO SELLER:**	
101. Contract Sales Price	98,500.00	401. Contract Sales Price	98,500.00
102. Personal Property		402. Personal Property	
103. Settlement Charges to Borrower (Line 1400)	1,901.60	403.	
104.		404.	
105.		405.	
Adjustments For Items Paid By Seller in advance		*Adjustments For Items Paid By Seller in advance*	
106. County Assessments to		406. County Assessments to	
107. County Taxes to		407. County Taxes to	
108. Assessments to		408. Assessments to	
109.		409.	
110.		410.	
111.		411.	
112.		412.	
120. GROSS AMOUNT DUE FROM BORROWER	100,401.60	*420. GROSS AMOUNT DUE TO SELLER*	98,500.00
200. AMOUNTS PAID BY OR IN BEHALF OF BORROWER:		**500. REDUCTIONS IN AMOUNT DUE TO SELLER:**	
201. Deposit/earnest money $250.00 RETURNED		501. Excess Deposit (See Instructions)	
202. Principal Amount of New Loan(s)	96,715.00	502. Settlement Charges to Seller (Line 1400)	10,174.25
203. Existing loan(s) taken subject to		503. Existing loan(s) taken subject to	
204.		504. Payoff of first Mortgage to U. S. Home Mortgage	102,786.82
205.		505. Payoff of second Mortgage	
206.		506.	
207.		507. Courier Docs & Wire Payoff fee to Safemark Title A	85.00
208.		508.	
209.		509.	
Adjustments For Items Unpaid By Seller		*Adjustments For Items Unpaid By Seller*	
210. County Assessments to		510. County Assessments to	
211. County Taxes 01/01/09 to 04/30/09	541.07	511. County Taxes 01/01/09 to 04/30/09	541.07
212. Assessments to		512. Assessments to	
213.		513.	
214.		514.	
215.		515.	
216.		516.	
217.		517.	
218.		518.	
219.		519.	
220. TOTAL PAID BY/FOR BORROWER	97,256.07	*520. TOTAL REDUCTION AMOUNT DUE SELLER*	113,587.14
300. CASH AT SETTLEMENT FROM/TO BORROWER:		**600. CASH AT SETTLEMENT TO/FROM SELLER:**	
301. Gross Amount Due From Borrower (Line 120)	100,401.60	601. Gross Amount Due To Seller (Line 420)	98,500.00
302. Less Amount Paid By/For Borrower (Line 220)	(97,256.07)	602. Less Reductions Due Seller (Line 520)	(113,587.14)
303. CASH (X FROM)(TO) BORROWER	3,145.53	*603. CASH (TO)(X FROM) SELLER*	15,087.14

15. The borrower must have cash at closing in the amount of

   A. $541.07.

   B. $3,145.53.

   C. $97,256.07.

   D. $100,401.60

16. How much was the mortgage that the seller will pay off?

   A. $113,587.14

   B. $102,786.82

   C. $98, 500.00

   D. $97,256.07

Name: _____ Date: _____

▶ Directions: Determine whether each of the following statements is true or false. If the statement is true, write T. If the statement is false, write F. Then rewrite the false statement to make it true.

FORM **W-2 Wage and Tax Statement**
Copy C For EMPLOYEE'S RECORDS (See notice on back of copy B)

Dept. of the Treasury • Internal Revenue Service
This information is being furnished to the Internal Revenue Service. If you are required to file a tax return, a negligence penalty or other sanction may be imposed on you if this income is taxable and you fail to report it.

These substitute W-2 Wage and Tax Statements are acceptable for filing with your Federal, State and Local Income Tax Returns.
If you worked in multiple locations, or had several forms of special compensation, you may receive more than one of these documents.

All four copies of your W-2 are on this page, separated by perforations. The white copies are for your tax returns; the blue copy is for your records. General instructions for these forms, including an explanation of the letter codes used in box 12, are on the other side of the page.

To the right is an explanation of the contents of the wage boxes on your W-2. Please note that the Gross amount shown may include adjustments.

	Federal Box 1	Soc. Sec. Box 3 & 7	Medicare Box 5	State Box 16	Local Box 18
Gross	35048.26	35048.26	35048.26	35048.26	35048.26
Sect. 125 Plan	657.54-	657.54-	657.54-	657.54-	657.54-
W-2 Wages	34390.72	34390.72	34390.72	34390.72	34390.72

A. CONTROL NUMBER 3052008289	This information is being furnished to the Internal Revenue Service	**2005**	OMB NO. 1545-0008	1 WAGES, TIPS, OTHER COMPENSATION 34390.72	2 FEDERAL INCOME TAX WITHHELD 3259.11
B. EMPLOYER IDENTIFICATION NUMBER 42-5559782		D. EMPLOYEE'S SOCIAL SECURITY NUMBER XXX XX XXXX		3 SOCIAL SECURITY WAGES 34390.72	4 SOCIAL SECURITY TAX WITHHELD 2132.22
C. EMPLOYER'S NAME, ADDRESS, AND ZIP CODE				5 MEDICARE WAGES AND TIPS 34390.72	6 MEDICARE TAX WITHHELD 498.67
MAZER 6680 POE AVE DAYTON OH 45414	13 Statutory Employee [ ] Retirement Plan [X] Third-Party Sick Pay [ ]			7 SOCIAL SECURITY TIPS	8 ALLOCATED TIPS
				9 ADVANCE EIC PAYMENT	10 DEPENDENT CARE BENEFITS
E. EMPLOYEE'S FIRST NAME AND INITIAL LAST NAME				11 NONQUALIFIED PLANS	12 a-d
RON L YEARLING APT 23 166 LORETTA AVENUE FAIRBORN, OH 45324				14 OTHER	

15 STATE OH	EMPLOYER'S STATE I.D. NO. 51-087895 2	16 STATE WAGES, TIPS, ETC. 34390.72	17 STATE INCOME TAX 1099.05	18 LOCAL WAGES, TIPS, ETC. 34390.72	19 LOCAL INCOME TAX 601.82	20 LOCALITY NAME VANDALIA

17. W-2 forms list all taxes withheld from your wages by that employer.

_____

_____

18. The income subject to federal taxes is the same as income subject to Social Security and Medicare taxes.

_____

_____

Chapter Review

▶ Directions: Write your answer to each question on the lines below.

2009 Tax Table–Continued

If line 43 (taxable income) is—		And you are—				If line 43 (taxable income) is—		And you are—				If line 43 (taxable income) is—		And you are—			
At least	But less than	Single	Married filing jointly *	Married filing sepa-rately	Head of a house-hold	At least	But less than	Single	Married filing jointly *	Married filing sepa-rately	Head of a house-hold	At least	But less than	Single	Married filing jointly *	Married filing sepa-rately	Head of a house-hold
		Your tax is—						Your tax is—						Your tax is—			
32,000						**35,000**						**38,000**					
32,000	32,050	4,386	3,969	4,386	4,206	35,000	35,050	4,944	4,419	4,944	4,656	38,000	38,050	5,694	4,869	5,694	5,106
32,050	32,100	4,394	3,976	4,394	4,214	35,050	35,100	4,956	4,426	4,956	4,664	38,050	38,100	5,706	4,876	5,706	5,114
32,100	32,150	4,401	3,984	4,401	4,221	35,100	35,150	4,969	4,434	4,969	4,671	38,100	38,150	5,719	4,884	5,719	5,121
32,150	32,200	4,409	3,991	4,409	4,229	35,150	35,200	4,981	4,441	4,981	4,679	38,150	38,200	5,731	4,891	5,731	5,129
32,200	32,250	4,416	3,999	4,416	4,236	35,200	35,250	4,994	4,449	4,994	4,686	38,200	38,250	5,744	4,899	5,744	5,136
32,250	32,300	4,424	4,006	4,424	4,244	35,250	35,300	5,006	4,456	5,006	4,694	38,250	38,300	5,756	4,906	5,756	5,144
32,300	32,350	4,431	4,014	4,431	4,251	35,300	35,350	5,019	4,464	5,019	4,701	38,300	38,350	5,769	4,914	5,769	5,151
32,350	32,400	4,439	4,021	4,439	4,259	35,350	35,400	5,031	4,471	5,031	4,709	38,350	38,400	5,781	4,921	5,781	5,159
32,400	32,450	4,446	4,029	4,446	4,266	35,400	35,450	5,044	4,479	5,044	4,716	38,400	38,450	5,794	4,929	5,794	5,166
32,450	32,500	4,454	4,036	4,454	4,274	35,450	35,500	5,056	4,486	5,056	4,724	38,450	38,500	5,806	4,936	5,806	5,174
32,500	32,550	4,461	4,044	4,461	4,281	35,500	35,550	5,069	4,494	5,069	4,731	38,500	38,550	5,819	4,944	5,819	5,181
32,550	32,600	4,469	4,051	4,469	4,289	35,550	35,600	5,081	4,501	5,081	4,739	38,550	38,600	5,831	4,951	5,831	5,189
32,600	32,650	4,476	4,059	4,476	4,296	35,600	35,650	5,094	4,509	5,094	4,746	38,600	38,650	5,844	4,959	5,844	5,196
32,650	32,700	4,484	4,066	4,484	4,304	35,650	35,700	5,106	4,516	5,106	4,754	38,650	38,700	5,856	4,966	5,856	5,204
32,700	32,750	4,491	4,074	4,491	4,311	35,700	35,750	5,119	4,524	5,119	4,761	38,700	38,750	5,869	4,974	5,869	5,211
32,750	32,800	4,499	4,081	4,499	4,319	35,750	35,800	5,131	4,531	5,131	4,769	38,750	38,800	5,881	4,981	5,881	5,219
32,800	32,850	4,506	4,089	4,506	4,326	35,800	35,850	5,144	4,539	5,144	4,776	38,800	38,850	5,894	4,989	5,894	5,226
32,850	32,900	4,514	4,096	4,514	4,334	35,850	35,900	5,156	4,546	5,156	4,784	38,850	38,900	5,906	4,996	5,906	5,234
32,900	32,950	4,521	4,104	4,521	4,341	35,900	35,950	5,169	4,554	5,169	4,791	38,900	38,950	5,919	5,004	5,919	5,241
32,950	33,000	4,529	4,111	4,529	4,349	35,950	36,000	5,181	4,561	5,181	4,799	38,950	39,000	5,931	5,011	5,931	5,249

19. How do you read a federal income tax table? Describe steps below. How much in taxes would a single person who made $32,804.35 owe?

_____

_____

_____

_____

20. How does filing status affect a person's federal income taxes?

_____

_____

_____

21. How much more in taxes would a single person pay compared to a married couple filing jointly on income of $38,417.95?

_____

NOTES

Answer Key

CHAPTER 1: Consumer Documents

Chapter Review

PAGES 33–42
1. From your boarding pass, you can learn important information about your flight, such as the time of take off, the gate from which it will depart, and your seat on the plane.
2. FWA stands for Ft. Wayne
3. 0182759235
4. This form should be thoroughly completed.
5. F; You only need to include child support payments as part of your income if you rely on that money to make credit payments.
6. Kealoha's monthly fee would be $5.04.
7. The interest rate on this card is 25.99%. It can change over time. The application says the rate will vary with the market based on the Prime Rate.
8. One pound of green peppers would cost $1.99.
9. C; return or exchange an item at a store.
10. If the cookware item cost $20, the sales tax on the item would be $1.65.
11. T
12. F; The price of the car without additional equipment or features would be $21,988.
13. According to this report, the car is worth $190 less than the retail book value.
14. F; Car insurance policies vary greatly in what they cover.
15. T
16. When you take your car in to be serviced, you also have to pay for sales tax and for the disposal of your old oil.

CHAPTER 2: Personal Documents

Chapter Review

PAGES 101–110
1. F; Kathi's federal taxable wages for this period were $386.15.
2. T
3. Deandra is responsible for paying $52.27.
4. You can pay this hospital bill online, over the phone, or by mailing in this portion of the form with payment.
5. This form should be thoroughly completed.

6. This form should be thoroughly completed.
7. When applying for a driver's permit, you must give your name, address, date of birth, height, Social Security number, telephone number, and eye color.
8. This application might allow you to drive a car, truck, bus, or motorcycle.
9. F; An applicant's parent or legal guardian may submit an application for a Social Security number of the applicant's behalf.
10. B; when you end the lease entirely
11. C; repairs needed due to the tenant's carelessness.

CHAPTER 3: Business Documents

Chapter Review

PAGES 131–140
1. This form should be thoroughly completed.
2. Because she entered "1" on line "A," you know that no one else can claim Janelle as a dependent.
3. Yes, Janelle has chosen to have an extra $27.50 withheld from each paycheck.
4. Alicia worked 6.5 hours of overtime in the week ending 11/18/11.
5. Alicia does not get paid for lunch because she clocks out before she leaves and clocks back in when she returns.
6. F; Different company healthcare benefit plans usually offer varying levels of coverage.
7. T
8. A; $10
9. Option 3 offers the best prescription drug coverage because it has the highest maximum annual benefit.
10. All the plans will pay 100% up to the maximum annual benefit amount.
11. D; half of the person's base pay up to $125 a week
12. The contract is in effect for a period of three months or until the job is done.
13. The employer has more rights, such as being able to end the contract early.
14. T
15. F; The first step of the grievance process is to discuss the complaint informally with the employee's direct supervisor.
16. F; The two parties should agree on an Arbitrator.

17. F; If the grievance is not filed in a timely manner, it will be dismissed.
18. T
19. F; An employee would be in violation of the dress code if he wore nice jeans and a polo shirt to work. According to this policy, jeans are inappropriate work attire.
20. C; maintain files so that they are easy to find.
21. A; when they are needed for immediate use.

CHAPTER 4: Financial Documents

Chapter Review

PAGES 199–208
1. C; balance forward
2. F; This bill charges Arturo for the water he used, and it also charges him for sewer fees and a storm drain fee.
3. F; The period for the bill above is one month.
4. T
5. This bill also charges for HBO channels, residential Internet, a pole attachment fee, an administrative fee, and several taxes.
6. Kwame paid an extra $7.38 on his bill because he was charged a 10% late fee.
7. A home buyer could use this form for a VA, FHA, conventional, USDA/Rural Housing Service, or other type of mortgage.
8. The interest rate on this loan is 5.25%.
9. The applicant's interest rate will not rise over time because the mortgage is fixed rate.
10. C; Prepaid items and closing costs are added to the total.
11. D; has no outstanding judgments against them.
12. There are two time limit provisions on this offer letter. First, it requires that the owner turn over possession of the house to the buyer by 2 PM, two days after the closing. Second, this letter states that the offer is good for a little less than a month, until the closing date.
13. F; If the borrowers make all the payments as scheduled, they will have paid $206,693.14 for their house.
14. F; The borrower must pay $30.50, or 4 percent of the total payment due.
15. B; $3,145.53
16. B; $102,786.82
17. T

18. T
19. First, you find your taxable income level category on the left. Second, you read down the column for your filing status. The place where the two meet is your federal income tax. The taxes owed are $4,506.
20. Your filing status directly affects how much you owe in taxes. Single people and married people filing separately pay the most in taxes. Someone filing as head-of-household pays less. Married couples filing jointly pay the least amount in taxes.
21. A single person would pay $5,794 in taxes, while a married couple filing jointly would pay $4,929 on income of $38,417.95. So a single person would pay $865 more in taxes.

Index

Index

Index